MDM:
Fundamentals, Security, and the Modern Desktop

MDM:

Fundamentals, Security, and the Modern Desktop

Using Intune, Autopilot, and Azure to Manage, Deploy, and Secure Windows® 10

Jeremy Moskowitz

SYBEX®
A Wiley Brand

For all the strong women in my life.

Acknowledgments

I want to start out by thanking Cathy Moya from Microsoft, without whom this book would not be possible. Thank you so much for reaching out to help find the right people to help answer the tough questions and help me believe that this book was necessary and possible. Seriously, this book wouldn't have existed without your help.

My next big thanks goes to Panu Saukko, Enterprise Mobility MVP who did the very un-glamorous job as my Technical Editor and made sure I didn't "make stuff up," called me on all my crunchy areas, and added his own deep wisdom on the subject. You're a strong, wise man, and I'm honored to have you by my side as my technical editor on this book. An additional tip of the hat goes to Yinghua (Sandy) Zeng, Enterprise Mobility MVP, who helped double-fact-check various items and help me find the light in the dark on more than a few subjects. I cannot believe how much information and knowledge the two of you have in your heads.

Additional thanks to Stephen Rose for graciously providing the Foreword and reviewing the OneDrive content.

Thanks to full chapter reviewers and question answerers from Microsoft: Michael Neihaus, Mahyar Ghadiali, Ken Revels, Christian Refvik, Craig Marl, Aisha Wang, Dilip Radhakrishnan, Riki June, Peter Kaufman, Chris Hopkins, Jan Ketil, Skanke, Joe Kim, Sreekar Mankala and other friends and reviewers at Microsoft. Just … wow. Thank you so, so much for taking time out of your busy workdays to help me and make this book the best it could be.

Thanks to my "dream team" at Sybex: Elizabeth Campbell, Judy Flynn, Christine O'Connor, Kenyon Brown, and Pete Gaughan. You guys are the reason why quality wins out in the end.

Thanks to my wife and family for putting up with me missing some nights and weekends. And thanks to my awesome team at PolicyPak and `MDMandGPanswers.com` for bringing your A game every single day. I simply adore working with all of you.

Finally, if you're holding this book (or reading it online), I want to thank you for taking a chance on learning something new, stretching to a new place, and putting your trust in me.

Thank you for buying the book, joining me at my live events and at `MDMandGPanswers.com`, and for using my PolicyPak software.

Meeting you in person is my favorite part of the job, and I look forward to hearing how this book has helped you out.

About the Author

Since becoming one of the world's first MCSEs, Jeremy Moskowitz has performed Active Directory, Group Policy, and MDM planning and implementations for some of the nation's largest organizations.

He is a 15-Year Microsoft MVP Awardee, first in Group Policy and Desktop Management, and now in Enterprise Mobility with an emphasis in Intune.

Jeremy is the founder of MDMandGPanswers.com and PolicyPak Software.

Computerworld magazine ranked MDMandGPanswers.com as one of the 20 most useful Microsoft sites for IT professionals. EnterpriseMobilityExchange.com placed Jeremy (@jeremymoskowitz) on its list of the "7 Endpoint Management Voices on Twitter" for IT pros to follow on social media.

His other book from Sybex is *Group Policy Fundamentals, Security, and Troubleshooting, Third Edition* date, which is on the Desktops of admins everywhere.

Get signed copies of his books, and learn more about Jeremy's Group Policy and MDM Master Class training at www.MDMandGPanswers.com.

Learn more about how to secure your Desktop and applications, manage all areas of Windows 10, and deploy all Group Policy settings through your MDM service at www.policypak.com.

Contents at a Glance

Contents

Foreword

Shortly after starting with the Windows team in 2009, I met Jeremy at a MVP mixer in Redmond. Within minutes he had me backed into a corner was inundating me with questions on Group Policy settings for the new Windows 7 beta that we just delivered.

I was thinking, "Who is this guy?" and more so, "How could any one person be so passionate about Group Policy and desktop management?" What is most amazing is after all these years, his passion around helping IT pros to manage their Windows desktops is just as strong as it was back in 2009!

Over the years I have been able to see the amazing impact that Jeremy has made. First upon how IT organizations look to manage the fundamentals, security, and troubleshooting of Group Policy. But Jeremy has also impacted how our own Microsoft engineering teams now look at problem sets based on his guidance with his audiences.

If you don't believe me, ask anyone who has sat one of his sessions at TechEd/Ignite. They are the stuff of geek legend. Packed to the gills with 400 level uber-admins with a plethora of questions for him.

In the past few years, he has moved from not just being the GPO guru, but now onward as the go-to guy for Intune and MDM. In this book, Jeremy provides industry standard guidance on how to best co-exist and/or transition from GPOs to MDM tools but continue to manage and secure your desktops.

As a reviewer on Amazon stated of one of his earlier books, "The difference between the good system engineer and the great system engineer is that the great system engineer reads the right book. This is the right book."

I can honestly say he's right. This is the right book. Enjoy!

Stephen L. Rose
Microsoft
@stephenlrose

Introduction

If you're picking up this book, it could be for several reasons:

- You keep hearing Microsoft talk about "Switching to a modern, managed desktop" at a conference, online, or in someone's speech.

- You have no idea what EMM and/or MDM is, but thought, "Hmm...interesting looking cover. Let me see what's inside it."

- You already subscribe to an MDM service, like Intune, Workspace ONE, or MobileIron, and you use it for phones and want to get started using it for Windows 10.

- You know what EMM and/or MDM is, see it on the potential horizon for your company, and are looking to get a handle on it.

- You purchased my "moderately famous" big, green Group Policy book, maybe even the first edition of *Group Policy, Profiles, and IntelliMirror* back in 2001, or maybe one of the more recent editions like *Group Policy: Fundamentals, Security, and the Managed Desktop, Third Edition*.

- Maybe the boss walked into your office and dropped this book on your desk and said, "Learn this EMM/MDM/Modern Management *whatever-it-is* and see if we should 'do this thing.'"

- Maybe your "boss' boss" struck a deal on the golf course, and now it's your job to learn MDM.

So what is EMM/MDM and Modern Management? And how is it different than on-prem, traditional management?

Let's define some terms so we can map our course and get on the road:

- EMM is Enterprise Mobility Management. It's a fancy term for "managing settings and applications and stuff over the Internet."

- MDM stands for two things. Officially, MDM is Mobile Device Management. It's more or less the guts, protocol, and moving parts that the concept that is EMM will use to perform the work.

- Modern management is a collection of overall features, concepts, how-tos, and step-by-steps of, well, rolling out, then managing a Windows Desktop (exclusively Windows 10) in a new way that opens up new opportunities and capabilities. Usually modern management also means managing (mostly) over the Internet; that is, by the cloud.

So, unofficially, MDM stands for *Modern* Device Management. You can see Microsoft really pushing the word *modern* into the conversation. So even though MDM originally had one meaning, it's really taken on two meanings at the same time.

To be clear, the lines are a little blurry here. And EMM and MDM (the official and unofficial definitions) mean so many different things to different people. As of this writing, here's what *Wikipedia* says:

> "Enterprise mobility management (EMM) is the set of people, processes and technology focused on managing mobile devices, wireless networks, and other mobile computing services in a business context."

And if you want to read Microsoft's definition of MDM, it can be found at `https://docs.microsoft.com/en-us/windows/client-management/mdm/`. But here's the important bit and opening sentence on the definition of MDM from Microsoft:

> "Windows 10 provides an enterprise management solution to help IT pros manage company security policies and business applications, while avoiding compromise of the users' privacy on their personal devices."

It's not super easy to find a unified definition of Modern Management anywhere. Maybe by the time you read this, some unified definition will be everywhere. But here's a quote from Microsoft's corporate vice president of management at Ignite 2018 that resonates with me reasonably well:

> "The modern desktop is a paradigm shift which takes things to a whole different level. In the modern desktop, everything, and I mean literally mean everything is connected to the cloud: Windows, Office, management security, it's all connected to the cloud.
>
> And that cloud connection makes your users more productive, gives you in IT security superior insights and control. Because it gives the full power of the Microsoft Intelligent Cloud behind you.
>
> As you cloud connect everything you have, you can take advantage of simplified management of your desktop devices, as well as compliance updates, updates which enhance your security, advanced data protection, and finally those cloud capabilities make your users far more productive."

Another place to go for understanding Microsoft's vision for a modern desktop can be found at:

`https://www.microsoft.com/en-us/microsoft-365/blog/2018/09/06/helping-customers-shift-to-a-modern-desktop/`

So, Modern Management is a shift not just from the traditional on-prem tooling of Active Directory, Group Policy, and SCCM toward something cloud-y. It's rather a shift in mindset to making Windows management more proactive and automated. Think "Drop a new system out of the box on someone's front door, and…bingo. They're all set up, and nicely managed, and the end user didn't have to lift a finger except for pressing the On button." That's the dream, anyway, of modern management.

Beyond that, the promise of modern management, in theory anyway, is that it should be simpler than traditional management with Active Directory, Group Policy, and/or SCCM. Why is that? Well, if you have zero on-prem infrastructure to babysit, that's going to be a plus. And, all the management options are all in one place: the MDM system you choose. So instead of 80 different ways to manage a device, using Group Policy, scripts, and so on, at least you have it all reasonably centralized in one management tool and portal.

Now, for me, I'm interested in this new modernly managed desktop world because EMM and MDM doesn't *replace* Group Policy; it opens up and augments new opportunities where Group Policy cannot go.

So, for me, I see a few categories of organizations. Maybe you fit into one of these categories right now, or your perspective might change over time:

- Maybe you'll stay exactly where you are; keep using on-prem Active Directory with domain-joined machines and keep using Group Policy to manage those machines. (In this case, this book might be interesting, if only to see where you could maybe stretch into the future.)

- Maybe you'll use EMM/MDM to augment your current world so you can do and accomplish new, interesting things (that you couldn't do before with Group Policy alone). Maybe you'll keep your traditionally managed machines for your headquarters but create a "Modern Managed parallel universe" for your non-domain-joined or far-flung machines where you have intermittent connectivity. In other words, you'll keep doing some (or many) traditional things in the original universe and spin up a parallel universe for some of the new scenarios we'll explore. (I foresee this scenario for many, many companies, by the way.)

- Maybe you'll completely walk away from the traditional management and rip and replace on-prem Active Directory and Group Policy and/or SCCM management. Then jump both feet in to EMM/MDM. (I call this the "Big Band-Aid rip.")

- Maybe you have zero on-prem infrastructure today and see that some of the world is heading toward a "let's put everything in the cloud" model. So, because you're starting with no on-prem infrastructure already, maybe it doesn't make sense to spin up a new on-prem Active Directory and/or SCCM. You're already all in on being a cloud-based company and this Modern Managed world would be a natural extension for your company.

So if you've already decided to go toward Modern Management or are still dabbling with the decision to open up some new doors that Traditional Management cannot, then this is the book for you. It could also be the book for you even if you are in the first camp; that is, you have no direct intention of walking away from Traditional Management (like on-prem Active Directory with Group Policy) but want to get a feel for what a EMM/MDM and Modern Management can do for you and start to get a handle on it.

In this book, I'm going to simply assume you're already familiar with existing traditional, on-prem paradigms, like Active Directory, Group Policy, and maybe a little SCCM. I'm not saying you need to have "wizard level" understanding of these items, but in looking forward to MDM and Modern Management, I will often refer *backward* to how things are done in a traditional sense and explain how they're different.

As such, if you haven't got a copy of my Group Policy book and think you might need a copy, head over to www.MDMandGPanswers.com/book and get your own "author signed" copy of the big green Group Policy book as this book's companion.

EMM and MDM Redefined

So EMM is Enterprise Mobility Management. It just means all the tools and people and stuff you need to manage your mobile devices in a modern way. So in short, EMM is the "concept."

And, MDM stands for Mobile Device Management.

Ask some people and they will say it stands for "Modern Device Management" or "Modern Desktop Management," which also kind of works.

I will always abbreviate it as simply MDM for short. MDM is a "cousin" to Group Policy. A newer cousin, with somewhat different goals, different parents, different upbringing, and so on. So, "cousin" is really the best analogy here. So, in short, MDM is the "worker bee."

You can also think of MDM like it's the moving part, or the transport for the ideas of EMM.

Like Group Policy, MDM has a moving part, or policy processing engine, inside the Windows 10 operating system. And actually, here's the thing: MDM isn't just inside Windows 10; that similar moving part is already embedded and inside mobile phones, tablets, and so on.

So if it's the similar moving part in both Windows and mobile devices, a new interesting opportunity opens up. use one management system, and leverage the in-box MDM engine (in Windows and also phones, etc.) as the moving part to receive "directives" (or policies) and have "one tool to rule them all."

Taking a step back, when you used Group Policy to manage your systems, Microsoft sold you everything, all at once, and it was all included in the box and worked "forever." Here were the general steps:

- You created an on-prem Active Directory and made a domain.

- You joined machines to the domain.

- You used a Microsoft MMC snap-in called the GPMC to make Group Policy Objects.

- Those GPOs contained policies.

- Those policies were downloaded through Ethernet or VPN.

- Those policies were processed by the Group Policy engine.

Now, with EMM, the deal is a little different:

- The expectation is that you walk away from or don't need your on-prem Active Directory anymore, but you might have Azure Active Directory for Office 365, for example.

- Machines are domain joined (maybe) because you had them historically joined. But the new idea is that you don't need to have them domain joined anymore but it's okay if they are.

- If you want to, you can get a bonus by "cloud attaching" your on-prem Active Directory and/or SCCM infrastructure to the cloud and gain additional benefits by leaning on the cloud.

- You purchase or otherwise acquire an MDM solution. Yes, you read that right: You have to buy something to make your EMM dreams a reality and purchase something to command the MDM moving part on your Windows and phones to perform actual work. And, if you opt for a cloud-based MDM service, you need to keep paying to keep your MDM service working.

- You make policies in your MDM service to deliver software and/or lock down settings.

- Those policies are downloaded through the Internet.

- Those policies are processed by the MDM engine.

So, some things are kind of the same, and some things are different.

But, the gist of MDM is the same as Group Policy: You have users and devices. You make "wishes" and store those wishes somewhere centrally, and endpoints download and process those wishes. What's majorly different is the need for being domain joined for Group Policy to work versus having zero on-prem infrastructure for MDM to work.

Group Policy and MDM have different goals and different upbringing, but we'll dig into that in Chapter 1.

Terminology

In this book, I'll be writing the letters (and terms) *EMM*, *MDM*, and *Modern Management* a lot.

I might say, "In your EMM environment" to talk about your business, or world at large.

I might refer to "an MDM system," "an MDM solution," or "your MDM." That's the thing, well, a service really, you purchase and maintain to perform the work of modern desktop management.

Modern Management will be the things we put in place after we get our MDM solution set up. Like the icing on the cake to get new machines rolled out and software deployed, locked down, and reported upon.

But of course, there's the other part as well, the MDM moving part that's pre-baked into Windows 10 (and also mobile phones, etc.). I'm going to refer to that as the MDM engine.

So in summary:

- **EMM:** This is about you and your business. your entire delivery ecosystem at large.

- **MDM solution or MDM system:** The thing you buy and pay monthly or yearly for.

- **MDM engine:** The moving part and guts built into Windows 10.

- **Modern Management:** The newer, (mostly) cloud-based way of performing similar activities you did with on-prem systems.

Other terminology, which I'll just say here, one time, and then assume you read this as I head onward in the book:

- AD or on-prem AD is Active Directory, as in the "stand up an on-prem domain with on-prem Domain Controllers." Ya know, the thing you've been doing since 2000.

- AAD is Azure Active Directory. This will be explored in more detail later, but this is Microsoft's cloud-based identity service.

- DJ++ is the shorthand terminology for when a machine is both joined to on-prem AD and also using AAD. I'll mention this again when the time comes.

- Workplace join means when the computer is not being managed by on-prem AD or by Azure Active Directory. This is a way to give people outside of your organization access to some resources and applications, but they are not fully managed.

A good blog article explaining all of these terminology items with good, if not blurry, screen shots can be found at:

https://blogs.technet.microsoft.com/tip_of_the_day/2016/08/
22/cloud-tip-of-the-day-determine-if-a-windows-10-pc-is-dj-
azure-ad-joined-or-workplace-joined/

What You'll Need to Get Started with This Book

As I just stated, and as we'll go into more detail in Chapter 2, you'll need to acquire an EMM system, which uses MDM as its transport. To keep things simple, I'm just going to call these "MDM solutions" like other people typically do. I guess some people might call them "EMM systems" or "EMM solutions," but that's not generally what my peers and I call these systems when we talk about them.

The main MDM solution gorillas on the block are as follows:

- Microsoft Windows Intune

- VMware Workspace ONE (formerly VMware Airwatch)

- MobileIron

These are all cloud-based, subscription based services.

To make the most of this book, you'll need one of these subscription-based services. Basically, I'll be using Microsoft Intune for most of my MDM examples. Not because it is or isn't the best, but because it's included with many Microsoft Enterprise customers' existing licensing and subscriptions.

There are also a handful of other MDM services that are less well known, and some that work (ironically) when they are deployed on-prem. I will not be covering those. That said, if you have another cloud-based MDM solution (SOTI, Citrix Endpoint Management [formerly XenMobile], and others), what we go over here should reasonably translate for you as well, even though I won't specifically be showing you any examples.

And, to be fair, for managing Windows 10 machines, they are all roughly equal. Some MDM solutions have different bells, others have different whistles. Ultimately, as I'll re-explain when the time comes, the MDM solution (the paid service) simply drives and directs the moving part (the MDM engine) on the endpoint.

Anyway, more on this in Chapter 2 when we do a little bit of comparison shopping, er...comparative analysis between the solutions.

What I Won't Be Covering in This Book

I'm focusing on managing Windows 10 in this book. I'm really not planning on covering phones, Macs, and/or other gizmos of various flavors. I'm also not spending a lot of time looking backward to Windows 7, but it might come up from time to time.

As of this writing, in 2019, if you ask 10 admins, what they are currently using an MDM service for. Most would say, "Managing phones." Because MDM, that is, it's very name—Mobile Device Management—does a great job for phones and remote lock and wipe and so on.

But of those 10 admins who are using an MDM service right now, almost none say, "And we're also using it to manage our entire fleet of Window 10."

But many of those admins are saying, "I think I'd like to get to know MDM and Modern Management to see if there are some interesting capabilities for my company with Windows 10."

So that's my focus for our time together. To help you see if EMM/MDM and Modern Management can open up new opportunities and do things you couldn't do yesterday with Group Policy and traditional tools.

Phones (of all kinds), iPads, Android, Macs, Chromebooks, and so on: for me—interesting, very interesting. And, yes, they would be controlled by your MDM system and fall under the umbrella of modern management. But, they're just not part of this book.

My expertise is in Windows endpoint management, and that's where I'm going to focus my attention.

Note, too, that there are also specific books on the EMM/MDM services themselves; their ins and outs and how to make a company portal, nuke a phone that Sally in Accounting left inside the taxi, share documents securely, and a lot of other items that you might or might not care about.

But if your main goal is to get on the road managing Windows 10 settings with MDM and learn to augment your traditional management skills and manage Windows 10 in a modern way, then this is the book for you.

Here's some other stuff I won't be covering:

MAM (Mobile Application Management)   This is a method to manage applications like Office on iOS and Android and prevent things like "Save as," cut/copy/paste, perform remote wipe of data, and more. This is nifty, and worth investigating because, while it does require an MDM service, it doesn't require any enrollment of users' devices in those services. Again: interesting, but not covered. Learn more about MAM here: `https://docs .microsoft.com/en-us/intune/mam-faq`.

Microsoft Identity Manager   Pretend for a moment you have multiple directory sources, like your existing on-prem AD, a human resources database, and some other custom database. Now imagine you need to sync identities across all those things and have them magically work in Azure AD. That's Microsoft Identity Manager, and I'm not covering it. In Chapter 2, I will be covering basic Azure AD Connect, which is an on-prem AD to Azure AD synchronization system and is in this ballpark. But to learn more about Microsoft Identity Manager, start here. https://docs.microsoft.com/en-us/microsoft-identity-manager/.

Azure Information Protection (and Rights Management)   Sally in HR just emailed "too many people" the organization chart with salary information embedded into it. Bad Sally, bad. Now what? Well, if you were using Azure Information Protection, or AIP, then you could automatically classify and protect documents based upon contents. For instance, say the word *Confidential* was in the document. When that gets emailed, the data actually stays with the originating company, not the receiving company. So Sally's "big oops" becomes Sally's big "nonevent." Learn more about Azure Information Protection (and Rights Management) here, because I won't be covering it in this book:

    https://docs.microsoft.com/en-us/azure/information-protection/

Single Sign-On   So right now, Sally in HR has a login to on-prem AD, soon also to have a login to Azure AD, and also to the external payroll system, another at Dropbox.com, and also (yet another) login at salesforce.com. Wouldn't it be great if she could have one single sign-on (SSO) to these external applications using her Azure AD account? You bet that's cool. But since I won't be covering that in this book, here's an example walk-through of how to use Azure AD to make a single sign-on with an external application like Salesforce:

    https://docs.microsoft.com/en-us/azure/active-directory/saas-apps/
    salesforce-tutorial

User Self-Service   Users love forgetting their passwords. And doing another password reset is booooriing. So both Office 365 and Azure AD has a way to enable users to perform self-service password resets. Since I won't be covering it, if you want to set this up and/or see a quick walk-through of it, check out:

    https://docs.microsoft.com/en-us/azure/active-directory/authentication/
    quickstart-sspr

Two-Factor Authentication   Azure AD has a way for some resources to require a second authentication. Either a biometric authentication, like a fingerprint or YubiKey, or accepting phone calls or texts. This is Azure multifactor authentication and you can learn more about it here:

    https://docs.microsoft.com/en-us/azure/active-directory/authentication/
    concept-mfa-licensing

To me, these additional Azure services are super, duper interesting. But they are not part of my focus for you and this book. Our job: We'll be focusing on using an MDM service and other Azure services to manage Windows 10 PCs.

How Do You Know This Book Won't Be Out-of-Date 80 Seconds after You Buy It?

If there's one thing we can be sure about, it's that this new world of cloud services seems to move faster than most of us can handle it.

But don't panic.

I agree that it's hard to keep up with all the magic cloud coders spin out every day. Literally. Every day. For on-prem infrastructure, that's not the deal. You download, you install, you let it sit until you do an upgrade.

For this book though, my plans are to show you things I *think* won't be changing too, too much. I cannot know for sure, of course. But my plan is to explain concepts that seem like they will be entrenched for a while; those I think will likely be the most used concepts over the long haul.

No guarantees. I don't work for Microsoft, I dont directly influence its road map. So it's possible some steps might be a little bit different in the Azure or Intune portals from the time I wrote this to the time you get the book. And then after the book is out, and it's, say, two or three years on.

But the stuff I'm planning on guiding you through with examples is *reasonably* solid with regard to the basic steps and examples. And I'm not going to be heading down too much *experimental* territory. I'll be explaining stuff that's already been working for some real-world companies for some length of time and stuff I'm pretty sure will continue to be foundational in the world of modern management for the foreseeable future.

I could be wrong, and I could make some mistakes and talk about some concept *today* that gets killed or supplanted *tomorrow*. But I have a reasonably high degree of confidence in the specific chapters and concepts I've chosen to write about along with the examples.

The point is this: Yes, any specific step-by-step or screenshot might change a little bit, but I think you'll be reasonably safe with what I'm publishing now, and it should work into the reasonable future. So, with what you learn here, even if the steps and names of things are a little different in a year or two, you should be able to figure it out.

I believe in you.

You are, after all, an IT professional.

A Final Note about Group Policy vs. MDM

I realize this may be my last chance to grab your attention in the bookstore, or more likely, Amazon or Safari or whatever you are using to read this introduction. And if you know me, and you've seen me speak, and know my body of work, right now maybe you're thinking, "I guess he's done with Group Policy and now Jeremy's on to MDM?"

For total, 100% clarity, let me repeat a common mantra I have espoused for years: Group Policy is not dead. The irony though, the more I (or others) say, "Group Policy is not dead," the more people think Group Policy is dead.

It is, in fact, not dead. Microsoft has not "turned off" Group Policy usage for on-prem scenarios, nor have product teams stopped producing new functions that can be controlled by Group Policy.

Au contraire. Group Policy continues to be supported, and new settings for the OS, Edge, and more ship each and every time Windows is revised.

Indeed, many scenarios will *always* require on-prem Active Directory and Group Policy, like non-Internet-connected machines, ultra-secure scenarios, and for the foreseeable future, RDS, Citrix, and on-prem VDI scenarios.

I wrote a pretty famous "off the rails" blog post called, "Why Group Policy is Not Dead Manifesto." It would be a good read at this point if you have a moment. Here's the link (or Goog…, I mean, Bing for, "Group Policy Not Dead."):

```
https://www.gpanswers.com/blogs/view-blog/
the-why-group-policy-is-not-dead-manifesto
```

"Why then, Jeremy, are you writing a book on modern management with Microsoft's cloud solution for settings management, MDM, and Intune?" I hear you ask.

The answer is that I feel there is room for both a traditional management model with domain joined machines (with Group Policy and other on-prem management systems like SCCM) and for something new with EMM/MDM and the Modern Management scenarios that are brought to the table.

It would be foolish for me to close off my mind to new possibilities that an MDM system can add, and what solutions modern management will solve. But it would be equally foolish to walk away from almost 20 years of a proven technology like Group Policy, which is currently in use in just about every single company on the planet.

So this book is to enable you to explore the EMM/MDM/Modern Management route for yourself; try some examples, and see if it's right for you.

You can make a plan to walk away from the old, have some kind of hybrid with old and new, or jump all in with the new.

I'll leave that to you.

A Little about Me, This Book, PolicyPak, and Beyond

I've been managing Windows systems since I was a toddler. Well, not quite, but almost. I was one of the first MCSEs in the world back in 1994, and I spent lots of time being a consultant to organizations of all sizes for many years.

Then I found and fell in love with Group Policy, wrote my popular Group Policy book, and became a Microsoft Group Policy MVP for 15 years. And, more recently, I have been anointed as a Microsoft MVP in Enterprise Mobility (with a focus in Intune). Additionally, I've been helping companies try to understand this new MDM world and what it means to the original Group Policy world.

I also founded and run a company called PolicyPak Software, which extends both Group Policy and MDM to do more amazing things than what is possible with what's in the box alone. For instance, here are some of the things you can do with the products from PolicyPak:

- Manage third-party applications like Java, Flash, Firefox, OpenOffice, and hundreds more.

- Take on-prem Group Policy and Group Policy Preferences settings and use them with your MDM service.

- Marry a website to a specific version of Java.

- Manage "which website should open in what browser."

- Copy files down from cloud services and keep them up-to-date.

- Remove local admin rights and elevate processes and applications that require UAC prompts.

- Dynamically manage the Windows 10 Start Screen and Taskbar.

...and a whole lot more.

So I'm going to try to walk a fine line here. With your permission, I'm going to, from time to time, describe when something from PolicyPak could enhance a situation or solve a problem that cannot be solved out of the box. I'll show you real examples of how to solve real problems.

And I'm not doing it to sell you something, but if that happens, that's okay too. The point, really, is to demonstrate a problem or situation that might not have any other way out of it. So basically, if I didn't explain that the "PolicyPak possibility" to fix a particular problem existed, you wouldn't know about it, and you'd always be stuck in a rut.

And if there's an alternative or other third-party way to achieve the same goal, I'll do my best to explain that too.

As you read this book, it's natural to have questions about Modern Management, MDM (or Group Policy). For that, I have a blog that can be found at MDMandGPanswers.com.

I usually post a "Tip of the week" and send it through email. You'll also find download-able PowerShell scripts, tips and tricks, and lots more.

If you want to meet me in person, book me for onsite training, or attend my live public MDM and Group Policy courses, my website at MDMandGPanswers.com shows my upcoming scheduled events. I'd love to hear how this book met your needs, got you started with MDM, or helped you out.

Start out by following and/or tweeting me @jeremymoskowitz. Use the hashtag #mdmbook and let me know what's helping you out today.

Thanks for being part of the journey.

MDM:
Fundamentals, Security, and the Modern Desktop

Chapter 1

Enterprise Mobility and MDM Essentials

In this first chapter, we'll get to know what MDM is, where it came from, and how it's different than its cousin Group Policy.

I think the best place to start is right at the top of a new page. Like this one.

And that's kind of what Microsoft did when they decided to dedicate their efforts with EMM and MDM and not continue down the path of investing more features into existing core on-prem Active Directory and Group Policy technologies.

Again, as I stated in the book's Introduction, Group Policy is not dead. And Microsoft has not "turned off" Group Policy usage for on-prem scenarios, nor should you live in fear that your favorite new, "Windows 10 gismo," will lose the ability to be controlled by Group Policy.

But, going forward, you can expect that nearly all Windows 10 (and related settings like Edge) should be controllable with either Group Policy or MDM. There are some exceptions, but Microsoft is committed to adding new settings to GPO. That said, don't expect new major Group Policy features (like enhanced Group Policy reporting new Group Policy Preferences, or additional troubleshooting tools). But do expect more Group Policy settings to be born each and every time Windows 10 ships, and you'll see these as the Group Policy Admin Template policy settings (ADMX settings) you've come to know and love for umpteen years.

 For new Group Policy features, like managing the Start Screen and Taskbar and File Associations, while there is some rudimentary stuff in the box, I heartily suggest you take a look at PolicyPak Group Policy edition, which will supplement the missing features most on-prem AD admins are looking for.

The reality is that the concept of Enterprise Mobility and thus using MDM to manage Windows is Microsoft's new focus, and it's not looking backward to bolster core Group Policy functions anymore. But at the same time, it is also not killing Group Policy either for use with your existing domain-joined machines.

Microsoft is expecting you to keep using traditional management like Group Policy for some scenarios and modern management with MDM for other scenarios.

Getting Ready to Use This Book

To go through some of the exercises in this book, you will need to own or get evaluations of some software. Or not, and just read the book and see the pictures and get a general feel for what would be involved.

You don't have to do this now, but to take advantage of the walk-throughs in this book, you will be acquiring the following:

- Azure AD (free) or Azure AD Premium (preferred for this book). And, if you have Office 365, you already have Azure AD.

- An MDM service, like Microsoft Intune, VMware Workspace ONE, or MobileIron. Most of the main services have 30 day (or longer) evaluations.

Again: Don't do this step now; we'll tackle that in the next chapter.

If you did want to follow along with all the ideas I'll be showing, you can take some time now to have some representative on-prem infrastructure to simulate what you might already have now. So if you don't already have a test lab you can beat up, here's my recommendation of the following computer names, with the following operating systems:

- DC01 (I recommend Server 2019 or Server 2016.)

- `WIN10Computer.fabrikam.com` joined to DC01. If you have other machines joined to Fabrikam.com too, that would be okay and likely useful as well.

- WIN10-NDJ-1 not domain joined at all

- WIN10-NDJ-2 also not domain joined at all

You might need more as we go along, but these are a good start.

I suggest you use VMware Workstation or Hyper-V on Windows 10 to make a simulated lab environment. That being said, fair warning, some of the scenarios in Chapter 8, "Rollouts and Refreshed with Configuration Designer and AutoPilot," won't work unless you have real hardware. I'll call those scenarios out when the time comes.

I'm not going to provide any step-by-step instructions for you to bring up your own domain and Domain Controller. But one of my PolicyPak teammates created a video on how to do it here if you're unfamiliar:

```
https://www.policypak.com/video/
policypak-cloud-how-to-create-a-dc-for-editing-purposes.html
```

Then join at least Win10Computer to the domain you create; in my examples, I'll be using the domain name Fabrikam.com.

You might want to have a small gaggle of on-prem AD users pre-created in an OU called Sales. Name your test users anything you like, but you'll see mine in the book like EastSalesUser1, WestSalesUser7, and so on.

Additionally, as I go along, you might see me manually create other users (in on-prem AD and in Azure AD).

If case you're curious on the backstory of Microsoft's fake names, like Fabrikam.com, check out this old blog entry:

https://blogs.msdn.microsoft.com/oldnewthing/
20061013-05/?p=29393

Why the Need for MDM

Throughout the years, I kept hearing the supposed death knell of Group Policy. But, it's more than 19 years since Windows 2000, and, well, it's still here, and seems pretty darned popular.

So much so that I went a little bananas in 2016 and 2017 and wrote a blog post called "The 'Why Group Policy is Not Dead' Manifesto." I mentioned this in the book's introduction, but if you didn't read it then, take a moment to read it now. It can be found by moseying over to MDMandGpanswers.com at:

https://www.GPanswers.com/blogs/view-blog/
the-why-group-policy-is-not-dead-manifesto

I highly recommend you take a moment and read it and then come back here to continue. It's long, so maybe it takes two moments.

So, if Group Policy is so great, then why do we need MDM as something to look to for the future? Because as I said in the introduction, Group Policy cannot be the only transport if we want to solve for new scenarios and use cases.

Because in some ways the future is already here. Here are the key factors I see why people are looking at MDM:

New Workstyle: Constantly on the Go   You have one. A cell phone. And it's "constantly on the go." In fact those are literally the words that Microsoft uses when it explains its position of the benefits of MDM. And yes, cell phones are the primary device that's always on the go, but we can all agree that carrying around your laptop is easier than ever.

Note that you can see some of Microsoft's position with regard to MDM if you read this blog entry called "Managing Windows 10 in your organization - transition to modern management." It's found at:

https://docs.microsoft.com/en-us/windows/client-management/
manage-windows-10-in-your-organization-modern-management

New World: Internet Everywhere   If not everywhere, pretty darn close to everywhere. There are always going to be third-world countries and submarines and dead spots. And broken Wi-Fi hot spots. But the prospect of LTE and 4G and (coming soon) 5G everywhere is, well, pretty darned good and getting better all the time.

Now that there's "Internet everywhere," it makes more sense to have an always on, always connected system to manage our "constantly on the go" devices.

New Paradigm: No Domain Join   We've been joining devices to domains since LanManager and NT 3.1 days. Domain joined, however, means that you have all your eggs in the same basket so to speak, which at the time, made a lot of sense. You only really needed to talk to printers and file shares and the occasional SNA device to talk to a bigger mainframe. It made perfect sense.

Today? Not as much.

Endpoints just connect directly to the web-y thing they need and go on with their lives.

The other part of this idea of "no domain join" is a more subtle point, which is the idea that the bad guys could maybe already be inside your on-prem network at any/all times. In days of yore we would assume having a firewall to protect us from the bad guys out on the Internet was enough. But now it's an actual reasonable assumption that the bad guys are already inside your network, like, right now. And if that's true, having machines domain joined could actually *exacerbate* the problem.

If the bad guys break through to the DCs, they could do a big password dump of the hashes of your users and then do a brute force attack. And they could also break into one end-point, become an admin through an exploit or via a tool like Mimikatz, and then hop from machine to machine in what is known as a "pass the hash" attack.

In my Group Policy book (www.GPanswers.com/book), I show you how to set up Microsoft Local Admin Password Solution (LAPS) to create unique, rotating passwords to mitigate these kinds of attacks.

But having machines that are *not* domain joined gives you at least these security advantages, perhaps more.

New Reality: New Windows Every Six Months   There is only one Windows 10. Except that is totally and completely untrue. The "pitch" we got was that there would be one, final, and total Windows...ever again.

But, as you know by now, there's a brand-new Windows 10 version every six months. (Microsoft tries to ship new Windows around every March and October.) And each version adds new features. But if you stop to smell the roses for, say, 6 to 12 months, and look backward—holy cow. It becomes a huge evolution of "old Windows 10" to "newest Windows 10."

Seriously, try it yourself. Go backward and try out Windows 10 1507 compared with say, whatever is latest as you read this book. You'll feel totally lost and see how dramatically different "old Windows 10" feels to today's Windows 10.

New Needs: New Versions of Windows   To start with, there are the normal desktop and laptop versions we've been using for a long time. Like Windows 10 Pro and Windows 10 Enterprise. There's also Windows 10 Home, but it couldn't do Group Policy before, and it's still not designed to integrate with any MDM system.

Beyond that there are a myriad of new sub-versions of Windows. Here are at least five interesting ones:

- **Windows on ARM:** ARM is a processor type that's normally found in phones. Before they were reasonably powerful and had reasonable battery life. Now, ARM processors are even more powerful and have even better battery life. As such, Microsoft caught wise to this trend, reengineered the Windows you know and love, and figured out a way to translate x86 instructions on an ARM processor (also known as Snapdragon processors). Result? New laptops without Intel/AMD chips. These laptops run all day and then some. You can learn more about the platform here:

  https://docs.microsoft.com/en-us/windows/arm/

  And an initial test of some ARM laptops here:

  https://www.zdnet.com/article/
  windows-10-on-arm-tests-say-snapdragon-845-could-bring-big-speed-boost

- **Windows 10 in S Mode:** A secure version of Windows 10 that is restricted to only running Windows Store apps. A one-way upgrade path is possible from Windows 10 in S Mode to Windows Pro or Enterprise, which is available as a one-way trip. If you wish to go backward again, you need to format the hard drive. If you want to learn more about Windows 10 in S Mode a talk from Ignite 2017 can be found here:

  https://www.youtube.com/watch?v=BkGURA_ywRI

- **Windows HoloLens (and HoloLens2):** You've seen this thing; it looks like twenty-second century ski goggles. I've used this thing two or three times in demo situations, and, who knows. Maybe they'll take off. Regardless, the HoloLens has MDM built-in.

- **Windows 10 IoT (Internet of Things):** MDM is built into this version as well, so what you're doing with the "normal" Windows, you could also do with a PC running Windows the size of a business card. Here's a homegrown video of a guy installing Windows 10 IoT edition on a Raspberry Pi3:

  https://www.youtube.com/watch?v=DxeasYy6kqs

- **Windows (codename) Polaris:** This might be a version that comes out without any legacy Windows pieces at all. So no Win32 subsystem at all. It doesn't exist yet as I write this, but maybe in a year or two or three. Or never. But it's possible.

New Things That Aren't Windows (Like Macs and Chromebooks)   Look at what the kids are using nowadays at school. It could be a real Windows PC, or it could be a Mac or Chromebook. And all of these things have MDM built into them. Instead of having disparate tools to manage the Windows world and the non-Windows world, there's an advantage of having one unified tool to deal with all the devices in one place.

New Things That Aren't Windows (That Don't Exist Yet)   Who knows what the future brings. As such, it does seem reasonable that placing an MDM engine inside it will remain a standard for things that are and aren't Windows, for devices that exist today and also those that haven't been dreamed up yet.

Group Policy and MDM Compared

It's natural to want to compare old versus new. Tried-and-true versus something growing and burgeoning. And in this section I'm going to explain where Group Policy does great, where MDM does great, and also where each of them needs a little work and a little boost of help.

Before I go into details of implementation, the main thing people want to talk about, and quickly learn about most, is where new MDM "stacks up" versus the Group Policy they already know and love.

Let's start right there: As of this minute (2019), there is no debate. There are more, more, way more Group Policy settings than is possible with MDM.

MDM has about 2000 "curated settings," that is, settings that are guaranteed to work. Ironically, many of these MDM settings are focused on one legacy piece of software: Internet Explorer. Almost 200 policies alone are for dealing with IE zone settings. Some are what is known as "ADMX backed" (more on this in Chapter 3, "MDM Profiles, Policies, and Groups") and some are specific and called by the MDM engine.

As of this moment, the official list of settings that Group Policy has in Admin Template settings is 4256, and there are heaps more available configurable items in Group Policy Preferences-land. That said, since Group Policy Preferences isn't getting any fixes, some major areas, like the Start Menu Group Policy Preferences item, don't work anymore in Windows 10, and thus their usefulness is reduced. But in short, from a strictly settings perspective, Group Policy is the "winner."

But, here's the secret: It's not a contest.

It seems like it *should* be a contest, but in reality, it's not supposed to be a contest at all. In other words, if you were strictly looking at Group Policy "versus" MDM, you might think, "Wow, MDM has a long way to go." But the MDM philosophy is expressly *not* to try to take on all of Group Policy's functionality. Besides, since MDM is only for Windows 10 devices, it wouldn't make sense to backport, say, Group Policy settings from Windows XP into MDM. So, by design, MDM will always have fewer settings than Group Policy.

MDM is being rebuilt to handle modern scenarios. And, yes, some of those scenarios overlap with existing scenarios we know, love, and need to deal with today (as we did yesterday). But MDM's philosophy is to analyze each scenario and *then* come up with a way to tackle it. Again, the goal is *not* to replicate all of Group Policy's settings, guts, and complexity (real and perceived).

Another angle and way to think about MDM is that it's trying to enable control of only what's needed instead of "throwing the book at managing everything" in the style that Group Policy did. So, fashions change, and the winds might be blowing toward less controlled settings on your PC now than you needed 10 years ago.

So as I write this, it's true that some admins are looking at what settings are in MDM and throwing their hands up in the air and saying, "Well, I can't do X with MDM, so I have no way to deal with that."

There are some answers here: One (shameless plug) answer would be to check out PolicyPak MDM, where one key feature is to enable you to export real Group Policy ADMX, Group Policy Security, and Group Policy Preferences settings and utilize (almost all of) them with your MDM service. That is definitely an option. See https://www.policypak.com/products/policypak-mdm-edition.html for details.

Another option, is to "live without." This sounds crazy, but stay with me here for a second. Pretend you were to move from a big house with horse stables and downsize to a nice, curated condo. There would be some ups and some downs here. Your big house with the horse stables was awesome, and you had unlimited land and could do whatever you wanted to your house. But when things broke, you had to figure out how to fix it. When you move to your condo, on the one hand, you would necessarily have to downsize (that is, less stuff to bring over), but that might be okay for the trade-off of having less to go wrong. If your condo is nicely curated, new benefits just pop in every so often, like a new clubhouse, new gym equipment, and so on. Heck, maybe this condo doesn't have horse stables like you're used to, but it has free built-in bowling! And for a small upcharge, you can take dance classes. And if the plumbing goes bad, someone else fixes it. You just pay your bills every month, and...hey, maybe you could get used to this. So living without the same exact setting or process you used in Group Policy-land might be okay. Maybe you really didn't need that setting after all, or maybe it makes no sense in a non-domain-joined world. Or maybe there's a workaround with a PowerShell script (though I personally really don't love that option compared to a real setting). But again, living without should be analyzed and dealt with as part of your new "condo living reality."

A third option is to lobby Microsoft with your need and see if they will build it into a future version of Windows. The premier way to do this (as of right now) is via Uservoice: https://microsoftintune.uservoice.com/forums/291681-ideas. You might be able to up-vote a feature or start your own feature and get noticed. Remember, democracy takes time.

And, it should be noted that the "interesting thing you want" requires two pieces:

- Your feature has to be policy enabled in the first place by the Windows 10 product team.
- That policy needs to then be implemented in MDM.

It's. Gonna. Be. Slow.

Setting coverage in MDM will increase over time. It will. But don't expect it to "take on" or "take over" all that on-prem Group Policy has been able to do. That's not part of the deal; at least that's specifically stated from the MDM team to me as their philosophy.

Now that I've talked about the most important aspect, settings, let's explore the other differences between Group Policy and MDM.

History and Development Time   Group Policy has been around since 2000, when Windows 2000 came out. It had some crunchy areas in the engine, which were ironed out around when Vista shipped. Group Policy also scooped up a company called DesktopStandard and rereleased its PolicyMaker program as the Group Policy Preferences, increasing what's possible in Group Policy to thousands of possible settings with nearly infinite configurations to many of the most commonly configured Desktop areas.

After this major release, not a lot happened in Group Policy-land. Group Policy kind of stagnated from a "getting more features" perspective. And, now, all this time later, Microsoft is still committed to "Group Policy engine" bug fixes as well as delivering the ability to manage new feature settings as Admin Templates, such as managing the Windows 10 Start Menu and Taskbar, Windows Edge, and other new Windows 10 features.

But they are clearly not fixing other well-known bugs in Group Policy, mostly in Group Policy Preferences land. There are many Group Policy Preferences items that simply do not work when delivering settings to Windows 10 machines, and these are not ever going to be fixed. In short, other than Group Policy engine bug fixes, security fixes, and adding new settings via Admin Templates, Group Policy's upward growth and development status has stopped, but it's not dead. At Microsoft, it's in the hands of the "Sustained Engineering Team" within Windows, which means...not dead, but not getting drastically improved.

In contrast, the guts for MDM showed up in Windows 8.0, but even by Microsoft's own account, didn't really get fully baked until Windows 10 shipped, which was July 29, 2015. Since then, MDM has increased its coverage of some of the most important settings admins want and the MDM engine has been getting increased development.

Targeting Policies   If you've used Group Policy, you surely know the idea of LSDOU targeting, Group Filtering, WMI Filtering, and Group Policy Preferences Item Level Targeting. These items provided a huge amount of ways to target your policies to specific users, groups, and conditions on the computer.

MDM, on the other hand, has a way to include or exclude groups, minimum and maximum OS version, Windows health attestation, and some others. We'll see this in Chapter 3.

Required Infrastructure and Purchases   So Group Policy "comes in the box" with on-prem AD. You just stand up on-prem AD and get Group Policy for free. AD is the directory and identity service, and Group Policy is the user and device management engine.

In general, to make the most of MDM, you'll need some kind of identity directory service. The most common one would be Azure AD, and just to make things complicated, there's not just one version, there's at least three versions. You can see the differences between AAD Basic, AAD Premium P1, and AAD Premium P2 here:

```
https://docs.microsoft.com/en-us/azure/active-directory/fundamentals/
active-directory-whatis
```

A little later, to get started, we'll sign up for a free 90-day Azure AD Premium account so you can work through the exercises in this book. We'll get Azure AD Premium when we sign up for our "cloud meal plan" in the next chapter.

MDM: Guts, Protocols, and Moving Parts

MDM is the name we give the moving part of the endpoint to receive settings and perform work. But underneath it all, on the endpoint, there are protocols and moving parts that do the actual work.

Let's break it down to understand the parts of MDM.

OMA-DM: The Protocol

Group Policy uses Kerberos and SMB to coordinate its efforts of authenticating a user or computer, then downloading directives.

MDM uses a much lighter weight system based upon XML.

The protocol is called OMA-DM (sometimes spelled out as OMA DM). This is an open standard protocol. The OMA part stands for Open Mobile Alliance. And the DM part stands for Device Management.

OMA-DM deals with the joining aspect of a machine to an MDM system, which is properly known as *enrollment*. And OMA-DM deals with sending messages down in real time, say, to deliver a new policy via push, gather its status, or perform a remote wipe.

Honestly, it's too freakin' boring to go into details for OMA-DM. You really don't want to read about computer-to-computer XML-specific commands to enroll a device, get the acknowledgment, and so on.

The good news is that this is dealt with for you by Microsoft, who supports the OMA-DM protocol inside the Windows 10 MDM engine, and by each MDM vendor. They just "talk the same language" and magic occurs.

And this is also why you can pick any MDM vendor. As long as they've written their specs to the OMA-DM standards, Windows 10 will pick it up and run with it. Again, you don't want to read these boring details. But if you did, here would be the two places to get that gnarly XML information. The OMA specs themselves can be found at www.openmobilealliance.org/wp/.

Microsoft's supported specs for Windows 10 can be found at:

```
https://docs.microsoft.com/en-us/windows/client-management/mdm/
oma-dm-protocol-support
```

CSPs: Configuration Service Providers

To me, the interesting part of MDM is the CSPs, or Configuration Service Providers. These are the build-in mini-receivers within Windows 10's implementation of MDM. They accept OMA-DM directives as XML, process them, and...bingo, something happens on the client.

In Group Policy-land, we used CSEs, or Client-Side Extensions. If you'll remember, there are 39 "in the box" CSEs for Group Policy. Things you know and love, like Admin Templates, Folder Redirection, Group Policy Preferences Printers, and so on. Group Policy CSEs are only available on real Windows versions, and even then, not every Client-Side Extension is available on all real Windows versions. For instance, the Group Policy Preferences CSEs (21 of them) are not available on Windows Home.

Now in MDM-land, we use CSPs. And here's the thing: CSPs are in real Windows (like Pro and Enterprise) and also in these new alternative Windows types, like Windows Mobile and Windows IoT, and...whatever comes next.

And they're in non-Windows devices too. Like iOS, Android, Macs, Chromebooks, and more.

This means you'll need to stay up-to-date with any new CSPs that come out from Microsoft, but really, only for the Desktop versions you need to worry about. Remember that with every Windows 10 release, there might be either new settings to existing CSPs or even new CSPs.

An example of three CSPs and a matrix of which version of Windows 10 they would apply to can be seen in Table 1.1.

TABLE 1.1   Example CSPs and which versions of Windows they apply to

	Home	Pro	Business	Enterprise	Education	Mobile	Mobile Enterprise
AppLocker CSP	✓	✓	✓	✓	✓	✓	✓
Firewall CSP	✗	✓	✓	✓	✓	✗	✗
Policy CSP	✓	✓	✓	✓	✓	✓	✓

These are all detailed inside Microsoft's Configuration Service Provider Service reference, found at:

https://docs.microsoft.com/en-us/windows/client-management/mdm/
configuration-service-provider-reference

There is one CSP you should get to know, like, really well, before you head charging down the road of using an MDM service.

It is called the PolicyCSP and it has two abilities. On the one hand, it can drive settings indirectly. On the other hand, it can do what's called ADMX-backed policies. As you might imagine, ADMX-backed policies tie back to real Group Policy settings.

I'm not really ready to talk about the PolicyCSP in detail yet—until you've selected an MDM service, and you can see how to interact with it. So, stay tuned; this topic will come back soon enough in Chapter 3.

For more about CSP details for IT Pros, read:

```
https://docs.microsoft.com/en-us/windows/configuration/
provisioning-packages/
how-it-pros-can-use-configuration-service-providers
```

WMI-to-CSP Bridge

Windows 10 has a small trick up its sleeve for when a machine has no MDM service to talk with. It's called the WMI-to-CSP Bridge.

This is a way to deliver some CSP commands via scripts, C#, and/or WMI. You can deliver these commands using…well, whatever you like. You could write a login script or deliver the commands via SCCM or have some custom program that did the job.

The point is that if you look at the CSP list, there are a lot of MDM settings you can poke and manage…without subscribing to any MDM service at all.

Okay, sure, you then have to do everything yourself, with a script or some way to program it. Anyway, it's in the box if you want it. The two resources to check out here would be as follows:

MDM Bridge WMI Provider docs found at:

```
https://docs.microsoft.com/en-us/windows/desktop/DMWmiBridgeProv/
mdm-bridge-wmi-provider-portal
```

Using PowerShell scripting with the WMI Bridge Provider found at:

```
https://docs.microsoft.com/en-us/windows/client-management/mdm/
using-powershell-scripting-with-the-wmi-bridge-provider
```

MDM Service

Picking an MDM system as a service is discussed in the next chapter; but there's a big insider secret. This secret is so big, so protected, and I kind of cannot believe it's been kept as long as it has.

Ready for the secret?

Here it is: no single MDM system can fundamentally manage Windows better than any other MDM system.

Did I just blow your mind?

"Why is this?" I hear you cry! Because ultimately all MDM services are limited to using the CSPs that Microsoft provides for Windows 10 in the MDM platform, and, as of this writing, writing custom CSPs isn't permitted.

So all the MDM providers must be pushing the same buttons, remotely using the OMA-DM protocol and twiddling the bits of the CSPs to do the same work. And that's it.

There is an interesting caveat here though, which is that different MDM vendors could expose and "pretty up" the available CSP settings in their UI. We'll see more about this in Chapter 3. But the quick story is that some vendors do a better job than others about lighting up the available CSP settings in a pretty clickable MDM UI.

I've heard this referred to as "First Class" settings. So if your MDM provider doesn't make a particular setting available as a "First Class" clickable setting, you can always poke and set the setting manually. I've heard this called "Third Class" settings. Again, this is something we'll see in Chapter 3.

It is possible to squint a little bit and extend your MDM service to do more than it was originally intended to do. In fact, there are some add-on products to MDM services. See the next section to see how that's done.

But fundamentally, "any MDM will do."

Because they're all pushing the same buttons and pulling the same switches because they're all eventually poking the settings of the in-box CSPs of Windows 10.

Extending Your MDM Services with Third-Party Tools

Even though all MDM services are limited to using the same CSPs, it's possible for an MDM service (or anyone really) to extend Windows management in some other way and use MDM as the transport for doing so.

For instance, MobileIron has a paid add-on product called MobileIron Bridge that is a fancy way of deploying PowerShell scripts. It simply uses the MDM's built-in CSP for deploying MSI files and, then, drops a PowerShell script on the machine and has a little "runner program" to execute the PowerShell scripts.

And Intune itself is also made up of its own "built-in" third-party tool of sorts. It's called the Intune Management Extension. And right now, it bolts on two pieces of functionality that customers kept asking for: running PowerShell scripts and installing Win32 apps (.EXE and .MSI apps with multiple files). It does this by installing a service into Windows, after Windows 10 enrolls into Intune. Maybe the Intune Management Extension will grow in the future to do more things, but as of this writing, that's what it does right now. You can learn more about running PowerShell scripts at:

https://docs.microsoft.com/en-us/intune/intune-management-extension

You can learn more about Win32 app management at:

https://docs.microsoft.com/en-us/intune/apps-win32-app-management

Another instance of how MDM can be extended is how we do it with PolicyPak MDM. For 200 percent clarity, PolicyPak MDM is *not* its own MDM service like Microsoft Intune or Workspace ONE. Instead, PolicyPak MDM's goal is to add onto your existing MDM service (whichever you've picked) and "do more" with it.

So, for example, we let you take your on-prem Group Policy directives (and other magic PolicyPak settings for Windows 10 management) and get them onto your Windows 10 machines. How do we do this? We wrap the directives up into an MSI and then leverage the MDM's CSP for deploying MSI files to get your desired configurations onto the machine. This delivery magic via MSI enables you to deliver the full range of both Group Policy settings and PolicyPak's extra settings (managing browsers, removing admin rights, taming Java, etc.)—all things that neither MDM nor Windows in the box could naturally do.

Additionally, installing the SCCM agent through an MDM service extends your MDM service as well. Wherein you then get to do all the SCCM things you did before as you're used to, like getting detailed inventory of MDM machines rolled up into your SCCM console.

The point is that any given MDM service itself is restricted in what's possible with what Microsoft provides within the CSP list. But as I've shown in this section, the workaround for MDM's shortfalls is to add on a booster rocket….delivered as a bolt-on and delivered via the MSI CSP method when needed, like what I've shown here in these examples.

Final Thoughts

In this chapter I explored the essentials of MDM.

You should now have a grip on why MDM is interesting for scenarios that cannot be covered with on-prem solutions like Group Policy and SCCM. Additionally, I hope you got the memo that I'm not beating up either Group Policy or MDM in any way: Group Policy is great for what it does, and MDM is great for what it does. And, as I said, it's not a "contest" to see when MDM will take on all of Group Policy's settings, because that's not in the game plan.

I also hope going through MDM's guts and moving parts helps you understand how it's all put together. And the good news is, it's not complicated, which is a nice plus.

Additionally, since MDM is always being updated and taking on new settings, you should check in from time to time to see what's new, especially when Windows is updated. The best URL for that is:

```
https://docs.microsoft.com/en-us/windows/client-management/mdm/
new-in-windows-mdm-enrollment-management
```

Hit me up on twitter at @jeremymoskowitz and tell me the one thing you learned in this chapter, Chapter 1. Use the hashtag #mdmbook.

Like … "@jeremymoskowitz, in Chapter 1 of your #mdmbook I learned…." Then just tell me one neat thing.

I can't wait to get your tweets.

And I'll remind you at the end of each chapter, too.

Last, flip back to the beginning of this chapter to see my suggested on-prem test lab details. If you haven't got those set up yet, now would be a good time. In the next chapter, we're going to test-drive Azure AD and select an MDM service. So, best to get the on-prem test lab set up and ready to go before we dive into new waters.

See you there.

Chapter 2

Set Up Azure AD and MDM

In this chapter, we have three main goals:

- Checking out the major players and choices in the MDM space
- Getting started with one of them
- Getting Azure AD set up and having Windows 10 machines auto-enroll to our MDM service

Optionally:

- Use a custom domain name (instead of Microsoft's default one).
- Connect our on-prem AD and have those users sync to Azure AD.

So, let's get started.

Comparative Analysis of Different MDM Services

The following services are the biggest MDM services out there:

- Office 365 with its own "micro" MDM management
- Microsoft Intune
- VMware Workspace ONE
- MobileIron

There are others you might want to check out; I know some organizations using SOTI as an alternative (www.soti.net/solutions/enterprise-mobility-management/), and some using on-prem deployed Meraki (https://meraki.cisco.com/solutions/mobile-device-management), which isn't a cloud service at all. There's also Citrix Endpoint Management (it was called Citrix XenMobile), which I hear is pretty good, but I haven't personally used it.

There's also a "Free for 25 devices" solution from ManageEngine called Mobile Device Manager Plus (www.manageengine.com/mobile-device-management/).

In other words; you might want to find one that makes sense for you, your company, your needs, and your budget...*not* simply going with the big gorillas on the block because you see other people doing it.

That said, I will be showing screen shots and scenarios from only the big guys, mostly Intune. But the concepts you learn with what I show should translate to most MDM solutions because they all, by definition, are driven by what's possible with the MDM guts within Windows 10, which every MDM vendor must use.

Azure AD Premium, Enterprise Mobility + Security, and Microsoft 365

Remember, your MDM management system might or might not be able to do it alone. By that I mean an MDM service might rely on you having an identity service to house your user accounts and create some identity around who is who at your company.

Microsoft's cloud-based identity service is Microsoft Azure AD, which comes in four flavors: Free, Basic, Premium P1, and Premium P2. And a fifth, which can be used exclusively with Office 365 (though that one may be upgraded to one of the Premium versions if needed).

Cutting right to the chase, to do MDM "right" (what we'll learn a little bit later), the only Azure AD flavors that matter are Premium P1 and Premium P2. This is because only the P1 and P2 account types do what's called MDM "auto-enrollment." This (as you'll see) is the magic when a user goes to enroll their device in MDM and that request is forwarded from Azure AD to your MDM service. Additionally, Dynamic Groups—that is, the ability for computers or users to meet criteria and magically get into groups—is also only available in P1 or P2.

So for me, the other Azure AD account types are literally nonstarters with regard to working with MDM. You really must get an Azure AD P1 or P2 account type in order to be successful with MDM. You can see Microsoft's chart at https://azure.microsoft.com/en-us/pricing/details/active-directory/.

Maybe in some future world, there will be more offerings to choose from. But as of this writing, if you zip down to the last row comparing all the features and versions, you should see the feature "MDM auto-enrollment, Self-Service Bitlocker recovery, Additional local administrators to Windows 10 devices via Azure AD Join, Enterprise State Roaming."

If Microsoft changes its Azure AD plans in the future, by the time you read this, that's fine. Here's Jeremy's MDM Rule #1:

> To do MDM right, always get an Azure AD plan that provides MDM auto-enrollment and enables Dynamic Groups.

The end.

Meanwhile, you might be curious about how to buy Azure AD Premium and/or start a free trial. Indeed, to make the most out of the examples in this book, you'll need to start an Azure AD Premium trial. Don't buy or do anything with Azure AD just yet! But if you wanted to, just look at the trial page at `https://azure.microsoft.com/en-us/trial/ get-started-active-directory/`. Again, don't do this now, but if and when you're ready to purchase Azure AD, I recommend you work with your Microsoft licensing person to help you set an Enterprise Agreement. Or you can work with a reseller or partner. Microsoft is pushing a new idea, which can make sense if you're starting to get "all in" on the cloud and want to use Microsoft as the one-stop shop for modern management. Microsoft 365 is a "meal combo" that comes with the following offerings:

- Azure AD Premium. (Again, the Premium part is what's needed to do the auto-enrollment.)

- Enterprise Mobility + Security, which in and of itself contains a huge gaggle of cloud services:

  - Microsoft Intune (Manage PCs and phones; this is the product we'll be using the most in this book.)

  - Azure Information Protection (Prevent Sally in HR from sending out confidential information.)

  - Microsoft Cloud App Security (Know which cloud services like Dropbox and Salesforce are being used and set policies about who can do what.)

  - Microsoft Identity Manager (Synchronize on-prem AD to Azure AD and let users reset their own passwords.)

  - Azure Advanced Threat Analytics (Detect suspicious activity, such as if someone just logged in while in New York and also somehow magically in Helsinki within 2 minutes.) This is sometimes called "impossible travel."

  - Azure Advanced Threat Protection (detects abnormal behavior like Pass-the-Hash attacks and various brute force attacks against your on-prem and cloud)

- Office 365
- Windows 10 Enterprise use rights

So, my plan in this book is not to go into all these things. But I want you to be able to start talking about, and making the right decisions about, what to buy.

If this Microsoft 365 "all in/meal combo" sounds appetizing, I would actually start out by taking a step back and analyzing *only* the Enterprise Mobility + Security features and pricing plans, since that's the most germane to the focus of what we're doing together.

As of this writing, there are only two Enterprise Mobility + Security options: the E3 plan and the E5 plan. For me, the E5 plan is stronger, but more expensive. You can see the plan comparisons at `www.microsoft.com/en-us/cloud-platform/ enterprise-mobility-security-pricing`.

Remember, if you like the idea of being "all in" with Microsoft's cloud services, then you shouldn't really be gunning to buy Enterprise Mobility + Security alone (even though it includes Azure AD). But rather, you would be researching Enterprise Mobility + Security plans to then guide your decision about which Microsoft 365 plan you wish to purchase, because Microsoft 365 plans contain Office 365 and Enterprise Mobility + Security.

The rundown of major items can be seen in Figure 2.1.

FIGURE 2.1   Features and options with E3 vs. E5

ENTERPRISE MOBILITY + SECURITY (EMS)		E3	E5
Mobile device management	Microsoft InTune	✓	✓
Identity management	Azure Active Directory	P1	P2
Threat detection	Advanced Threat Analytics	✓	✓
Information protection	Azure Information Protection	P1	P2
App security	Microsoft Cloud App Security	✗	✓

WINDOWS 10		E3	E5
Windows 10 upgrade	Windows 10 Business or Enterprise	E3	E5
Device Deployment	Windows AutoPilot	✓	✓
Security: biometric, credential, malware	Windows Hello, Credential Guard, Device Guard, AppLocker, Enterprise Data Protection	✓	✓
Antivirus	Windows Defender Antivirus	✓	✓
Threat protection	Windows Defender Advanced Threat Protection	✗	✓

Then after you make that decision, you can work with your partner or reseller, and get an Enterprise Agreement (EA) for Microsoft 365 that suits your needs. And it should be cheaper overall to buy a Microsoft 365 subscription than to buy all the parts separately (as with any good deal).

Again, though, for the "base hit" exercises in this book, you don't need to go bananas or even buy anything at all.

Just get the Azure AD Premium trial, again, from here: https://azure.microsoft.com/en-us/trial/get-started-active-directory/.

If you wish to follow along with the exercises, do this step before continuing.

Office 365's Built-In MDM Management

If your company is already an Office 365 customer, then you already have some degree of MDM built in. Cutting to the chase, the Office 365's built-in MDM management has a single goal: to replace Exchange ActiveSync and try to get into the twenty-first century.

And it does.

It's a perfectly fine MDM for phones, tablets, and so on.

It's not really trying to be a "grown up" version of MDM like Microsoft Intune is trying to be. But it's free, and it's built into all business and enterprise versions of Office 365.

By default, the MDM features of Office 365 are not active; you must manually activate them. After you do, it takes between zero minutes and a few hours before they are actually ready to use.

The step-by-steps of setting up Office 365 MDM can be found here:

```
https://support.office.com/en-us/article/
set-up-mobile-device-management-mdm-in-office-365-dd892318-bc44-4eb1-af00-
9db5430be3cd
```

I've shortened the link to `https://bit.ly/2ttf3bc` if you want to use that.

You can see the device security policies that are available in Figure 2.2.

FIGURE 2.2 Office 365's built-in MDM

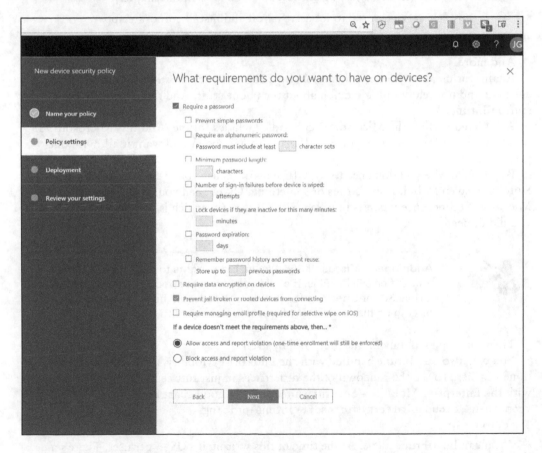

And, it's really not that much. Fine for small needs, and "basically okay" for phones and general protection.

But it's Intune, which is Microsoft's stronger way to manage Windows 10, and that's where I'm going to focus my attention.

Microsoft Intune

Intune is Microsoft's premier cloud way to manage Windows 10 and other MDM-capable devices. From a Windows 10 perspective, you get the following items, which are not present in the Office 365 MDM (many of these topics we will cover in subsequent chapters):

- Deploying applications (like MSI, MSIX, etc.)
- Securing content with MAM (mobile application management)
- Running PowerShell commands
- More PC management and policies, including ADMX-backed policies
- Connect to SCCM for co-management (explained later in the chapter).
- Company self-service portal to let users enroll and install corporate apps
- Provision Wi-Fi and VPN profiles

And more.

Again, for me, and you, and this book, my goal is to stick mostly to Windows 10 management and not really talk too much about the phone stuff. And there's a lot of phone stuff in Intune.

As I stated earlier, the Microsoft 365 bundle includes Intune. And this Microsoft 365 bundle makes a lot of sense if you're "all in" with Microsoft and want it all, with one price tag.

But, hey, maybe you don't need, say, Office 365 because you've already got Google's G Suite or, heaven forbid, Lotus Notes or something. Okay, then you wouldn't want to buy Microsoft 365 because it comes bundled with Office 365, which is something you just said you didn't need.

 Additionally, Microsoft 365 also includes rights to use Win10 Enterprise and Office 365 ProPlus. It could even be cost effective if you don't need Office 365 or OneDrive for Business. You would have to check out the pricing on that with your Microsoft sales rep.

Therefore, you can buy Intune alone, all by itself.

You can also buy Intune bundled with the Enterprise Mobility + Security suite I mentioned earlier. To see the rundown of the differences in just Intune alone or Intune along with the Enterprise Mobility + Security suite, there's a good chart here: www.microsoft.com/en-us/cloud-platform/microsoft-intune-pricing.

So, to recap:

- You can buy Intune alone. At the time of this writing it's US$6 per user. There's a special "per device" license (when no users are on the machine, like digital signs) for US$2 per device.
- You can buy it as part of the Enterprise Mobility + Security E3 suite.
- You can buy it as part of the Enterprise Mobility + Security E5 suite.
- You can buy it as part of Microsoft 365.

I found two ways to try Windows Intune.

Way #1: Find the Microsoft Enterprise Mobility + Security pricing page I noted earlier, and in the E5 block, click Try Now.

Way #2: Go to the "Sign up for a Microsoft Intune free trial" page: `https://docs` `.microsoft.com/en-us/intune/free-trial-sign-up`.

For this book, I am going to use Way #1 and sign up for an E5 trial and connect it to my Azure AD trial that I made in the previous step. So, again, go here: `www.microsoft.com/` `en-us/cloud-platform/enterprise-mobility-security-pricing`.

Just look for Try Now. I did create a fake `Outlook.com` address to get started, and that took about 80 seconds. After that, the basic steps I used can be seen in Figure 2.3 to get started.

FIGURE 2.3   The signup page for EMS E5

Then, it's time to create your first user and company name. What I used can be seen in Figure 2.4. Note that the company name must be unique across all the special ".onmicrosoft.com" domains in the world. I'm claiming `Fabrikam1000.onmicrosoft.com` as my domain name to use throughout this book and my ongoing examples at `www.MDMandGPanswers.com`.

FIGURE 2.4   Create your first user and company name.

Then just sit back and wait a moment or two, and   bingo. You're ready to rock, like what's seen in Figure 2.5.

FIGURE 2.5   EMS E5 trial success message

ActiveSync, Office 365 MDM, and Intune MDM Feature Comparison

You might be wondering what features are available in what product. To that end, I found and re-created a public Microsoft document that spells out the major differences.

You can see that in this table here if the boss ever asks why the MDM for Office 365 isn't enough and you have to start spending on Intune or another MDM service instead.

Device management feature comparison

Category	Feature	Exhange ActiveSync	MDM for Office 365	Intune
Device configuration	Inventory mobile devices that access corporate applications	●	●	●
	Remote factory reset (full device wipe)	●	●	●
	Mobile device configuration settings (PIN length, PIN required, lock time, etc.)	●	●	●
	Self-service password reset (Office 365 cloud only users)	●	●	●
Office 365	Provides reporting on devices that do not meet IT policy		●	●
	Group-based policies and reporting (ability to use groups for targeted device configuration)		●	●
	Root cert and jailbreak detection		●	●
	Remove Office 365 app data from mobile devices while leaving personal data and apps intact (selective wipe)		●	●
	Prevent access to corporate email and documents based upon device enrollment and compliance policies		●	●
Premium mobile device & app management	Self-service Company Portal for users to enroll their own devices and install corporate apps			●
	Deploy certificates, VPN profiles (including app-specific profiles), and Wi-Fi profiles			●
	Prevent cut/copy/paste/save as of data from corporate apps to personal apps (mobile application management)			●
	Secure content viewing via Managed browser, PDF viewer, Imager viewer, and AV player apps for Intune			●
	Remote device lock via self-service Company Portal and via admin console			●
PC management	PC management (e.g. inventory, antimalware, patch, policies, etc.)			●
	OS deployment (via System Center ConfigMgr)			●
	PC software management			●
	Single management console for PCs and mobile devices (through integration with System Center ConfigMgr)			●

Additionally, this was the latest page where I found the side-by-side comparisons of MDM for Office 365 and Intune:

```
https://support.office.com/en-us/article/
choose-between-mdm-for-office-365-and-microsoft-intune-c93d9ab9-efb2-
4349-9b93-30c30562ee22
```

Another ugly link, so I made a short link at `https://bit.ly/2E20PWe`.

Intune for Education

There's another version of Windows Intune that should be mentioned here, in case this is your scenario. There is Windows Intune for Education, which has a special superpower.

That is, it can read data from Microsoft School Data Sync (`https://sds.microsoft.com/`) and automatically create and keep groups of users and computers up-to-date.

The other interesting part of Windows Intune for Education is that it has two licensing methods.

> Method #1 is that you can buy it outright for $30 per device. This includes unlimited users on the devices you license.
>
> Method #2 is that you can pay per user at $8.28 per year. Before you flip out, students are free! You only count staff and faculty.

The sweetheart part of the deal is the included Azure AD type that comes with Windows Intune for Education. It's got its own flavor called Azure AD EDU, but it hits the mark with the most needed features you'll need, including auto-enrollment.

You can always upgrade to Azure AD Premium and get some additional AD security features, like two-factor authentication, which is only available there. But, Azure AD EDU hits the mark for what I think most schools would need to marry up with Intune.

Start out by reading

```
https://www.microsoft.com/en-us/education/intune/default.aspx and
https://blogs.windows.com/windowsexperience/2017/01/24/
announcing-intune-education-new-windows-10-pcs-school-starting-189
```

Last, and I think it's worth mentioning, in the same way that there's a full bore bundle of stuff for businesses called Microsoft 365, there's also a full bore bundle of stuff for education (Office 365, Azure, Intune) and some other stuff like Mindcraft.

And, no surprise, it's called Microsoft Education. So if you wanted to try out Windows Intune for Education in conjunction with the other pieces of the Microsoft Education suite, the trial page for the whole enchilada can be found here:

```
https://docs.microsoft.com/en-us/education/get-started/
get-started-with-microsoft-education
```

Note that once you sign up for a Microsoft Education trial, they do some verifications to see that, yes, you really are a school, so you cannot just start a trial without some scholastic affiliation.

VMware Workspace ONE

VMware is also in the game for MDM management with its product called VMware Workspace ONE. It used to have the catchy name "AirWatch," and now it has a more boring name with Workspace ONE, and it's harder to type.

That said, it's the same product, and a solid MDM solution. You have to pick the edition of VMware Workspace ONE to use. There's a medium-long comparison chart at www .vmware.com/products/workspace-one.html, but if you dig for it, there's a PDF you can download when you click on View Complete Feature Comparison.

In checking out the table, there is one line item row that sticks out. "Advanced Desktop Management" which touts "Includes custom scripting, BitLocker encryption, desktop / Win32 app management, Windows 10 Enterprise polices (including Credential Guard Device Guard)." And for those features, it's going to be Advanced Edition, Enterprise Edition, and Enterprise for VDI Edition.

Computers managed with Workspace ONE can also auto-enroll in Azure AD when taught to do so. but Azure AD is not strictly required if you want to experiment with VMware Workspace ONE. VMware also has its own identity service in VMware Identity Manager, which you can learn about here: www.vmware.com/products/workspace-one/identity-manager.html.

If you want to get started, as of this writing, the AirWatch brand is transitioning to Workspace ONE. As such, the way to get started with AirWatch, I mean, Workspace ONE, might be different by the time you read this. I was able to find a 30-day trial at www.air-watch.com/lp/free-trial/. But then trying to find a Workspace ONE trial, I could only find a hands-on lab, which is fine, but not really what I was after. Anyway, you can try that out here if you like: https://www.vmware.com/go/workspace-hol.

Since it's a sandboxed hands-on lab, I didn't try to connect it to a real Azure AD, which might or might not work. The step-by-steps for marrying Workspace ONE (still called AirWatch on this page) to Azure AD can be found at https://docs.microsoft.com/en-us/azure/active-directory/saas-apps/airwatch-tutorial.

For me, I have a full account for Workspace ONE, and that's what I'm going to use for any examples in the book. If I have my story straight, you can get your own full account through a VMware reseller or account manager.

MobileIron

MobileIron's website is the most confusing of the bunch. It took me a while to find their page talking about Windows 10 management. But I did, and it's here: www.mobileiron.com/en/unified-endpoint-management/operating-systems/windows-10.

Then, if you want to start a 30-day trial of MobileIron, you can do so here: https://info.mobileiron.com/30DayTrial.

To connect MobileIron to Azure AD, complete step-by-steps are on Microsoft's website here: https://docs.microsoft.com/en-us/azure/active-directory/saas-apps/mobileiron-tutorial.

Setting Up Auto-Enrollment and Enrolling Your First Machines

Okay. Let's recap:

- You signed up for a free Outlook account.
- You signed up for a free Enterprise Mobile Suite + Security E5 plan.
- You got Azure AD Premium P2 at the same time.

Now it's time to turn on your Intune inside your Azure AD.

Start out by signing out of everything: Outlook, Azure AD, and/or any other Microsoft services you might have open.

Then, head over to portal.office.com and you might be prompted as shown in Figure 2.6. Pick the one with the .onmicrosoft.com address and log in.

FIGURE 2.6 Log on using your onmicrosoft.com account.

Turning On MDM Enrollment

There are two steps to MDM Enrollment:

- Users
- Computers

Let's do the user side first and the computer side second.

MDM Enrollment for Users

Click Azure Active Directory as seen in Figure 2.7.

FIGURE 2.7   Click to open Azure Active Directory.

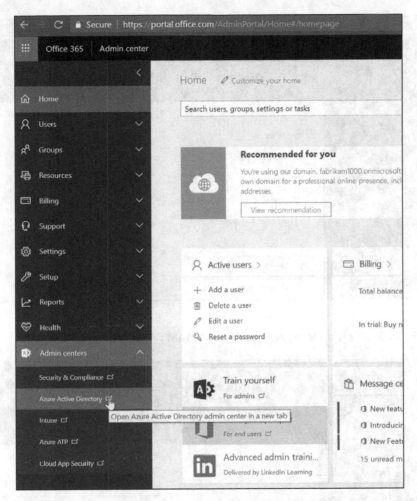

In a new tab, you'll be seeing Azure AD and can click Mobility (MDM and MAM), then Microsoft Intune, as seen in Figure 2.8. Then, in the Configure Microsoft Intune dialog box that appears next, as seen in Figure 2.9, you specifically need to enable MDM user scope. For our examples, I recommend selecting All (also seen in Figure 2.9).

FIGURE 2.8   This is where you click to turn on Intune.

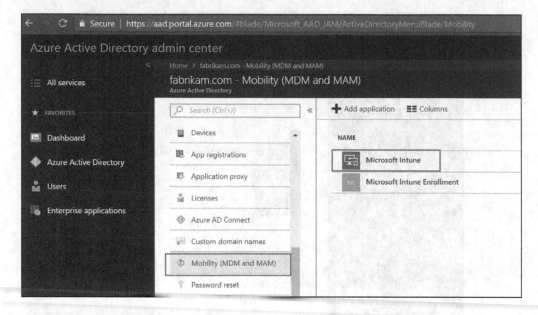

FIGURE 2.9   Turn on MDM and, optionally, MAM for all users.

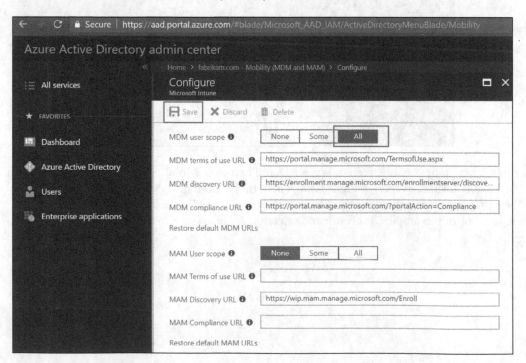

Then, back at the Mobility (MDM and MAM) page (again, Figure 2.8), you'll click Microsoft Intune Enrollment. This gets you to the "Microsoft Intune Enrollment" page seen on Figure 2.10. For MDM user scope, click All again and click Save.

FIGURE 2.10   Turn on MDM for Intune Enrollment.

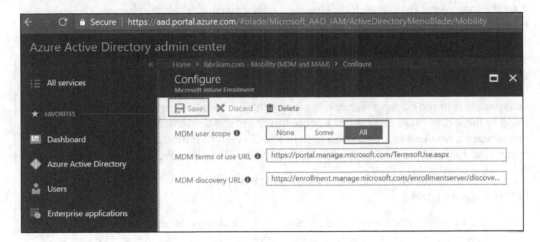

What you just configured was the user side of the MDM equation. Users need to be prompted to acknowledge the terms of use and so on.

But the real magic is in devices. You need to configure the device registration authority.

MDM Enrollment for Computers

Just 10 seconds ago you were in the Azure AD Console. Now it's time to get into Intune and tell it that you wish to have it accept requests and perform auto-enrollment.

As I write this, there are three ways to jump into Intune. Way #1 is from the main Admin center, as seen in Figure 2.7. within the Admin center, you could click Intune.

But if you're still in Azure's portal, you might not see a link to Intune.

My favorite way to just "go to Intune" is just to search as shown in Figure 2.11. Just click the search spyglass, type **Intune,** and click the word Intune when it pops up, like I'm doing in Figure 2.11.

FIGURE 2.11   If you ever get lost in the Azure portal, just search for Intune.

So if you ever get lost and just want to go to Intune (or you cannot *find* Intune), use the spyglass as seen in Figure 2.11.

Bingo.

Another way to add Intune to the list of Azure resources is to click "All services" (seen also in Figure 2.11). Then find Intune and click the star next to it. This will magically add it to the long menu list on the left. This then puts it (basically) on every page, and makes it much easier to just click on to jump to Intune.

Some Notes and Tips about the Intune UI

I suspect that in the coming months, Intune might just be a nice easy-to-find clickable thing in the Azure main page. After I wrote this chapter, Microsoft already came back and announced a preview of a new page to help you zip toward Intune and device management even faster once you're logged on: `https://devicemanagement.microsoft.com`.

So, be on the lookout for that. I likely won't be able to retake screen shots for the book before it goes to press.

But, again, the methods here should continue to work alongside any new method as well. Going forward, in the book, I might just say, "Go to the Intune console" and I'll assume you can find your way there: from the Azure portal, a nifty new icon on the Azure portal (if they do that), or at `https://devicemanagement.microsoft.com`.

Additionally, and unrelated, each little window that slides to the right as you expand to do something interesting in Azure or Intune has a nifty name.

It's called a *blade*.

Doesn't it feel so super cool saying that?

Say it again: *blade*.

Not a window, not a pane. No, no. Those terms are so retro.

Now it's a *blade*.

Ahem. Okay. Sure. I'll call it a *blade*.

Once you're in Intune, the first stop will be "Device enrollment," as seen in Figure 2.12. This is where you'll explain to Intune what's allowed and not allowed. For instance, if you wanted to allow Apple phones and Windows devices but disallow Android devices, this is the right place.

FIGURE 2.12   In Intune, use "Device enrollment" to specify the MDM authority.

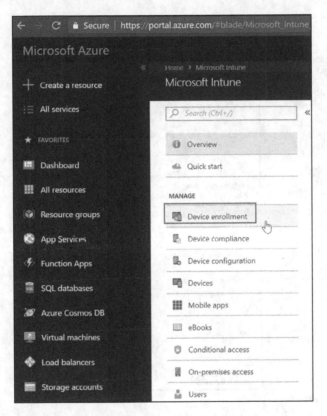

Then, you'll see the Choose MDM Authority blade, shown in Figure 2.13. You will only see Choose MDM Authority if you have not done this step ever before.

The correct option to select is Intune MDM Authority as I've selected here. Configuration Manager MDM Authority would enable what's known as Hybrid Intune + SCCM and is going away. (I talk more about Hybrid Intune and SCCM, why it's going away, and what replaces it in Chapter 4.)

FIGURE 2.13   Choose Intune MDM Authority to manage devices.

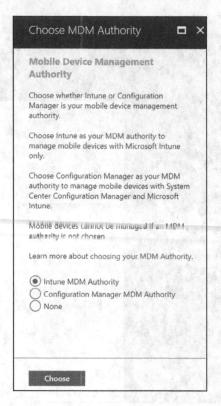

 If you want to learn more about the MDM authority, there is a detailed article here: https://docs.microsoft.com/en-us/intune/ mdm-authority-set. For instance, you may want to later set it to SCCM or some other MDM service.

When you do you'll get a toast notification that it was set correctly.

 What is *toast*? It's like a pop-up. Read this if you never heard that term before: https://ux.stackexchange.com/questions/11998/ what-is-a-toast-notification.

Add Your First User to Azure AD

Adding your first user to Azure AD, manually, takes just a moment.

Back in the Azure portal, start out by clicking Users or "Add a user" as seen in Figure 2.14. If you're lost, and cannot find Azure AD, just type in aad.portal.azure.com. and you should be teleported back to Azure land.

FIGURE 2.14   Adding a user by hand to Azure Active Directory

Then, enter information for a user. I'll be adding someone named Jack Tors as seen in Figure 2.15. Note that I have to explicitly spell out his username, which must (for now) end in fabrikam1000.onmicrosoft.com. Later, we'll set up optional custom domain names.

FIGURE 2.15   Create your first user in Azure AD.

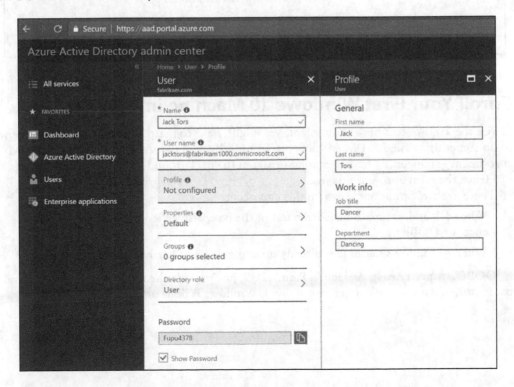

Jack is now created but has no licenses. To assign him licenses, click back to Users ➤ Active Licenses and find the user you just created, Jack Tors. Then specify a location and that he gets a license, as seen in Figure 2.16.

FIGURE 2.16   Each user needs a license.

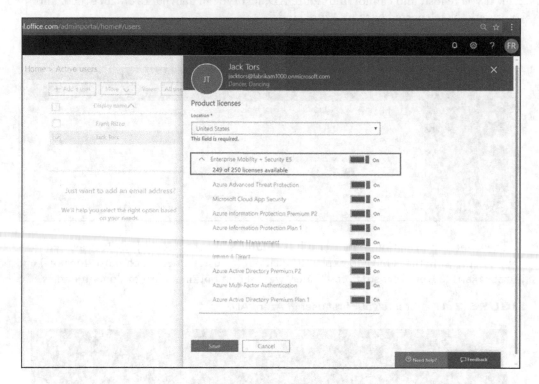

Enroll Your First Windows 10 Machine into MDM

Here's the kind-of bad news. You might, yes might, have to (gasp!) actually teach users how to do something called MDM enrollment. Technically, you join Azure AD, and the MDM enrollment is happening for you automatically in the background.

Hence the term *auto-enrollment*.

There are two situations in which this can occur:

- When a Windows machine is fresh out of the box, also called the out of box experience, or OOBE
- When a Windows machine is already up and going and has been used for a while

OOBE is...pretty easy. As seen in Figure 2.17, just provide the user with a username and password, and a few clicks later (not shown), Windows is done and ready to rock.

FIGURE 2.17   You can give someone a username and password to enroll a machine "out of the box" aka OOBE.

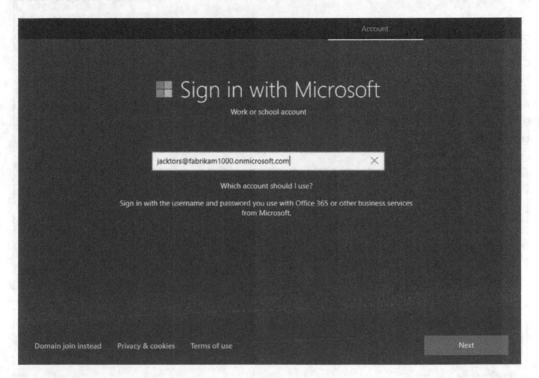

But after this is over (don't shoot the messenger), the person who enrolls the machine becomes a local admin. Wait, wait...don't panic. You can change this behavior if you want; see the sidebar "Restricting Users and Devices in Azure and Intune."

And, additionally, we will overcome this problem when we talk about distributing new machines using Autopilot. But that's all the way in Chapter 8! But for now, it's true: If someone enrolls the machine in this way using the out of the box experience, they become the local admin on the box.

Okay. Take a deep breath and let's move onward.

Now, the next methods I want to show you will be for when the Windows 10 machine is already up and running, maybe having been used for some time. I'm going to teach you three things in this scenario:

- The first thing is what *not* to teach your users. Yep, what *not* to do comes first.

- The second thing is "all the manual clicks" a user would have to do in order to get MDM enrolled.

- The third thing would be a little shortcut method to minimize the steps a user would have to perform.

Restricting Users and Devices in Azure and Intune

Having anyone who just enrolls a machine with their username and password automatically become a local admin of the Windows 10 machine: crazy bad idea.

Crazy good news: You can fix this with Azure's Device settings, in a section called device type restrictions.

First, in Azure's portal (not in Intune), when you click Devices and then "Device settings," there are a handful of interesting options you may want to know about. You can see them here.

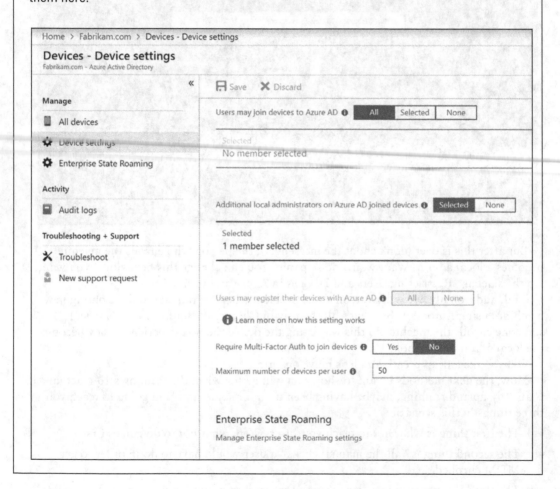

You can use the items on this page as follows:

- To limit which users may join devices to Azure AD

- To add which Azure users will also be local administrators on your AAD joined devices

- To specify how many devices a user can have. Could be handy to set it to 1 or 2 instead of 50 or unlimited.

The second, related idea is how you can use the Intune console to prevent personally owned devices from being able to make their way into Intune. When you do this, you ensure that devices you know about are coming into Intune and not random machines purchased at Best Buy or Amazon.

Okay then, if you block personally owned devices, then what is the definition of personally owned, versus, say, corporate owned?

The web page on the subject is here: `https://docs.microsoft.com/en-us/intune/ enrollment-restrictions-set#set-device-type-restrictions`, and here are the relevant characteristics:

- The enrolling user is using an admin style account, also known as a device enrollment manager account. A nice step-by-step is found at `https://prajwaldesai.com/ adding-microsoft-intune-device-enrollment-manager/`.

- The device is enrolled through Windows Autopilot (discussed in Chapter 8).

- The device enrolls through a bulk AAD Token via a provisioning package (also discussed in Chapter 8).

- The device enrolls through automatic enrollment via SCCM for co-management.

There are some other restrictions too, but these are the big ones.

If you want to tweak Intune to block personally owned devices, which would then prevent (what should be) standard users from becoming local admins on the Windows 10 machine, then in Intune, go to Device Enrollment ➢ Enrollment Restrictions. Inside Device Type Restrictions, you can click Properties and select the "Configure platforms," then within the "Personally Owned" column, click Block upon the type of device you want to restrict; in our case Windows 10, as seen here.

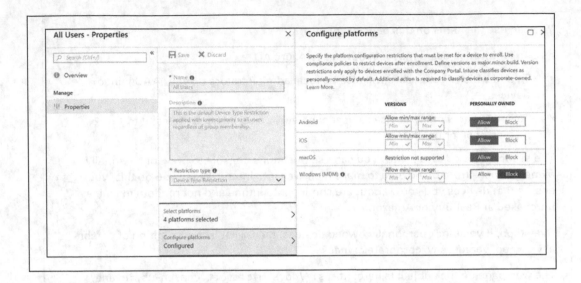

What Not to Do: Azure AD Join, but No MDM Enrollment

Why am I showing you what *not* to do first? Because, it seems like the most obvious path you (or your users) would take. Trust me, you'll see what I mean.

These examples are using a Windows 10 1809 machine; your experience may be a little different in future versions of Windows. But this is what I've got to show you today.

Pretend to be a Standard User (that is, one without any local admin rights), and go to the Start bar and type in **MDM**. For me, and I swear I'm not making this up, I also got some nice recommendations about the mind-altering drug MDMA. But, erasing the recommended A in MDMA will get you what you see in Figure 2.18.

FIGURE 2.18 Using Windows search to look for MDM settings

This enables the user to click either "Enroll in MDM only" (two choices) or "Access work or school."

Again, maybe it's just me, but in 1809, clicking "Enroll in MDM only" (the left side or the big right-side link) actually did *nothing* at all except bring me to the Windows Settings page (yippee). (I even tried this as a local admin, and nothing occurred at all.)

Now as this pretend user, inside Windows Settings I have to type **MDM** again, where you'll see what's in Figure 2.19.

FIGURE 2.19   Use the Settings app

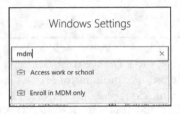

Once again, trying "Enroll in MDM only" again from here gives me…exactly nothing again. Literally. It goes nowhere at all.

Okay. (Remember, you're trying to think like the user, and a Standard User at that.) So let's try "Access work or school." Okay! That works. On that page is a big + (plus) with the word *Connect*. Great, let's click on that.

Then the big, beautiful dialog box you'll see next is seen in Figure 2.20, where you would expect a user to put in their Azure AD account information.

FIGURE 2.20   The "Set up a work or school account" dialog box. Just waiting to eat your end users for lunch.

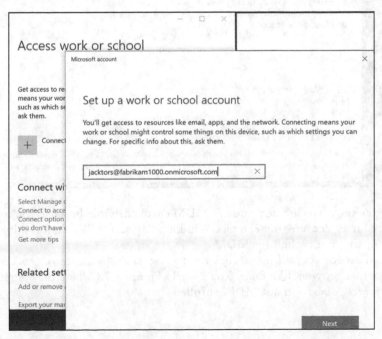

Then, they log on with the username and password they got from email. As it's cooking, it will look like Figure 2.21.

FIGURE 2.21   As the connection to Azure AD occurs, you'll see something like this.

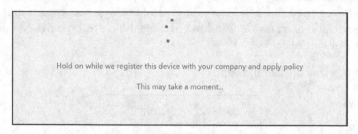

You'll get an "All set" message and a chance to click Done. When you do, you'll fall right, directly, squarely into the snake pit, like Indiana Jones does in *Raiders of the Lost Ark*.

Here's an example of the wrong icon, seen in Figure 2.22. It looks like the Windows flag icon. This is <u>not</u> what you want to see if you wish to be MDM enrolled.

FIGURE 2.22   The Windows icon after enrollment means you're "Workplace joined" and not really MDM enrolled.

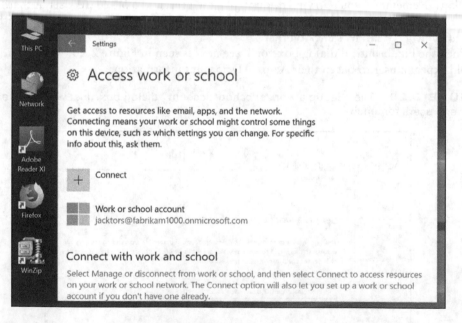

How do you know you are not *actually* MDM enrolled? Only because you're reading this book of course. Because to me, a nice Windows flag seems like a good thing. But it's actually wrong and not enough for MDM.

But you can see for yourself if you click on the flag, click "Manage your account," and open the page in a browser, like Edge. You'll see in Figure 2.23 where the computer is merely *Workplace joined* and not MDM enrolled.

FIGURE 2.23   You *don't* want to be Workplace joined. You want to be MDM enrolled, which is explained next.

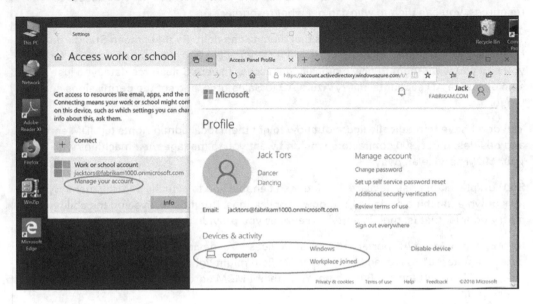

To understand what you've just done, which, again, is called Workplace Join, see the sidebar "What Is Workplace Join?"

What Is Workplace Join

If you're not MDM enrolled in Figure 2.22, then what *have* you done there?

As you can see in Figure 2.23, after you click into it for further inspection, it's called Workplace Join and it's really part 1 of the 2 part process to really be MDM enrolled. Said another way, there are two parts to MDM enrollment: joining Azure AD (aka Workplace Join) and Enrollment into MDM.

That big, inviting window is where you put in the username, that literally only takes care of part 1, the Workplace Join part and not the MDM enrollment part.

So what is Workplace Join and why would you want it?

Again, for clarity, it's not MDM, so for the purposes of this book, you really don't want it. But its function is to enable people who bring their own device to join your Azure AD, where you can then provide single sign-on to apps like Box, Salesforce, and so on.

And that's it.

With Workplace Join, you're not able to deliver applications, manage settings, or perform any other MDM function.

It's really there just to, well, join your Azure AD, and then when you provide access to resources, you can dictate who can get what resources.

The other upside of Workplace Join is that anyone can do it. By that I mean Standard Users (aka non-admins) can do it. So if you've already got 300 contractors working for you and you want them to now magically get access to your Salesforce data, you just spin up Azure AD accounts, marry Azure AD to Salesforce, and set the permissions and... bingo.

You don't have to magically figure out how to get them local admin rights to MDM enroll, and besides, those 300 contractors wouldn't want you to manage *their* machines with *your* MDM service anyway.

So Workplace Join has its place, but it doesn't enable you to actually control, manage, or lock down a machine or deploy Windows applications. But it does give you the ability to marry people (that is, their identity) to services you provide through Azure AD.

If you go into Azure AD portal and look at Devices ➤ All devices, you will see the computer "registered" to AD, and even the MDM field might light up saying your MDM service, like Microsoft Intune. But, oh no. You are not MDM enrolled, you are "Azure AD registered."

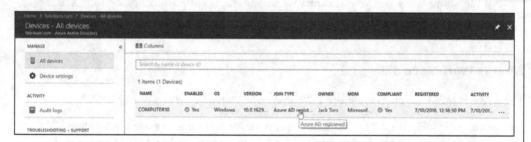

If you followed me down the snake hole, let's get a clean slate. First, back at the client, click the Windows flag icon, like what you saw in Figure 2.22 (and 2.23). Then click Disconnect and then Yes. Then, here inside the Azure AD portal, click on the computer itself, then click Delete and say Yes.

Poof. Out of the snake pit.

What to Do: MDM Enroll

Snake pits: bad. Treasure: good.

To get to the MDM treasure you need to knock on the secret door.

And, Indiana Jones is no regular user, he's a hero…a Local Admin. (I'll just call him an Admin, but you'll know I mean Local Admin.)

So, log off the machine as a Standard User and back in on as an Admin. When you do, you'll be able to knock three times and find the secret door. Indeed, Figure 2.24 is the secret door and the X marks the spot. Well, not an X, but an oval.

FIGURE 2.24   Just click "Join this device to Azure Active Directory" for MDM enrollment.

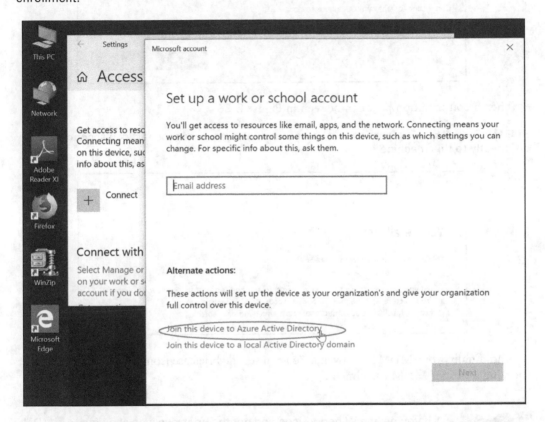

Before you continue, take a look at the difference between Figure 2.24 and Figure 2.20. See that as a Standard User, you don't even get the chance to find the treasure (labeled as "Join this device to Azure Active Directory."

Now, because you're an Admin, click on the treasure "Join this device to Azure Active Directory."

Then, and only then, on the next page (not shown), you will put in Jack's username and password. Once you do, you'll get a pre-confirmation of what is about to occur as seen in Figure 2.25. Click Join to enroll.

FIGURE 2.25   The pre-confirmation for MDM enrollment

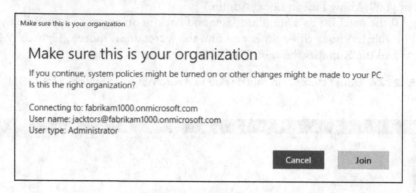

Then a confirmation page can be seen in Figure 2.26.

FIGURE 2.26   Explanation that you can now use the `onmicrosoft.com` account to log on directly to this machine

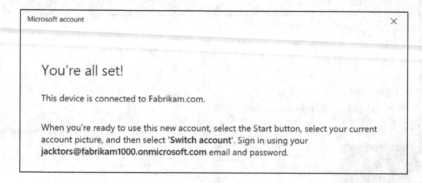

And, finally, your MDM gold awaits. You can see the briefcase icon, as seen in Figure 2.27, showing a proper MDM enrollment.

If you get the Windows icon and not the briefcase icon showing true MDM enrollment, try waiting a day and retrying. Sometimes after telling Azure AD who the MDM authority is takes some time. Like 24–48 hours.

Now on your Windows 10 machine, log off, and log on as `JackTors1000@fabrikam1000 .onmicrosoft.com` as seen in Figure 2.28.

FIGURE 2.27   The briefcase icon means you are successfully enrolled in MDM.

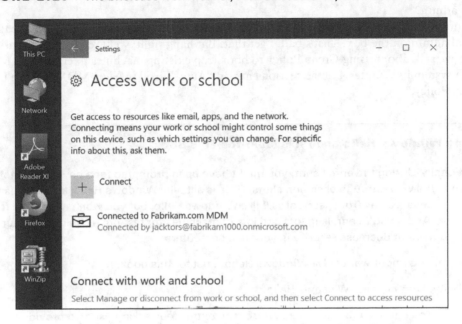

FIGURE 2.28   Now you can sign on with your Azure AD credentials to this machine.

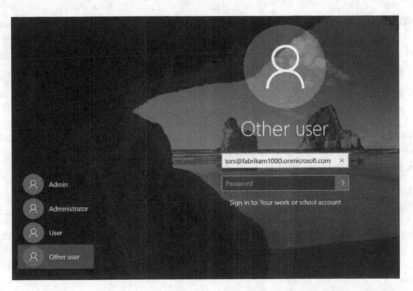

Remember when enrolling using the "out of the box experience" made the person a local admin?

Bam. Same problem here too: The user who just enrolled the machine is automatically a local admin on the box. That's bad. I get that. But hang tight; we'll rectify this situation when we talk about using Group Policy to bootstrap existing machines to enroll into MDM as the system in Chapter 4 in the section entitled "Auto-Enroll in Your MDM Service Using Group Policy."

Killing Windows Hello and PINs (Just for This Book)

Additionally, during the enrollment, you might have been prompted for a device PIN (not shown in the walk-through or screen shots). This is actually Windows Hello, a mechanism to help you walk away from passwords. I like Windows Hello, but you won't need PINs for this book. And if you're enrolling lots and lots of machines for testing, it could slow your testing down but decrease security in your test computers.

That said, you might want to kill Windows Hello...just for this book.

For clarity: I am *not* anti–Windows Hello.

But when you enroll a machine, there are several extra steps asking users to provide a PIN (which can replace a password), and it just generally takes longer to perform your test enrollments.

Counterintuitively, using PINs instead of passwords is safer, because the PIN is bound only to the device. On the other hand, if someone has eight devices, they may have to remember eight unique PINs instead of one password. If you want to read a good article on the subject, check out:

```
http://www.brucebnews.com/2016/08/
logging-in-with-a-pin-is-easier-than-a-password-and-safer-too/
```

For our purposes, if you wish to turn it off, just for now, the global way to do this would be Intune ➤ Device Enrollment ➤ Windows Enrollment ➤ Windows Hello for Business. Then click the one entry in there for All Users, then Settings.

You can, if you want to, have multiple Windows Hello for Business profiles. It means that you can disable Windows Hello from your test users but enable it for your real users.

But, since this whole book will be about testing, go forth and disable Windows Hello for Business, as shown in the following image.

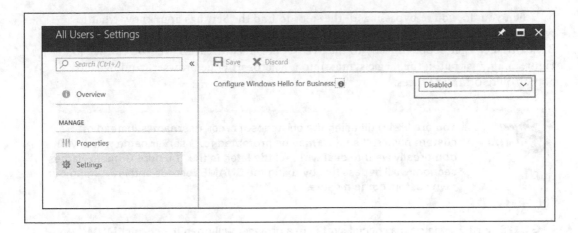

MDM Enrollment via Shortcuts (aka Deep Links)

In the previous example, we used the Windows 10 Settings app to find the Azure AD/MDM enrollment section of the universe.

But what if you wanted to:

- pre-create the Azure AD accounts, and

- email everyone with step-by-step join directions, and

- pray to the universe people follow your steps correctly, and not Azure Workplace join, but actually perform the MDM enrollment?

There's a better way. Again, though, MDM enrollment can only be done by Admins and not Standard Users.

That said, you can use a magical shortcut, also known as a deep link. There are a few ways to do this. You can send your people (the people who have Azure AD accounts now) an email telling them to click on a link, say, in an email specified like this:

```
ms-device-enrollment:?mode=mdm
```

You can copy and paste that string into a browser (as seen in Figure 2.28), or use Windows + R (to bring up the Run dialog box) and type it in directly like what's seen here.

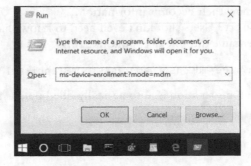

When you do, you're bypassing all the steps to find the Settings app, know what to type to discover the MDM section within the Settings app, and also avoid the snake pit. Basically: Let's get people directly to the MDM enrollment treasure. As you can see in Figure 2.29, just put in the magic syntax into a Microsoft Edge browser window, and… poof. You're off to the races.

WARNING   You are likely still using the `onmicrosoft.com` usernames instead of custom names. If so, you may be prompted for a server name which you don't really want to deal with. A little later, in the "Custom Domain Names" section, we'll bypass this by fixing the CNAME records and leveraging our own custom domain name.

FIGURE 2.29   Using the special syntax in a browser will open the correct MDM enrollment dialog box.

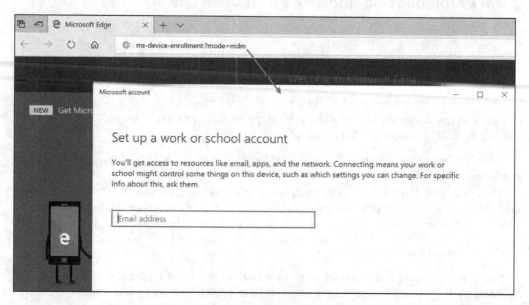

Then the user must know their account information.

What's that I hear you cry? Users shouldn't even need to know that much? No problem. You can embed their username into the deep link like this.

```
ms-device-enrollment:?mode=mdm&username=jacktors@fabrikam1000.onmicrosoft.com
```

And when you do, that information is automatically filled out, as seen in Figure 2.30.

FIGURE 2.30   Using MDM deep links to pre-fill in user information

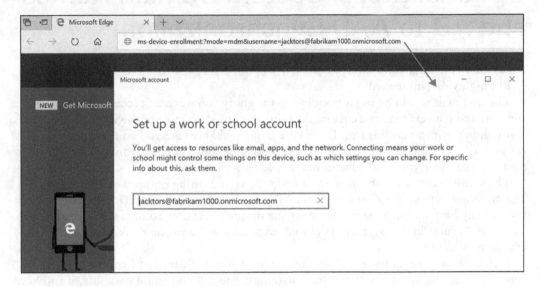

And, for some MDM systems, like Workspace ONE, you might be required to enter in a specific server name (if you're doing all the steps manually). You can bypass all that as well, by entering in the server name inside the deep link like this:

```
ms-device-enrollment:?mode=mdm&username=mdmuser1@fabrikam1000
.com&servername=https://techp-ds.awmdm.com
```

The result might look like Figure 2.31 where the user's name and server, which is pre-placed on the special link, can be seen in the dialog box.

FIGURE 2.31   When you specify both the username and server in the deep link, then both are shown to the user during enrollment.

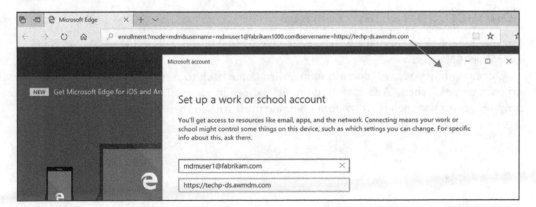

Optional Steps: Custom Domain Names and AD to AAD Synchronization

These next two walk-throughs are completely optional and not required.

But highly recommended.

The first item would be to say goodbye to the goofy "onmicrosoft.com" domain name you got, and convert that to a custom domain. You could do most of the work in the book if you didn't want to do this step. In real life though, chances are you don't want your users walking through life having to remember this domain name. Instead, you'll likely want them to remember your real domain name, whatever that is.

The second item would be to connect and sync your existing on-prem AD to Azure AD. The goal here is to sync existing on-prem AD user accounts to Azure AD because it's likely you already have an on-prem process to create on-prem AD user accounts, and you want to get those AD accounts magically synchronized to Azure AD so you don't have to keep adding them manually.

Again, neither is required, but I will recommend you do them, and I will be doing them here and continue onward with the book assuming you did do them. In real life, if you have no on-prem AD, or plan to walk away completely from on-prem AD, then maybe you really don't need to sync any on-prem AD to Azure, because…well, in your case there would be no point.

For me, in these next steps, I'm going to do the following:

- Change over my fabrikam1000.onmicrosoft.com domain to simply fabrikam1000.com.

- Sync my on-prem AD, which is named Fabrikam.com, to my Azure AD world, which is (about to be called) fabrikam1000.com.

Custom Domain Names: Goodbye to "onmicrosoft.com" Names

For me, I went to my domain registrar (like GoDaddy) and purchased the rights to own Fabrikam1000.com.

Once you buy your real domain name, then come back to Azure AD and select "Custom domain names," then "Add custom domain" as seen in Figure 2.32. At this moment, you'll only see your onmicrosoft.com domain name until you do these next steps.

FIGURE 2.32   Use Azure AD to see and add custom domain names.

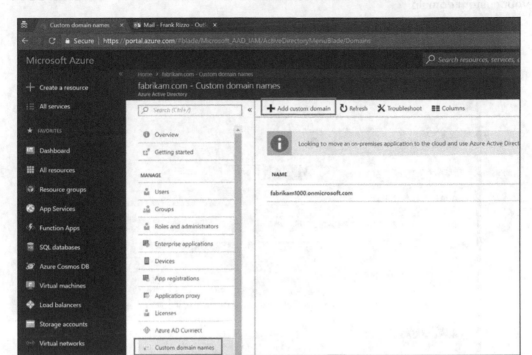

After you click Add, enter in your purchased name as seen in Figure 2.33.

FIGURE 2.33   Adding a custom domain name into Azure AD

Next, you'll be instructed how to configure your domain name registration so the whole marriage works. You'll see something like what's seen in Figure 2.34 from Azure AD.

FIGURE 2.34 The parameters you'll need to inject into your domain registrar about your custom domain

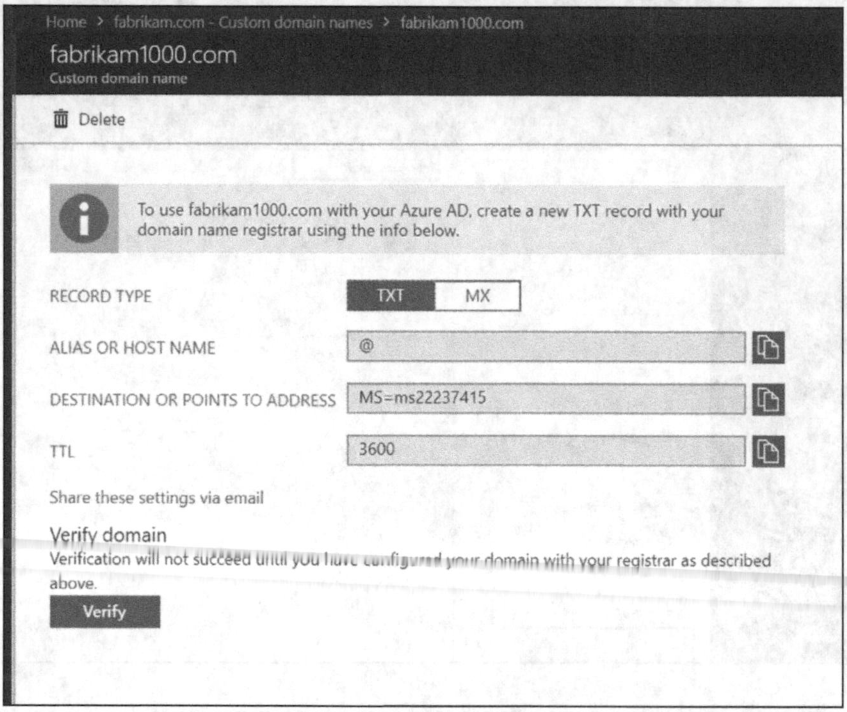

Then, within the record inside your domain registrar, you're going to plunk in that same information. You can see I did exactly that in Figure 2.35 using GoDaddy.

There are also two entries that should be present so auto-enrollment is perfectly smooth, first time, every time. Without these entries, it might not be perfect. Users may be prompted for a server name during enrollment, which is not optimal and just another thing to remember, explain, and go wrong.

You can see the basic gist of the CNAME adds in two places. The official docs are here:

```
https://docs.microsoft.com/en-us/intune/
windows-enroll#enable-windows-enrollment-without-azure-ad-premium
```

And a good blog entry on the subject is here:

```
https://blogs.technet.microsoft.com/intunesupport/2017/03/04/
which-cnames-to-use-for-auto-discovery-during-mdm-enrollment/
```

FIGURE 2.35   Using GoDaddy to place your Azure AD custom information

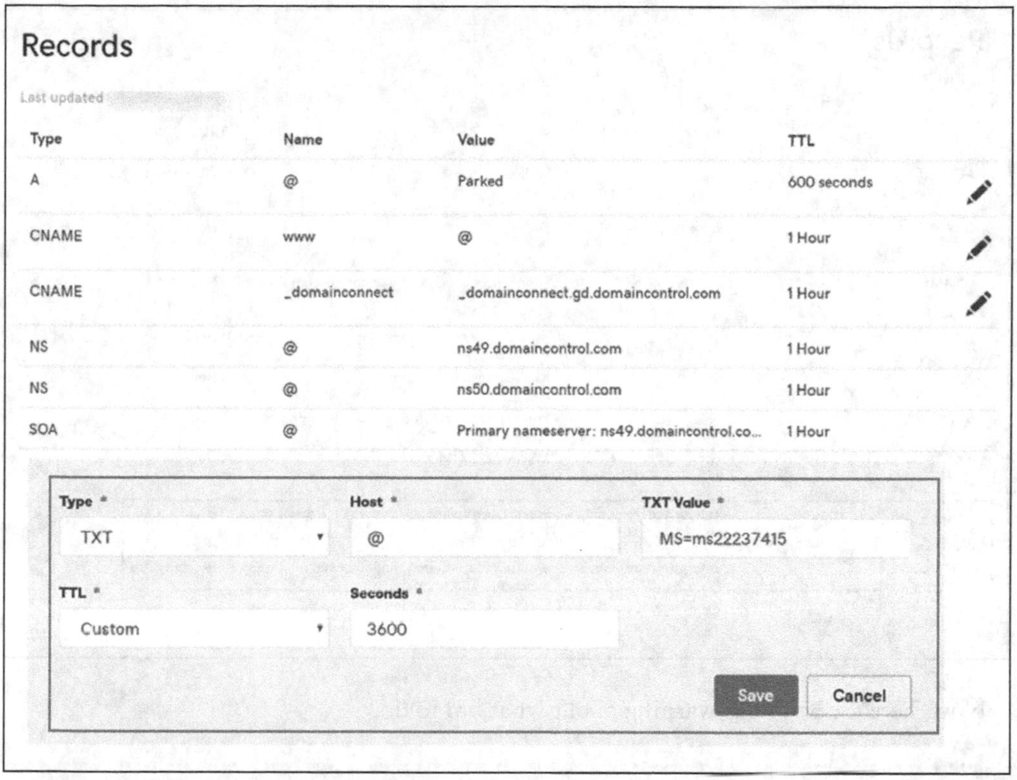

In short, you're going to create two entries in your registrar. See the following table for the essentials.

Type	Host name from your domain (like Fabrikam1000.com)	Points to	TTL
CNAME	EnterpriseEnrollment	EnterpriseEnrollment-s.manage.microsoft.com	1 hour
CNAME	EnterpriseRegistration	EnterpriseRegistration.windows.net	1 hour

The final result will look like what's seen in Figure 2.36.

FIGURE 2.36 Adding the CNAME records for smooth auto-enrollment

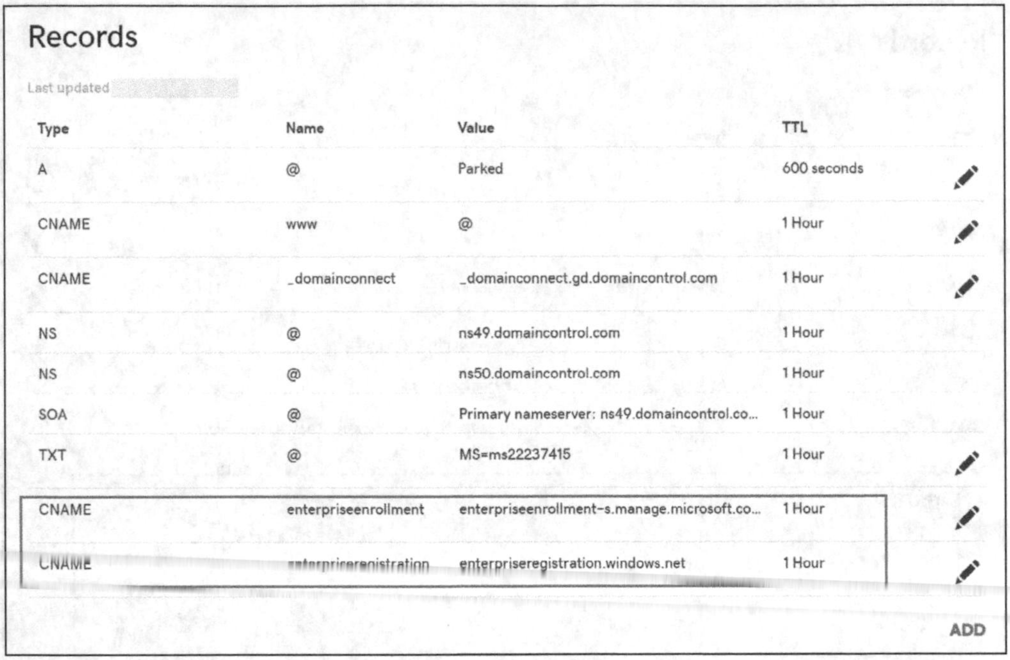

Records

Last updated

Type	Name	Value	TTL	
A	@	Parked	600 seconds	✎
CNAME	www	@	1 Hour	✎
CNAME	_domainconnect	_domainconnect.gd.domaincontrol.com	1 Hour	✎
NS	@	ns49.domaincontrol.com	1 Hour	
NS	@	ns50.domaincontrol.com	1 Hour	
SOA	@	Primary nameserver: ns49.domaincontrol.co...	1 Hour	
TXT	@	MS=ms22237415	1 Hour	✎
CNAME	enterpriseenrollment	enterpriseenrollment-s.manage.microsoft.co...	1 Hour	✎
CNAME	enterpriseregistration	enterpriseregistration.windows.net	1 Hour	✎

ADD

Now, here's a big, huge warning about what *not* to do.

WARNING If you look at the Microsoft documentation, they might say to put **EnterpriseEnrollment.company_domain.com** into the CNAME host field. This is totally wrong. That's more than you need to put into the field. Because at GoDaddy (or whatever), you're already editing the domain itself, say Fabrikam1000.com. So you don't need to enter the full FQDN of EnterpriseEnrollment.fabirkam1000.com into the CNAME host field; just enter in **EnterpriseEnrollment**. Likewise for the guidance saying to put in **EnterpriseRegistration.company_domain.com**. Again, wrong. Just put **EnterpriseRegistration** into the CNAME host field. Not understanding this cost me many hours the first time I set this up.

You might need to wait a few minutes before this propagates, but I found it took effect right away once I got it right. Then you're ready to test.

Going in reverse order, you'll first want to run the CNAME tests first.

This is found in the Intune portal ➢ Device enrollment ➢ Windows enrollment ➢ CNAME Validation as seen in Figure 2.37.

FIGURE 2.37   Testing the CNAME before continuing

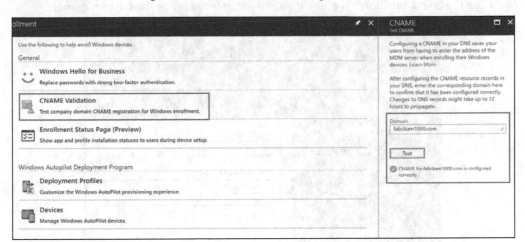

Back in Azure AD ➢ "Custom domain names" and then your domain, like Fabrikam1000.com, click the Verify button (not shown). In Figure 2.38 (left), you should see "Verification succeeded" but Primary Domain is set to No. Simply click on Make Primary and you'll get what's seen in Figure 2.38 (right).

FIGURE 2.38   The goal is to validate the domain first (left). Then change the default primary domain to the custom domain (right).

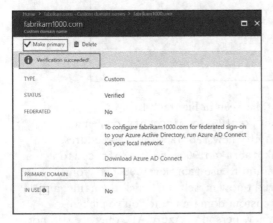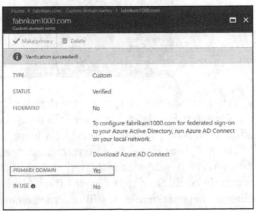

Now when you go to manually enter a new person into Azure AD, the custom domain name (in my case @fabrikam1000.com) will be accepted into the person's username as seen in Figure 2.39. Feel free to add a new user like Anthony Kissel (kissel@fabrikam1000.com) as also seen in Figure 2.39.

FIGURE 2.39   The user name field will not permit you to add a domain you don't own. You'll see the check box light up green if you have correctly made the custom domain.

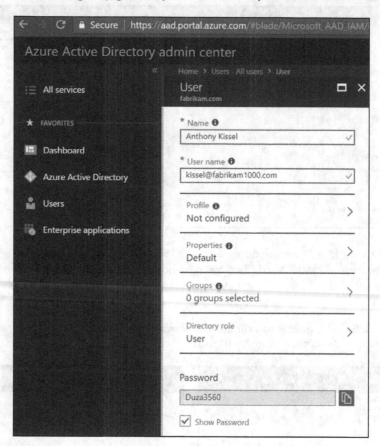

After saving the user, you'll see the user list, las seen in Figure 2.40.

Note that Frank and Jack are still using fabrikam1000.onmicrosoft.com email addresses. But Anthony Kissel is now using a spiffy new fabrikam1000.com address!

At this point if you wanted to change frank@fabrikam1000.onmicrosoft.com to frank@fabrikam1000.com as well as Jack's account to use fabrikam1000.com, you certainly could, and that's what I'll be doing right now myself. Just click the name, and change their username. It will accept the new custom domain name you've picked.

Remember that even though you added the new person to Azure AD, they are still not licensed to use any services. I find it easiest to just type in https://portal.office.com to jump to the place user licenses are configured. Then click Users ➢ Active Users then select a user to edit. ➢ Edit a User, then click on "Licenses and Apps." You will see something like what's seen in Figure 2.41 (although yours could be different). Then pick a location (like United States), and assign a license to the new person.

FIGURE 2.40   You can see your new user with the custom domain name.

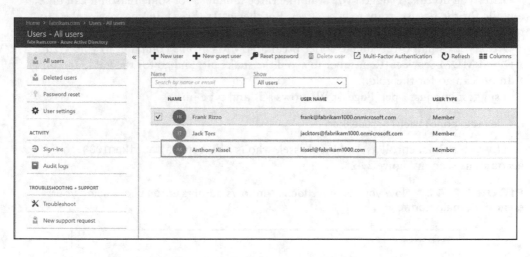

FIGURE 2.41   Assign your new user a license.

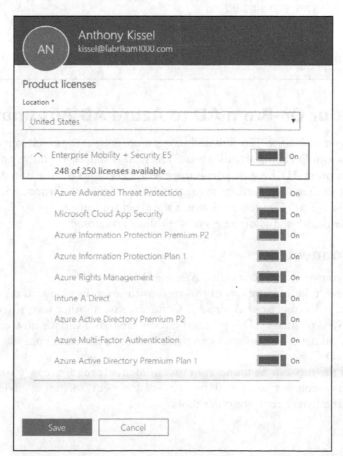

After you do this, I suggest you wait like three minutes. For some reason it can take a while for the license grant to take effect. But then after three minutes, you're clear for takeoff.

After your small three minute coffee break, retry to enroll a computer to your Azure AD and MDM service. (Remember to avoid the snake pit, and go for the gold, and only Admins can go for the gold.)

I suggest you just open Edge or Windows + R and type in:

```
ms-device-enrollment:?mode=mdm
```

Now, this time, enroll as Anthony Kissel, who is now using a `fabrikam1000.com` account, as seen in Figure 2.42.

FIGURE 2.42   Now you can have local Windows admins enroll users using your custom domain name!

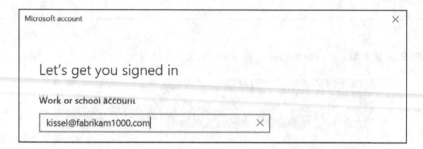

Syncing Your On-Prem AD to Azure AD Automatically

If you're already in the Office 365 club and have an on-prem AD as well, chances are you know about this tool I'm about to talk about. The goal is simple: If you've got a zillion on-prem users in on-prem AD, how do you auto-generate accounts for them in Azure AD (so you can do stuff to them, like settings management or offer them Office 365, and so on)?

Simple: Use Azure AD Connect to perform the synchronization.

And know the health/status of these syncs if things go wrong.

Azure AD Connect

Again, the tool you want to find is called Azure AD Connect.

There have been a lot of iterations of this tool, with several versions and name changes. But this is it, this is the tool now: Azure AD Connect. Said another way, if you have or had the old DirSync or Azure AD Sync...those tools are toast, and it's now only Azure AD Connect. The good news is that if you had these old tools, there are upgrade options from them to Azure AD Connect.

The basics of the tool can be found at `https://docs.microsoft.com/en-us/azure/active-directory/connect/active-directory-aadconnect`, including advice for those who are upgrading from one of the older tools.

In this example, I'm going to assume you have a single on-prem domain, named Fabrikam.com (as I recommended in the opening pages of this book). If you have something more complex in real life, that's fine; you can use the aforementioned URL to find your scenario and give it a go.

Do *not* start out by downloading the Azure AD Connect tool. No. Don't. Don't start there. Instead, inside your on-prem AD, run the Active Directory Domains and Trusts tool. Then right-click over the root node and select Properties. Then in the UPN Suffixes tab, add the name of your (now verified) Azure AD domain. In Figure 2.43, I added fabrikam1000.com and clicked OK.

FIGURE 2.43   You need to add the name of your verified Azure AD domain here in on-prem AD Domains and Trusts. It took me eight hours to figure this out, and I could find no documentation on this. So, I hope this step saves you those eight hours.

Alternatively, you could have added your onmicrosoft.com name, like fabrikam1000 .onmicrosoft.com. That would work as well, but since I went to the trouble to purchase and verify Fabrikam1000.com, I'm using that.

Next, after adding the UPN suffix, you can now continue by downloading Azure AD Connect and installing it directly upon the DC of your on-prem AD domain. You can use a spare server as well, but for me, and this book, I'm installing it right onto the Domain Controller. The download can be found at http://go.microsoft.com/ fwlink/?LinkId=615771.

After you run it, you'll start out with a welcome screen. The next screen can be seen in Figure 2.44 explaining Express Settings.

FIGURE 2.44   Use Express Settings to connect your (simple) on-prem AD to Azure AD.

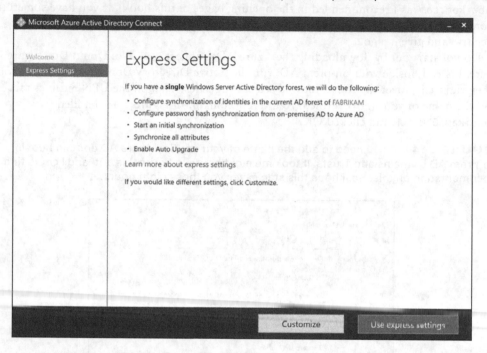

I would also say that Express settings are good for the book exercises and to get you up and running but might be suboptimal for "real life." Typically you want to point it toward specific OUs, so you don't sync all accounts to Azure AD, like your admin and/or service accounts.

That said, so I don't have to go down every rat hole with the tool, and I can get you on the road with examples quickly, the Express Ssettings should be fine for our use.

On the next screen, you'll provide your Azure AD creds (as seen in Figure 2.45); this is what you used to set up your E5 trial. Then you'll provide your on-prem AD creds as seen in Figure 2.46.

FIGURE 2.45   Give it the credentials you used when setting up your E5 account.

FIGURE 2.46   Provide the on-prem AD domain administrator credentials.

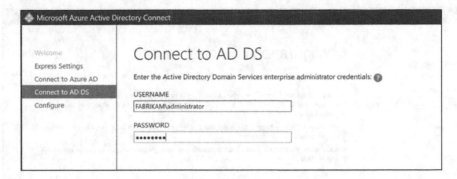

Now when you get to the Azure AD sign-in configuration page, you should see the UPN name you added to on-prem AD marry up to the Azure AD domain name as seen in Figure 2.47. Also in Figure 2.47, a small bug in the Azure AD Connect program requires you to select the "Continue without any verified domains" check box, even though you do have a verified domain. It might be fixed by the time you read this.

FIGURE 2.47   Be sure your UPN and Azure names match as Verified.

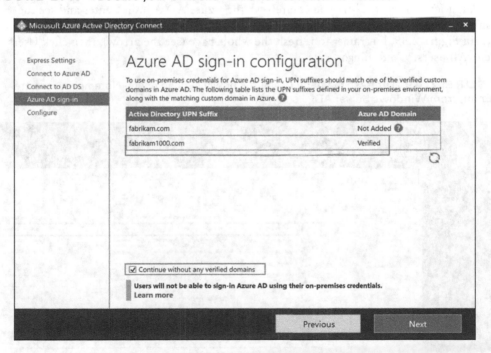

Click Next and then start the process going. You will be notified when the process is complete, as seen in Figure 2.48.

FIGURE 2.48   The AD Connect sync wizard is complete.

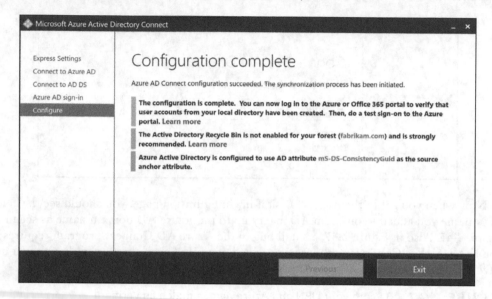

Wait a few minutes. Then, you can refresh the Azure AD Admin Center and see the results. I found that the best way to get results was not to hit the refresh button, circled as seen in Figure 2.49, but rather to refresh the whole page (see the arrow), then click Users then "All users." And, bingo.

FIGURE 2.49   Refresh the page to see the newly synced users. Note new users are coming from Windows Server AD.

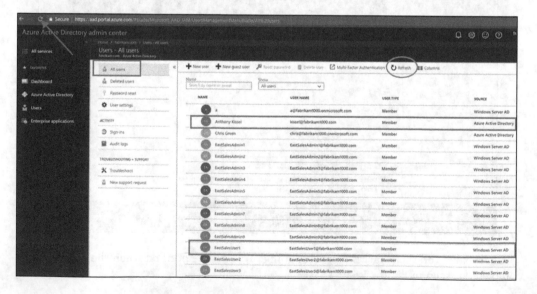

You'll also see in Figure 2.49 in the Source column which users were created from which source: Azure Active Directory versus Windows Server AD.

Changing Over the Users' Suffixes

But, wait a second! After the synchronization occurs, synchronized users from on-prem AD will not have the the nice, pretty fabrikam1000.com as part of their username but instead still have the ugly fabrikam1000.onmicrosoft.com as part of their username.

Why would this be? Because your on-prem AD users need to already be expressly using the suffix, *and only then* will you see it after synchronization.

To change it, for one user, use Active Directory Users and Computers, find an account, like EastSalesUser1, like what's seen in Figure 2.50. Then click the Account tab so you can perform two steps:

- **Step 1:** Actually enter in a name in the "User logon name" field. Usually this will be the name they already use, know, and love.

- **Step 2:** Pull down and select the custom domain name you specified within Active Directory Domains and Trusts earlier. In my case, it's Fabrikam1000.com.

FIGURE 2.50 Each user needs to have the correct suffix in on-prem AD for it to be synchronized to Azure AD.

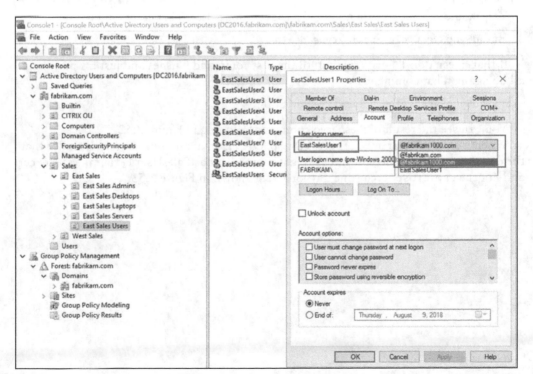

You can wait a while, and the changes will naturally occur.

Or you can see the changes happen in real time. To see them, find the Azure AD Connect folder and launch Synchronization Service as seen in Figure 2.51.

FIGURE 2.51 Launching the Synchronization Service

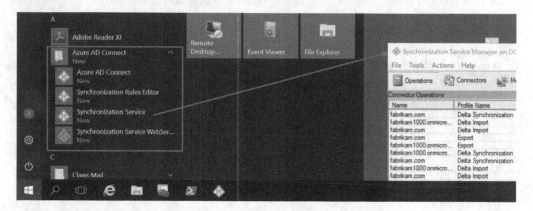

Then, the tool itself doesn't seem to have a big "Click Here to Sync" button. But there's a PowerShell way to do it.

You should be able to push up just the changes, or deltas. That command is:

```
Start-AdSyncSyncCycle -policytype delta
```

If that doesn't do the trick, wait until the first command finishes and just try pushing it all up again. That command is:

```
Start-AdSyncSyncCycle -policytype initial
```

You can see the result of these two commands running in Figure 2.52.

When it's complete, refresh Azure AD and look again at all users. Carefully notice that the one user you specified now has the right username: EastSalesUser1@fabrikam1000.com and not the onmicrosoft.com one any longer, as shown in Figure 2.53.

FIGURE 2.52   Using PowerShell to force an AD to AAD sync

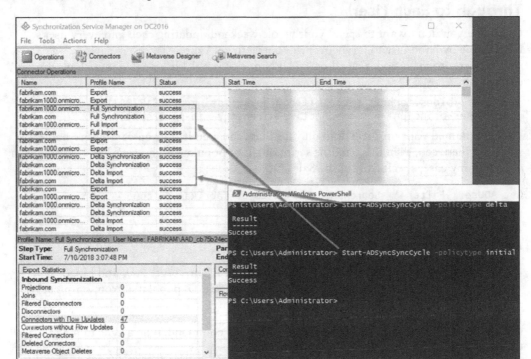

FIGURE 2.53   See that your one user has successfully come over from on-prem AD to Azure AD.

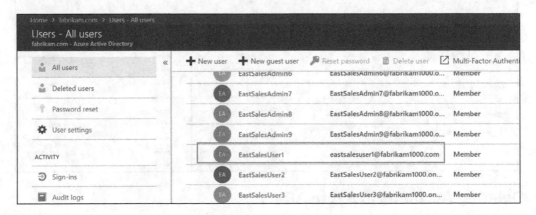

Mass Updating the UPN for On-Prem AD (Instead of Clicking Through to Each User)

Of course you don't want to spend your whole weekend updating each and every user's UPN name by hand just so it synchronizes correctly to Azure AD.

The secret to mass updating all users' UPN names is quickly revealed in a blog entry here:

```
https://blogs.technet.microsoft.com/heyscriptingguy/2013/08/13/
add-user-principal-names-in-active-directory-via-powershell/
```

If you named your on-prem domain fabrikam.com, and if your custom Azure name is say, Fabrikam.com, then this one-line script ought to populate each user's UPN attributes in a jiffy. In my case, specifically in the Sales OU.

```
Get-ADUser -Filter * -SearchBase 'ou=Sales,dc=fabrikam,dc=com'
-Properties userPrincipalName | foreach
{ Set-ADUser $_ -UserPrincipalName
("{0}@{1}" -f $_.name,"fabrikam1000.com")}
```

Then, use the technique earlier to re-sync on-prem AD to Azure AD, and bingo.

Everyone now has the exact right username in Azure AD, populated from on-prem AD, as seen in Figure 2.54.

FIGURE 2.54   After the on-prem AD PowerShell command, then a sync to Azure AD, all accounts now show your custom domain name.

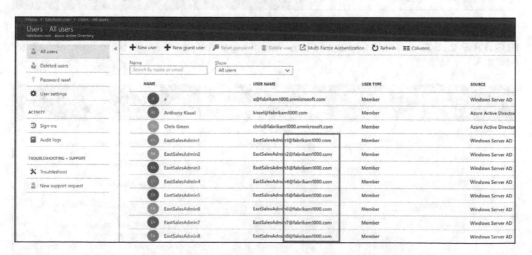

Deleting Accounts in Azure AD

For fun, inside the Azure AD Admin Center try to click on an existing Windows Server AD user and click Delete user from the menu command bar.

Spoiler alert: you cannot.

The synchronized user is born, lives, and dies inside on-prem AD and is only synchronized here. And you can try this yourself. Create a new user in on-prem Active Directory Users and Computers. Then wait a while, and bingo. You should see it in Azure AD.

And nothing ever, ever goes wrong when syncronizing things. Not ever. Ahem. So, if you do get caught in a jam, I learned a little PowerShell trick that can nuke a record inside Azure AD. The commands are:

```
Install-Module msonline
Connect-MSolService.
```

This will prompt you for your Azure admin creds; in our case, Frank@fabrikam1000 .onmicrosoft.com.

```
Remove-MsolUser -userprincipalname yourguy@fabrikam1000.com
```

The result can be seen in Figure 2.55.

FIGURE 2.55   How to nuke a user who is syncronized from on-prem AD

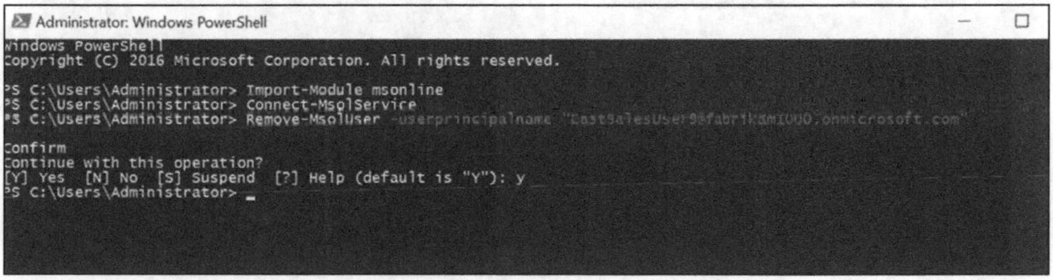

Then a refresh of Azure AD will show the user now nuked but remaining in on-prem AD.

A good article on removing objects synchronized from on-prem AD can be found at:

https://support.microsoft.com/en-us/help/2619062/
you-can-t-manage-or-remove-objects-that-were-synchronized-through-the

Yep, this URL just ends in the word *the*.

Get Windows 10 to Automatically Join Azure AD (Hybrid Azure AD-Joined Devices)

Again, All the steps in this section are optional, but over the long run you might want to consider this interesting idea. That is, you can teach your on-prem AD to synchronize all the existing Windows 10 accounts from on-prem AD, and push them up to Azure AD.

Big, big sort-of warning here: While this gets all your Windows 10 computers registered into Azure AD, it doesn't magically *also* get them enrolled into your MDM service. Don't worry: We set that up in Chapter 4 (and, ironically, we use Group Policy to do it).

And, speaking of Group Policy, you can use it to pre-block some Windows 10 machines from being synchronized from on-prem AD to Azure AD. The policy setting is Computer ➤ Policies ➤ Admin Templates ➤ Windows Components ➤ Device Registration ➤ **Register domain-joined computers as devices** (as seen in Figure 2.56). When you set this policy to Disabled (yes, Disabled), then computers that pick up this policy will ignore the magic trick we're about to perform.

So, I suggest you pre-deliver the **Register domain-joined computers as devices** Group Policy setting to the machines you want to exclude *before* performing the next steps. (And, as another blatant plug, if you wanted to know and verify the setting made it to all your intended machines, you could utilize the paid version of the PolicyPak Group Policy Compliance reporter, which tells you which on-prem machines got which GPOs and settings, so the guesswork is removed...but I digress.)

FIGURE 2.56   Use the **Register domain-joined computers as a devices'** policy to prevent Windows 10 computers from being synced from on-prem AD to Azure AD.

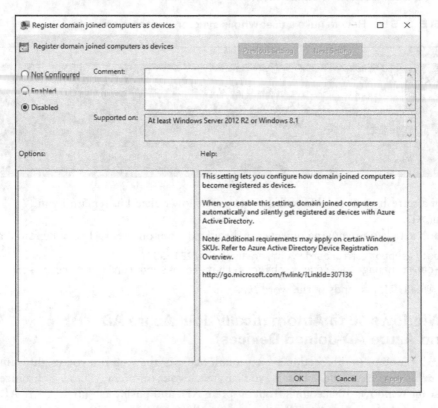

Anyway, when you're ready to start the Vulcan mind-meld between on-prem Azure AD and Azure AD, here is each PowerShell command to type, one on each line. You'll do this on the machine running the Azure AD Connect program.

In case you want to copy and paste these, instead of typing them in, I'll tell you where I found them, which is this URL (which I'll mention again a little later): https://docs.microsoft.com/en-us/azure/active-directory/devices/hybrid-azuread-join-manual-steps.

Here are the PowerShell lines of code:

```
Import-Module -Name "C:\Program Files\Microsoft Azure Active Directory
Connect\AdPrep\AdSyncPrep.psm1";

$aadAdminCred = Get-Credential;

Initialize-ADSyncDomainJoinedComputerSync -AdConnectorAccount
frank@fabrikam1000.com -AzureADCredentials $aadAdminCred;
```

The result of these PowerShell commands can be seen in Figure 2.57 in the first section. Then, if you want to see that it really took effect, you could run a sort of verification check, which would be the following PowerShell commands (again, these lines are also in the aforementioned URL at Microsoft):

```
$scp = New-Object System.DirectoryServices.DirectoryEntry;

$scp.Path = "LDAP://CN=62a0ff2e-97b9-4513-943f-0d221bd30080,CN=Device
Registration Configuration,CN=Services,CN=Configuration,DC=fabrikam,DC=com";

$scp.Keywords;
```

FIGURE 2.57   You need to specifically set up Azure AD to also sync Windows 10 computers.

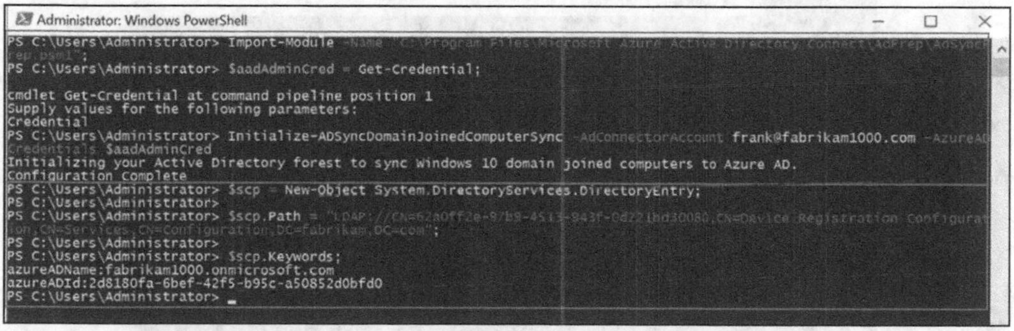

You can see the result of that in the second block in Figure 2.57, where it spits out some stuff, including my domain name fabrikam1000.onmicrosoft.com!

Now your Windows 10 machines (1607 and later) on your network will automatically get the memo and self-register in Azure...when they're domain-joined fresh, or existing Windows 10 machines, when they're rebooted and/or logged into.

And you can see it happen too. After your Windows 10 systems are rebooted, and after some synchronizations happen naturally using Azure AD Connect, you should see new Windows 10 computers pop into Azure AD when you examine all devices, as seen in Figure 2.58 with a W10-1703-PRO-64 computer. If you look at Join Type, it says "Hybrid Azure AD joined."

FIGURE 2.58   How to see Hybrid Azure AD joined machines

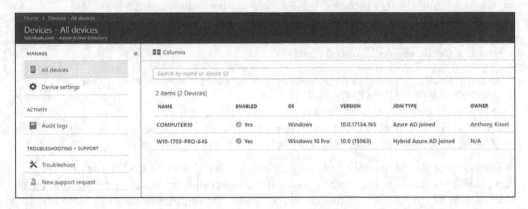

Back on the Windows 10 machines, you need to see if they get the signal to magically perform their Azure AD join. When you go to a Windows 10 machine and run the command dsregcmd /status, you might see what I have in Figure 2.59, where it clearly shows AzureADJoined is NO.

FIGURE 2.59   Before a machine is automatically Azure AD joined

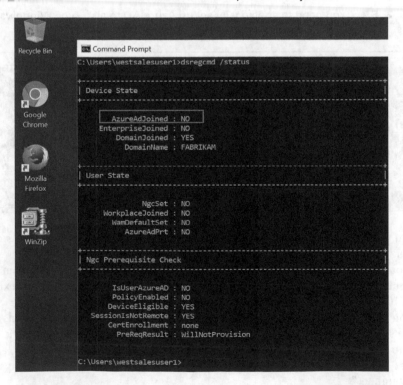

Then, after some time, the change occurs on the Windows 10 machine.

You can see the change in Figure 2.60 as you keep running and rerunning `dsregcmd` `/status`. The command will show you a ton of information you don't care about. But it's the first line that counts: `AzureADJoined` is set to YES as seen in Figure 2.60.

FIGURE 2.60   After a machine is automatically Azure AD joined

Again, this only happens after the Azure AD sync happens once or twice. If you want to goose it, then see the earlier commands on how to run a delta sync. That worked for me to "rush" things.

Additionally, if you want to see all the computers that are now joined to Azure AD, you can use a few PowerShell commands.

- `Install-Module msonline`

- `Connect-msolservice` then give Frank's admin credentials when prompted.

- `Get-MSoLDevice -all` will show you the machines joined in Azure AD.

- Or use `Get-MSOLDevice -all | Select displayname, objectid` for a prettier view, like what's seen in Figure 2.61.

FIGURE 2.61 You can see computers joined to Azure AD through the get-msoldevice PowerShell cmdlet.

```
PS C:\Users\Administrator> get-msoldevice -all | Select displayname, objectid

DisplayName     ObjectId
-----------     --------
W10-ENT-64      02dc208c-92bc-49de-8e08-d6d3c6f42129
COMPUTER3       2edf1b7b-5d18-43d2-8eea-7daa287e6c15
DC2016          50d3ffcb-8bfc-4e46-93b9-39cbac8f0e3d
W10-COMPUTER2   5ea82305-b093-4c02-a455-04ba02857fc5
COMPUTER10      7a503a76-8a99-4c0e-b4b6-b257f6263109
COMPUTER10      af64de65-d7aa-4c00-aef1-7b09712d85c3
W10-PRO-64      c28c2cd3-f939-40ea-bb36-1b55c1c358db

PS C:\Users\Administrator>
```

That's the basics, and that's how you get machines to be both AD joined and Azure AD joined. Again, that's got a nifty lingo we call DJ++. You can drop that acronym at a cocktail party now that you're badass and got it set up.

That said, there is more information, including all sorts of additional magic tricks like the following:

- Dealing with multiple forests syncing to Azure AD

- Using older 2008 Domain Controllers instead of Server 2016 and later

- Including Windows 7 machines into Azure AD

Then that guidance (again) can be found at:

https://docs.microsoft.com/en-us/azure/active-directory/
devices/hybrid-azuread-join-manual-steps

Azure AD Connect Health

If you'd like, you can also do nice, ongoing monitoring of the synchronization. This is beyond the scope of the book, but if you wanted to check it out, it's included in the Azure AD subscription.

Here are three good links on the subject:

https://docs.microsoft.com/en-us/azure/active-directory/connect/
active-directory-aadconnect

And

https://docs.microsoft.com/en-us/azure/active-directory/connect-health/
active-directory-aadconnect-health.

And finally, the most important one:

https://docs.microsoft.com/en-us/azure/active-directory/connect-health/
active-directory-aadconnect-health-sync

Final Thoughts

Okay. You did it. Let's recap all you did:

- You got your Azure AD account, either stand-alone or with Enterprise Mobility + Security or with Microsoft 365.

- You got your MDM service and married it to Azure AD.

- You set up all the pieces to enable auto-enrollment to MDM.

- You went down into the snake pit with Workplace join and learned it wasn't really MDM.

- You actually enrolled some machines with MDM, the long manual method or with deep links.

- And optionally, you...

    - Got out of the "onmicrosoft.com" name business and into custom names.

    - Synchronized on-prem AD to Azure AD.

    - Got your Windows 10 machines to automatically do a DJ++ join.

I think it's fair to say you did a lot in this chapter. And we're just getting started.

Tweet me @jeremymoskowitz with the hashtag #mdmbook and tell me what you got out of this chapter. I love getting your tweets !

Chapter 3

MDM Profiles, Policies, and Groups

Last chapter you set up Azure, chose an MDM service, purchased a domain name, and hooked up all the wires so your on-prem AD user accounts synchronized to Azure AD.

This chapter is a little less hectic. In this chapter, we have four goals:

1. Create your first MDM policies.

2. Get to know some of the inner workings of how the guts of MDM policies are constructed.

3. Utilize third-party ADMX files.

4. Learn how to create and leverage MDM groups to target policies.

So, let's get started.

MDM Policies and the Policy CSP

People like to say that MDM is like Group Policy because they use Group Policy as the original model of what can be done with a machine with Group Policy.

For instance:

- Group Policy can deploy look-and-feel policies to your Windows machines. MDM can deploy look-and-feel policies to your Windows machines.

- Group Policy can deploy security settings to your Windows machines. MDM can deploy security settings to your Windows machines.

- Group Policy can deploy custom application settings (also known as ADMX settings) to your Windows machines. MDM can also deploy custom ADMX settings to your Windows machines.

- Group Policy can deploy software to your Windows machines. MDM can deploy software to your Windows machines.

Wow. No wonder people equate MDM with Group Policy. They learned all their original tricks inside Group Policy-land, and now they want to convert those tricks over to MDM and Modern Management-land.

Let's set up some policies to our machines using an MDM service, in my case Intune. Then a little later we'll deploy software as well.

MDM: Getting Started with Policies

You enrolled some machines in MDM last chapter. I don't know if you saw this, but immediately after you enroll your machine into MDM, you get a little hurray message, like what's seen in Figure 3.1.

FIGURE 3.1 After you enroll a device, you get a success message.

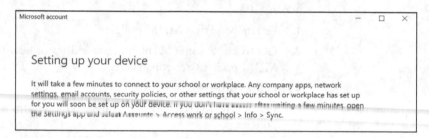

If you read that message closely, it basically says, "Hang tight, and at some future point, any policies you set up will eventually make it there."

But you're a busy IT professional.

In MDM-land, you can run the equivalent of a GPUpdate, called an MDM sync. You find this magical sync button by first returning back to the Windows 10 Settings ➤ Access Work or School section. Then find your little briefcase, seen in Figure 3.2 (left) and click Info. Note that if you're logged in as a Standard User, you'll see the Windows logo icon (Figure 3.2 right), and not the briefcase icon, which is a little inconsistent in my opinion.

FIGURE 3.2 The Info button within Access Work or school. Local Admins see what's on the left. Standard Users see what's on the Right.

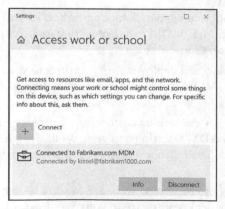

After you click Info, you'll see the Sync button (Figure 3.3).

FIGURE 3.3   The Sync button is like GPUpdate for MDM.

The Sync button is going to be similar to the GPUpdate command, but this time for MDM. Feel free to sync it now, even though you have no policies for MDM.

I teach you this now so I don't have to give you the step-by-step directions each time you want to see a change. I'll just say something like "....and sync with your MDM service." And now you'll just know what I mean.

And, as I've seen it, the Sync button works, but not always the first or even sometimes the second time. I don't know if it's a delay between the time the MDM service is sending the policies and the time they're applying, or what. But don't be totally surprised if you have to click Sync a few times before the sync actually occurs. It could also be that the policy isn't totally ready yet in the MDM service and it's getting its gears grinded and ready. Or maybe I'm just impatient.

Profiles and Policies

Let's run a quick test and verify that all is right in the world and thus you can create your first policy. First, some nomenclature.

There is no GPO in MDM-land. That's not a thing.

Let me say it again: There are no Group Policy Objects in the new world. Not in Azure, not in Intune, nor in any other MDM systems. For complete clarity, there are some items that do the same things as some Group Policy settings, but the concept of a GPO doesn't exist within MDM.

See Chapter 11, "MDM Add-On Tools: Free and Pay," to see how you use PolicyPak MDM to take GPOs and their settings and leverage them using your existing MDM service. But an MDM service has no inherent concept of GPOs.

Also, kind of unrelated, if you ever need to take existing Intune policies and export them for others to use, then import, this blog article is invaluable: http://techgenix.com/export-intune-policies/.

Instead, the thing you create to contain your policies is called a *profile*. It's not the name I would have given it, but, hey, that's just me.

So, for clarity, in MDM land you:

- Create profiles, then….

- Stuff policies into profiles, then…

- Target those profiles to specific computers.

Let's try this now.

So the first step in creating an MDM policy is to create the container, or profile, for those policies to slip into.

Using Intune, click into Device Configuration, the Profiles. In the Device- Configuration - Profiles blade, click Create profile. You can see me creating a profile to change the Edge Home Page in Figure 3.4. Note the myriad of profile types available to you. For right now, click "Device restrictions."

FIGURE 3.4   Click a profile type to see policies' types within that profile type.

When you select the Device restrictions drop-down, a new blade called Device restrictions will appear, with a bunch of possibilities. Just focus on the Microsoft Edge Browser as seen in Figure 3.5. Then find the policy called "Start pages" and type in in your domain name (or any valid URL really), like http://www.fabrikam1000.com, and click OK (also seen in Figure 3.5).

FIGURE 3.5 Making your first Device restriction policy to manage Microsoft Edge Browser

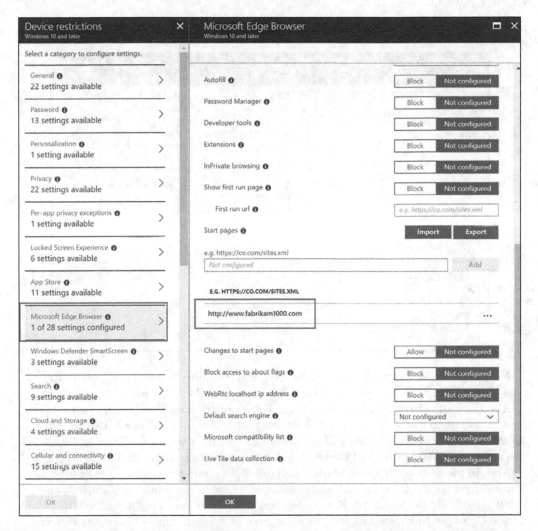

Click OK again to save the profile and you'll get a notification like the one shown next, which is really two messages.

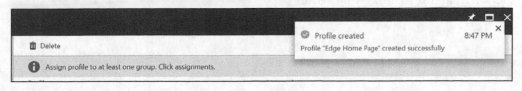

The messages are that, hey you did it. You've saved your first policy. But, it's not assigned to actually work anywhere.

Like in Group Policy-land, you need to "link" a GPO over to a location; in MDM-land you need to *assign* it to a group.

In MDM-land, there's a handy All group. And that's who we're going to target first: All. All Devices, to be specific. To do this, click Assignments and then specify All Devices as seen in Figure 3.6. Then click Save to save it.

FIGURE 3.6   Use the Assignments blade to assign your policy to All Devices.

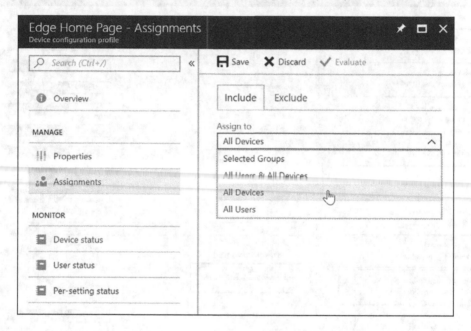

Now it's time to sync with your MDM service. (Remember I said I would say that?) Launch the Edge browser and see if your URL made it as the home page.

And, here's the best part. You made this a Device restriction. So all the users on these devices will get the same thing. Try it! Log on as any other user on your MDM-enrolled Wnidows 10 machine. Everyone will get the same home page setting for Edge. In Figure 3.7, you can see an MDM sync and then me opening up Microsoft Edge. And there it is!

And, in the settings Window (shown in Figure 3.8), if you scroll down a little more, you will first see a section called "Areas managed by <your domain>" (not shown), and you'll see that Browser is listed. Keep going down to a section called "Advanced Diagnostic Report" (as seen in Figure 3.8) and you'll see a big ol' "Create report" button (also seen in Figure 3.8). Try this out now and you'll see an MDMDiagReport.html file created. This is kind of like what you'll remember from a GPresults report, but now for MDM.

Open it, and you can see your setting!

FIGURE 3.7   Your first MDM policy sets the Windows Edge home page to the value of your choice! A success!

FIGURE 3.8   Use the MDM Advanced Diagnostic Report to see your settings.

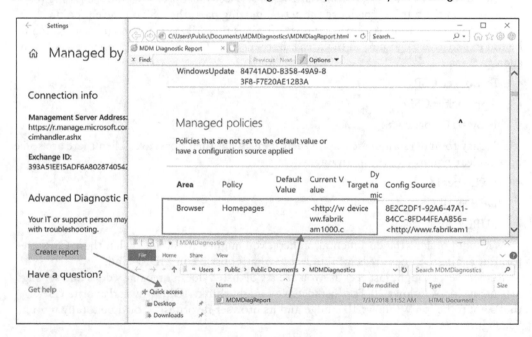

We'll come back to the MDM Advanced Diagnostic Report a bit later, but it's good to know it's here if you want to check it out from time to time during the examples in this (and other) chapters.

What Makes an MDM Policy?

So earlier, in Figure 3.5, you saw a gaggle of policy settings that you can choose from. Where do those come from?

Well, again, the MDM team at Microsoft decides which policy settings can be available to use and makes them available for all MDM providers (Intune, Workspace ONE, MobileIron, etc.) to utilize.

There's a giant, ever-changing, but generally up-to-date list available at:

```
https://docs.microsoft.com/en-us/windows/client-management/mdm/
configuration-service-provider-reference
```

There you'll see all the possibilities in MDM-land. Take a minute and bookmark this in your browser for future reference; chances are you'll come back here again and again to get ideas of what to configure on your endpoints.

Investigating and Discovering CSPs

We talked about this idea in Chapter 1, "Enterprise Mobility and MDM Essentials," in the section "CSPs: Configuration Service Providers."

The editor and view we get from our MDM service is just pretty window dressing (if you'll pardon the pun) to configure the actual moving part, the CSP on the endpoint.

You're welcome to look at the giant list of things that MDM can configure; it's going to be too exhaustive to go into all the areas. But you'll see CSPs that will configure CSP items such as these:

- BitLocker CSP
- AppLocker CSP
- BrowserFavorite CSP

It's easy to understand based upon their name what their goals are. Then there are some not-as-clear names like the following:

- PXLogical CSP
- DevDetail CSP
- SUPL CSP

Without going to the documentation here, you might have no idea what these CSPs are for. But again, the docs are helpful to know what's possible in MDM-land.

Remember, though, just because you see a CSP listed doesn't mean its docs and settings are meant for Windows 10. For instance, you might think, "Oh, BrowserFavorite CSP... that's got to be for Windows 10's Edge and its browser favorites!" You'd be totally wrong. See Figure 3.9.

FIGURE 3.9 Don't be fooled: Not every CSP with familiar names will work as expected on Windows 10.

BrowserFavorite CSP						
Home	Pro	Business	Enterprise	Education	Mobile	Mobile Enterprise
X	X		X	X	X	X

Indeed, there is a way to use MDM to tell Edge what favorites to populate, but those settings are in another CSP, the PolicyCSP in a category called Browser/ProvisionFavorites.

The point is, don't judge a CSP name by its display title: Check the docs to make sure what you want to set actually exists within a CSP.

So, it's the job of a good MDM system to abstract the settings and make a pretty GUI for these settings for you to click upon. In the biz, they call this "surfacing" a setting within an MDM system; that is, to bring this low-level CSP function to the surface in a pretty clickable UI button or check box or whatever. I've also heard these called, "First Class" settings.

Sometimes an MDM system will not surface a possible CSP setting, and that's a real bummer. When this happens, or rather, doesn't happen, then we as the IT admin of our MDM system have to strap on the gear and perform what's called a "custom URI," which we'll try out in a bit. I've heard the term, "Third Class setting," used for settings like these. That is, the MDM system on Windows 10 will do the thing, but there's simply no easy, peasy way to click-click-click to do that simple thing.

One more, pretty darned important bit. Remember earlier when we set the browser home page? And on Figure 3.6 we had to decide if this setting was to apply to users, devices, or both. The only way you would know if your setting would work for users or devices (or both) would be to check out the documentation.

Here in Figure 3.10, you can see the documentation for the Browser/HomePages setting, and the scope is listed as okay for both User and Device.

FIGURE 3.10   Some MDM policies will work for both User and Device.

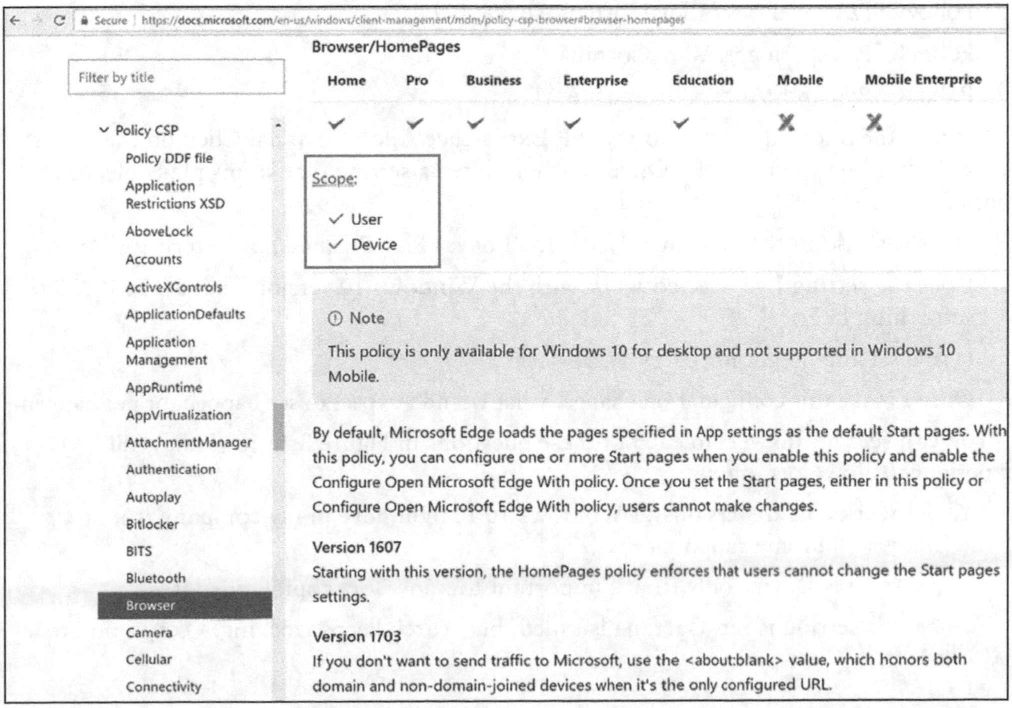

Other settings will show as User or Device only.

I haven't inspected all MDM services, but it doesn't seem like the MDM services give any indication if you're about to shoot yourself in the foot and try to apply, say, a device-side-only policy setting to a group of users. It's up to you to pre-read the docs and know what to aim for.

Policy CSP

Arguably the most exercise your MDM service will have with Windows 10 will be pushing down policies that exist in the Policy CSP. Indeed, you can see an abbreviated list of some of the categories in the Policy CSP in Figure 3.10, starting with Autoplay, then Bitlocker, BITS, Bluetooth, and so on.

Again, the Policy CSP is simply one of the many CSPs that the MDM engine can take directives from. But it's the one most closely aligned with the common items you might do in Group Policy-land and the one that has the most Windows 10 configuration items.

Some MDM systems have a way to search through or filter the settings and find the setting(s) you want to deploy. Others don't. So for me, I like to start my investigation of interesting settings in the Policy CSP documentation here and look for the task I want to perform: https://docs.microsoft.com/en-us/windows/client-management/mdm/policy-configuration-service-provider.

For instance, maybe the boss walks into your office and says, "Cortana? Bah!" Then it would be up to you to be a murderer and kill Cortana.

Okay, you've agreed to kill Cortana. Now how do you do that?

Start by going to the Policy CSP docs and look for items with Cortana in the name. There's going to be a handful of them on the page. As of this writing there are these:

- PolicyCSP/AboveLock/AllowCortanaAboveLock
- PolicyCSP/Experience/AllowCortana
- PolicyCSP/Search/AllowCortanaInAAD

Clearly, the one you want is PolicyCSP/Experience/AllowCortana. Click on that one to see if it's going to fit the bill. Once you've isolated a setting that seems plausible, ask yourself:

- Does it work on the Windows 10 edition I have? Pro, Business, or Enterprise?
- Does the setting I've selected work with the Windows 10 version I have (1703, 1709, something later)?
- Is this setting meant for Users or Devices?
- Once I make this configuration change, what would I expect to see happen (or not happen)?

You can see the answers to each of these questions in Figure 3.11 for PolicyCSP/Experience/AllowCortana:

- Yes, it works on all versions of Windows 10 I might have in my company (so, no Windows 10 Home support).
- The setting is Device only (that's important to know for scoping purposes).
- Once this setting is set, Cortana is killed, but search keeps working. Okay, good to know.

FIGURE 3.11   Getting to know a setting before deploying and testing it

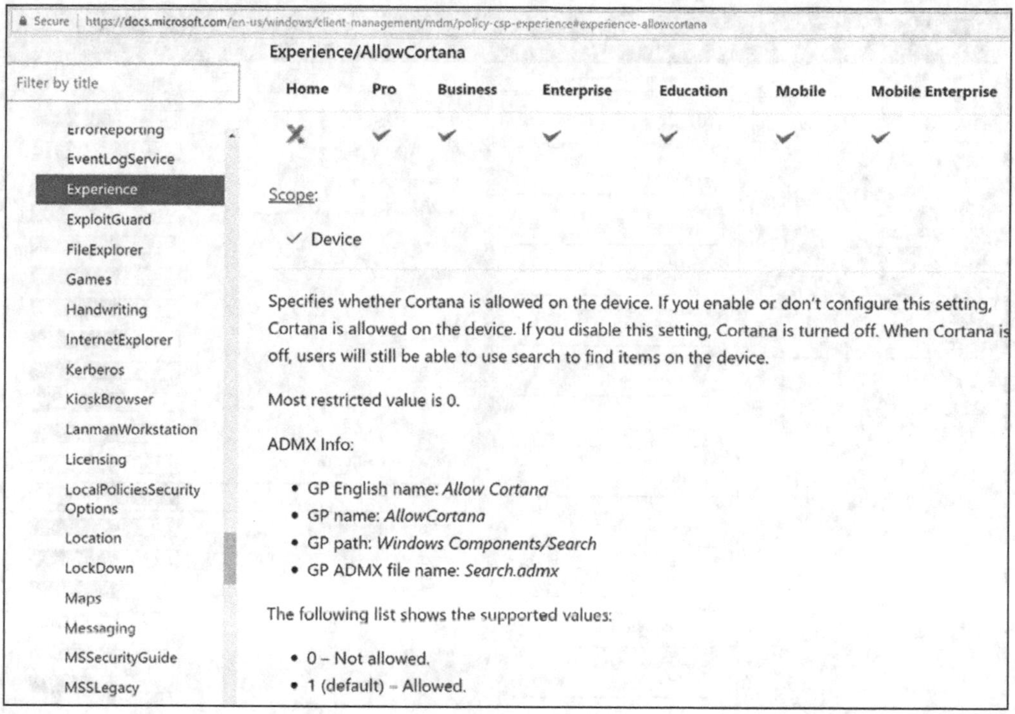

Let's kill Cortana now.

Back in Intune, click Device configuration, then Profiles and Create Profile. Then provide a name, like Kill Cortana. In the Platform drop-down, select Windows 10 and later. In the "Profile type" drop-down, select "Device restrictions." Then in the "Device restrictions" section, click on General, and locate the Cortana policy.

You can see that Cortana's policy is "Not configured" by default, which means that it must be enabled by default.

Now, let's select Block.

All of this can be seen in Figure 3.12. Then, assign to All Devices (not shown). And, remember, if you assign this profile to Users, this isn't going to work because the Kill Cortana setting is Device only.

Back at the endpoint, in the MDM section click on Sync last seen in Figure 3.3. You should see the time jump to now, and if all went well Cortana should disabled. That said, after syncing, sometimes it takes a while, and also sometimes it takes more than one sync.

But you'll know it's done after you investigate the Registry on the Windows 10 machine. In Figure 3.13, you can see AllowCortana is set to 0 after traversing to HKEY_LOCAL_MACHINE\Software\Microsoft\PolicyManager\current\device\Experience.

FIGURE 3.12   Using Microsoft Intune to block Cortana

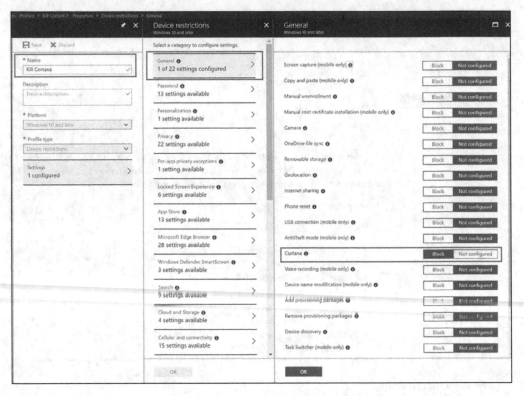

FIGURE 3.13   See MDM setting AllowCortana in the PolicyManager section of the Registry.

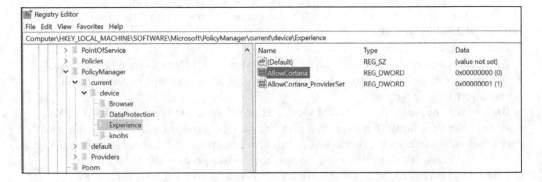

If you then remove the profile, and resync, you would get what's seen in Figure 3.14, where AllowCortana is then reverted, and set back to 1.

FIGURE 3.14   When the MDM profile is removed AllowCortana returns to 1 (Enabled).

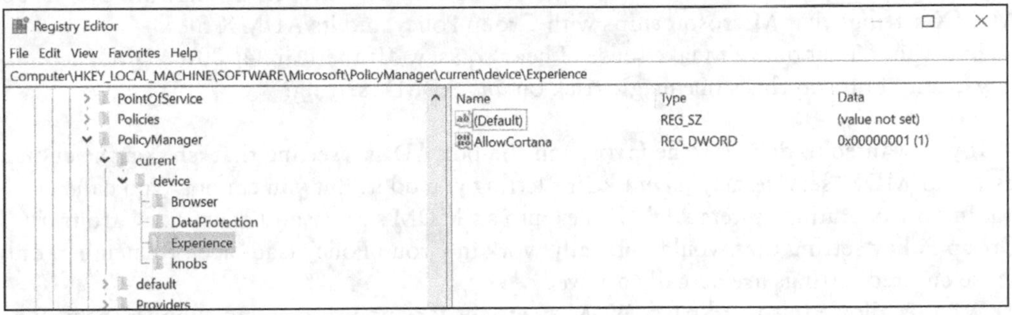

You might not see Cortana pop back to life until you log off and back on.

ADMX-Backed Policies

So in the previous section, we found a policy setting in the documentation, then happened to also find it as something we could graphically click on in the MDM user interface. And poof: It worked.

But not every MDM provider is the same, and not every MDM provider will GUI-enable every interesting policy setting. And sometimes new settings will only be available for testing when some future version of Windows makes an appearance. (Note: Future versions of Windows can be downloaded through the Windows Insider program.) And if you want to see those yet-to-be-born MDM settings take effect, you'll be testing with settings that the MDM providers definitely won't have placed into their GUIs yet.

As such, there's a little "backdoor" way to configure a gaggle of Policy CSP settings that might not be GUI-enabled (yet). I say yet because it's only a matter of time, usually, between when an MDM policy is shipped into Windows 10 and the MDM service then gets the memo and makes a GUI-enabled version of that policy setting. As I mentioned before, these GUI-enabled settings are sometimes called, "First Class" settings.

Or maybe the MDM provider never gets the memo and never GUI-enables the policy setting, and you'll be glad you know about this technique to deliver these settings. These settings, again, are therefore called "Third Class" settings.

You likely wouldn't want to use this backdoor method unless you actually need to. If it's possible to set settings using the GUI, you should strive for that. Not only is it easier to do, but ultimately reporting on the settings is easier as well.

The settings we'll be dealing with in this section are called ADMX-backed policies. There are only a handful (but a nice-sized handful) of these ADMX-backed policy settings. I call these "curated ADMX" settings.

The list of the curated ADMX settings can be found here:

```
https://docs.microsoft.com/en-us/windows/client-management/mdm/
policy-configuration-service-provider#admx-backed-policies
```

As of this second, as I write this, the documentation shows that there are 386 special, curated ADMX-backed policy settings. Again, I call them curated because that's what they are. They are special, and hand-picked by the MDM team as something they want to support and they have guaranteed results. So the complete list of ADMX-backed policy settings is at the URL above, but as you might remember from Chapter 1, there are over 4000 ADMX settings that Microsoft ships with Group Policy and its ADMX files.

But wait, "That doesn't make sense" I hear you say. "If there are 4000+ ADMX settings, can't I just do this same magic trick on *any* ADMX setting?"

No.

If you wanted to deliver some favorite in-the-box ADMX setting that isn't on the curated list, your MDM service may *seem* like it's letting you do it. But you cannot. You cannot import operating system ADMX files into an MDM service and deliver any arbitrary Group Policy setting that would naturally work in Group Policy (sad face). Remember, only those curated settings are actually allowed.

What is allowed, is third-party ADMX settings for applications that support them. We will explore that as well.

Throw that sad face into outer space. If you do have some favorite ADMX setting (or really, any Group Policy setting at all) and you wish to get it delivered using your MDM service, then it's (shameless plug again) PolicyPak MDM to rescue. Check out PolicyPak MDM edition and see some videos on how to deliver real Group Policy, Group Policy Preferences, and Group Policy Security settings that Microsoft won't let you deploy, by visiting www.policypak.com/products/policypak-mdm-edition.html. Videos showing how it's done are right on that page.

So there are two ways to poke these curated ADMX settings through Intune (other MDMs may vary) : the Administrative Templates node and Customer URIs.

Let's explore both now.

Administrative Templates Node through Intune

At Microsoft Ignite 2018, Microsoft announced some initial click-click-click through to some Admin Template settings inside Intune in a technical preview. In the preview, the Administrative Templates node lives within a Profile type as seen in Figure 3.15.

FIGURE 3.15   The preview of Administrative Templates node in Intune

Once an Administrative Templates profile is created, the possible settings appear in their own blade, as seen in Figure 3.16. The curated ADMX settings appear as a flat but searchable list. In Figure 3.17, I'm searching for the word *desktop*, and the settings that are relevant appear.

FIGURE 3.16   The list of curated ADMX settings in a flat list in Intune

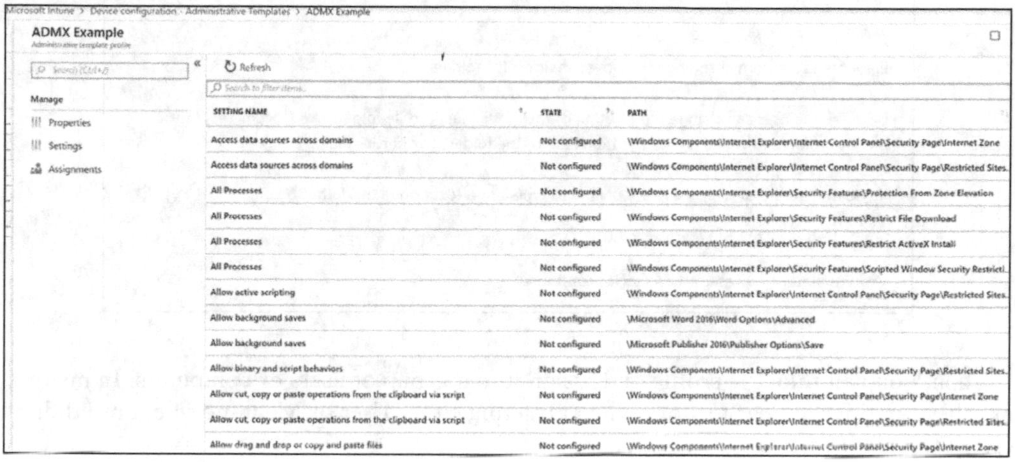

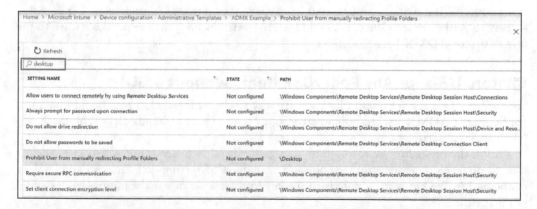

FIGURE 3.17   Searching for relevant ADMX settings

You might notice that the list is not hierarchical, as we have come to recognize it in Group Policy-land. I don't know if Microsoft will keep the current stance, or make it more Group Policy-like by making it hierarchical. For me, I like to see related settings grouped together in a hierarchical way. You can sort by Path, which will kind of do that, but it's not my first choice. Anyway, my guess is that this is subject to change since this feature is in preview and might change before the book goes to press.

Clicking on any policy setting opens another blade that should be familiar to Group Policy users. You can see the "tri-state" selection of Not configured (default), Enabled, or Disabled.

Prohibit User from manually redirecting Profile Folders   □   ✕
\Desktop

Prevents users from changing the path to their profile folders.

By default, a user can change the location of their individual profile folders like Documents, Music etc. by typing a new path in the Locations tab of the folder's Properties dialog box.

If you enable this setting, users are unable to type a new location in the Target box.

Supported on: At least Windows 2000

◉ Enabled   ○ Disabled   ○ Not configured

Then, you can take the profile and assign it to a group of users or computers. In my testing, these settings appear to work when targeting either User or Machine side, but I didn't test all the settings.

I will end this section with a little confession/question: If there are 386 special, curated settings, why aren't they *all* here? My rough count is that only 231 items are listed in the preview, and some of them are for Office, which wouldn't count anyway.

I know this is a work in progress, so keep your eyes on this as it progresses. I expect this section to get better for Office, IE, and OneDrive settings first, then expand outward to the other curated ADMX-backed settings.

Custom URIs for Any PolicyCSP Items without a GUI

So if your MDM service doesn't have a nifty way to click-click-click through and find and configure the ADMX-backed policy settings, it's time to get our hands dirty with these, "Third Class" settings.

I think the procedure we're about to do together is fairly onerous but worth knowing how to do (even if, at some future point, all available CSP settings get surfaced and GUI-enabled). It's like knowing how to turn the key to start a car or use the jumper cables and jump-start it.

Let's jump-start it.

Again, the procedure I'm about to show you is only required when there isn't a GUI method from your MDM that will perform the same function. The one I'd like for us to use as an example is PolicyCSP/InternetExplorer/DisableAdobeFlash, and it's seen in Figure 3.18.

FIGURE 3.18   An example ADMX-backed setting

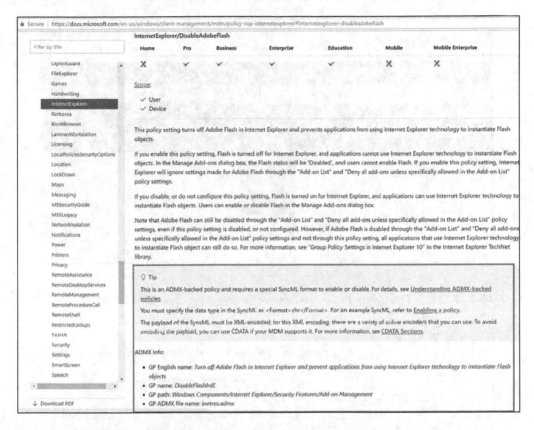

I poked around Windows Intune for about 20 minutes and couldn't find a way to click on it and make it happen with a GUI. Doesn't mean that tomorrow the Windows Intune team won't wake up and say, "Hey, let's GUI-enable the Disable Adobe Flash setting and give it to the people!" It's just that they haven't…yet.

So, before we start down the road at all, let's verify that Flash is happy, working, and enabled on our Windows 10's IE…before we kill it. (Seems like we're doing a lot of killing in this book. Don't tell my mom.)

On Windows 10, launch IE then head over to `http://get.adobe.com/flashplayer/about/`. Do you get the energetic Adobe bouncing box as seen in Figure 3.19?

Great, now let's kill Adobe Flash with a custom ADMX-backed MDM policy.

Now, if I was to use Group Policy to do this work, which I know I'm not, the setting would be found in both the User and Computer side. I can see the User side example in Figure 3.20, after I open the Group Policy editor and find it within User Configuration ➢ Admin Templates ➢ Windows Components ➢ Internet Explorer ➢ Add-on Management ➢ **Turn off Adobe Flash in Internet Explorer and prevent applications from using Internet Explorer technology to instantiate Flash objects**. (And, yes, unbelievably, that's the full name of the policy.)

FIGURE 3.19   Adobe Flash enabled by default within IE

FIGURE 3.20   The Group Policy setting we're going set, but using MDM

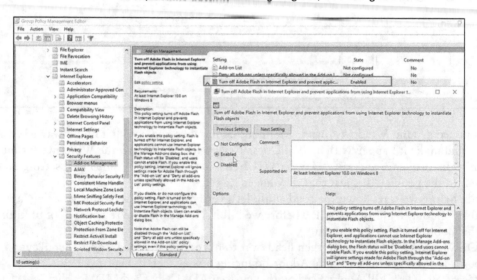

And, if you look at Figure 3.18, you'll see the documentation spells out where this setting lives in Group Policy's ADMX guts.

Here's what it says in the ADMX Info block in the documentation:

- GP English name: Turn off Adobe Flash in Internet Explorer and prevent applications from using Internet Explorer technology to instantiate Flash objects

- GP name: DisableFlashInIE

- GP path: Windows Components/Internet Explorer/Security Features/Add-on Management

- GP ADMX file name: inetres.admx

Now, in the same way that Group Policy settings can be user or computer side, so can MDM settings. And there's a format, and way to express that in MDM speak. It goes like this:

- ./User/Vendor/MSFT/Policy/Config/*AreaName*/*PolicyName*
- ./Device/Vendor/MSFT/Policy/Config/*AreaName*/*PolicyName*

Note the leading dot (.) before the /User and /Computer.

Now, when we look at Figure 3.20, it's a simple policy with just Enabled and Disabled. Nothing fancy about it, and that's where we're going to go first. So our job is to deliver "Enabled" to this policy setting, but by using MDM and not Group Policy.

We now need to put together all the pieces of information we know and what we need to use and smash them all together.

- We know the PolicyCSP location and name of the policy: `InternetExplorer/DisableAdobeFlash` (seen in Figure 3.18).
- We know the way to express that (generally) in MDM speak.
- We know we want to do this on the User side.

Putting it all together we get this:

`./User/Vendor/MSFT/Policy/Config/InternetExplorer/DisableAdobeFlash`

And, it has to be capitalized exactly right or the thing doesn't work. So, write that down, or keep it handy as we make the profile and policy inside MDM.

This specially formatted line is called a custom OMA-URI. Remember, OMA is the Open Mobile Alliance and now URI means Uniform Resource Identifier. It's basically the address, or value, you want to poke with MDM.

Using Intune, you would create a Custom profile type, as seen in Figure 3.21.

FIGURE 3.21   Create a Custom profile type for ADMX-backed policies with no GUI.

The last two pieces of information you need are buried in the MDM docs, so I'm just going to tell you what you need for "Data type" and Value.

▪ For "Data type," use String.

▪ For Value, use <enabled/> (with no spaces).

You can see these in Figure 3.22.

FIGURE 3.22   Creating a custom OMA-URI setting

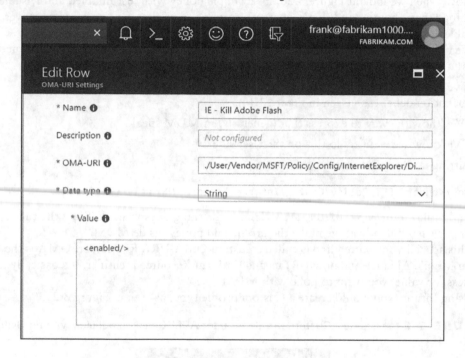

 Some documentation I've seen shows <enabled />. That's the less-than symbol, the word *enabled*, a space, a slash, then a greater-than symbol. When I did this syntax (adding the space), it failed to work for me, but it might be required for some MDM services.

After the policy is saved, perform the assignment to All Users (not shown).

Back on your Windows 10 machine, close IE if it's still open. Then sync again with MDM to get this setting from your MDM service. Then return to the Flash player test URL, and, before the advertisement pops up, you should see what's seen in Figure 3.23 and no bouncing Adobe Flash animation.

FIGURE 3.23   Flash should stop functioning in IE now.

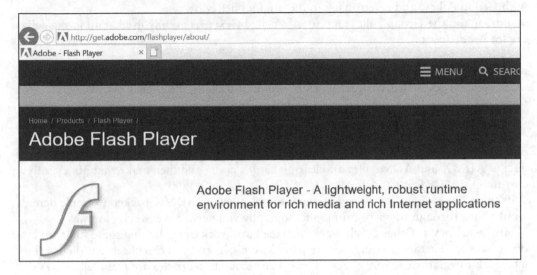

Here's the very nifty, under-the-hood thing that's happening here. Remember, there's no Group Policy involved in this. You made a custom OMA-URI to deliver an ADMX-backed setting. Well, if it's an ADMX-backed setting, that means it has to lay down a Group Policy–style Registry item, right? Yep. And you can see the resultant example in Figure 3.24 within HKCU\Software\Policies\Microsoft\Internet Explorer. It sets DisableFlashInIE to 1.

FIGURE 3.24   No Group Policy involved, yet the Policies keys are manipulated.

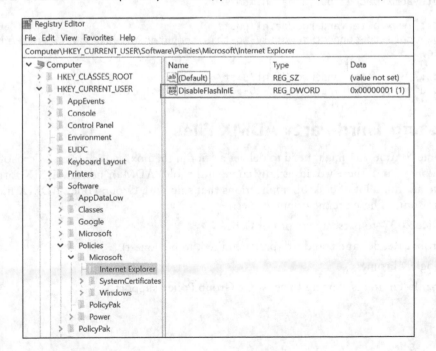

And, when you delete the profile or kill the policy setting, the setting disappears, just as with Group Policy, and reverts back to the original behavior.

But, again, the Group Policy engine (also called GPsvc) is not involved at all in the delivery (or un-delivery).

Nifty.

Now, that being said, not every ADMX-backed policy setting is a simple Enabled/Disabled value. Some ADMX items can get pretty complex, and again, the hope is that you won't need to dig inside the ADMX's guts in order to discern how it's built in Group Policy-land and basically "rebuild" it in MDM land. The MDM service should be abstracting you from it.

But if you find an ADMX-backed setting that has a myriad of text-based options, or other configurable options, you're going to have to strap on even more gear and dig into the guts of ADMX and ADML files and learn what it's doing and then make that policy into a custom OMA-URI.

It's just too arduous for me to even go into one complex ADMX-backed example here. It would burn through the page count, and hopefully you never have to do it anyway.

But, good news. Other people have done the hard work of explaining these steps, so I don't have to. The first two articles are from Microsoft, and you can check out the excellent walk-through video in the second one. The second two articles are from fellow MVP Peter van der Woude, who writes excellent how-to articles about MDM and Intune. Those four resources show how to tear into an ADMX and ADML file and create a more complex ADMX-backed policy:

https://docs.microsoft.com/en-us/windows/client-management/mdm/understanding-admx-backed-policies

https://docs.microsoft.com/en-us/windows/client-management/mdm/enable-admx-backed-policies-in-mdm

https://www.petervanderwoude.nl/post/allow-users-to-connect-remotely-to-this-computer-via-windows-10-mdm-admx-style/

https://www.petervanderwoude.nl/post/deep-dive-configuring-windows-10-admx-backed-policies/

Ingesting Third-Party ADMX Files

From time to time you might need to deliver a "not in the box" policy from Microsoft. In Group Policy-land, these would usually come in the (old) ADM or newer ADMX format.

There are not a lot of desktop applications that ship with Group Policy ADMX files. But there are some. These are the popular ones:

- Office 2007–to present versions of Office
- Acrobat Reader and Standard (pretty limited, to be honest)
- Google Chrome
- Mozilla Firefox is starting to get some Group Policy support.

There are some others, but these are the heavy hitters you might already be using with your existing Group Policy. And your MDM service has a way to ingest third-party ADMX files and deliver those settings to your Windows 10 machine.

In Group Policy-land, this idea of sucking in ADMX files was called *consuming* ADM or ADMX files. Now, in MDM, *just to be different* it's called *ingesting*, which to me sounds a little more gross. But that's just me.

Anyway, remember the deal earlier: All the ADMX-backed policies that Microsoft curates are, well, from Microsoft, and, as I said, they're (pretty much) guaranteed to work as expected. But for third-party ADMX files, Microsoft is more loosey-goosey and doesn't curate and therefore doesn't guarantee that they're going to work as expected. Remember, Microsoft shipped the Administrative Templates technical preview I mentioned earlier. As of this moment, there's no way to point and click to add your ADMX templates via ingesting. I heartily suspect they will add this feature. It seems reasonably easy to do. I cannot show you any step by steps for it, because again, there's nothing to show. But keep your eye on that likely possibility.

So, this means the steps right now are pretty onerous (again).

So, buckle up, here's how to do it.

There are two steps to ingesting third-party ADMX:

- Copying the third-party ADMX file into a custom OMA-URI

- Setting the value from the ADMX file you want (pretty much exactly like what we just did in the previous section)

So, to get started with this example, I'll be using Foxit Reader's ADMX, but again, most third-party ADMX files should work here.

You might be wondering why I didn't choose either Adobe Acrobat Reader or Chrome for these examples, and I have a good reason for each:

- Google Chrome and its ADMX: Just as we were going to press, Chrome got the wherewithal to start honoring its ADMX via MDM. The official step-by-steps can be found at https://support.google.com/chrome/a/answer/9102677. Note that not every Chrome setting will actually work when machines are non-domain joined. (One of my team members at PolicyPak took the time to figure out which items should work "a-ok" for non-domain joined machines. If you want to check it out, it's here: https://kb.policypak.com/kb/article/ 284-which-items-in-chrome-will-and-will-not-work-when-nondomain-joined.)

- Adobe Reader's policy support is downright pathetic. I don't understand it, but it has very few policies, several I tested failed to function at all as expected, and many of them are what's called preferences and not policies. As such the UI doesn't lock down, so I'm not going to use that here.

- Microsoft Office has some policies that lock out and others don't. Besides, the ADMX files are all over the place and complex for a simple example.

You might be wondering how the MDM engine knows what to accept and what to throw out. And the answer is pretty simple and elegant. If you look at the ADMX items that Microsoft ships in the box for the operating system, all the policy settings will write Registry items like `HKLM` or `HKCU / Software / Policies / Microsoft / <something>`.

Well, Adobe, Chrome, Firefox, Office, PolicyPak, and so on all ship ADMX files to do some kind of final tweaking of their products, but as you might expect, don't write values to the Microsoft operating system subkeys. So all of those are written and honored by MDM because the MDM system isn't there to curate these settings.

For our working example I've chosen Foxit Reader and its ADMX files. If you want to join along and test this, on your Windows 10 endpoint, install the latest Foxit Reader by hand (as of this writing, it's version 9.2). Just go to `www.foxitsoftware.com/pdf-reader/` and download the standard version and install it. Again, install this on your Windows 10 endpoint managed by MDM and take all the defaults. (Not shown.)

After you run Foxit Reader on your Windows 10 machine, take a second to see the Automatically Update status by going to File ➤ Preferences and then clicking Updater. You should see what's in Figure 3.25, where the program is set to download updates and let users choose to install them.

We will be using our MDM service to set this to "Do not download or install updates automatically" and also lock it down so users cannot change it.

FIGURE 3.25 Foxit Reader's default update behavior

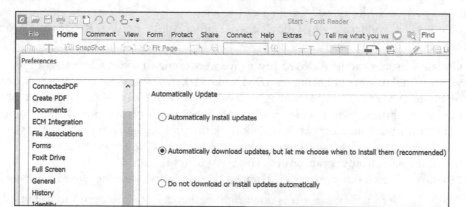

Next, on your management station, download and have handy the Foxit ADMX files. At last check you can find them here: `https://help.foxitsoftware.com/kb/available-gpo-templates.php`.

Now, if I was going to be using Group Policy to manage Foxit Reader (I'm not), it would look like what you see in Figure 3.26. The setting I might want to use would be **Disable the Automatically Update** policy setting, also seen in Figure 3.26.

FIGURE 3.26 How you would use Group Policy to set Foxit Reader to stop automatic updates

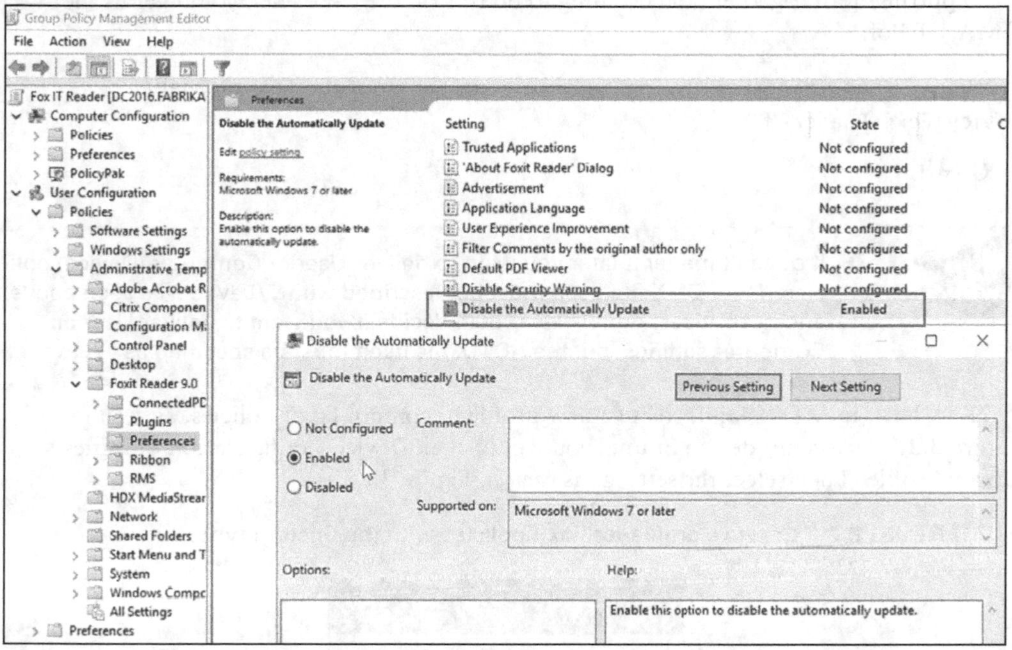

So, to do this with MDM, start with opening up the Foxit ADMX file in Notepad and have that ready. Then using your MDM service like Intune, create a new profile, then another custom OMA-URI policy as we did earlier; just this time make it obvious you're doing something for Foxit Reader.

In the OMA-URI field, you need to specify a special syntax that signifies you're about to feed it a whole ADMX file. The syntax would be:

```
./Device/Vendor/MSFT/Policy/ConfigOperations/ADMXInstall/{AppName}/
{SettingType}/{FileUid or AdmxFileName}
```

Okay. This gives us a little puzzle to sort out. We need to find and place in the following values:

- AppName: This can be anything, but best to give it the name of what we're doing. I'll call it FoxitReader.
- SettingType: Even though this seems like it could be different keywords, in practice, when ingesting ADMX, this must always just be the word Policy.

- `FileUid` or `AdmxFileName`: This can also be anything, but it's recommended to name this the same as the ADMX file you are using. So I'll use the value `FoxitReaderADMX`.

So putting it all together (and deciding to do this on the User side) would get us the OMA-URI of:

`./Device/Vendor/MSFT/Policy/ConfigOperations/ADMXInstall/FoxitReader/`
`Policy/FoxitReaderAMX`

Great!

> It doesn't matter if later you want to deliver User or Computer (Device) policies. The ADMX file itself must be described with `./Device` (as seen above) and not `./User`. Again, later you'll decide if you want to deliver User or Computer settings; but the ADMX file itself must be specified as `./Device`.

Now, back in MDM-land, create a new profile to contain Foxit policies, as seen in Figure 3.27. As a reminder, in Intune, you would click Device Configuration - Profiles ➤ Create Profile. Then select the settings as seen in Figure 3.27.

FIGURE 3.27   Create a profile for Foxit policies with the Custom type.

Then, in the OMA-URI settings view, give it a name, paste in the OMA-URI you crafted 10 seconds ago, provide the data type of String, and then, here's the fun part…paste *all* of the Foxit ADMX into the Value field (seen in Figure 3.28) and click OK (not shown). This will save the entire ADMX file into the profile.

Then all these possible ADMX definitions get delivered to the endpoint. (This is an interesting and obscure point that is about to become really important in a few pages. See the sidebar "Replacing Existing ADMX Settings on the Endpoint" for the details.)

FIGURE 3.28   Adding an ADMX file as a custom OMA-URI. The whole ADMX file gets downloaded to the client.

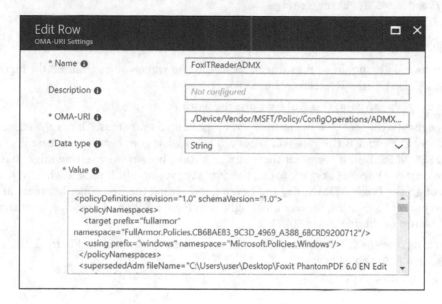

Next, you need to do a little digging inside the ADMX file and find the value you want to deliver. In Figure 3.29, I think I found the right one, since it's got the words *Disable* and *Updater* in the name. So, I'm reasonably sure that PREF_DisableUpdater has to be the right one.

FIGURE 3.29   Find the policy setting within the ADMX you want to deliver.

```
Foxit Reader.admx - Notepad
File Edit Format View Help
            <text id="PREF_UserManualPath" valueName="UserManualLocalPath" />
        </elements>
    </policy>
    <policy name="PREF_DisableUpdater" class="Both" displayName="$(string.
    <parentCategory ref="PREFERENCES" />
    <supportedOn ref="SUPPORTED_WINXPSP2" />
    <enabledValue>
        <decimal value="0" />
    </enabledValue>
    <disabledValue>
        <delete />
    </disabledValue>
</policy>
```

We need to translate this to MDM-land. The way to express what we need would look like:

```
./Device/Vendor/MSFT/Policy/Config/
{AppName}~{SettingType}~{CategoryPathFromADMX}/{SettingFromADMX}
```

or

```
./User/Vendor/MSFT/Policy/Config/
{AppName}~{SettingType}~{CategoryPathFromADMX}/{SettingFromADMX}
```

Great. Another puzzle to figure out. Here are the pieces:

- AppName: This should be the same name as the app when you configured the ingestion of the ADMX-file. Remember, I used FoxitReaderADMX.

- SettingType: Again, this is always just the word Policy.

- CategoryPathFromADMX: In Figure 3.29, I highlighted two areas. One is the name of the policy. The other is the parentCategory. This is what goes here; in our case it's called PREFERENCES. But, it turns out there's more to this, because any setting might have one or more parentCategory (or no parentCategory at all). It took a while to trace through the Foxit ADMX file, and I even got it wrong the first time. But there are two parent categories, the one I highlighted in Figure 3.29 and one more (not shown) at the top of the file called FOXIT.

- SettingFromADMX: This is what we want to configure, also seen in Figure 3.29. In our case, PREF_DisableUpdater.

Putting it all together we get:

```
./User/Vendor/MSFT/Policy/Config/
FoxitReader~Policy~FOXIT~PREFERENCES/PREF_DisableUpdater
```

or

```
./Device/Vendor/MSFT/Policy/Config/
FoxitReader~Policy~FOXIT~PREFERENCES/PREF_DisableUpdater
```

Note that not every ADMX file will nicely have the same setting on both the user and the computer side, but this one from Foxit Reader does.

Now, you can add your second policy into the profile. To do this, click Add in the OMA-URI settings blade, then when Add Row appears, you can add the policy to disable Foxit Updater.

You'll put in the Name, user, or device OMA-URI you created 10 seconds ago (I'll use device in my example), give it data type of String, and then for Value, type in **<enabled/>** with no spaces. You can see the policy in Figure 3.30 (left) if you wanted to deliver the setting on the computer side and Figure 3.30 (right) if you wanted to deliver the setting on the User side.

FIGURE 3.30 Add the value to disable Foxit Updater. You can deliver the value to Device (left) or User (right).

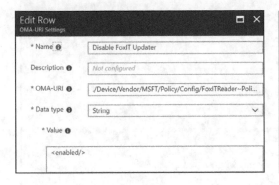

Click Save to save the value, then again to save the profile. Then assign it to All Devices. Note that you must assign the profile to Devices, even if you want the settings to affect the User side. Weird, right? It's because the URI of the ADMX setting itself (./User or ./Device) does the magic after the setting is delivered to the device side.

Back on your Windows 10 machine, if Foxit Reader is still open, close it. Then sync with the MDM service. You should see what you see in Figure 3.31, showing your custom ADMX ingested settings.

FIGURE 3.31 You can see the ingested custom ADMX policies in the MDM sync (after you close and reopen the page).

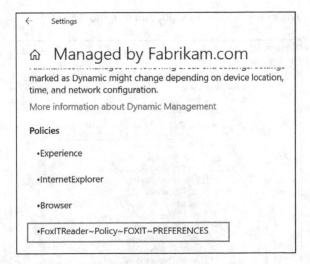

Then open Foxit Reader and go to File ➤ Preferences ➤ Updater.

You should see the UI for Foxit Reader locked out and not configurable by the user as seen in Figure 3.32.

FIGURE 3.32   Successful lockout of Foxit reader with ingested ADMX file

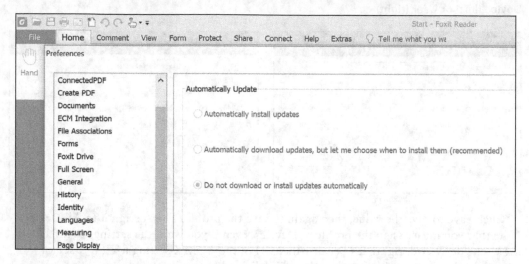

And you can check a few locations to see if your settings are being written to the Registry (and note these are good troubleshooting steps too).

Remember that the ADMX definitions themselves are basically delivered to the client and then stored locally. Where is this? In `HKLM\Software\Microsoft\PolicyManager\ AdmxDefault\{GUID}` as you can see in Figure 3.33. You should see the entire Foxit Reader ADMX we sent down.

FIGURE 3.33   The entire ADMX downloaded into the Registry

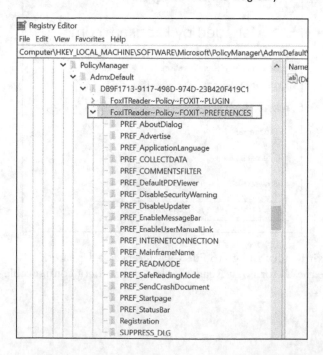

Then, the actual thing we want to verify, the Group Policy location of the write, can be seen in Figure 3.34. You're going for HKLM\Software\Policies\Foxit\Reader 9.0\Preferences and see that DisableUpdate is set to 0 (which is a little unusual; most well-written ADMX files would usually be something like DisableUpdate set to 1, but, I can roll with it).

FIGURE 3.34 The Group Policy location is written to by the ADMX.

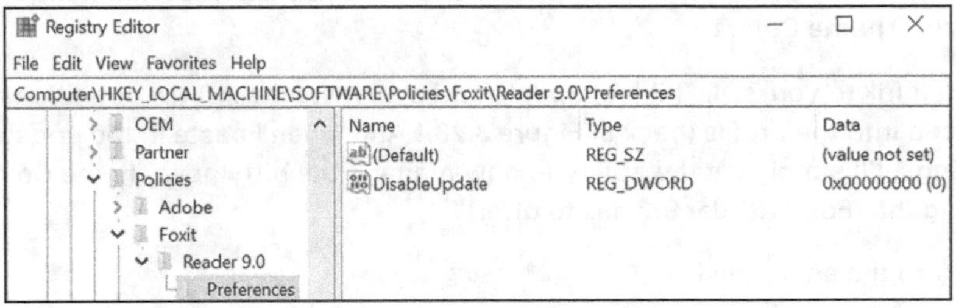

Registry Editor			
File Edit View Favorites Help			
Computer\HKEY_LOCAL_MACHINE\SOFTWARE\Policies\Foxit\Reader 9.0\Preferences			
	Name	Type	Data
> OEM	(Default)	REG_SZ	(value not set)
> Partner	DisableUpdate	REG_DWORD	0x00000000 (0)
∨ Policies			
> Adobe			
∨ Foxit			
∨ Reader 9.0			
Preferences			

If this seems like an insane amount of work, well, you're right, it is. Again, at least Intune will likely have some kind of ADMX "ingesting" routine for third-party ADMX settings. But also note that PolicyPak MDM can do this as well, for just about every application, and lock those settings down (even for many applications that don't have built-in lockdown). This is with our PolicyPak Application Manager component within PolicyPak MDM. And those lockdown settings for applications can be deployed using Group Policy or your MDM service. Check out www.policypak.com/products/policypak-application-manager-including-policypak-designstudio.html for some demo videos that greatly reduce the frustration in this process.

You can learn more about ingesting ADMX files into an MDM service with the following URLs:

- https://docs.microsoft.com/en-us/windows/client-management/mdm/understanding-admx-backed-policies (search for the word Ingest)

- https://docs.microsoft.com/en-us/windows/client-management/mdm/win32-and-centennial-app-policy-configuration

- https://www.petervanderwoude.nl/post/deep-dive-ingesting-third-party-admx-files/

Replacing Existing ADMX Settings on the Endpoint

Okay, let's jump ahead into the future a little bit.

You've deployed Foxit Reader 9.2 and used the ADMX setting that came out with it.

Then you use your MDM service to roll out Foxit Reader 9.3, and it has some features in it that can be controlled by ADMX. Maybe Foxit Reader 9.3 has a new setting (and I'm making it up here), Theme Colors.

"Nifty!" You think to yourself, "I'll just update and overwrite the ADMX definitions I've already placed into the profile (back in Figure 3.28)! And when I paste in the updated ADMX settings, I'll simply get the ability to now manage the nifty new Theme Colors policy setting that Foxit Reader 9.3 has to offer!"

Bam. Right into the snake pits!

I wouldn't have guessed this behavior either, but apparently the MDM engine cannot handle this situation.

When you attempt to wholesale-replace the ADMX definitions for the custom application, it simply doesn't work.

Chasing this down, I found a very "fine print" kind of reasoning in the PolicyCSP docs:

```
https://docs.microsoft.com/en-us/windows/client-management/mdm/
policy-configuration-service-provider
```

Here's the quote:

> Policy/ConfigOperations/ADMXInstall/AppName/Preference/UniqueID
> Added in Windows 10, version 1703. Specifies the unique ID of the app
> ADMX file that contains the preference to import. Supported operations
> are Add and Get. Does not support Delete.

Do you see the problem? "Does not support Delete."

So you've upgraded (really, replaced) the ADMX definitions with newer ones. And the MDM engine sees the change and says, "Can't help ya, man."

The result (at least) is an error in the Microsoft ➢ Windows ➢ DeviceManagement-Enterprise-Diagnostics-Provider logs like what's seen here in Event 454.

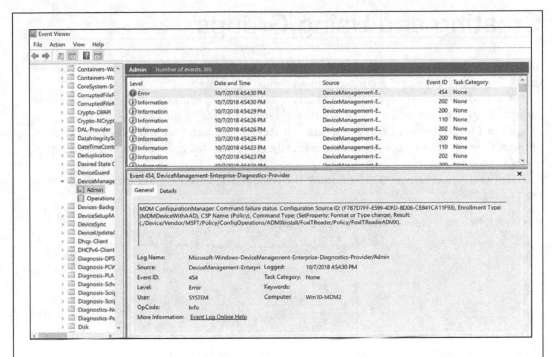

Because the existing ADMX definitions cannot be deleted, they cannot be replaced. So the engine kind of goes into a stalemate, and you don't get your updates.

Note this story is not limited to Foxit Reader; it could be referring to the idea of upgrading Office 2016 ADMX with a slightly newer one or Firefox ADMX with a slightly newer one, etc.

So how do you get out of this jam? There are three answers as I see it today:

Choice 1: Create a new profile expressly for the newer application.

Choice 2: Pre-run some kind of custom cleanup PowerShell script to scrape the data out of the Registry manually. Your goal would be to remove the `HKLM\Software\Microsoft\PolicyManager\AdmxDefault\{GUID}` data that stores the ADMX contents.

Choice 3: Use PolicyPak MDM to deliver the setting using PolicyPak Admin Templates Manager, PolicyPak Preferences Manager, or PolicyPak Application Manager (depending on the situation). When the value is needing to change, *PolicyPak just changes it.*

Maybe this just gets fixed in some later version of Windows. Maybe it gets resolved by the time you read this…or maybe not. But I wanted to make sure you did know about it if it's "one of those things" that doesn't get a quick fix.

Creating and Using Groups

So far in the book, we've made some test profiles and then linked them either to All Users or All Computers, the two default groups that exist in Intune.

An MDM service also enables you to create specific *Assigned* groups and also *Dynamic* groups. Assigned groups are where you directly dictate that specific users or computers are put inside. Dynamic groups are where you set criteria, such that when the condition applies, then the user or computer automatically gets evaluated to be contained within the group.

In Intune, you create groups by finding the Groups node off the main Intune blade, as seen in Figure 3.35.

FIGURE 3.35   How to start to create groups in Intune

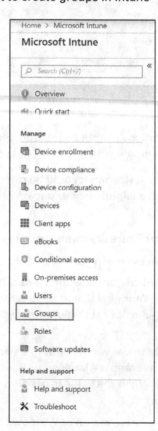

Creating Assigned Groups

Assigned groups, again, simply means you're directing which users or computers are inside. These are akin to on-prem AD Security Groups, but they're used mostly for targeting where Intune profiles will used.

To create an Assigned group, simply pull down the group type as Security, provide a group name and optional description, then specify the membership type as Assigned as seen in Figure 3.36. Then, simply select members to add to the group.

Couldn't be easier.

FIGURE 3.36   Creating Assigned groups (containing users)

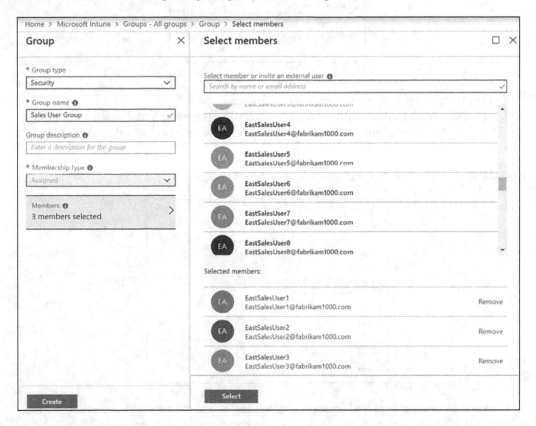

Creating Dynamic Groups

Dynamic groups are another story.

As in Figure 3.36 earlier, you have to specify the group type (as Security) and group name, provide an optional description, and then specify Dynamic User or Dynamic Device as seen here.

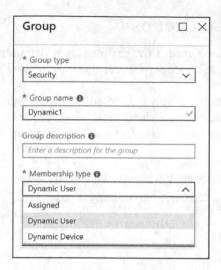

There are two types of rules: Simple and Advanced.

Simple rules have limited abilities and it's generally easy enough to discern what's going on. In Figure 3.37, I'm creating a Dynamic group for devices where `displayName Contains Computer`.

FIGURE 3.37   Creating a Dynamic computer or user group

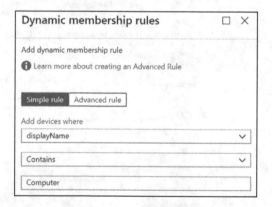

It would be great if Intune showed you right there which computers (or users) would be added; but it doesn't. Instead, you have to go back to Groups - All groups and select the new Dynamic group you just created.

Then, you can see the number of devices (or users) the group contains at a glance or see the actual members by clicking Members (both seen in Figure 3.38).

Creating and Using Groups

FIGURE 3.38 See the number of devices or users in a Dynamic group and/or click Members to see all of them.

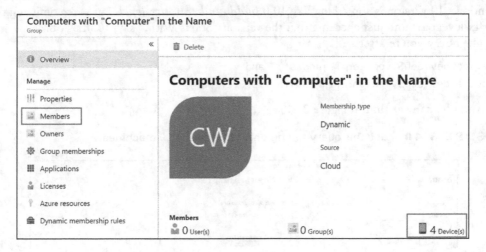

Advanced Dynamic Rules

I also mentioned Advanced rules, which can kind of be a bear to set up but, as you might expect, have a lot more power. Luckily for all of us, Microsoft has an excellent reference on the subject, which they advertise right inside the rule creator as seen in Figure 3.39.

FIGURE 3.39 Advanced rules utilize a query language, and you can learn more about the query language at the link.

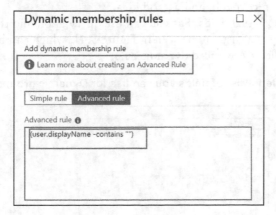

A Somewhat Deeper Dynamic Group Example

In case you need to do it, here's a common dynamic query example that might help you out. For instance, here is how to find all Windows 10 1809 devices. The first part of the rule is to make sure we query only for Windows devices. Then, the second part of the rule will include only Windows 10 devices with a build number that starts with 10.0.17758. The actual Windows 10 version is something like 10.0.*buildnumber.hotfix-level*. But we're omitting the hotfix-level part and just checking that the version "Starts With," say, 10.0.17758.

The query you're after is:

```
(device.deviceOSType -eq "Windows") -and
(device.deviceOSVersion -startsWith "10.0.17758")
```

And you can see that in Figure 3.40.

FIGURE 3.40   Use this query to find only Windows 1809 machines.

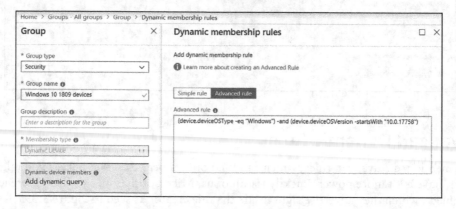

Limitations of Dynamic Group Fields

Dynamic groups are a nice touch, and a good idea.

That being said, the actual fields that you can use query upon and then make Dynamic groups is a little paltry. The list can be seen in Figure 3.41, which can be seen when performing either a Simple or Advanced dynamic rule.

FIGURE 3.41   The full list of fields you can use for Dynamic groups

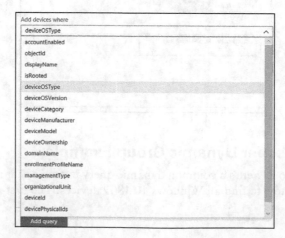

Inspecting Dynamic Group Membership Last Updated

Because Dynamic groups, are, well, dynamic, that means the membership is constantly evaluated for new, matching items. And that could take a bit.

In Figure 3.42, you can see the "Membership last updated" value. When it updates, you can be reasonably sure your correctly formed query will find and sweep new computers in.

FIGURE 3.42 You can see the "Membership last updated" value for your Dynamic group.

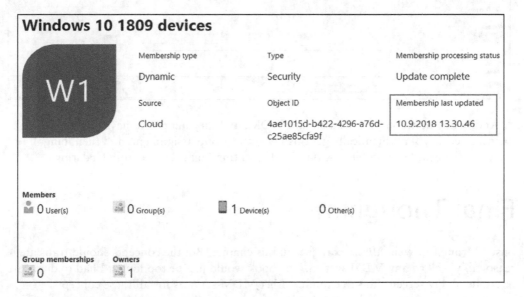

Troubleshooting Dynamic Groups

If you have trouble with Dynamic groups, a good Q&A about troubleshooting can be found at `https://docs.microsoft.com/en-us/azure/active-directory/users-groups-roles/groups-troubleshooting`.

Key findings from that document include that the smaller the directory, the faster the change. And large directories could take up to 30 minutes to populate.

So, you might need a little patience as you add more and more computers.

Here are some good resources and articles on Dynamic groups:

`https://blogs.technet.microsoft.com/pauljones/2017/08/28/dynamic-group-membership-in-azure-active-directory-part-1/`

`https://blogs.technet.microsoft.com/pauljones/2017/08/29/dynamic-group-membership-in-azure-active-directory-part-2/`

Utilizing Groups in Intune

Now that you've got either Assigned or Dynamic groups handled, you could use them as I'm doing in Figure 3.43. That is, instead of targeting All Devices, I'm now using my nifty group entitled **Computers with "Computer" in the Name.**

FIGURE 3.43   You can select groups which will accept settings.

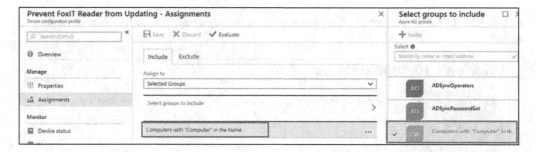

And, when new computers enroll into MDM, and they happen to have Computer in their name, they'll automatically get this Dynamic group assignment, and then, bingo! They get the profile or profiles I want, like **Preventing** Foxit Reader from Updating.

Final Thoughts

I used Intune for, well, *all* the examples in this chapter. But the concepts should translate reasonably well to any MDM system. The book would just be too long if I had to duplicate or triplicate my screen shots to examine other MDM services for all these concepts

As I tried to express in the introduction of the book, I'm reasonably sure that most of the concepts here should stay put and work for years to come. But it's also true that the user interface will certainly shift in some places as the folks at Microsoft change their mind about placement of buttons, icons, drop-downs, and so on.

Not to mention maybe they change their mind about showing the Administrative Template settings in a hierarchy (maybe?) as well as ingesting custom and third-party ADMX files in some nifty not-yet-delivered interface.

That said, a little side note, which is that you can always see what's new in Intune at https://docs.microsoft.com/en-us/intune/whats-new.

This was another big chapter where you learned the following big, big, super big concepts:

- Profiles vs. policies
- How to create a simple MDM policy
- What is the Policy CSP, and how ADMX-backed policies fit in (along with Administrative Templates UI preview)

- How to create custom OMA-URI settings when there isn't a GUI way to do the action
- How to ingest third-party ADMX to manage third-party applications
- How to create and use Groups for targeting (Assigned and Dynamic)

Tweet me @jeremymoskowitz with the one killer thing you learned in this chapter. Be sure to use the hashtag #mdmbook and mention Chapter 3.

Next up: More integration with on-prem SCCM and Group Policy.

See you in the next chapter.

Chapter 4

Co-Management and Co-Policy Management

When Intune first shipped, the party line was clear: A machine shouldn't be managed by, say, Active Directory with Group Policy and by SCCM and also Intune. That would be a disaster because how would you know what setting was coming from where?

That was the "Story 1.0." I want to explain that story first and then go onward to "Story 2.0," which happened around September of 2017, and explain where that's different and now evolved.

This "Story 1.0" was called Hybrid MDM.

This "Story 2.0" is called co-management and it involves your MDM service alongside both SCCM and Group Policy.

Indeed, using Group Policy alongside MDM has some interesting advantages and pitfalls. First, you can use Group Policy to "bootstrap" your existing machines to join your MDM service. But then, once machines are getting both Group Policy and MDM settings, who is going to win?

It's a lot to explain and explore, and that's what this chapter is all about.

Co-Management of SCCM and Intune

So again, back when Intune was launched, it just made sense: Blocking the registration of a device in both SCCM and Intune (or any MDM service) was a perfectly sensible decision at the time.

You wouldn't want to have settings be delivered from multiple sources when those two sources couldn't really talk to each other. Not to mention, administrators who were already invested in SCCM as their "big management system of choice" didn't want to have to run to two consoles to do things. So Microsoft created the Intune Connector.

The Intune Connector enabled an administrator to keep using their on-prem SCCM console and perform the same tasks as if they had simply logged onto Microsoft Intune and done it in that other console. And Microsoft called this the hybrid design, which you can see in Figure 4.1.

FIGURE 4.1 The old Microsoft Intune and SCCM hybrid design with the Intune Connector

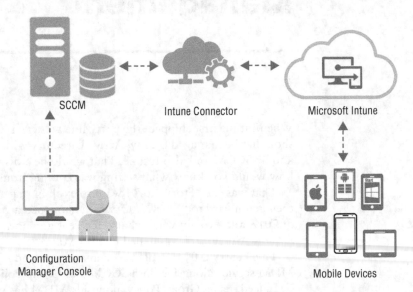

But at Microsoft Ignite 2017, Microsoft announced a shift in its thinking. Instead of actively preventing a machine from independently picking up directives from on-prem Active Directory (that is, Group Policy) and SCCM and/or an MDM service (like Microsoft Intune), they showed a graphic that is a lot like Figure 4.2, a very simplified version of a concept called *co-management*. Co-management's terminology started out specific to Microsoft Intune, but as you'll see in a bit, other MDM services have jumped onto the bandwagon using the same terminology.

FIGURE 4.2 Simplified version of on-prem and cloud co-management

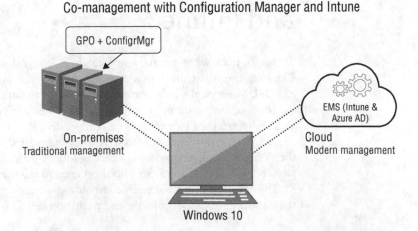

Indeed, Microsoft has explained that they are turning off the lights on hybrid as explained in this blog entry:

`https://blogs.technet.microsoft.com/intunesupport/2018/08/14/`
`move-from-hybrid-mobile-device-management-to-intune-on-azure/`

Co-management turns the initial rules on its ear. Instead of actively blocking registration of a device in SCCM and Intune (at the same time), as well as Active Directory (with Group Policy), now they are downright permitting and encouraging it.

The idea and rationale to enable co-management came to Microsoft after they realized that organizations simply wouldn't "jump" from all their entrenched on-prem solutions (primarily SCCM) over to Intune (or any MDM). And the idea is that co-management is a way to first connect "all the wires" from Windows 10 to your on-prem systems and also to your MDM system. Then, over time, decide which *workloads* (as Microsoft calls them) will be handled by what technology (either SCCM or Intune).

Co-management has quite a few steps to go through to get enabled if you've got an existing on-prem SCCM infrastructure. But the key screen in SCCM can be seen in Figure 4.3, where the SCCM admin gets to make some decisions about "which tool will manage what policies."

FIGURE 4.3   Microsoft SCCM co-management screen to decide which technology will handle what workload

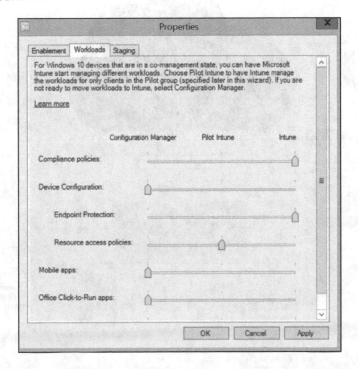

The Workloads screen, shown in Figure 4.3, enables an SCCM admin (where they have pre-configured co-management to work) to simply slide a slider or sliders and decide that

one or more workload policy types is now going to be handled by either Configuration Manager (SCCM) or Intune.

The endpoint then gets directives from the MDM channel as well as the traditional SCCM client. Best of both worlds, until you decide to cut the SCCM cord. That's the idea anyway. That said, Microsoft's latest stance is that SCCM co-management might stay a relatively long time. So you might not even cut the SCCM cord at all.

And, as you can see in Figure 4.3, there are really two positions for Intune: Pilot Intune and Intune. The idea is that you can have a pilot group first to make sure things are operating as expected. Then, throw the switch all the way, and blammo! You've cut the wires for that workload from your on-prem SCCM and are now just using Intune for that workload. At some future point, you've moved all the sliders, and all workloads are being handled by Intune, and, hey, look at that! You can maybe walk away from SCCM (or rely upon it a lot less).

I think it's worth mentioning that the real picture of co-management has more moving parts than the simplified graphic I showed to get us started on the topic in Figure 4.2. Said another way, co-management can be better described graphically by exploding all of its parts, as seen in Figure 4.4.

FIGURE 4.4   Co-management with all of its moving parts

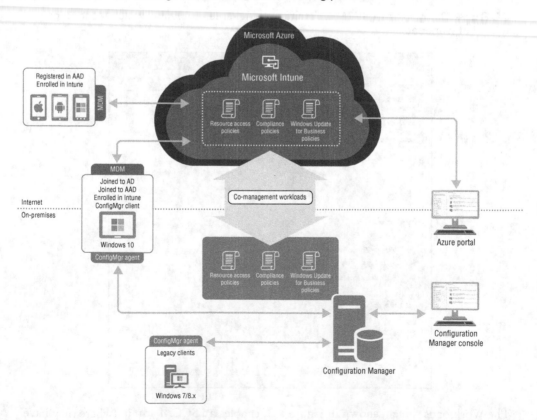

So, fleshing out all of what Microsoft co-management would be is beyond the scope of the book and what I want to cover. But you might actually have on-prem SCCM and want to enable SCCM and Intune co-management and need to get a handle on what Microsoft is talking about and be conversant in understanding their goals and why they want you to start down the road with SCCM and Intune co-management.

In this book, I'm *not* going to assume you have SCCM. I mean, maybe you do, and that's great for you if you do. But I think it's a bit of a burden to ask you to set up an SCCM environment just to try out co-management. But if you've already got SCCM and the idea of co-management is interesting for you, a great (if not long and arduous) six-part walk-through of enabling SCCM and co-management can be found, starting here: www.scconfigmgr.com/2017/11/23/how-to-setup-co-management-part-1/.

The Microsoft marketing efforts on this is called "Just 4 clicks," which is a little… well, it's more than four clicks, that's for sure. But you can see their take on it here, using the link to the official documentation:

https://cloudblogs.microsoft.com/enterprisemobility/2018/04/10/co-management-is-instant-and-easy-with-just4clicks/

Co-management and Third-Party Integrations

If you'll forgive the pun, it's worth mentioning that at least VMware is also trying to co-opt the term *co-management*. They are trying to also make a connection between traditional on-prem SCCM and Group Policy management and their Workspace ONE product. You can see more about that here: https://blogs.vmware.com/euc/2018/04/sccm-workspace-one-co-management.html.

They have an add-on to Workspace ONE called Airlift for Windows 10, which is an SCCM connector. Then the SCCM data you know and love can be seen inside Workspace ONE. At least, that's the idea.

So, in my opinion the VMware goals appear to be more like rip and replace on-prem SCCM to MDM as opposed to the Microsoft goals, which appear to be more aligned with letting the IT and business decide which workload is being managed by which technology.

When trying to find the co-management story with MobileIron, I came up a little short. There's a marketing page here: https://www.mobileiron.com/en/blog/new-sccm-and-emm-co-management-capabilities-windows-10 and then not much else. I know there is also a MobileIron SCCM "connector," but its goals appear to have the opposite approach. That is, the MobileIron SCCM connector takes MobileIron data and places it in SCCM. That way, you have all your mobile information data in one database and can take actions on them.

As usual, technology doesn't stand still, so be on the lookout for new advancements here from the non-Microsoft players.

Co-Policy Management: Group Policy and Your MDM Service

So, no one at Microsoft has come out and used any specific words with regard to your existing on-prem AD and Group Policy alongside an MDM service, but it's my book and I'm going to do just that.

I'm going to give it a name: Co-Policy Management.

There are two parts to Co-Policy management with Group Policy and your MDM service:

- Using Group Policy to do the heavy lifting for you to get machines enrolled into MDM service

- Dealing with settings conflicts between your MDM and Group Policy

Let's explore both of those topics now.

Auto-Enroll in Your MDM Service Using Group Policy

So, Co-Policy management with Group Policy and your MDM service is also possible. This involves doing what is called AADJ, or joining both on-prem AD and Azure Active Directory and then enrolling into an MDM service.

Back in Chapter 2, "Set Up Azure AD and MDM," in the section titled "Get Windows 10 to Automatically Join Azure AD (Hybrid Azure AD-Joined Devices)," you did just that. You got your existing (and newly domain-joined) Windows 10 machines to automatically join Azure AD. But, joining Azure AD is exactly half of the process here. The other equally important thing is to enroll the device into your MDM service.

But why oh why would you want to be both AD joined and AAD joined at the same time? Because this way you can get some Group Policy settings and some MDM settings. And, maybe in some future world, if MDM evolves to a place where you no longer need Group Policy, you're already connected to both and could (maybe, at some point in the distant future) cut the cord on Group Policy if that's something you want to do.

And you can utilize Group Policy as the bootstrapper to get your existing machines auto-enrolled in your MDM service. But you can only do these steps if your Windows 10 machines are preenrolled in Azure AD (again, which we set up in Chapter 2). The last prerequisite is that the following little magic trick only works for Windows 10 1709 and later.

As we saw in Chapter 2, machines that are pre-joined to Azure AD through Azure AD sync can be verified with the dsregcmd /status command, which is shown in Figure 4.5.

FIGURE 4.5   The dsregcmd /status command can tell you if your Windows 10 machine is AzureAdJoined.

So again, the problem is if you have 500, 5000, or 50,000 machines and you want to force enrollment into your MDM service, what are you going to do? Run around to each of them? Are you going to email each owner the local admin account name and password so they can join the MDM service themselves? No way, dude!

If the machine is pre-joined to Azure AD, you can leverage the Group Policy infrastructure you already have to get those machines enrolled into your MDM service. The basic steps to leverage Group Policy to auto-enroll gaggles of existing on-prem AD joined machines into AAD and then also perform MDM enrollment would be as follows:

1. Create a GPO and link it to the OU containing computers already AAD joined that you also want to MDM enroll. Again, these computers must be Windows 10 1709 or later.

2. In the Group Policy Management Editor, find the setting Administrative Templates ➤ Windows Components ➤ MDM ➤ **Auto MDM Enrollment with AAD Token** as seen in Figure 4.6 and set to Enabled.

FIGURE 4.6   Use the Auto MDM Enrollment with AAD Token policy to bootstrap a mass MDM enrollment.

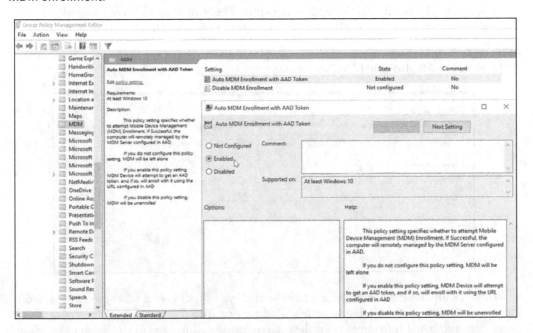

After Group Policy refreshes, a scheduled task is created on the Windows 10 machine to run every five minutes for the duration of one day. The task will self-destruct after it's successful.

To see the task, you need to be an admin or use an elevated command prompt. Then open Task Scheduler, open Microsoft ➤ Windows, and click EnterpriseMgmt (which won't exist until the Group Policy gets there). The task is then called "Schedule created by enroll-ment client for automatically enrolling in MDM from AAD" and can be seen in Figure 4.7. You might have to refresh a bunch of times before the EnterpriseMgmt node appears.

FIGURE 4.7 The scheduled tasks created by the Auto MDM Enrollment with AAD Token policy

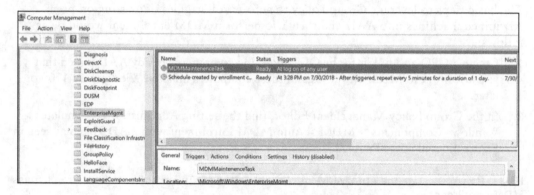

Underneath the hood, what's happening is this: The Windows 10 Task Scheduler is attempting to call a program called deviceenroller.exe. You can see this in Figure 4.8.

FIGURE 4.8 The scheduled task showing that deviceenroller.exe is what does the lifting to Azure AD and your MDM service

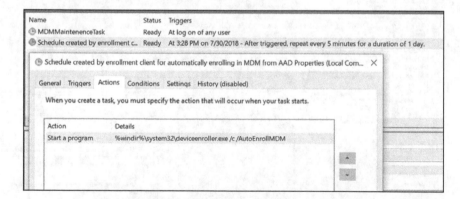

When it's all complete, and the dust has settled, you should see a machine auto-joined in Azure AD and auto-enrolled in your MDM service. You'll know it happened because an extra button labeled Info appears on the domain information page in the Settings window. You can see this in Figure 4.9.

FIGURE 4.9 The on-prem AD now has an Info button.

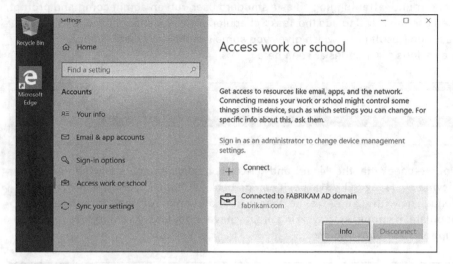

Then, clicking the Info button, you can see that you are MDM enrolled and your MDM policies should have come down.

Troubleshooting Hybrid MDM Enrollment

To be honest, I had a lot of trouble making hybrid MDM enrollment work the first time. New machines seemed to work great for me. By which I mean I would first take a fresh machine, not enrolled into MDM or joined into on-prem AD. And then I would just perform an on-prem domain join. Those worked great: They picked up the GPO, got the Scheduled Task, and performed the enrollment.

But some existing, already-AD-joined machines were giving me fits. For some of these already-AD-joined machines, de-joining on-prem AD and rejoining helped, as did performing Azure AD delta syncs.

If you have errors or the auto-enrollment doesn't happen, here are some things to try:

- Remember first that the AD user—well, their "mirrored" account in Azure AD—needs to be licensed for Azure AD Premium and Intune. So, if you're trying to get standard user EastSalesUser2 at (on-prem) Fabrikam.com to do the auto-enrollment, then EastSalesUser2@fabrikam1000.com needs to have their Azure license activated. You do this inside office.portal.com and give the EM+S, E3, or E5 license to the equivalent AD user logging on.

- A standard user cannot see the tasks in Task Scheduler, which is a bummer because that's where all the interesting information about the last run of the task is. As a workaround, after logging on as a standard user, run an admin command prompt, then use the MMC to add the Task Scheduler. Now you should be able to see the Last Run Result field, which gives you some insight into what is happening with the various error codes as seen here.

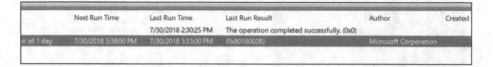

	Next Run Time	Last Run Time	Last Run Result	Author	Created
		7/30/2018 2:30:25 PM	The operation completed successfully. (0x0)		
n of 1 day.	7/30/2018 3:38:00 PM	7/30/2018 3:33:00 PM	(0x8018002B)	Microsoft Corporation	

- Double-check that the `MdmUrl` and `MdmtoURL` fields are populated when being viewed by `dsregcmd /status`. If not, go back to Chapter 2, and see how to do a delta sync with Azure AD sync, then wait another hour or two. Once these fields populate, it should start working. If they never populate, you might want to open a support case with Microsoft.

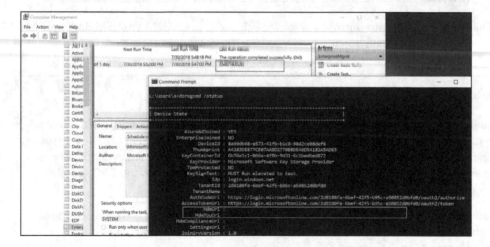

Here are some other links I used when troubleshooting the hybrid Azure domain join with automatic MDM enrollment:

```
https://social.technet.microsoft.com/Forums/en-US/
d2bda796-eef4-452a-b622-7c7463218555/mdm-enrollment-error-0x8018002b-
on-windows-10-1709?forum=microsoftintuneprod
```

```
https://docs.microsoft.com/en-us/windows/desktop/mdmreg/
mdm-registration-constants
```

```
https://docs.microsoft.com/en-us/intune-user-help/
troubleshoot-your-windows-10-device-windows
```

```
https://t3chn1ck.wordpress.com/2018/07/09/
auto-mdm-enroll-failed-the-system-tried-to-delete-the-join-of-a-drive-
that-is-not-joined/
```

The framework I just provided should be enough for you to try this out yourself. That said, Microsoft's official walk-through on this, with some extra information and basic troubleshooting steps, can be found at:

```
https://docs.microsoft.com/en-us/windows/client-management/mdm/
enroll-a-windows-10-device-automatically-using-group-policy
```

Co-Policy Management...Who Wins: MDM or Group Policy?

So let's pretend you set the same exact setting or settings with MDM or Group Policy. Like, you Kill Cortana with MDM and try to resurrect it (her?) using Group Policy.

Which technology wins when there's a conflict?

Who *should* win?

Well, the "who should win" seems a little undecided. My opinion is that Group Policy should win.

And the answer to "who will win" is very, very complicated (as of right now). Before I dive into the nitty-gritty details here, I will say that I believe this unusual-to-understand behavior may change over time and just be rectified one day with some future version of Windows. So, I'll explain the story for now, then explain where I hope (and kind of expect) this to end up.

About MdmWinsOverGp

In Figure 4.10, you can see the DeviceManagement-Enterprise-Diagnostics-Provider logs, specifically the Operational log, which shows event ID 2220 where it says "MdmWinsOverGp Policy value is (0x0)" which means, "You cannot know who is going to win."

FIGURE 4.10   Event ID 2220 shows who wins, Group Policy vs. MDM.

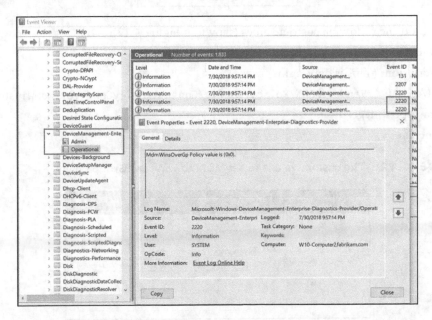

Really.

Let me say it now (and explain it further in a bit): The default behavior of Windows is that if you have both a Group Policy setting and an MDM setting gunning for the same value, you literally cannot know what the final value is going to be.

That said, there's a way to make MDM "win" over Group Policy.

The setting is in the PolicyCSP and is called `ControlPolicyConflict/MdmWinsOverGP`. When set to 1, any Group Policy settings that have the equivalent setting in the Policy CSP (but only the Policy CSP) will be ignored for processing.

If you want to check this out, here are the steps, but do me a favor and read all the way through to the end of this section before giving this a try.

You would start out by creating a new profile, or using an existing one. I'll create a new one as seen in Figure 4.11.

FIGURE 4.11   Create a new profile to house the new MDM policy.

Then, add the following custom values (shown in Figure 4.12):

- Name: ControlPolicyConflict
- Description: (This is optional.)
- OMA-URI: `./Vendor/MSFT/Policy/Config/ControlPolicyConflict/MdmWinsOverGp`
- Data-type: Integer
- Value: 1

FIGURE 4.12   The custom values to set MDM to win over Group Policy

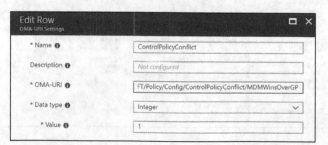

Then you would save this and assign to Devices.

I wouldn't recommend you do this at this time; I'm just showing you how you *would* do it.

You'll know you did it right (again, when you opt in to do this) because you'll see the results seen in Figure 4.13 when looking at the MDM report.

FIGURE 4.13   How to know you've turned on MDM to win over Group Policy

  An extra big ol' warning here about this setting: In Windows 1803, when you write this value to endpoints, you can never go backward. This setting doesn't support "delete." It's a one-way bridge. That said, 1809 and later, you can change your mind and change the setting, which will return to the original behavior.

MdmWinsOverGp: Real Tests with Windows 1809

As I was testing this, I ran into some unusual findings. Sometimes Group Policy would win. Sometimes MDM would win. Sometimes, I couldn't tell who was winning or why.

So I asked for help. Special thanks to another MVP, Sandy (Yinghua Zeng), who had time to test this issue. Her findings correspond with what I found. Here are some of our test results (again, today, with Windows 1809, and again, this is something I think could possibly change in the future).

Test 1: When MDMWinsOverGP is not configured, set the MDM item to Disabled, and set the corresponding Group Policy settings to Enabled.

1. Assign MDM policy such that Cortana is **Disabled**.
2. Refresh MDM and see that Cortana is, in fact, disabled.
3. Create a Group Policy setting such that Cortana is **Enabled**.
4. Assign Group Policy setting to the same Win10 1809 device. Refresh Group Policy.

Test 1 results: Cortana appears Disabled. Feels like MDM wins.

For me, this was totally unexpected. Since MdmWinsOverGp is not configured, my expectation would be that Group Policy would win (by default).

But that's not true.

Because the MDM policy for Cortana got written first and the Group Policy got written second, something in MDM's brain is locking the setting in place with MDM winning, which doesn't make much sense to me right now.

Test 2: When MDMWinsOverGP is Not Configured, set the Group Policy setting to Enabled, then the corresponding MDM setting to Disabled.

In this test, Group Policy value will be set first and set to Enabled. Then MDM will set the same value as Disabled.

1. Create and link a GPO that would **Enable** Cortana.

2. Refresh Group Policy and verify that Cortana is, in fact, enabled.

3. Create MDM policy to **Disable** Cortana.

4. Assign MDM policy to Win10 1809 device. Refresh MDM.

Test 2 results: Cortana remains Enabled. Feels like MDM loses.

This feels like the correct result.

Group Policy got there first, MDMWinsOverGP is Not Configured (or specifically set to Disabled to lose). And what happens? The Group Policy setting you expected was on the box.

Test 3: When MDMWinsOverGP is Enabled, set the Group Policy setting to Enabled, then the corresponding MDM setting to Disabled.

1. Create and link a GPO that would **Enable** Cortana.

2. Refresh Group Policy and verify that Cortana is, in fact, enabled.

3. Create MDM policy to **Disable** Cortana.

4. Assign MDM policy to Win10 1809 device. Refresh MDM.

Test 3 results: Cortana becomes disabled. MDM wins.

This also feels like the correct result.

Group Policy got there first; MDMWinsOverGP is set to Enabled (to win). And what happens? The MDM setting written second overrides the Group Policy setting, and the MDM setting you expected was on the box.

In case your head is swimming a little bit, here's a table showing a grid which enumerates the key cases in an easy-to-digest format.

Case	MDMWinsOverGP	MDM Value	Group Policy Value	Item State	Result / Feeling
1	Not set or 0 (Disabled)	Disabled	Enabled	Can't know.	Can't know.
2	Not set or 0 (Disabled)	Enabled	Disabled	Can't know.	Can't know.
3	Not set or 0 (Disabled)	Disabled	Enabled	Can't know.	Can't know.
4	Not Set or 0 (Disabled)	Enabled	Disabled	Can't know.	Can't know.
5	Set to 1 (MDM wins)	Disabled	Enabled	Disabled	MDM wins.
6	Set to 1 (MDM wins)	Enabled	Disabled	Enabled	MDM wins.
7	Set to 1 (MDM wins)	Disabled	Enabled	Disabled	MDM wins.
8	Set to 1 (MDM wins)	Enabled	Disabled	Enabled	MDM wins.

So how do we interpret these seemingly contradictory results?

- MDMWinsOverGP is *not* a two-way street. It is only for controlling when MDM wins over GPO. It is not about controlling when GPO wins over MDM.
- If MDMWinsOverGP is not configured (or Disabled), Group Policy versus MDM world is non-deterministic.

Non-deterministic is just a fancy way of saying you might not be able to predict what is going to happen over the long haul.

Why is this?

Well, in the real world, sometimes you're going to have Group Policy settings that were applied first; then MDM settings are going to apply second. Sometimes you're going to have MDM settings apply first, and Group Policy settings are going to apply second.

As of right now, here are the final rules of the game if you want to attempt to make your MDM and Group Policy co-managed world to be as deterministic as possible:

- Turn on the value to force MDM to win over Group Policy (./Vendor/MSFT/Policy/ Config/ControlPolicyConflict/MdmWinsOverGp to 1).
- Use MDM to define policies whenever possible.
- Actively avoid Group Policy versus MDM conflicts for good measure, though with the MdmWinsOverGP set to 1, the engine will make MDM win in a conflict when the same MDM value is set against the same Group Policy setting.
- Use Group Policy for those setting that cannot be configured by MDM "First class" settings. You can always back out of a Group Policy ADMX setting easily, should that value become a first class setting within MDM.

MdmWinsOverGp: Final Thoughts and Notes

As I said, I believe this complicated "non-deterministic" behavior will have to be eventually rectified. I have no insider knowledge, and no one is telling me anything as I write this; it's just a hunch. But here's what I think could happen:

- Microsoft could change the default to MDMWinsOverGP set to "on" and therefore MDM would just win over a Group Policy conflict. (Again, this would only kick in when the Group Policy value is also deployed to the same target value anyway.)

- Microsoft could make it more deterministic when MDMWinsOverGP is not set. They could just decide that "whoever gets there first" is the expected behavior, until MDMWinsOverGP is set.

Again, no timeline yet, because no one is telling me anything. But in some future world, these are two possibilities. There are likely other things that the engine could do to help resolve and report conflicts.

Since I cannot predict the future, I promise to write about it on MDMandGPanswers.com. But then beyond that, you can read more about this at:

```
https://docs.microsoft.com/en-us/windows/client-management/mdm/
policy-csp-controlpolicyconflict
```

You may want to check this website every time Windows ships an update, because it might be irrelevant if Microsoft just "goes ahead" and makes MDM win over Group Policy...always. My guess is that this page will tell you in what version of Windows this will have transpired.

Two other good write-ups on this subject can be found here:

```
https://osddeployment.dk/2018/02/12/
how-to-control-both-mdm-and-gpo-settings-on-windows-10/
```

```
https://blogs.technet.microsoft.com/cbernier/2018/04/02/
windows-10-group-policy-vs-intune-mdm-policy-who-wins/
```

What Is Microsoft Azure AD Domain Services (and What Does It Have to Do with Group Policy)?

Don't get confused about real on-prem Group Policy with your MDM service and another, completely unrelated idea called Microsoft Azure AD Domain Services (AADDC for short).

AADDC is a way to make a "pretend" domain in the cloud for your existing on-prem servers to leverage if you decide to "lift and shift" some of your servers to Azure. And, when inside Azure, they still need to talk to something that is pretending to be a domain. So AADDC helps these machines join something...it's like a mini-real on-prem AD domain, but in the cloud.

But for 10000% clarity: This mini on-prem AD domain in the cloud is not for Windows 10 machines to join but instead only for servers to join.

I explain this concept here only so you don't search for, say, "Joining Azure AD and Group Policy" and come across AADDC and wonder, "What the heck is this thing?"

And when you see AADDC, you'll see information about managing these servers with AADDC's built-in Group Policy editor—again, to manage those servers that would usually be managed on-prem with AD and Group Policy.

In short: This AADDC thing is only for servers and not for endpoints.

Now you know.

So AADDC's URL to learn more is:

```
https://docs.microsoft.com/en-us/azure/
active-directory-domain-services/active-directory-ds-admin-guide-
administer-group-policy
```

Final Thoughts

Even if you don't have SCCM, you're going to hear a lot from Microsoft about co-management. Sometimes, I'm hearing them also say, "Cloud attached," as in, "You can get your on-prem infrastructure 'Cloud Attached' and then co-manage your environment with SCCM and Intune." I don't know if Microsoft is going to stick with that phrasing, but I thought I should mention it in case you hear it.

And, since you likely have on-prem AD and Group Policy, it's good to know all about Co-Policy management (my phrase, not Microsoft's) and about working together.

Remember, to ensure that the values are deterministic, you must flip the switch to make MDM specifically win over Group Policy or else you literally cannot know the final state of the machine.

Tweet me @jeremymoskowitz and mention Chapter 4 with the hashtag #mdmbook. Let me know what you got out of this chapter. I love getting your tweets!

See you in the next chapter, where we talk about tools to help with an actual migration of Group Policy to MDM and some tips and tricks to troubleshoot MDM.

Chapter 5

MDM Migration and MDM Troubleshooting

In previous chapters, you learned about the Policy CSP and its relationship to Group Policy: some policies are baked into the Policy CSP, and others are ADMX backed.

But if you already had an on-prem Group Policy infrastructure, how would you determine what Group Policy settings are even possible to convert over?

And, once you've got your MDM service up and running (like Intune, Workspace ONE, etc.), how can you figure out what's going on? How can you best get to the bottom of problems?

MMAT: Microsoft MDM Migration and Analysis Tool

To help you evaluate what you already have in Group Policy-land, and help you determine if you can migrate some of those settings over to MDM-land, Microsoft provides a free, downloadable tool called MMAT, the Microsoft MDM Migration and Analysis Tool.

The key word in this tool is *Analysis* and not really *Migration*. The tool doesn't write anything you can use in MDM-land, but rather analyzes what you have in Group Policy-land to see if it can possibly be converted to MDM-land.

You can find the tool here: `https://github.com/WindowsDeviceManagement/MMAT`.

You can see the web page and how to download it in Figure 5.1.

FIGURE 5.1   Download MMAT from GitHub.

Here's the idea: Whenever Windows 10 is upgraded to a new version (1703, 1709, 1803, 1809, 19H1, etc.), invariably there are going to be more MDM settings available than there were available the last time. Remember, even though MDM isn't trying to take on Group Policy's breadth, it's still true that MDM settings growth will be happening regularly.

Soon after the next Windows 10 has gone live, then this tool, MMAT, gets updated with the latest known Group Policy and MDM. You then can use this tool to analyze a single machine's already applied GPOs and pop out a report of settings that can transfer over to MDM perfectly, those that definitely won't, and those that are a bit of a mystery.

So that means that the tool needs to be run on an example machine you want to test to see if those settings could possibly come over. And that means you would have to run around from "representative machine to representative machine"—say, Sally in Marketing to Bob in Engineering—to get a feel for what policies might or might not come over from Group Policy-land to MDM-land.

To get started, you need to be running MMAT on a machine that also has the RSAT and GPMC. This presents a littttle bit of a challenge because it's likely that neither Sally in Marketing nor Bob in Engineering has the RSAT tools installed on their machine. But the good news is that you can get away with only having *your* machine with RSAT because you can run MMAT remotely against Sally's or Bob's machine and they won't need RSAT installed then.

You can also tell MMAT to read every freakin' GPO you have (in the whole domain) and see what it thinks about *all* of them. That's interesting too, because then you can buzz through all your GPOs at once and learn a lot in one shot. But, of course, MMAT isn't trying to see if these GPOs are used or not, where they are targeted or filtered, and so on. It's just sort of a "mass flyover" to see if the values that are in GPO-land can get to MDM-land.

To be fair, so far, in this book, I haven't asked you to create too many GPOs, so this tool won't have a lot to report on in your test lab. But this is a really safe tool to run in your real world; it's just reading settings and not writing anything back into GPO-land. So you might want to just try this out on your real-world machines or on another test lab you have set up that maybe already has a bunch of GPOs applying to your machines.

So on a Windows 10 machine with the RSAT installed, download MMAT and then unpack it to your location of choice, say, c:\MMAT. Then it's time to run it and see what it comes up with. Run PowerShell as Admin. Then run the following PowerShell commands, as seen in Figure 5.2.

```
Set-ExecutionPolicy Unrestricted -Scope Process
$VerbosePreference="Continue"
./Invoke-MdmMigrationAnalysisTool.ps1 -collectGPOreports -RunAnalysistool
```

FIGURE 5.2   Run MMAT with these PowerShell commands.

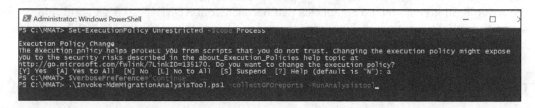

In addition to the flags above:

```
-collectGPOreports -RunAnalysistool
```

Here are some other optional flags:

- If you want to inspect all the GPOs across the whole domain, add -targetdomain fabrikam.com on the end of the last command.
- If you want to inspect Bob's machine, add -targetComputer BobsPC on the end of the last command.
- If you want to inspect Sally the last time she used Bob's computer, add -targetUser Sally -targetComputer BobsPC on the end of the last command.

MMAT will churn on Bob's machine's Group Policy guts for a while, then be done, as seen in Figure 5.3.

FIGURE 5.3   The PowerShell of MMAT completes.

```
VERBOSE: Importing cmdlet 'Set-GPLink'.
VERBOSE: Importing cmdlet 'Set-GPPermission'.
VERBOSE: Importing cmdlet 'Set-GPPrefRegistryValue'.
VERBOSE: Importing cmdlet 'Set-GPRegistryValue'.
VERBOSE: Importing alias 'Get-GPPermissions'.
VERBOSE: Importing alias 'Set-GPPermissions'.
VERBOSE: About to query <root\rsop\computer> for RSOP GPO list
VERBOSE: Completed query of RSOP GPO list.  See file <.\MachineRsop.log> for RSOP data
VERBOSE: About to query <root\rsop\user\S_1_5_21_934088035_149717768_3671783038_500> for RSOP GPO list
VERBOSE: Completed query of RSOP GPO list.  See file <.\UserRsop.log> for RSOP data
VERBOSE: Querying Machine GPO ids
VERBOSE: +++++ Scanning {31B2F340-016D-11D2-945F-00C04FB984F9} from fabrikam.com +++++
VERBOSE: +++++ Scanning {6011B62E-B62D-4A5E-B1D9-93B337730687} from fabrikam.com +++++
VERBOSE: +++++ Scanning {6AC1786C-016F-11D2-945F-00C04FB984F9} from fabrikam.com +++++
VERBOSE: +++++ Scanning {CF8CC3D0-2E93-482C-8ACB-307FC9AD010A} from fabrikam.com +++++
VERBOSE: +++++ Scanning {E1548F7C-0133-481A-9102-64F87666B3E0} from fabrikam.com +++++
VERBOSE: Querying User GPO ids (that haven't already been queried as part of machine)
VERBOSE: +++++ Scanning {320F1D0E-A806-4899-B812-B7D1AC099AAA} from fabrikam.com +++++
VERBOSE: Completed querying GPO list
VERBOSE: Removing the imported "Get-GPPermissions" alias.
VERBOSE: Removing the imported "Set-GPPermissions" alias.
VERBOSE: Starting analysis tool: <C:\MMAT\Invoke-MdmMigrationAnalysisTool.ps1\..\MdmMigrationAnalysisTool.exe>
MDM Migration Analysis Tool. Copyright (c) Microsoft 2016.
Completed MDM Migration Analysis Tool
VERBOSE: Completed running analysis tool
PS C:\MMAT>
```

The output from MMAT will be in a file called `MDMMigrationAnalysis.html`, and you can check it out in any browser.

The output is split into Computer and User side. Then, you will see supported settings in green (shown in Figure 5.4) and unsupported settings in red (not shown). Later in the report, in light green, you'll see "Policies that need Custom ADMX," so it's a good thing we covered that topic already. Finally, at the end is a list of the GPOs that MMAT read, because it could be different depending on how you run MMAT (against one machine or against all GPOs in the domain, for instance).

FIGURE 5.4   Example MMAT output

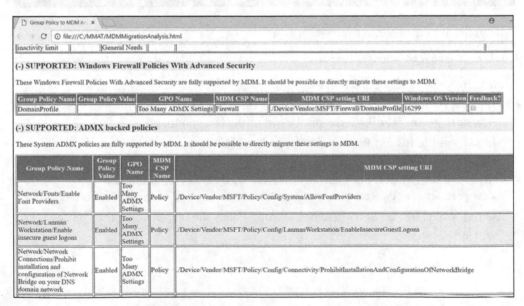

Also, I said this before, but it bears repeating:

- Not every setting in Group Policy will convert to MDM, nor should you even want them to. For instance, settings that only apply, say, to XP and not Windows 10 make no sense being migrated to MDM-land.

- Just because you see that you do have a particular Group Policy setting that you have already deployed doesn't mean you should convert it over to MDM. You need to analyze your situation and see if it makes sense to bring it over or leave it behind if you go to MDM.

- Some settings might seem reasonable and desirable to get to MDM, but those settings maybe simply aren't available yet as curated settings in MDM.

- MMAT isn't going to read GPOs and magically write pretty MDM settings for you. You have to do that part, hard work and all, if that's what you want to do.

- Be sure to already re-download MMAT every time Windows goes out the door and it's re-updated. When both Windows and MMAT are updated, you should see settings that wouldn't convert yesterday now ready to be available in MDM-land. Note that this doesn't mean the setting is a First class clickable setting in the MDM service's UI; it could be Third class that you need to manually construct an OMA-URI for.

MMAT is a useful tool, and I would encourage you to check out the following MMAT resources for more information:

- The PDF guide for MMAT is only seven pages, but it is full of useful information and tricks.

- Video from Ignite 2017: `www.youtube.com/watch?v=QtqLW2Rp2lU`

- `https://www.petervanderwoude.nl/post/mdm-migration-analysis-tool/`

Troubleshooting MDM

An MDM problem isn't going to just jump up and down and show itself. Troubleshooting MDM comes down to knowing where to look for the right stuff. We'll explore those locations in order:

- Analyzing MDM service reports
- Looking at "MDM Advanced Diagnostic Report" from the MDM engine
- Investigating event logs for interesting information
- Using Microsoft and third-party web resources to help us out

Let's check these angles out now.

MDM Service Reports, Diagnostic Logs, and Event Logs

In this section we'll go over the three main places in the order I would generally recommend you start troubleshooting. You could bounce around and investigate these areas in a different order than I present. But I think I've got a good roadmap to get you on the path toward successful troubleshooting.

Delivery Reports from Your MDM Service

So MDM works great with machines that are always on and does a pretty good job with machines that are not always on. In other words, the MDM server and Windows 10 machines are always talking (provided they are turned on), so you should always have some insight into what's happening.

The first thing to do to check to see how things are going would be to click on any profile and then look at the built-in reporting. There are two panes to check out: the graphs and the tables.

In here you can discover if MDM thinks the settings made it out the door and onto your users or devices, which failed or have errors, and so on. There is a graph for "All profiles" (not shown, and also not particularly helpful). And graphs per profile.

You always have information on device and user status. Device status tells you all the device and user combinations that have received the profile. User status tells on how many devices the user has received the profile.

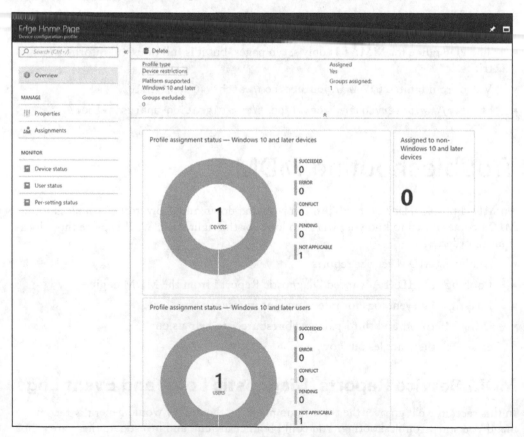

You can also click on "Device status" or "User status" to see if that profile made it there and at what time, as seen in Figure 5.5.

FIGURE 5.5   Looking inside a report for Last Status Update

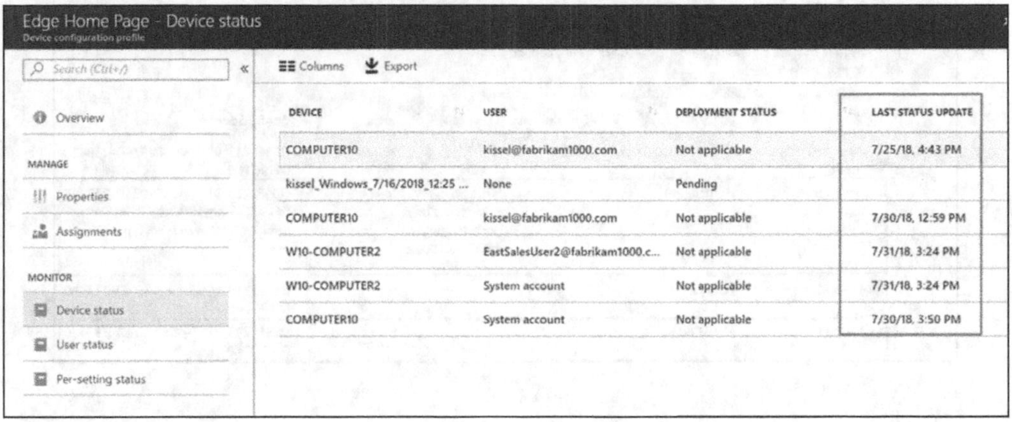

If you target a user setting to devices, then all users on those devices get the settings. If you target a device setting to users, the setting will be applied to all computers the users will log on to.

Advanced Diagnostic Reports and Resolving Conflicts

Twice now we have checked out the MDM Advanced Diagnostic Report that appear on the Windows 10 endpoints. Again, this is like GPResult, but for MDM.

As a reminder, to create an MDM Advanced Diagnostic Report, you would start in Windows Settings. Then click on Access Work or School, click on the MDM connection, then click on Info. Once there, scroll down to "Create report."

There are a bunch of categories in this report, but you need to focus on these three:

- **Managed Policies:** Seen earlier, this will show a list of what is configured on the device that's different than the default values.

- **Blocked by Group Policy:** This will show a list of items that are configured in Group Policy, also configured in MDM, and who wins.

- **Unmanaged Policies:** Everything else. This is interesting, actually, because if there's anything (non-custom) that you want to change, this list is always up-to-date!

Let's check out each of these three sections now.

The Managed Policies Portion of the Advanced MDM Report

In Figure 5.6, you can see me focusing in on the "Managed policies" part of the report. There are two ways I go about using this section. The first way, I can see which values I want specifically set with MDM. For instance, in Figure 5.6 you can see that I set my Browser Homepages and I also killed Cortana.

FIGURE 5.6 Using the Advanced MDM report to see set values

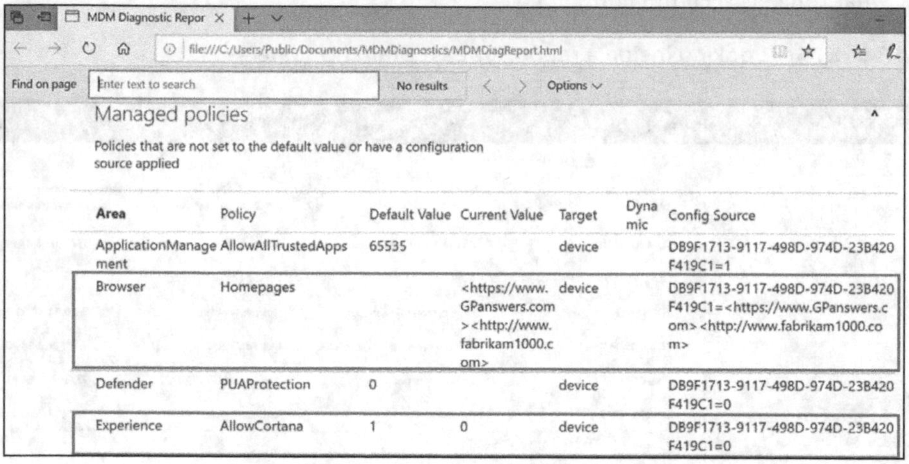

Area	Policy	Default Value	Current Value	Target	Dynamic	Config Source
ApplicationManagement	AllowAllTrustedApps	65535		device		DB9F1713-9117-498D-974D-23B420F419C1=1
Browser	Homepages		<https://www.GPanswers.com><http://www.fabrikam1000.com>	device		DB9F1713-9117-498D-974D-23B420F419C1=<https://www.GPanswers.com><http://www.fabrikam1000.com>
Defender	PUAProtection	0		device		DB9F1713-9117-498D-974D-23B420F419C1=0
Experience	AllowCortana	1	0	device		DB9F1713-9117-498D-974D-23B420F419C1=0

The Blocked Group Policies Portion of the Advanced MDM Report

Back in Chapter 4, we talked about how to specifically force MDM to win over Group Policy. When you opt in to this and deliver the MdmWinsOverGP setting, the Blocked Group Policies report lights up.

Not to be pedantic, but there are no such things as "Group Policies." There can be "Blocked Group Policy Settings," which would be most accurate, but I'll have to breathe in and breathe out and let it go.

Anyway, as you can see in Figure 5.7, when you flip the switch where MDM wins over Group Policy, the report section lights up showing conflicts. Remember, by default, Group Policy and MDM on the same box is non-deterministic. Only when you flip the switch to make MDM win will you know the actual result.

FIGURE 5.7 You can see which Group Policy settings are being overridden by MDM.

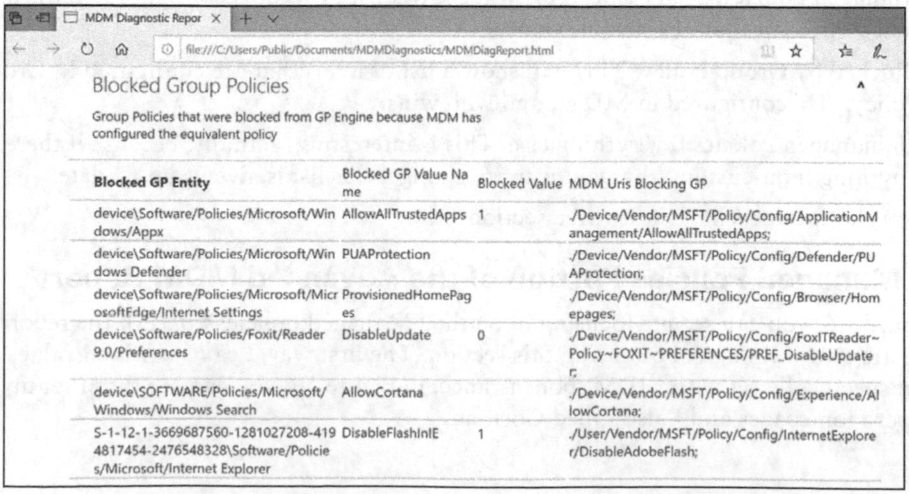

Blocked GP Entity	Blocked GP Value Name	Blocked Value	MDM Uris Blocking GP
device\Software/Policies/Microsoft/Windows/Appx	AllowAllTrustedApps	1	./Device/Vendor/MSFT/Policy/Config/ApplicationManagement/AllowAllTrustedApps;
device\Software/Policies/Microsoft/Windows Defender	PUAProtection		./Device/Vendor/MSFT/Policy/Config/Defender/PUAProtection;
device\Software/Policies/Microsoft/MicrosoftEdge/Internet Settings	ProvisionedHomePages		./Device/Vendor/MSFT/Policy/Config/Browser/Homepages;
device\Software/Policies/Foxit/Reader 9.0/Preferences	DisableUpdate	0	./Device/Vendor/MSFT/Policy/Config/FoxITReader~Policy~FOXIT~PREFERENCES/PREF_DisableUpdater;
device\SOFTWARE/Policies/Microsoft/Windows/Windows Search	AllowCortana		./Device/Vendor/MSFT/Policy/Config/Experience/AllowCortana;
S-1-12-1-3669687560-1281027208-4194817454-2476548328\Software/Policies/Microsoft/Internet Explorer	DisableFlashInIE	1	./User/Vendor/MSFT/Policy/Config/InternetExplorer/DisableAdobeFlash;

And that's what this report is all about. It's telling you, specifically, which settings are now winning by MDM, where before they were non-deterministic.

Again, for me, it's a big bummer I cannot see with GPO (that is the Group Policy Object itself) which is involved in "losing," nor can I see which MDM profile is involved in the "winning." Maybe this report will be fleshed out in some future world.

The Unmanaged Policies Portion of the Advanced MDM Report

The other way to use this report is to find *interesting* values in the "Unmanaged policies" portion of the Advanced MDM Settings Report, as seen in Figure 5.8.

FIGURE 5.8   The "Unmanaged policies" section

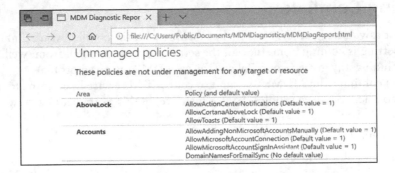

So for instance, you can look through the unmanaged policies and think, "Hmm, *interesting*...I didn't know I could customize the warning messages for RemoteAssistance." But, there it is, so you know it should be reasonably straightforward.

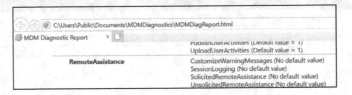

Final Thoughts about the Advanced MDM Settings Report

The MDM Advanced Diagnostic Report needs a little extra work to catch up to Group Policy's reporting. For me, in Group Policy-land, reporting of conflicts is reasonably easy. When you run GPresult /h and look at the settings report, it tells you which GPO "wins" and the settings therein.

In MDM-land, this is (today) not really possible by walking up to some affected machine and just checking on the client side.

Yes, the Advanced MDM report tells you the final setting, which is nice. But there doesn't seem to be any way to say, "Oh, you got the Edge Homepage setting from MDM Profile 'My Test Settings.'" Strangely, GUID value in the Config Source field to the value as seen in Figure 5.6, which looks like it should correlate to something (an MDM profile or inner policy setting). But I asked, and it doesn't seem to correlate to anything at all, at least nothing yet.

This is a bummer, because when you have a lot of profiles and possibly lots of settings within them, and then you have conflicts, that's going to make troubleshooting just that much harder if you *only* have access to the machine with the conflict.

But there is a way you can take a stab at resolving conflicts, and that's coming up next.

Resolving Conflicts

So as we just saw, having access to only the machine with the conflict won't illuminate where the setting is coming from. Indeed, the setting could be coming from, well, a lot of sources, including any given Group Policy Object MDM (any given profile).

But if it is coming from MDM, you can use your MDM service like Intune to try to illuminate conflicts between profiles. So, for instance, in this example, I have two profiles, shown in Figure 5.9:

▪ "Start Menu: Hide videos on Start"

▪ "Start Menu: Show videos on Start"

FIGURE 5.9 Two profiles can have different settings and target the same user or device.

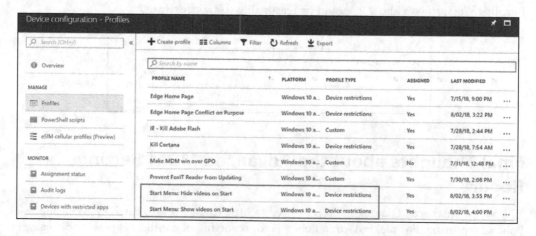

A conflict report does work nicely when you have conflicting settings defined within Intune UI. If you traverse to "Device configuration - Profiles" and click "Device status," you can see devices that report conflicting settings, as seen in Figure 5.10.

FIGURE 5.10 Any given device might have profile conflicts.

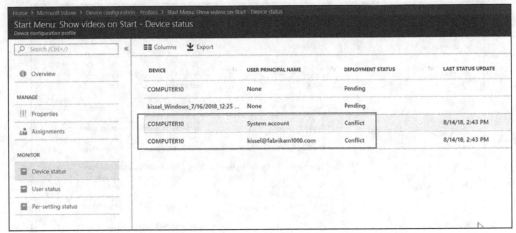

Then, click into the computer itself where you can then see the Monitor section for items like hardware, discovered apps, and more. The item you're after is Device Configuration, seen in Figure 5.11.

FIGURE 5.11 Click "Device configuration" first (before you get to see the various profiles placed upon the machine).

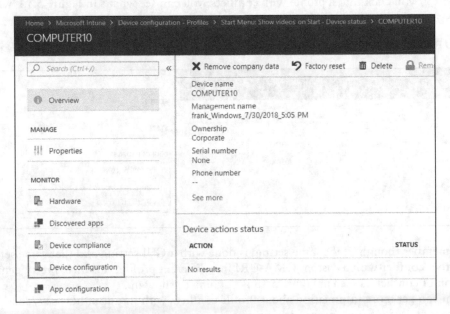

Then, you will see any profiles with any conflicts, as seen in Figure 5.12.

FIGURE 5.12   All the profiles and any conflicts can be seen on the device.

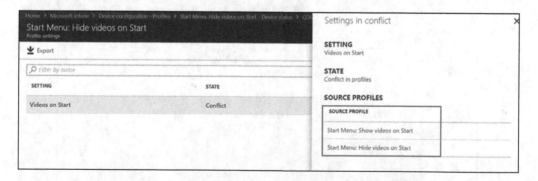

Next, if you click into a profile with conflicts, you can see what's in Figure 5.13, where it shows you which source profiles are competing.

FIGURE 5.13   Competing source profiles are illuminated.

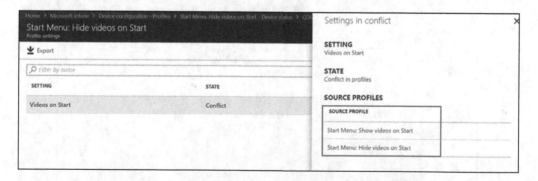

Remember though, if the same setting is done with a GUI setting *and* that same setting is set to a conflict with a custom OMA-URI in a different profile, this nice, pretty demonstration of conflict as seen in Figure 5.13 isn't going to show up.

You can get more information about Profile conflicts with Intune at https://docs .microsoft.com/en-us/intune/device-profile-monitor.

How *Not* to Troubleshoot MDM

You might be tempted to just fire up the ol' Google or Bing and start to search for "MDM Troubleshooting" when you get into a jam.

In doing so though, you could get into a lot of hot water, fast. Why? Check out this page if you want a chuckle: https://technet.microsoft.com/en-us/library/dd252836.aspx. If you don't want to type that in, just try Googling the phrase "MDM Troubleshooting" and for me, it's the first link (that's not an advertisement). Check it out here.

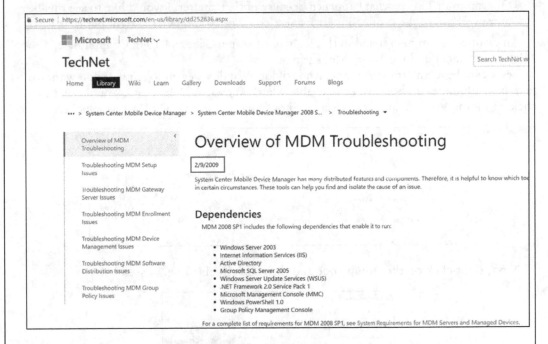

"What is this strange and interesting web page?" I hear you ask. "This seems like a reasonable place to start out with troubleshooting MDM, right?"

Wrong.

A hundred years ago, or really around 2009, there was an add-on to Group Policy and SCCM called System Center Mobile Device Manager.

And it's a dead product. Super, duper dead. But its bones (in the form of a web page) live onward.

This product was very innovative and ahead of its time: Use GPOs to store MDM settings, and use an on-prem server to send data to mobile phones and configure them using the MDM receiver inside the phones. This was way, way before Intune or any other MDM services existed. And before even Windows had an MDM receiver itself!

Anyway, just wanted to steer you away from that giant pothole straight away.

Investigating Event Logs

The next place to check out would be Event Viewer on a target Windows 10 machine.

Some events may appear in the System or Application log. I like to start there as a general rule. But then MDM has its own logs, which are found in Event Viewer ➤ Application and Services Logs ➤ Microsoft ➤ DeviceManagement-Enterprise-Diagnostics-Provider. Inside there you'll find two branches:

- **Admin:** This describes the communication chatter between the machine and the MDM service: When they started talking, what they said, and if there were any errors.

- **Operational:** This is what happened because of that chatter. I would like to see this be more verbose in the future, but errors here could get you down the right path.

An example of an item found in this log can be seen in Figure 4.10 in Chapter 4, "Co-management and Co-Policy Management."

Tesla cars have an "insane" mode. And so does Windows event logging. If you want to take it to 100 miles an hour, you can enable what's known as Debug logs. You do that by clicking on the View menu, then selecting Show Analytic and Debug Logs as seen here.

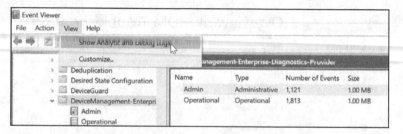

Next, right-click on the Debug node and then click Enable Log, as seen here.

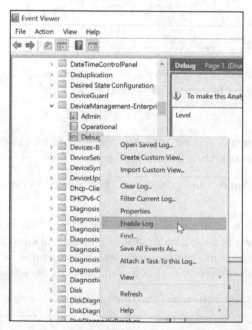

Then watch the fireworks when the events come in.

You can see a nice blog entry about debug logs at:

```
https://blogs.technet.microsoft.com/configmgrdogs/2018/08/09/
troubleshooting-windows-10-intune-policy-failures/
```

Remotely Collecting Logs from Windows 10

This is a built-in feature of the MDM platform, but as of this writing it has no First class clicky-click way to turn it on. Instead, you need a Third class OMA-URI setting to manually make the magic happen (right now).

This feature was announced just as this book was going to print. It's only valid for Windows 1903 (19H1) or newer builds. A good walkthrough can be found here:

```
https://oliverkieselbach.com/2019/04/23/
on-demand-windows-diagnostic-logs-via-intune/
```

You can see it in the MDM spec docs here:

```
https://docs.microsoft.com/en-us/windows/client-management/mdm/
diagnose-mdm-failures-in-windows-10
```

There are some caveats to making this work, and I didn't get a chance yet to try this myself.

Remember MdmWinsOverGP Setting and Gotchas

Remember in the previous chapter the discussion about MdmWinsOverGP and how the final outcome could be non-deterministic.

Whenever MDM settings are already applied (before the same setting is set with GPO), MDM always wins, regardless of how MdmWinsOverGP is configured or not. If, however, both MDM settings and GPO settings are applying at the same time to the same setting, the following rules apply:

- If MDMWinsOverGP is enabled, MDM wins.

- If MDMWinsOverGP is not configured or disabled, you don't know what is going to win.

Other Miscellaneous Notes, Traps, and Gotchas

In this section, I want to provide some interesting websites and items I found that can help troubleshoot MDM. Then for each URL, I want to give you the most interesting insights and quotes I found.

Here we go, in no particular order.

The Myriad of Ways a Device Can Be Enrolled into MDM

```
https://micro-scott.azurewebsites.net/2018/08/31/
managing-windows-10-with-intune-the-many-ways-to-enrol/
```

```
https://micro-scott.azurewebsites.net/2018/12/27/
troubleshooting-intune-device-enrollment-types/
```

The first URL shows a quick reference to some items we've covered already (like utilizing the user account to enroll into MDM) as well as the oodles of ways you can enroll a machine using Autopilot (what we'll cover in Chapter 8).

The second URL shows a way to use the downloadable Intune PowerShell module to query which machines are enrolled and output what enrollment type got them there.

I ran the steps myself because I wanted to see what it looked like. You can see an example of the output here.

```
PS C:\SHARE\IntunePowershell> Import-Module .\Microsoft.Graph.Intune.psd1
PS C:\SHARE\IntunePowershell> connect-msgraph -adminconsent

UPN                     TenantId
---                     --------
frank@fabrikam1000.com  2d8180fa-6bef-42f5-b95c-a50852d0bfd0


PS C:\SHARE\IntunePowershell> Get-IntuneManagedDevice | select devicename, deviceenrollmenttype

deviceName      deviceEnrollmentType
----------      --------------------
COMPUTER10      windowsAzureADJoin
COMPUTER10      windowsAzureADJoin
COMPUTER4191    windowsAzureADJoin
COMPUTER4287    windowsAzureADJoin
COMPUTER5408    windowsAzureADJoin
COMPUTER9639    windowsAzureADJoin
COMPUTER-FR3    windowsAzureADJoin
DESKTOP-93CDH7N windowsCoManagement
DESKTOP-EUGDU94 windowsCoManagement
DESKTOP-POV83HV windowsCoManagement
DESKTOP-VK57380 windowsAzureADJoin

PS C:\SHARE\IntunePowershell>
```

Microsoft Intune Device Profile Troubleshooting

https://docs.microsoft.com/en-us/intune/device-profile-troubleshoot

Interesting Insights: This was the only place I could find that explained when a profile was deployed by Intune and when it's expected that an MDM device would then "phone home" to pick it up (iPhone, Android, Windows 10, etc.).

For Windows 10 timings, here's the quote from the website:

> Windows PCs enrolled as devices: Every three minutes for 30 minutes, and then every eight hours. For devices without user affinity, the sync frequency immediately following enrollment can vary from hours to a day or more. Intune sends requests at various intervals for a device to check in with the service. However, it is still up to the device to check in. After initial enrollment, depending on the type of device enrollment and the policies and profiles assigned to a device, the time it takes a device to complete the check-in is unpredictable. However, once the device is enrolled, and all initial policies are applied, the device typically checks for new policies about every six hours.

Microsoft Intune Policies Troubleshooting

https://docs.microsoft.com/en-us/intune/
troubleshoot-policies-in-microsoft-intune

Interesting Insights: Explains the possible statuses of a device configuration. Quoting from the website:

- **Conforms:** The device has received the policy and reports to the service that it conforms to the setting.

- **Not Applicable:** The policy setting isn't applicable. For example, email settings for iOS devices would not apply to an Android device.

- **Pending:** The policy is sent to the device, but hasn't reported the status to the service. For example, encryption on Android requires the user to enable encryption, and might show as pending.

Microsoft Guidance in Troubleshooting MDM in General

```
https://docs.microsoft.com/en-us/windows/client-management/mdm/
diagnose-mdm-failures-in-windows-10
```

Interesting Insights: Well, I already gave them to you earlier. But this would be a good URL to bookmark in case something new arises, like a new tool or update.

Talk from Ignite 2016 on MDM Troubleshooting

```
https://channel9.msdn.com/Events/Ignite/2016/BRK3331
```

Interesting Insights: Actually, I would steer you away from this one. The information is from a time when the MDM logs were XML and not HTML, and they appeared to want to use another tool called the Microsoft Message Analyzer for MDM troubleshooting, but that seems not to be the case any longer.

Disconnecting from the Management Infrastructure (Unenrollment)

```
https://docs.microsoft.com/en-us/windows/client-management/mdm/
disconnecting-from-mdm-unenrollment
```

Interesting Insights: This is great because it explains what happens if you want to walk away from an MDM service. Or maybe you want to switch from one MDM service to another and want to know what will happen during that time.

For me, the biggest insight on the page is this quote:

> When a device is enrolled into MDM through Azure Active Directory
> Join and then remotely unenrolled, the device may get into a state where
> it must be re-imaged. When devices are remotely unenrolled from MDM,
> the AAD association is also removed. This safeguard is in place to avoid
> leaving the corporate devices in an unmanaged state.

Yikes. That sounds tremendously scary, but at least now you know.

Steven Owen's MDM Error Code List

```
URL: https://foxdeploy.com/2017/08/04/
mdm-errors-failures-and-how-to-fix-them/
```

My MVP buddy Stephen Owen runs this blog, and in this particular post he notices something about MDM troubleshooting…

> Troubleshooting MDM issues presents a whole new set of difficulties, because where SCCM provides glorious log files with tons of community engagement and answers, MDM gives you hard to locate Windows Event logs. Every SCCM error code is meticulously documented on the web, where [Internet searching for] MDM error [codes] give you [oftentimes, zero returned results].

Basically, Steve's observation is that that pretty much every SCCM error code is well documented and will lead you down a path to get things fixed. And I feel the same way with Group Policy: Almost every problem that has occurred in nature has been accounted for, and someone has likely explained the fix somewhere already.

MDM though, not so much. It's still too new for thousands of possible conditions and problems to be chased down and fixed and someone putting pen to paper, or keyboard to pixel, and documenting all the outcomes.

But Steve does a good job here helping track down error MDM codes and gives good tips to take those dark, dank clues and lead upward and outward toward the sunlight for resolution.

Final Thoughts

And we made it through Chapter 5.

Now you know how to use the MMAT tool to discover what you're already using in Group Policy-land and see if it's even possible to determine if your existing GPOs can be converted to MDM.

We got to know how to troubleshoot MDM, revisited client-side troubleshooting, and looked at conflicts on your MDM server.

Last, I gave you a bunch of interesting places to get more help if you need it.

I hope you don't need this chapter, but it's here for if or when something goes wrong in your MDM-land.

Tweet me @jeremymoskowitz with the hashtag #mdmbook and mention Chapter 5 and let me know what you got out of this chapter.

Chapter 6

Deploying Software and Scripts

In this chapter, it's all about the apps.

And we have a lot of different application types. Here's the rundown of the application types we're going to install using MDM (specifically, Intune) in this chapter. Note that this rundown is different than the order in which we will be doing our examples:

MSIs   You know them and love them. MSI files. Most of the applications you have today are likely packaged as MSIs, and you might even have expertise in creating or repackaging applications to MSI.

Win32 Apps (EXEs)   Some apps just don't ship as MSI files. They are just totally fine as EXEs. Acrobat Reader and Firefox ship as straight EXEs. These are called Win32 applications and we'll see how to deploy those using an MDM service.

AppX, Windows Store, and Microsoft Store for Business Applications   Also known as *Metro*, or *Universal Windows Platform (UWP) applications*, AppX packages are the kind of applications you would typically find in the Windows Store. We'll explore the idea of deploying both line-of-business (LOB) apps and items that are already packaged and ready to rock in the Windows Store or Microsoft Store for Business.

MSIX   This is the new kid on the block. MSIX is Microsoft's new generation of application packaging. The idea is to combine the benefits of MSIs and AppX with additional cool features. The support of MSIX was first introduced in Windows 10 1809. That being said, it was then backported to 1803 and 1709 for customers still using those versions.

Microsoft Office   No discussion of deploying software could be complete without talking about Microsoft Office. Office has traditionally been one of the hardest things to deploy in the history of mankind. With MDM, they made this pretty point-and-shoot easy if you are using Office 365 ProPlus. It is a different story if you want to install MSI-based Office.

I'll also show you how to deploy PowerShell scripts to script one-off items and download packages that are evergreen (more on that later). And I'll show you how PolicyPak Scripts Manager and PolicyPak File Delivery Manager can add on to your MDM systems to fill in some file delivery and installation gaps.

Let's get started!

Don't Use It: The Old Intune Client Software

A quick side note about everything we'll be going over in this chapter: All of our software deployment tasks will be handled by the MDM channel.

I say this because Intune used to have (and some people still rely upon) the Intune "software client" that also has (had, really) its own method of installing software.

Some people call this the "Silverlight" method, but that's not accurate. What they mean when they say this is that this method was leveraged from the original Intune Portal, based upon Silverlight. But the Intune client software itself doesn't have any Silverlight in its veins.

Regrettably, there's still a lot of Microsoft content around this item (and again, we won't be talking about it). But if you want to see this old Intune client software, here are three links about it:

- https://docs.microsoft.com/en-us/intune/intune-legacy-pc-client

- https://docs.microsoft.com/en-us/intune/
  manage-windows-pcs-with-microsoft-intune

- https://docs.microsoft.com/en-us/intune/
  install-the-windows-pc-client-with-microsoft-intune

In short: you are *not* going to be installing or using the Intune client software to then assist you in any of the deployment types in this chapter. It's going be all MDM, all the way.

I say this now, in case you run into some problem with MDM software deployment and think, "I'll just do a search for the answer ..." But then you run across some old and outmoded information for deploying applications with Intune and the legacy software client.

And, that information would be totally inapplicable to you.

So, don't get caught in that trap.

Preparing for the Remainder of the Chapter

Again, the order in the previous section is not the order in which I plan on tackling things in this chapter. That being said, we will be tackling things in this chapter in this order:

1. MSIs
2. MSIX
3. AppX
4. Office 365 ProPlus
5. EXEs (aka Win32) apps

To prepare, let's take a look at what to download in advance, right now.

What to Download to Get Settled In for This Chapter

To prepare for the examples in this chapter, here's what you should download in advance for each segment.

We need two EXE applications: One we'll repackage into an MSIX (at the beginning of the chapter) and EXE application, which we'll deploy using the Win32 deployment technique at the end of the chapter.

Download Notepad++ from `https://notepad-plus-plus.org/`, and put the installer file, which should be named something similar to `npp.7.5.8.Installer.exe`, so that it's handy on your management machine.

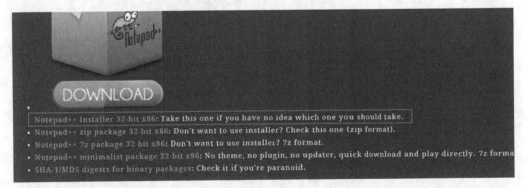

The second EXE application I'd like for you to download is Firefox ESR. ESR is the "Extended Service Release" and the one meant for IT departments. Start out on `https://www.mozilla.org/en-US/firefox/organizations/all/` and then find the language of your choice. I'll be using the English US, 64-bit download as seen here. Note that by the time you read this, there could be .MSI versions of Firefox ESR. But don't use that. Use the .EXE download for this chapter's exercises.

The filename I got was `Firefox Setup 60.3.0esr.exe`; yours might be similar but somewhat differently named. Again, double-check that you got the .EXE and not the .MSI for Firefox.

For our MSI application, I would like for you to download the latest and also next latest versions of 7-Zip from `https://www.7-zip.org/download.html`. You'll download either the 32-bit or 64-bit installer as seen here. I'll be using the 64-bit versions on my 64-bit machines in these examples.

As of this writing, here's how to find the latest version (18.05).

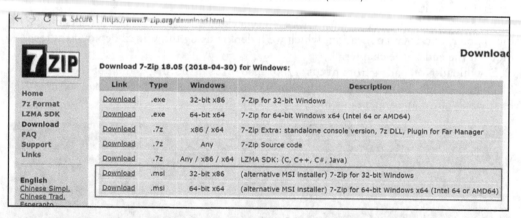

Then, also download an older version like 16.04, which can be seen here.

Download 7-Zip 16.04 (2016-10-04) for Windows:			
Link	Type	Windows	Description
Download	.exe	32-bit x86	7-Zip for 32-bit Windows
Download	.exe	64-bit x64	7-Zip for 64-bit Windows x64 (Intel 64 or AMD64)
Download	.7z	x86 / x64	7-Zip Extra: standalone console version, 7z DLL, Plugin for Far Manager
Download	.7z	Any	7-Zip Source code
Download	.7z	Any / x86 / x64	LZMA SDK: (C, C++, C#, Java)
Download	.msi	32-bit x86	(alternative MSI installer) 7-Zip for 32-bit Windows
Download	.msi	64-bit x64	(alternative MSI installer) 7-Zip for 64-bit Windows x64 (Intel 64 or AMD64)

For our AppX application, we'll be using an already-repackaged 7-Zip package found here: `https://github.com/UWP-Open-Source-Community/7zip`. Click Clone Or Download and then Download ZIP and keep that handy.

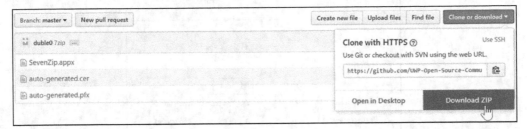

Also on your management station, you'll need a utility to take existing MSI and EXE packages and get them converted to MSIX format. Again, more on this later, but to prepare your machine for this, you need to use the Windows Store and download the MSIX Packaging Tool, which is seen in the next image. Note that the tool will only install on Windows 1809 and later.

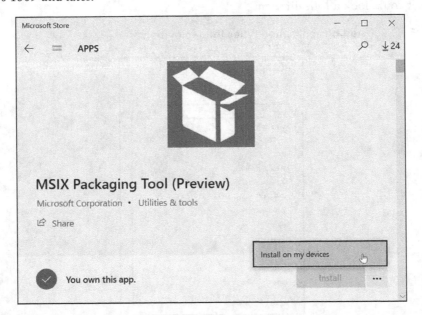

How to (Generally) Deploy Applications with Intune

So we'll be deploying different application types in the remainder of this chapter. That said, the general beginning steps to deploying applications of any type using Intune can be summed up in a few steps and a few screen shots.

In Intune, you would click Client Apps, then Apps, shown in Figure 6.1.

FIGURE 6.1   Windows Intune Client Apps and Apps panes

The next screen you'll see is the "Add app" pane, shown in Figure 6.2 (by the time you read this it could look a little different).

FIGURE 6.2   Adding application types for deployment

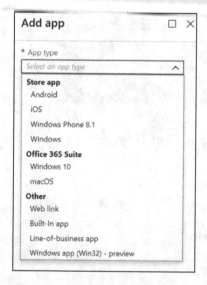

I won't show you these same steps over and over. When it's time to try another software deployment category, just refer back to Figures 6.1 and 6.2.

How to (Generally) Deploy Applications with WorkspaceONE

For the remainder of the chapter, I'm going to be showing Microsoft Intune for software deployment. But I wanted to at least show you one other service and how it's done there.

Using VMware Workspace ONE to deploy apps is pretty straightforward. In fact, deploying MSIs and EXEs is equally easy, which is a little bonus (compared to Windows Intune, where you'll see that we have to re-wrap EXEs first before uploading.)

The general steps are to click Apps & Books ➤ Native ➤ Add Application, as shown in the following image.

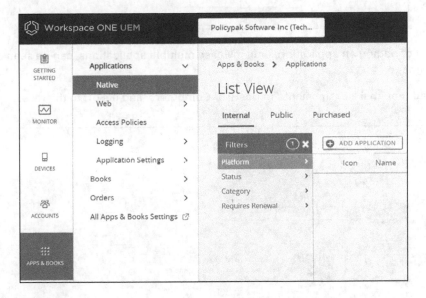

Then you click Upload to add the file, as shown in the following image.

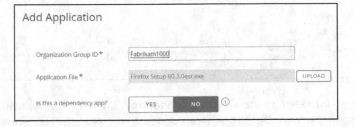

There a small myriad of questions to answer, like the Install and Uninstall command (the Install Command option can be seen in the following image).

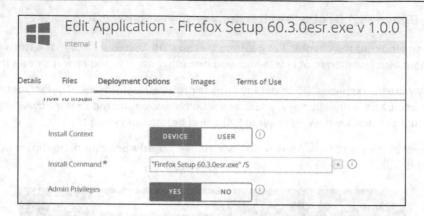

The result of adding an application, or in my case multiple applications, can be seen in the next image.

You would then make assignments to Users or Computers, and it's off to the races.

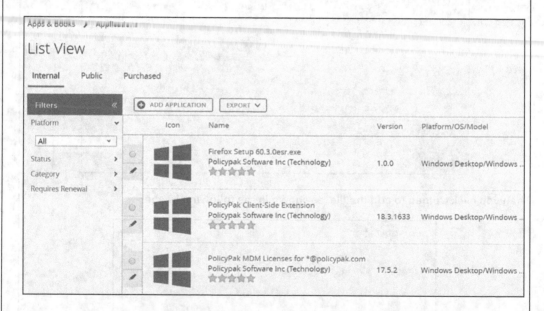

Again, I cannot go into step-by-step instructions for both VMware WorkspaceONE and Microsoft Intune in the book. But the general concepts we use in the remainder of this chapter should reasonably translate over to any MDM service, including VMware Workspace ONE.

Deploying MSI Applications with MDM

Let's begin our journey with deploying an MSI application with your MDM service like Intune or Workspace ONE.

The thing about deploying MSIs is that they must be what is called simple MSIs. What's a simple MSI? You've seen this a lot: a single, solitary MSI file, which is just a basic install. Okay, what's a complex MSI then? Office 2003 would be a complex MSI. It has multiple MSIs, this crazy thing called MSI chaining, and a gaggle of CAB files to boot. So, ya know, complex.

The method we'll be using here, in the following sections, only works with simple MSI applications. If you want to do medium-level complex .MSIs, then you should be using either the MSIX method or the Win32 apps deployment methods; both methods are described later.

With that in mind, let's get started and deploy a simple .MSI. Earlier I asked you to download the older and also the new version of 7-Zip as an MSI and keep it handy. It's time to use the older version first.

Deploying Your First MSI Application

In Intune, start out by clicking Client Apps, then Apps like what is seen in Figure 6.1. Then, in the new pane, click Add and then select Other ➤ "Line-of business app" (see Figure 6.2).

WARNING   Don't let the term *line-of-business app* fool you. In this case, it doesn't mean only an app that you might have developed in-house. It just means anything at all that you might want to install on the PC.

For MSI applications, you need to select a file and upload it to Intune. You'll choose the 7-Zip MSI you downloaded earlier and placed on your management station.

After selecting the file, but before uploading, you'll be asked to specify App information, as you can see in Figure 6.3. The only required fields are Description and Publisher. For this test, also specify "Device context" as the app install context, which will install it to the All Users profile on the system such that it can be used by every user on the system.

FIGURE 6.3 Only Description and Publisher are required fields for MSI applications.

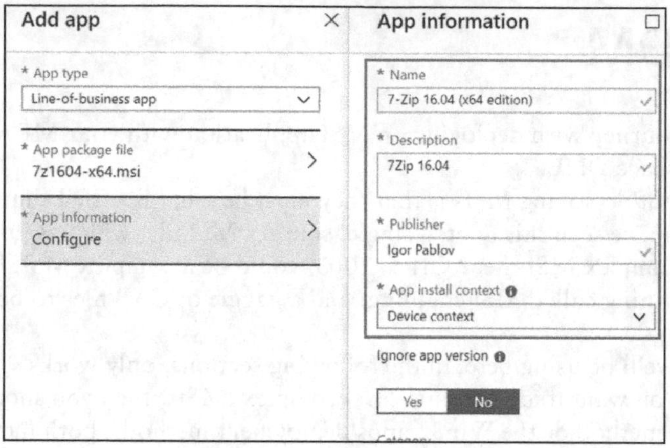

Targeting Users or Computers and Installation Context

In Figure 6.4, and in some other dialogs later in this chapter, you can see where you can assign a Line-of-Business application to "Make this app required for all users" or "Make this app required on all devices." Additionally, you can specify a specific group (of users or devices) to target.

Additionally, there's a pulldown underneath those options which enables the installation *context*. That is, if the application will be installed for users or for devices. Here's the quick guide on these settings:

Setting this to, "Make this app required for all users," will deliver the package on the device when a user with an Azure AD account and Intune license is logged in.

Setting this to, "Make this app required on all devices," will deliver the package on the device with any user logged in (valid Azure AD account or even a Local user).

As for User vs. Device *context*; this is how the app will actually get installed.

Device context will make the app installed such that any user who logged in will see the app. Device context installs the application for the entire device (including all current and future users).

User Context will make the app to be installed only per user, as long as the user is part of the group. But with user context, installation only happens for an application for one user at a time.

Here's what this means in practical terms.

For User context, if there are two Intune users and one non-Intune user (say, only a local account), there would be two installations, and the non-Intune user would *not* have access to the app. Furthermore, each new Intune user logging onto the device will require internet access to install the app.

For Device context, if there are two Intune users and one non-Intune user, there would only be *one* installation, and all *three* users will have access to the app. Furthermore, new users will still have access to the app, even if there is no internet access.

Device context is valid for all MSIX applications; learn more in the "Deploying MSIX with MDM" section.

MSI applications (unlike MSIX applications) may or may not get the choice of User Context vs. Device Context. Those decisions are pre-baked into the MSI itself, where an MSI file can be destined to be User-installed, Computer-installed, or both.

Additionally, and also importantly, don't try to target an application in a Device context set to target a group of users; that won't work.

You can learn more about User vs. Device targeting as well as User vs. Machine context at https://docs.microsoft.com/en-us/intune/apps-windows-10-app-deploy.

If you have an extra second, I recommend adding a logo to your software so it ends up looking nice in the company portal (which you will see later). It will take any standard PNG file.

Leave the remaining fields blank and click OK (not shown). Click "Add to finish" (also not shown). Then click Assignments ➤ Add Group to specify which users or computers should accept this package.

Let's just get it to all devices (which would then be all users on those devices). Note that in real life, you generally don't want to deploy most software to all devices, unless, of course you really, really want to. For our tests, sending this to all devices is A-OK. To do this, select Required under to "Assignment type" in the "Add group" pane as seen in Figure 6.4. Then, click Yes next to "Make this app required on all devices" as seen in the Assign pane. You can ignore the "Selected groups" and "Select groups to include" options as these are not needed since you've directed this package to all devices. Click OK in the Assign pane to continue (not shown). and OK to save in the "Add group" pane (also not shown).

FIGURE 6.4   Select Yes for the "Make this app required on all devices" option.

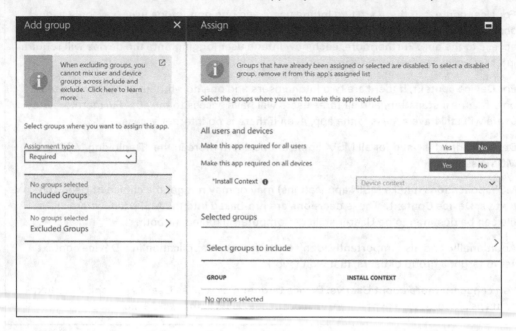

When complete, you should see your assignment showing Required for "All devices," as shown in Figure 6.5.

FIGURE 6.5   See that your application is required for all devices and installing in device context.

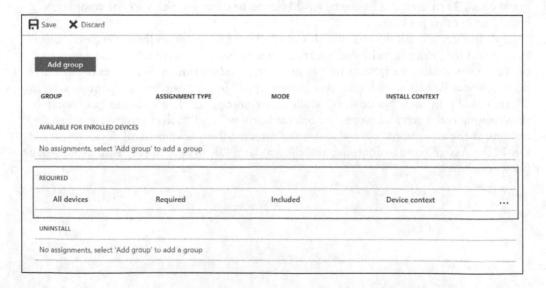

Back on your endpoint, if you're not logged on as any user in particular, log on as a user you created in Azure AD back in Chapter 1: Enterprise Mobility and MDM Essentials such as Anthony Kissel (`kissel@fabrikam1000.com` in my world).

Then if you need to, go into Settings ➤ Access Work or School, click on the briefcase or Windows flag and select Info. Then sync with your MDM service. If all goes well, in a little bit you should see what's in Figure 6.6 with 7-Zip installed (it bubbles right to the top because of the # in its name) and that applications are now installed in the basic MDM report.

FIGURE 6.6   See 7-Zip install to the Start Menu and appear in the basic MDM report.

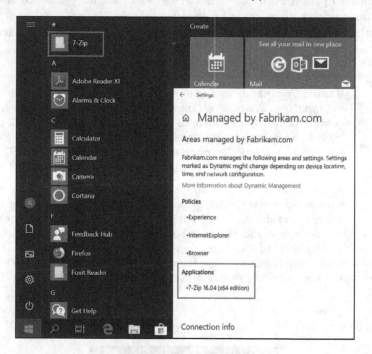

Note that in the Applications category, you might get a GUID instead of the pretty application name; I'm not sure why.

Run 7-Zip and select Help ➤ About, and verify that you got version 16.04.

MSI Application Deployment Tips and Tricks

Here are a few little side notes about MSI installations:

MDM can only (for now anyway) deploy what's known as basic or simple MSIs. Some MSIs are really, really complicated and call other MSIs (called nested MSIs) and perform other off-the-beaten-path tricks. MDM cannot handle those—not right now, maybe not ever. So if you're having trouble with any particular MSI, it might not be you; it could just be MDM.

Similarly, MSIs with MSPs (patches) or MSTs (transforms) cannot be deployed using this method. You can maybe (often) do it with the steps in the "Deploying Win32 Apps with MDM" section which I'll talk about later. And maybe you could use the final method I'll show you at the end of the chapter with PowerShell to "pull" applications, but the native MSI deployment method doesn't enable this function.

You might from time to time need to put switches to make your MSI package run silently or to perform an installation in a different way. Note that all applications are automatically run silently because the platform puts a /Q for quiet automatically on at the end.

This is supported, and the place for it would be the "Command-line arguments" block seen when editing a package's configuration items (refer back in Figure 6.3) but it's not shown there due to space. In my tests, I discovered that the "Command-line arguments" block didn't always work. I talked with the product team, and it should be fixed by the time you read this.

If using Command-line arguments doesn't want to work, check out the setting called *EnableUserControl,* which can be delivered by Group Policy custom OMA-URI or delivered by Registry key. For some MSI properties that are considered secure, you need to set the computer to allow the values to be overridden on the command line when MSIEXEC runs. That could be the case for some applications.

This is usually only needed for apps that are per-user or dual mode (per-user and per-machine). Per-machine apps are installed in the system context and should not be subject to (or need) this policy. For apps that do require this, if you don't pre-set this policy, the MSI install log will display a line similar to this: "Ignoring disallowed property INSTALLDIR." Details on EnableUserControl are found at https://docs.microsoft.com/en-us/windows/desktop/Msi/enableusercontrol.

An example of how you would use this, say, to install 7-Zip to a specific installation directory can be seen here.

MSI Updating

Once you have 7-Zip version 16.04 out there, let's try upgrading to 18.05.

To do this, go back to the properties of the 7-Zip package and select "App package file." Then simply select your newer version, as shown in Figure 6.7.

FIGURE 6.7   Replace an existing MSI with an upgrade package.

Then, as shown in Figure 6.8, go to "App information" and Configure and you should also nicely update the other information. Otherwise, in the MDM reports, you'll still see the old information.

FIGURE 6.8   Update the app Information or else you will see incorrect information in the MDM reports.

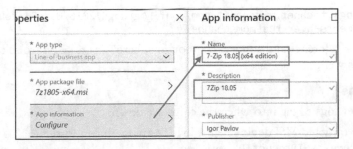

You can check your upgrade process by re-syncing with Intune and then re-running 7-Zip and checking Help ➤ About. You should now be running 18.05.

MSI Revoking

So I would have guessed that merely removing the assignment of the MSI from the group that houses computers (or users) would be enough to have the package revoke.

But that's not how it works.

To revoke applications deployed via MSI, you need to go back to the Assign pane and specify the group for which you specifically want to perform an *uninstall*, as shown in Figure 6.9. Of course it makes no sense to install, say, to "All devices" but also uninstall as well to Sales Desktops.

FIGURE 6.9 You need to specify which users or devices will have the application uninstalled.

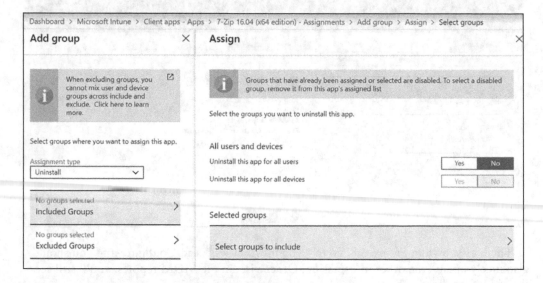

MSI Deployment Troubleshooting

Troubleshooting MSI installations can come in a handful of forms. To be honest, the definitive guide on the subject can be found here:

```
https://blogs.technet.microsoft.com/configmgrdogs/2016/08/03/troubleshooting-
msi-deployments-over-the-mdm-channel/
```

But for quick reference and some extra thoughts, here's my take on troubleshooting MSI deployments as well.

Log Locations

Here are the key logs to dig into when the chips are down:

- For device targeted MSI deployments, logs (if any) will be written to:
  `Windows\temp\<MSIProductID>.msi.log`

- For user targeted MSI deployments, logs (if any) will be written to:
  `%temp%\MSIProductID.msi.log`

Here's an interesting thing: You won't find logs if installation goes perfectly. If installation goes perfectly, log files are automatically cleaned up, and there's nothing there to see or inspect.

When an error occurs, MSI logging will almost assuredly yield the fastest information.

The trick is to find an error code here that you can Google/Bing for and find the underlying reason for failure.

Registry Snapshot of Deployment Status

For device targeted MSI deployments, look at the Registry items in:

```
HKLM\SOFTWARE\Microsoft\EnterpriseDesktopManagement\
S-0-0-00-0000000000-00000000000-00000000000-0000000000-00\MSI\<MSIProductID>
```

For user targeted MSI deployments, look at the Registry items in:

```
HKLM\SOFTWARE\Microsoft\EnterpriseDesktopManagement\<UserSID>\
MSI\<MSIProductID>
```

An example can be seen in Figure 6.10.

FIGURE 6.10   Cracking open the keys used in an MSI deployment

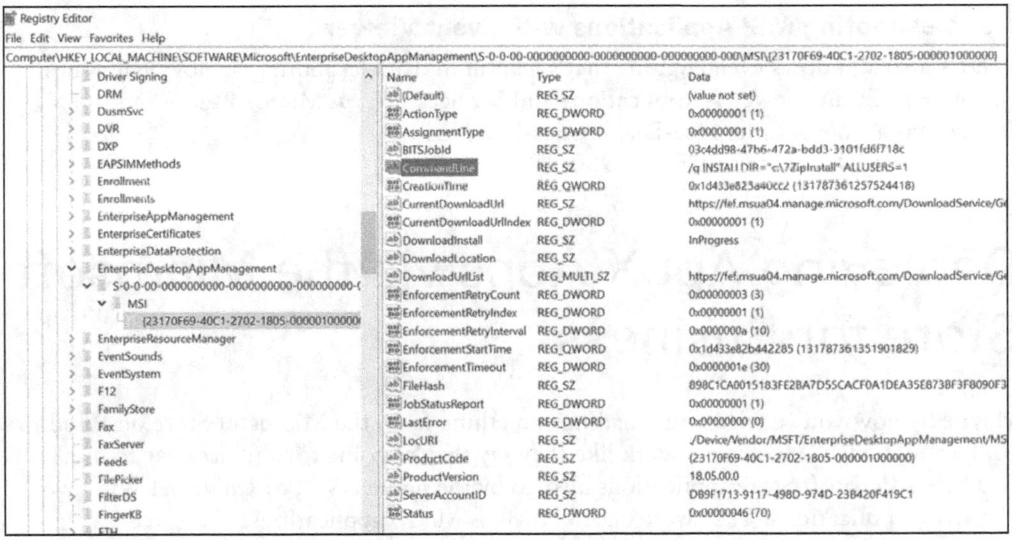

Windows Status Codes

Using the Registry information as described earlier, the Status and LastError Registry values can give you some clues as to what is going on. Again, from the blog entry (and seemingly no other place on earth), here are the codes to help you know what's going on.

Remember: It's the number in parentheses, like (70) for Status, and not 0x0000046, which is the hex value of 70.

The list of codes follows:

- 70 = Successfully installed/uninstalled
- 10 = Initialized
- 20 = DownloadInProgress

- 25 = PendingDownloadRetry
- 30 = DownloadFailed
- 40 = DownloadCompleted
- 48 = PendingUserSession
- 50 = EnforcementInProgress
- 55 = PendingEnforcementRetry
- 60 = EnforcementFailed
- 70 = EnforcementCompleted

The codes can be found in the documentation for the CSP that controls MSI deployments, the EnterpriseDesktopManagement CSP. The docs for this CSP are found at https://docs.microsoft.com/en-us/windows/client-management/mdm/enterprisedesktopappmanagement-csp.

Troubleshooting MSI Applications with Event Viewer

There's also Windows event logging that's helpful in troubleshooting deployment issues. Navigate to Event Viewer ➢ Applications and Services Logs ➢ Microsoft ➢ Windows ➢ DeviceManagement-Enterprise-Diagnostics-Provider.

The Event IDs you are after are 1900–1930.

Deploying AppX Apps via the Microsoft Store for Business

Maybe by now you've tried downloading something from the Microsoft Store on Windows 10. I know I have. Most items work like they say they're going to, and are easy to use.

These Microsoft Store applications also go by the name UWP, or Universal Windows Platform, applications. They were once known as Metro applications.

Instead of having your users each go directly to the Microsoft Store to download (and/or maybe pay for applications), there is a better way.

And the idea is that you, at your company, will curate specific items from the "wild wild west" Microsoft Store (free or paid). And you'll display the curated items for your end users.

This is called the Microsoft Store for Business. You can think of the Microsoft Store for Business as a big filter where your people can only see the stuff you provide for them.

Getting Started with and Activating the Microsoft Store for Business

Getting started with the Microsoft Store for Business isn't hard.

Head over to https://businessstore.microsoft.com and log on with the AAD Global Admin account, which in my case is Frank Rizzo. Then, accept the license terms.

Additionally, you may want to click Manage ➤ Settings ➤ Shop, and within Shopping Experience, set "Show offline apps" to On (the default is Off). This will enable applications that have a special licensing method called Offline Licensed apps to appear when users select one of these applications. Offline Licensed apps have a magic ability to deploy Store for business apps, well, offline, say during the image process, via DISM or Windows Imaging and Configuration Designer (WICD). WICD is shown in Chapter 8: Rollouts and Refreshes with Configuration Designer and Autopilot. Learn more about Offline Licensed apps at https://docs.microsoft.com/en-us/microsoft-store/distribute-offline-apps#download-an-offline-licensed-app.

Then after that, you need to connect the Microsoft Store for Business to Intune. Start out by going to Client Apps | Microsoft Store for Business. Then click Enable, then Save, then "Open the business store" as shown in Figure 6.11.

FIGURE 6.11   How to enable the Microsoft Store for Business within Intune

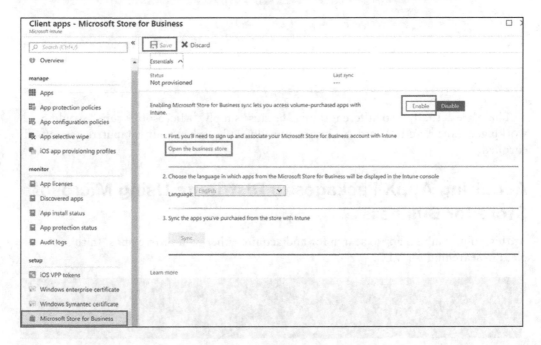

Once you're in the Microsoft Store for Business, you need to "teach it" that you want to marry it to your Intune or Workspace ONE, or whatever MDM you use. Click on Manage ➤ Settings ➤ Distribute (see Figure 6.12). Change the private store name if desired, but the "must do" item is to activate Microsoft Intune and Microsoft Intune Enrollment.

FIGURE 6.12   You must activate (at least) Microsoft Intune Enrollment, preferably both.

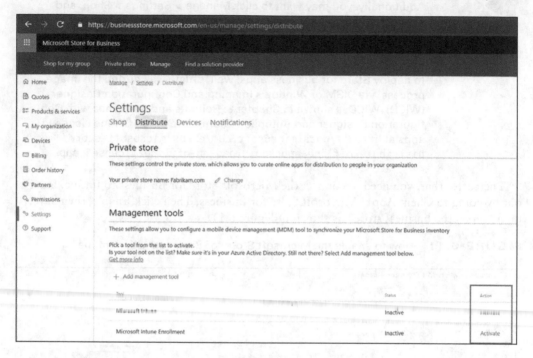

These are actually two different things, because simply "Microsoft Intune" would be workplace joined, and "Microsoft Intune Enrollment" is when your computers are actually enrolled.

Acquiring AppX Packages to Distribute Using Microsoft Store for Business

At this point you're ready to search for and acquire either paid or free apps. In this example, I'm searching for VLC.

Then, in Figure 6.13 I'm adding VLC Media player by clicking "Get the app."

FIGURE 6.13 The VLC app in the Microsoft Store (and getting it ready for Microsoft Store for Business)

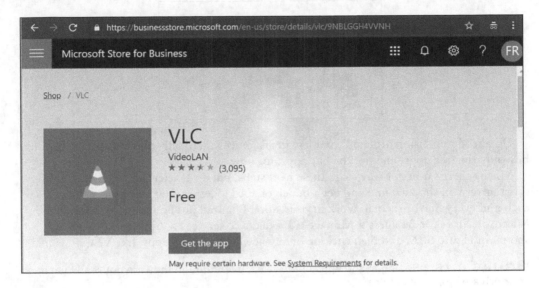

Also, while you're here, get the application named Company Portal (see Figure 6.14).

FIGURE 6.14 The Company Portal app in the Microsoft Store (and getting it ready for Microsoft Store for Business)

 You might be presented with a Microsoft Store for Business agreement after selecting an application.

And, in no time flat, you "own" an app, as shown in Figure 6.15.

FIGURE 6.15 You now have the application available for use within your company store.

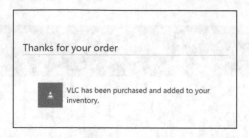

Go ahead and "shop around" for a few items. Since you're only playing around, I would buy only the free apps, and not the pay apps, for now.

Maybe there's a better way to do these next steps, but an efficient way eluded me. In short, after you shop around and get a bunch of apps together, you still have to bless each and every one of them to work in your store. I figured out how to do this inside the Microsoft Store for Business ➤ Manage ➤ Products & services ➤ Apps & software, as shown in Figure 6.16, and then clicking on my newly purchased apps, like VLC.

FIGURE 6.16 Seeing all the apps in the store, even though they are not ready yet in your private store collection

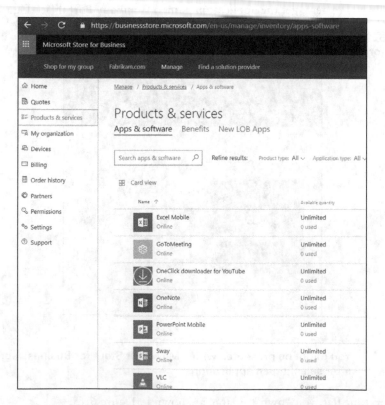

Then inside the application itself, you click on "Private store availability" and select Everyone to specify that anyone can get it, las shown in Figure 6.17.

FIGURE 6.17   Each application needs to be accepted into your company collection.

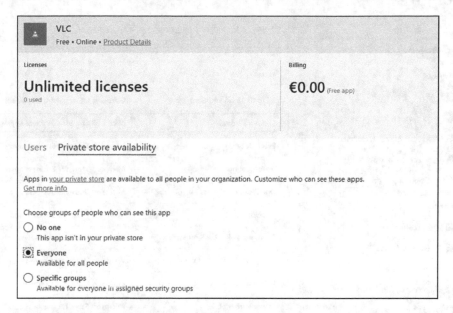

Back at the Intune's Microsoft Store for Business page, click the Sync button as back in Figure 6.11 (tucked under heading 3 in that window).

It will tell you it takes a while to sync, and for me, it always does. The year started at (not joking) 1969, then jumped up to modern days when it finally did the sync.

When the sync is done, go back to "Client apps - Apps" and you'll see any of the apps you've put into your private store, as shown in Figure 6.18 (and, yes, I know my screen shot has a few more items than yours might have).

FIGURE 6.18   See your Microsoft Store for Business apps available for delivery.

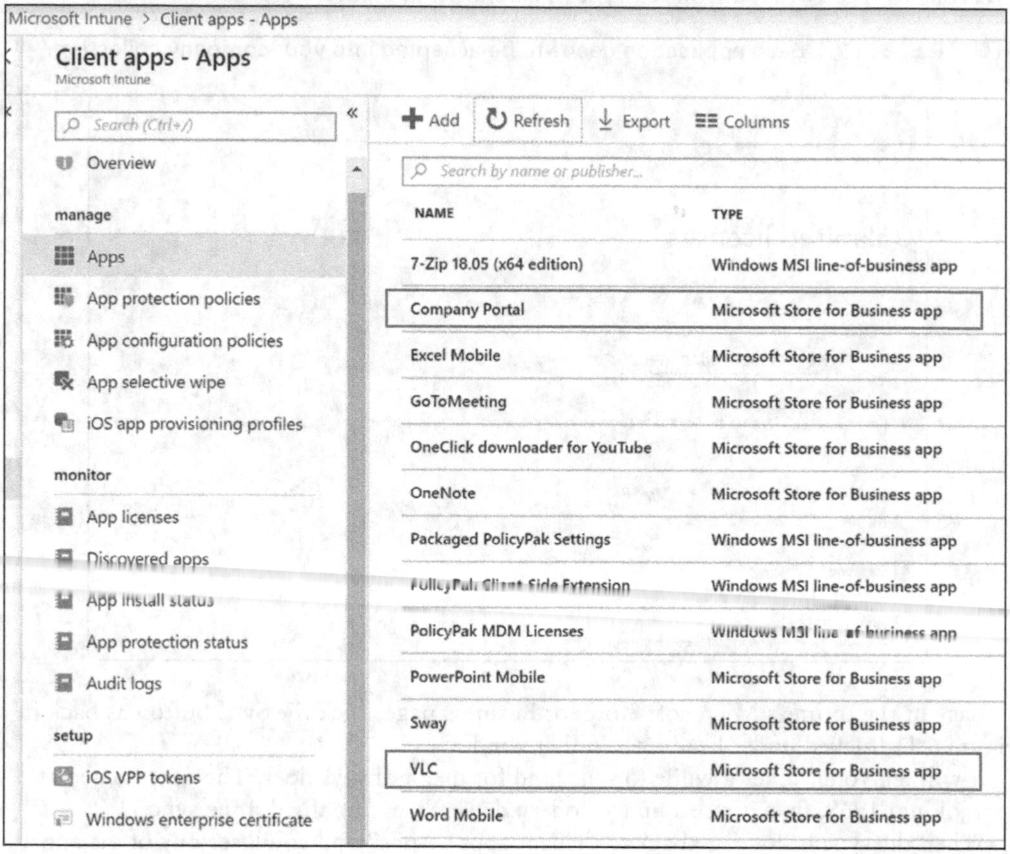

At this point, it's off to the races. You can assign to users, devices, or groups as we've done in previous discussions. Do this now for the VLC and the Company Store and assign it to "All devices."

The result of the application getting there is what you might expect after the MDM client syncs with the mother ship. Check out Figure 6.19 to see VLC get added quietly to the machine.

FIGURE 6.19   Applications delivered from the Windows Store for Business

The official guidance on this can be found at https://docs.microsoft.com/en-us/intune/windows-store-for-business.

You're welcome to run it, but we'll check out the Company Portal app we also deployed a little later. You can poke around in it for now, but hang tight, we'll get to it.

Blocking Consumer Windows Store Fully and/or Allowing Some Consumer Store Apps

Note also that deploying applications through the Microsoft Store for Business does not magically kill the built-in "consumer" Windows Store.

You might think this would just happen, but it doesn't.

So if you're deploying applications through the Microsoft Store for Business and then you want to kill the consumer Windows Store, here's how you would do it.

Using Group Policy, there's a setting Computer Configuration ≫ Administrative Templates ≫ Windows Components ≫ Store ≫ **Turn off the Store application**.

Using MDMyou need a custom OMA-URI.

- **OMA-URI**: ./User/Vendor/MSFT/Policy/Config/ApplicationManagement/ RequirePrivateStoreOnly

- **Value**: 1

There's a small, simple walk-through using MDM at:

> https://blogs.msdn.microsoft.com/beanexpert/2016/03/29/block-windows-10-
> public-store-using-microsoft-intune-but-still-allow-the-business-store/

Both the Group Policy and MDM magic *only* works for Enterprise or Education and not Pro.

But alas! There are two workarounds for Windows Pro, and I made two videos to demo.

Video #1 I made at https://www.youtube.com/watch?v=W3KJCIzhQ3U (or search for "Block Windows Store using Group Policy for Windows Pro"). This will fully put the smack down on the Windows Store for Business.

Video #2 requires PolicyPak Least Privilege Manager, and enables you to block the Consumer store fully; or, leave the Consumer store available, and dictate what vendors or specific programs are allowed from the Consumer store. It's super powerful (but not free). Check it out at https://kb.policypak.com/kb/article/ 624-policypak-manage-block-and-allow-windows-universal-uwp-applications.

Deploying MSIX with MDM

So, what the heck is an MSIX?

I'm going to make a prediction; if you're reading this book in 2019, you likely never heard of it, or you heard of it in passing. But I think as you read this book in 2020 and beyond, you're going to just know what MSIX is all about because you'll already be using them.

That said, the quickest way to explain MSIX can be summed up in Figure 6.20.

FIGURE 6.20   MSIX format enables you to take multiple package types, wrap them up, and then deliver them in MSI-like style.

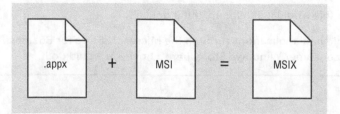

So I believe that the MSIX format will become the new gold standard package deployment type, in the same way that MSI was the gold standard from 2000 until now. Maybe not overnight, but I think pretty soon.

There are actually three main ways the MSIX format could get hot:

Way #1: Application vendors get on the bandwagon and just start using it. The main MSI repackaging tools (like Advanced Installer) are already enlightened to make MSIX packages.

Way #2: People use them to wrap up their existing Win32 .EXE applications and repackage them into the MSIX format. They then deploy those MSIX packages through MDM. However, there is a built-in to deliver Win32 .EXE files now with Intune, but not every MDM vendor has this method. So MSIX can be a bridge for those non-Intune customers.

Way #3: The MSIX format will be the new standard way to upload applications in the Windows Store. Existing .APPX store packages can be updated with a new MSIX version of the app. Neat!

What's great about MSIX format is that it fulfills several promises all in one shot:

- MSIs typically didn't install and then remove perfectly every single time. MSIX applications really should be genuinely sandboxed at install time and beautifully removed at decommission time.

- You can take many existing MSIs and convert them to MSIX format.

- Same for Win32 .EXEs; you can convert and get to MSIX format quickly. Again, though, as we'll see later, there's a Win32 EXE deployment method in Intune-land that we'll spend time on as well.

- You can also package UWP (AppX packages) into MSIX.

- Customers already familiar with App-V and packages in that ilk (like ThinApp) will already have a passing familiarity with what's going on with MSIX packages. MSIX applications have lightweight virtualization for files and Registry. And, in some future world, existing App-V packages can likely be converted to MSIX.

- MSIX is smart about packages that share the same files, and only one file is written to disk. And, over the network, any file duplicates between MSIX packages are not even downloaded, saving bandwidth.

- MSIX packages are downloaded in blocks, specifically changed blocks, and not as a blocky, massive file. So if your MSIX package changes, and you need to get it out the door fast, clients are only downloading the changes and not the whole thing (again).

- MSIX applications have better overall security: they have tamper protection and they rely upon being digitally signed by you (as you'll see a little later) so it's clear this is your app.

- MSIX (as a packaging technology) works not just on Windows but cross-platform on iOS, Android, MacOS, and Linux. (How's that for a mindblower?)

In summary, MSIX becomes kind of the universal package type for just about everything you might already have—for what you have on Windows (today), Windows (tomorrow), and other platforms.

The MSIX format was originally only valid on Windows 1809 and later. But as I said in the introduction, it was later backported for two earlier versions of Windows: 1803 and 1709.

Two good summaries of the benefits can be found in the following articles and blog posts:

https://redmondmag.com/articles/2018/08/07/microsoft-previews-msix-packaging-tool.aspx

https://blogs.flexera.com/application-readiness/2018/08/msix-the-new-super-package/

Additionally, if you want to see an expert's opinion on MSIX and how it relates to App-V, see http://www.tmurgent.com/TmBlog/?p=2778.

You might also be wondering: Why pick the MSIX method if the MSI method we already explored earlier works? And why use the delivery method of .EXEs (aka Win32 apps), which we'll explore later?

Here are the answers:

- Detecting and updating legacy MSI and Win32 app installations can be challenging. Repackaging MSI or Win32 apps as an MSIX app solves this detection and versioning problem by utilizing the native app identity and versioning scheme used for all UWP apps.

- Sometimes not every application is a perfect candidate for packaging into MSIX. The MSIX format is new and "up and coming." So I would recommend you at least try to get your .EXEs and .MSIs repackaged into MSIX format to get all the nifty MSIX format benefits. And remember, MSI packages (deployed through the MSI method) must be simple applications. If your application is complex, then it could be deployed easier when repackaged as an MSIX ... Or, maybe not.

- As you'll see, every MSIX package must be signed. So it could be somewhat more difficult to take an existing, ready-to-deploy application, and repackage it to MSIX. In other words, it's a quicker path for some applications to just "stay as they are" and then be deployed via the Win32 method (again, explored later).

That said, there are some key indicators that an application *is not* a good candidate for MSIX. Some of those problems would be apps with the following characteristics:

- Require admin rights after running.

- Create a service or must run as a service.

- Write to the install directory/directories.

So, in summary, it's going to be a best practice to try to get to MSIX land if you have the time. Try converting your application into MSIX format first and see if works nicely. If that doesn't work out, then hey … you can fall back to the .MSI deployment method or Win32 deployment method if need be.

Repackaging an App with the MSIX Packaging Tool

So to get started to make MSIX packages, you need a few things.

First you need the MSIX Packaging Tool.

You'll also need a code-signing PFX cert. Don't panic. Three lines of PowerShell later, you can have one for testing.

Let's get these two things out of the way first.

I suggest you first log off your Windows 10 machine and then back in as your admin user, in my case Frank Rizzo.

The MSIX Packaging Tool wants to run with admin rights, but even providing local admin rights when prompted didn't work for me. I actually had to be running as an admin on the Windows 10 computer to proceed.

Downloading the MSI Packaging Tool from the Windows Store

The MSI Packaging Tool is found in the Windows Store. You can see me finding and downloading it in Figure 6.21 (and, you can also, for instance, use the Microsoft Store for Business to push this app to, say, key admins and repackaging people).

FIGURE 6.21   Downloading the MSIX Packaging Tool

This app is updated from time to time with new features and compatibility fixes. You can check the MSIX Packaging Tool release history at https://docs.microsoft.com/ en-us/windows/msix/packaging-tool/release-notes/history to see latest updates.

Creating a PFX Code Signing Certificate for Signing the MSIX

The second thing you're going to need is a certificate to sign the MSIX. The MSIX Packaging Tool seems to imply you *don't* need a certificate, but in my testing it appeared to be required.

The certificate type is a .PFX file used for signing code. You and/or your in-house developers might have one already, but if you don't have one, and just want to quickly make one for the exercise, here's how to do it.

This example assumes you have a c:\Temp\ directory to dump the cert into. As an admin, run the following three lines of PowerShell code to make your own self-signed PFX certificate from Fabrikam1000.com with the password p@ssw0rd.

```
$cert = New-SelfSignedCertificate -DnsName fabrikam1000.com -Type CodeSigning
-CertStoreLocation Cert:\CurrentUser\My\

$CertPassword = ConvertTo-SecureString -String "p@ssw0rd" -Force -AsPlain

Export-PfxCertificate -Cert
"cert:\CurrentUser\My\$($cert.Thumbprint)"
-FilePath "c:\temp\test.pfx" -Password $CertPassword
```

The result of the PowerShell commands can be seen in Figure 6.22 where test.pfx pops out.

FIGURE 6.22   Creating a self-signed PFX certificate for testing

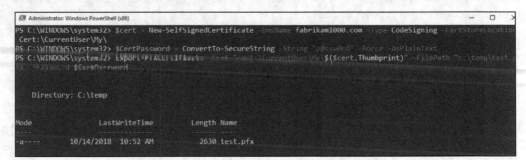

When test.pfx pops out, keep it handy. You'll need it right away to sign the MSIX you're about to create. And, that same cert will have to be delivered to the endpoints, which validates that the MSIX you're creating and signing is trusted because they're sharing the same certificate.

Repacking an Application to MSIX Format

Now that you have the tool and the certificate, you're ready to run the MSIX Packaging Tool as an admin. Select "Application package: Create your app package" as shown in Figure 6.23.

Then on the next screen, enter everything you have:

- Path to the Notepad++ .EXE installer
- Path to the test.pfx code-signing certificate
- Password to the code-signing certificate

FIGURE 6.23 Create your MSIX package by clicking on "Application package."

You can see this in Figure 6.24.

FIGURE 6.24 Create a new package by providing an existing application and certificate.

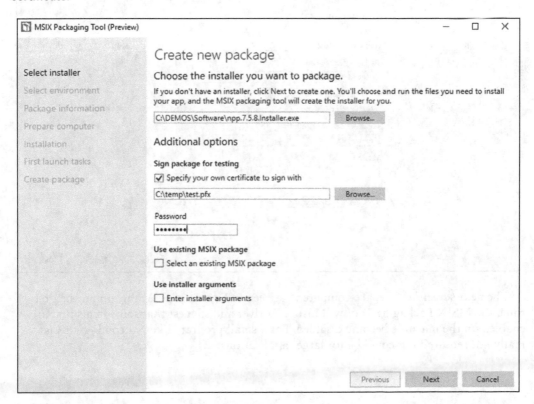

The next screen is titled "Select environment" but is not shown. This enables you to create the package in a virtual machine or on this computer. As of this writing, the virtual machine idea isn't a reality. I think the idea is that they'll let you download a preconfigured VM that you can then use as your "dumping ground" to set up complex applications. For Notepad++, using "this computer" is fine. Click Next.

The next screen is "Package information" and shown in Figure 6.25. On this page you'll enter in a package name and display name (could be the same or different), publisher name (which should automatically fill in from the certificate), publisher display name, version number, and target folder where you intend to install the application.

I've chosen `c:\NotePadPlusPlusMSIX\`.

Notepad++ is not typically installed in `c:\NotePadPlusPlusMSIX`, but that's where I plan to install it. And when I do, the MSIX Packaging Tool will see it and pick up the guts from there.

FIGURE 6.25 Enter the details of the package.

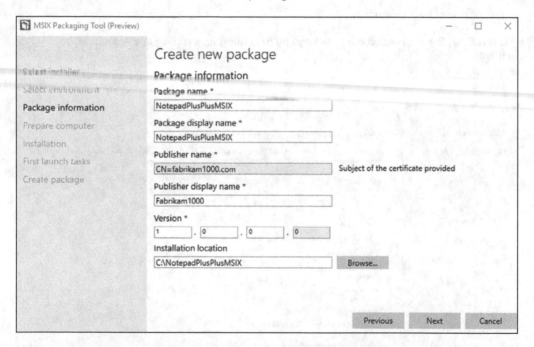

The next screen is "Prepare computer," as seen in Figure 6.26. At this point, the first time, the MSIX Packaging Tool will install a driver and suggest that some items that are enabled on the machine become disabled. For a small program like Notepad++, this is really not required but could be for larger applications.

Click Next to continue.

FIGURE 6.26   The MSIX Packaging Tool installs a driver and makes recommendations for the safest capture.

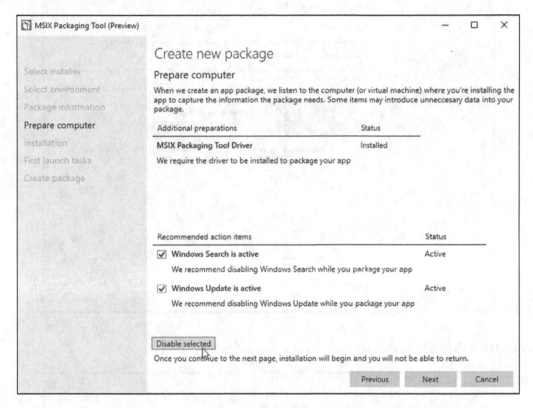

The next screen is the Installation screen, which is shown in Figure 6.27. The MSI Packaging Tool will automatically launch the Notepad++ installer. When it does, be sure to point Notepad++ to install in the installation location that will ensure the best capture.

Click through all the installation steps of Notepad++, and when asked to at the end, run it one time and then close it. When done, click Next in the MSIX Packaging Tool.

The next page is "First launch tasks" (see Figure 6.28). This page helps you verify that the capture tool actually captured the thing you wanted. You can see that Notepad++.exe is found as an *entrypoint*. Other applications might have more entrypoints, like sidecar applications, and so on. For now, this is fine, so click Next.

FIGURE 6.27   Run the application and deploy it to the target location.

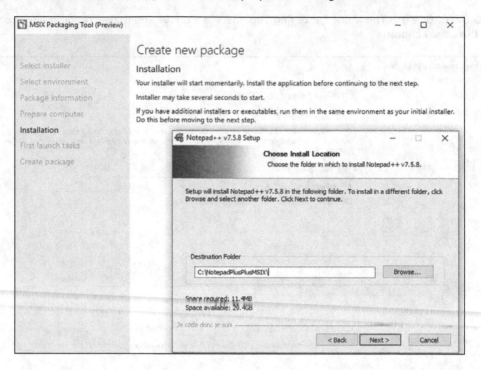

FIGURE 6.28   See the entrypoints of your application.

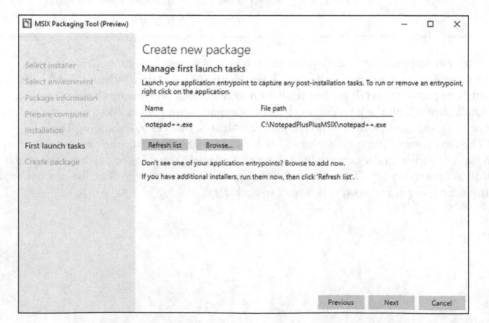

You may be prompted with an "Are you done" at this point. We are, so click "Yes, move on." Your package is prepared and you can dictate the save location.

The final screen is "Create package." Specify an output location for the MSIX package and click Create and a final confirmation (shown in Figure 6.29) will appear with a success message.

FIGURE 6.29   Success when creating an MSIX package

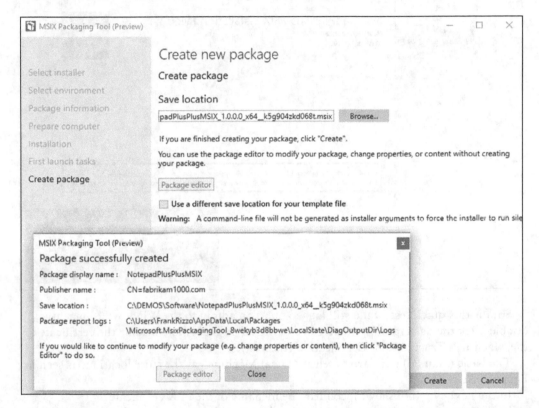

Now you're almost ready to test this out.

In fact, before proceeding, go to Add/Remove Programs and uninstall Notepad++, because during this process, well, you did just that.

Pre-testing Your MSIX

So, this isn't going to work, but I want you to try it anyway.

Now that Notepad++ is removed from your system, try to install it again, but this time from the MSIX package you created. Just double-click the install (which, again, will only work on a Windows 10 1809 and later machine, by the way).

You should see that the installation fails, as shown in Figure 6.30.

FIGURE 6.30 MSIX Installation fails because your computer doesn't trust the certificate that signed the MSIX.

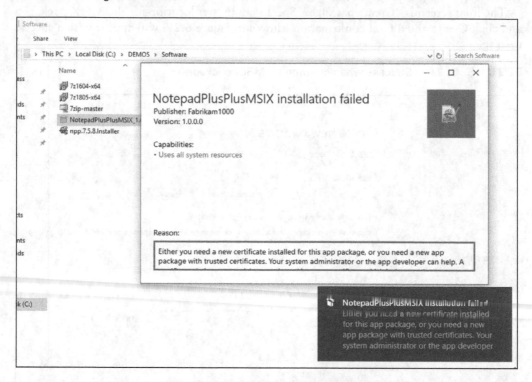

So, for this quick test, while still logged on as an admin to the Windows 10 machine, double-click the `test.pfx` file you created earlier. The goal is to consume the certificate to the Machine's Trusted Root Certification Authorities.

The basic (manual) steps are to select "Local Machine" as the store location, as seen in Figure 6.31.

In the next step (not shown), confirm the filename of the PFX certificate.

In the step after that (not shown), you need to provide the password for the certificate. In the PowerShell creation example we used `p@ssw0rd`.

Then on the Certificate Store page, do not automatically install the certificate, but rather specify to use the user's Trusted Root Certification Authorities as seen in Figure 6.32.

FIGURE 6.31   Starting the Certificate Import Wizard

FIGURE 6.32   Import the certificate into the Trusted Root Certification Authorities.

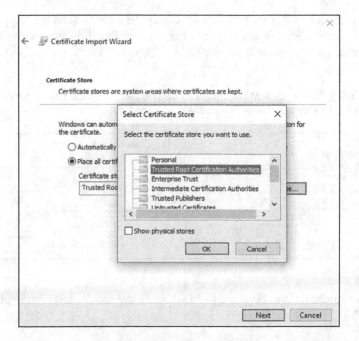

Then click Finish to complete the wizard and install the certificate.

Now re-click on the MSIX package you created earlier. It should install on the machine now (see Figure 6.33).

FIGURE 6.33   See your MSIX package install.

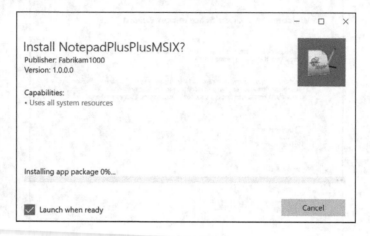

 These MSIX package installers can also be scripted via the PowerShell command Add-AppXPackage.

What's interesting now is that you will see the application in Settings "Apps & features" (on the left in Figure 6.34), but it's absent in the Control Panel Programs and Features (aka "Uninstall or change a program") (on the right in Figure 6.34).

FIGURE 6.34   Notepad++ MSIX package can be seen in "Apps & features" but will appear as missing in Control Panel Programs and Features.

At this point, uninstall the Notepad++ MSIX package so you can then deploy it with Intune.

Deploying Your MSIX Using Microsoft Intune

Let's recap:

- You created a certificate to sign your MSIX.
- You created the MSIX package.
- You installed it and removed it.

So what's remaining on the machine? Actually one thing: the PFX certificate in the machine's local store.

Which is good. Because I don't want to have to teach you how to use Intune to deliver certificates just to see your MSIX package run after installation. That's just ... too many steps right now. See the sidebar "Using Intune or Group Policy to Deploy Certificates" for a brief introduction on deploying certificates for applications.

Using Intune or Group Policy to Deploy Certificates

In this chapter, we had a .PFX certificate on the machine, and we pretended it magically got to the endpoint, but in reality we hand-installed it. You won't have this luxury in the real world. In the real world you'll need to get certificates to your machines in order to complete the certificate chain and enable the machine to run the MSIX installer.

If you want to use Intune to deploy certificates, there is a huge variety of certificate types and locations to do it. But, here, briefly, I'll explore two.

Note that in both cases, the certificate type has to be .CER, and in our working example it was .PFX. You'll need to open CertManager (via running `certmgr.msc`) and then find the PFX certificate and export as .CER.

The first type is the Windows enterprise certificate. As in Highlander, there can be only one. This is a .CER certificate type. Once you upload it, it will overwrite anything already there, so be careful if you choose to do this. You would do this in Intune ➢ "Client apps" ➢ "Windows enterprise certificate." The result can be seen here.

The second type of certificate is a code-signing certificate, which is more appropriate for ensuring that applications can complete their code-signing chains. This certificate type is found as an option within Device Configuration as a profile. As you can see the profile type is "Trusted certificate." Then you can select which store to place the file in; usually the Computer certificate store - Root is the right one, but you might have other needs.

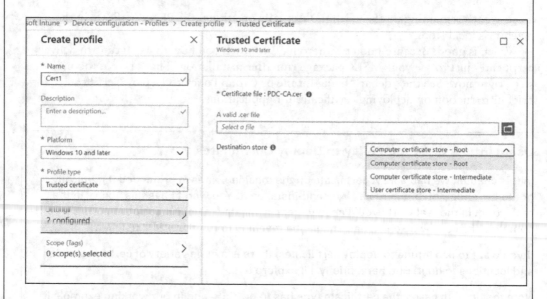

If you want some more details on how to use Intune to deploy these and other kinds of certificates, the link is https://docs.microsoft.com/en-us/intune/certficates-pfx-configure.

Alternatively, you could get the certificate to your domain-joined machines using Group Policy. There's a video (which I didn't make) on how do it here on YouTube: https://www.youtube.com/watch?v=5W96z46mKr0. (Search in YouTube for "Windows Adding Certificates With Group Policy.")

The point is, I need you to pretend that the PFX cert got on the target machine automatically somehow, because we're just *not* going to set up the automatic way that you would in real life.

What we will do, however, is deploy the MSIX using Windows Intune, but assume that the PFX certificate is already on the machine (which in our case is true).

Back in Intune, the steps are similar to what we've already seen back in Figure 6.2. In Client Apps, you'll add an app, specify the type as "Line-of-business app," then specify the Notepad++ MSIX you created in the previous steps. You can see all of this in Figure 6.35.

FIGURE 6.35   Importing your MSIX into Intune

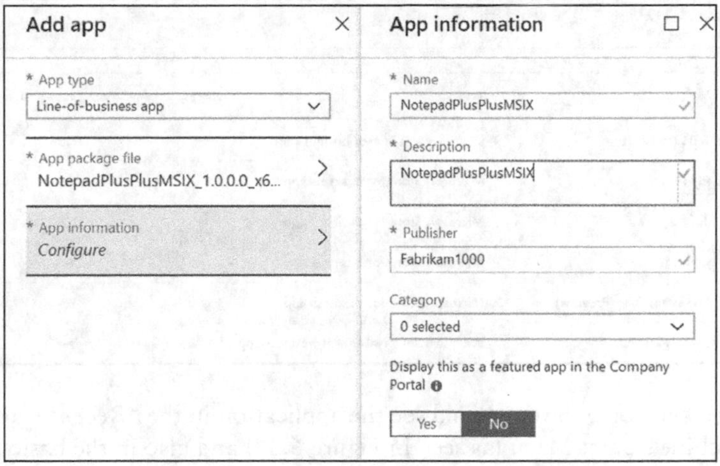

Then you'll make the assignment. In my example, in Figure 6.36, I'm assigning the MSIX package to all devices, but running the installation in the user context; this essentially makes the package installed to anyone who logs on to the machine. (For more details on this, see the previous sidebar entitled, "Targeting Users or Computers and Installation Context.")

FIGURE 6.36   Making the application required for all devices

The application will appear in the list, with a type of "Windows Universal line-of-business app" as seen in Figure 6.37.

FIGURE 6.37   Your AppX package in the application list in Intune

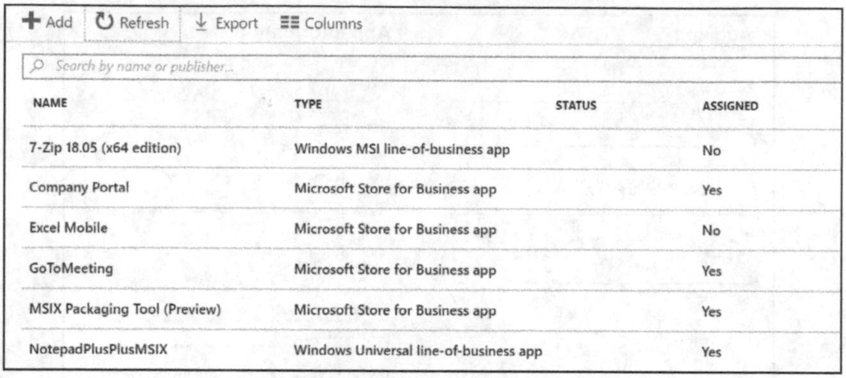

NAME	TYPE	STATUS	ASSIGNED
+ Add ↻ Refresh ↓ Export ≡≡ Columns			
🔍 Search by name or publisher...			
7-Zip 18.05 (x64 edition)	Windows MSI line-of-business app		No
Company Portal	Microsoft Store for Business app		Yes
Excel Mobile	Microsoft Store for Business app		No
GoToMeeting	Microsoft Store for Business app		Yes
MSIX Packaging Tool (Preview)	Microsoft Store for Business app		Yes
NotepadPlusPlusMSIX	Windows Universal line-of-business app		Yes

Then after a sync or two you should see the application in the "Recently added" list on the target machine's Start Menu (as seen in Figure 6.38) and also in the basic MDM report (as seen in Figure 6.39).

FIGURE 6.38   Result on Windows 10 deploying an MSIX app

FIGURE 6.39   Your MSIX application appears in the basic MDM report.

More MSIX Details (for the Real Go-Getters)

At Ignite 2018, there were myriad sessions on MSIX. The fastest way to watch these sessions is to open up YouTube, then search for the session ID.

And, badda-bing. More MSIX meat. Here are the sessions to check out:

- BRK2467: MSIX inside and out

  Presenters: John Vintzel and Nona Sirakova

- BRK3220: MSIX – Accelerating Windows 10 and app deployment
  Presenters: Andrew Clinick and Dian Hartono

- BRK2318: Updating your existing Configuration Manager apps to MSIX

  Presenters: Sharla Akers and Avi Prasad

- THR3097: Getting started with the MSIX Packaging Tool

  Presenters: Sharla Akers and Peyman Zanjani

Additionally, the official MSIX Documentation can be found at http://aka.ms/MSIX and the MSI Tech Community can be found at http://aka.ms/MSIXCommunity.

Deploying Office 365 ProPlus with MDM

Office can be one of the biggest pieces of software you deploy to your Windows machines. With the Microsoft 365 bundle you got started with in Chapter 1, you get Office 365 along for the ride.

But, just to be confusing, there's also Office 2016 and 2019, which are not the same as Office 365. Those are stand-alone, perpetual products that can be purchased and deployed as one-offs. You might have some unusual situation that requires per-machine licensing or offline installation. That's where you would pay for and use an Office 2019 license.

That said, the features and such within Office 2016 and 2019 (and whatever comes later) will always be just baked into Office 365 ProPlus. So once that train has left the station, it just keeps getting more fuel and supplies and it just keeps on delivering. You just do nothing, and computers keep getting updates.

A quick overview of the Office 2019 stand-alone product vs. the Office 365 ProPlus that comes with Microsoft 365 can be seen in Table 6.1.

TABLE 6.1 Office 2019 vs. Office 365 ProPlus

Office 2019	Office 365 ProPlus
Limited in-client collaboration	Real time co-authoring, @mentions, etc.
Limited cloud integration	Cloud and AI powered features
Static features; subset of ProPlus	Richer and better every month
Security and quality updates only	Security that evolves with threats
One PC per license	Five PCs/Macs + five tablets/mobile + web

At Ignite 2017 (and reiterated in the blog article https://techcommunity.microsoft .com/t5/Windows-IT-Pro-Blog/ Changes-to-Office-and-Windows-servicing-and-support/ba-p/151509), Microsoft explained that, going forward, all Office products will no longer ship anymore as an MSI.

And good riddance. See my Group Policy book (www.GPanswers.com/book) for a whole chapter in dealing with all the problems with Office as an MSI. That said, if I revise my Group Policy book, that chapter will be out the window.

Anyway, Office 365 is now only the "Click-to-Run" version, which will download what's needed on-demand directly from Microsoft and keep itself updated for features. Remember, the stand-alone Office 2019 is basically "done and baked" and won't update for features, only fixes. And once it's activated (Internet or offline), it doesn't have to check in with Microsoft ever again.

But, Office 2019 and Office 365 are sooooo closely related that if you already have Office 2019, it should be a reasonably quick jump to Office 365. You can learn more about this idea in the Ignite 2018 session BRK3260: What's new in Microsoft Office 2019 for IT deployment. (Remember to search for "BRK3260" on YouTube.)

Also, in that same session, they dropped a little micro bombshell (on me at least any-way). For years, and I mean years and years, Microsoft recommended installing the 32-bit versions of Office on 32-bit or 64-bit machines. In that same talk, at time index 26:00, you can see where they go on record and change that recommendation to now deploying 64-bit most of the time. Clean machines will get whatever you tell them, but existing machines will upgrade to the same bitness (I just love that word). And, as you might expect, if you want to add Visio or Project, be sure to add the same bit-level as the underlying Office software that matches what you're planting on the machine. You might be thinking of two questions:

- Should I switch?
- How do I switch?

Well, the answer to the "Should you switch?" question is maybe. Unless you have some known plug-ins that are 32-bit only (and actually break under 64-bit), then you should at least test-run 64-bit and then phase it in. As to the "How do I switch?" question, well, you'll see in a minute the flag to remove any, and I mean any, previous Office distributions. When that is checked, the machine is "Office naked" and then you can dictate whatever you want at that point: 32-bit or 64-bit Office 365.

Ironically, what was once one of the hardest apps to deploy is hovering toward the easi-est. Where it took maybe 80 billion clicks to get Office packaged in just the right way, it now takes mere moments to get (the basics) of Office rolled out via Intune, which should satisfy almost all requirements. I cannot guarantee that some obscure Office thingamabob your company needs isn't going to be missing in the Intune UI for deployment.

Here are the basic steps to deploy Office to a collection of computers or users.

In Intune, select "Client apps" (seen in Figure 6.1), and then select "Add app" (seen in Figure 6.2), and select "Office 365 Suite - Windows 10 (see Figure 6.40).

FIGURE 6.40   Selecting Office 365 Suite for Windows 10

When you do, you'll then have three categories of items to configure as seen in Figure 6.41:

- Configure App Suite ("Select Office apps to be assigned")
- App Suite Information ("Configure the app suite information")
- App Suite Settings ("Configure installation options for the app suite")

FIGURE 6.41   Preparing to configure an Office deployment

Let's go through each one by one.

 The page where Microsoft's descriptions of all these settings live is https://docs.microsoft.com/en-us/intune/apps-add-office365.

For the "Select Office apps to be assigned," I'm going to select only Excel, Word, and OneDrive Desktop (we'll use OneDrive Desktop later). You can see this in Figure 6.42.

FIGURE 6.42   Selecting which Office apps you want to deploy

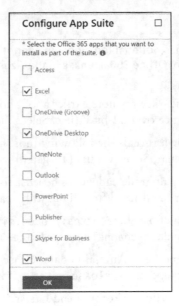

Most of the information on App Suite Information blade is either optional or self-explanatory. You can see my entries in Figure 6.43.

FIGURE 6.43   App suite Information

Then, on the App Suite Settings blade, you have the most decisions to make. Let's briefly check out each one in this blade.

WARNING   If this section is not enabled, and you cannot fill it out, then you might need to first specify Office 356 licenses in the Azure portal.

Office Version: 32-bit or 64-bit   See my note earlier about how the recommended tide has turned to now using 64-bit Office over 32-bit Office. Select the one you need.

Update Channel   This pulldown reveals the following (not shown) options, Monthly, Monthly (Targeted), Semi-Annual, Semi-Annual (Targeted).

This dictates the download and upgrade cadence. The least risky one is Semi-Annual, which is twice a year in January and July after all monthly features are rolled up.

You can learn more about each choice here: https://docs.microsoft.com/en-us/ deployoffice/overview-of-update-channels-for-office-365-proplus.

You can also see each month and Semi-Annual update release notes here: https://docs .microsoft.com/en-us/officeupdates/release-notes-office365-proplus.

Version to Install: Latest or Specific.   I recommend Latest. This way, you absolve yourself from having to worry about keeping computers up-to-date, it's just all automatic.

Remove other versions of Office (MSI) from end-user devices.   This is an amazing feature that's built into Office 365 and is a single toggle here in Intune. The underlying feature's doc can be found at https://docs.microsoft.com/en-us/deployoffice/ upgrade-from-msi-version.

This is also known as RemoveMSI (you'll see this in a bit).

The quick notes on this are that, yes, this will do what it says and seek and destroy many/most previously installed MSI versions of Office … all the way back as far as Office has ever gone.

This is a seriously smart move by Microsoft and a hugely powerful feature.

Think about it: In one click, you could be rolling out the latest Office across a whole fleet of machines with older versions of Office. But then, on the other hand, what if they are using some Microsoft Access 97 database that runs the whole accounting department? (Don't laugh. I *regularly* see this.)

As such, you should review the URL above because it explains in excruciating detail what will and won't be removed (such as it will remove Lync 2013 and Access 97 but won't remove the non-MSI click-to-run Office 2016).

Automatically accept the app end-user license agreement.   This does what it says and removes this small burden from the end user. Some companies require this to absolve their employees from accepting the EULA, and instead this shifts the legal stuff to the company deploying the software.

Use shared computer activation. If you have users who roam from machine to machine, this is the option for you. The page where Microsoft's descriptions of all these settings live is at https://docs.microsoft.com/en-us/DeployOffice/ overview-of-shared-computer-activation-for-office-365-proplus.

There are a lot of details here about sharing licensing tokens, what happens when no one logs on for 30 days, and other details you'll want to know about.

Languages Office will upgrade to the same language as already installed on the machine (if any) or the OS language. You can add additional languages if you need to here.

You can see my settings in Figure 6.44.

FIGURE 6.44 Office App Suite Settings blade

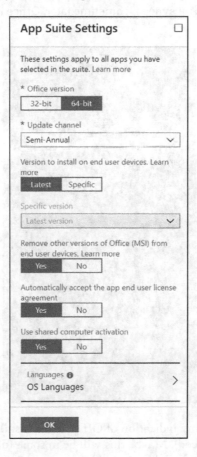

There's not much more to it than that, which is a nice change of pace.

What is missing, as you can tell, is the ability to make this more custom. For instance, maybe you want to uninstall every old Office application on the endpoint, but keep Access 97 so the accounting department doesn't lose their mind.

As of this writing, you cannot do that. There's no way to teach Intune that this is what you want. But, I'm reasonably sure that by the time you read this, you'll have some ability to feed Intune an Office configuration XML to perform special magic. See the sidebar titled "Office Deployment Tool and Office Policy Configuration Tool."

After you've got the profile, then assign it to users or machines, and ... wait for the magic to happen. In my example, I can see Word and Excel added to the Windows 10 Start Menu as seen in Figure 6.45 as well as Settings ➤ Apps & Features (or the older Add/Remove Programs in Control Panel).

FIGURE 6.45   After you've synced, sometime later, Office is installed according to your specifications.

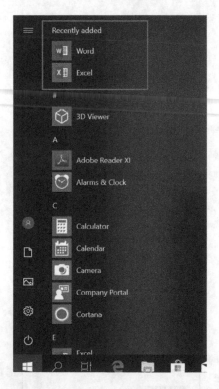

However, I didn't notice any indication of Office being installed via MDM in the settings reports (basic or advanced). Maybe this will be in some future Windows MDM reporting update, but I really don't know.

But, you can see some leftover breadcrumbs from the install. One place to go is the Registry of the endpoint (as admin) and check out HKLM\Software\Microsoft\OfficeCSP\ and look at anything in there. Here's what mine looks like:

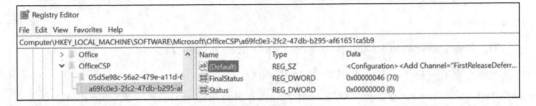

In my examples, I have two keys with GUIDs and in those keys some values. The one I have highlighted here shows three things:

Default   If you look inside this, you'll see all the parameters you used to install the software, like release channel, edition, the flags used for `RemoveMSI`, and so on. Copying and pasting here so you can see what I mean, it looks like this:

```
<Configuration><Add Channel="FirstReleaseDeferred" ForceUpgrade="TRUE"
 OfficeClientEdition="64"><Product ID="O365ProPlusRetail">
<ExcludeApp ID="Access" /><ExcludeApp ID="Groove" />
<ExcludeApp ID="InfoPath" /><ExcludeApp ID="Lync" />
<ExcludeApp ID="OneNote" /><ExcludeApp ID="Outlook" />
<ExcludeApp ID="PowerPoint" /><ExcludeApp ID="Publisher" />
<ExcludeApp ID="SharePointDesigner" /><Language ID="MatchOS" />
</Product></Add><Display Level="None" AcceptEULA="TRUE" />
<RemoveMSI All="TRUE" /><Property Name="SharedComputerLicensing" Value="1" />
<LastExecuteTime>1/1/2019 3:50:15 AM</LastExecuteTime></Configuration>
```

Status   My status is 0. That is reasonably common to mean "good" or no errors.

FinalStatus   My final status is 70, which everyone *also* knows is "succeeded."

Wait a minute. You mean you didn't know that error code 70 meant succeeded?

Okay. I didn't either. But I looked at the Office CSP and the codes are right in there! Other error and status codes can be found on that page too, which is quite useful if you're wondering why things are failing or not installing as you expect.

That page for reference is found at https://docs.microsoft.com/en-us/windows/ client-management/mdm/office-csp.

Office Deployment Tool and Office Policy Configuration Tool

Office configuration is going to the cloud.

In two pieces:

- The way you create an XML to manipulate Office's configurations
- The way you can possibly set policy settings

Let's talk about creating Office XML configuration files first. Instead of downloading a deployment tool, then massaging an XML file to death, now the tool is online at `https://config.office.com/`. You can start fresh and make customizations, or import an existing file and then after you're done, export those customizations. You can see the Office Customization Tool here.

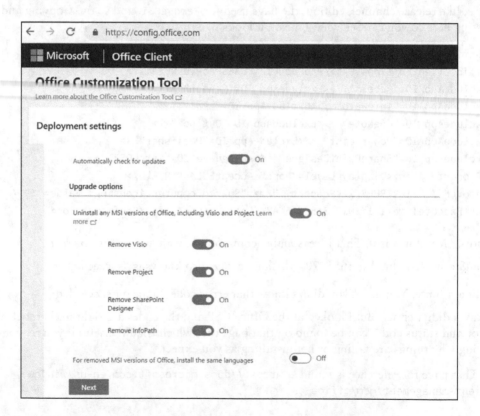

As of now, this tool is only able to configure Office 2019, because only with Office 2019 can you pass it an XML file. For Office 365 with Intune, there's no way to do that now—*now* being the operative word.

Most of the UI you would need that configures Office is already in Microsoft Intune. It's not *all* of the bells and whistles, but quite a few. For the remaining weird things, you should (soon) be able to craft an Office XML using this tool and then pass the XML file to Intune.

The second Office-in-the-cloud tool is the Office Client Policy Service, or OCPS for short. OCPS enables domain-joined and non-domain joined machines, MDM or no MDM. Basically, it's a way to centrally create and manage Office policies for any Office in your control. In order to access the OCPS, your Azure tenant needs Office 365 ProPlus, and you must log on with your Global Admin, Security Admin, or Desktop Analytics admin credentials. (If you try this without having an Office 365 ProPlus subscription, you will get an indiscriminate error message.)

The OCPS is found at `https://config.office.com/officesettings`. When you're there, you get to select an Azure AD group, as seen here, and then select some policies to configure.

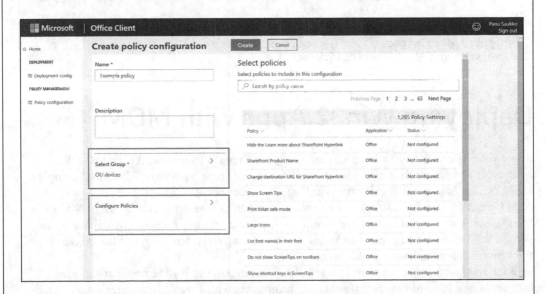

Now your computers running Office 365 anywhere just "phone home" and check for policies (using the same mechanism that Office itself uses to check for updates). It will check in every 90 minutes. The ports and URLs are documented at `https://docs.microsoft .com/en-us/office365/enterprise/urls-and-ip-address-ranges` (just look for "Office policy management").

Note also that if there's a conflict between OCPS and Group Policy, then OCPS wins.

Note that not all settings are in OCPS, today, only user-side items, and only user-side items that have basic values.

OCPS is only for Office 365 and isn't for volume licensed versions of Office like Office 2019. For those versions of Office, you'll still need to use the Office Customization Tool and XML files.

Last, if you want to learn more about deploying Office 2019 in a traditional way (as opposed to Office 365 via Windows Intune), here are the resources:

- **YouTube:** What's new in Microsoft Office 2019 for IT deployment - BRK3260

- https://docs.microsoft.com/en-us/deployoffice/office2019/deploy

- https://config.office.com/

And if you wanted to learn more about the Office Client Policy Service (with a good video), check out:

    https://techcommunity.microsoft.com/t5/Office-365-Blog/
    Announcing-the-new-cloud-based-policy-management-service-for/ba-p/310405

The official docs are at:

    https://docs.microsoft.com/en-us/deployoffice/
    overview-office-client-policy-service

Deploying Win32 Apps with MDM

Every year Microsoft has a big announcement with regard to Intune. At Ignite 2018, Microsoft's big announcement was the ability to use Intune to deploy .EXEs and complex MSIs, which Microsoft is collectively calling Win32 applications.

Where is this useful? Well, lots of applications don't come prepackaged as an MSI or MSIX. Some key ones like this are Adobe Reader (and up until recently, Mozilla Firefox). Why some vendors don't ship as an MSI is a bit of a mystery, since almost the whole rest of the universe ships software as MSIs, but … okay.

Back to the announcement at Ignite 2018 about deploying Win32 applications via Intune. When I heard that this was the big announcement, I was a little puzzled, because there was nothing stopping us from already (pretty much) doing this by wrapping up our EXEs into an MSIX, and that was already supported before the announcement.

The general idea (to repeat something I expressed before) is that I would still recommend attempting to use an MSIX to do your deployments first, instead of what we're about to talk about in the following section. While it takes a little while to wrap a .EXE or your complex .MSI application into an MSIX, there is a big benefit in (near guaranteed) proper removal of the MSIX package, not to mention delta downloads and the other MSIX benefits I already mentioned.

But again, not every package will be a great candidate for MSIX wrapping as I expressed earlier.

What's interesting about the Win32 deployment capability is that it's something that's not native to MDM (like .MSI or .MSIX), but something that Intune added on *to MDM*.

I know this is weird, because both of these things (the MDM engine and Intune) are both from Microsoft, right? But it doesn't really work that way internally. Internally, there's the MDM engine folks (and their technology is generally available for any MDM vendor). And then there's the Intune folks who use what the MDM engine folks provide and also from time to time need to sidestep and/or add on their own functionality.

Back in Chapter 1, in the section entitled "Extending Your MDM Services with Third-Party Tools," I talked about this. The idea that anyone can add a little magic to Windows itself via the MDM platform. I mentioned that Intune is already doing this through the Intune Management Extension. And I mentioned that (today) the Intune Management Extension has two features: One is running PowerShell scripts, and this is the second feature, deploying Win32 applications. Maybe in the future they will add more features, but these are the two that ship right now.

Here's the basic steps to get this to work:

- Download an .EXE application. At the beginning of the chapter, I recommended Firefox ESR for this purpose, but you should be able to download anything that's an .EXE installer and have it handy.
- Download the Win32 Content Prep Tool to wrap up the .EXE (more on this in a second).
- Repackage the application.
- Configure Intune to consume the application.
- Deploy the application to a target group.

So, that's the gist. Let's get started.

Note that I'll use the terms *EXE* and *Win32* interchangeably in the following sections.

Microsoft Intune Win32 Content Prep Tool

Because the MDM engine itself doesn't have a native way to consume Win32 applications, Windows Intune needed to enable Win32 application deployments as a reality.

That is, the Intune team enlightened Intune to accept a new package format called .intunewin.

How do you get .EXEs into the .intunewin format? Well, the Microsoft Intune Win32 Content Prep Tool, of course! (Note that this tool was initially known as a the Win32 App Packaging Tool.)

So start out and download it at:

```
https://github.com/Microsoft/Intune-Win32-App-Packaging-Tool
```

You can see how to do that in Figure 6.46.

FIGURE 6.46   Downloading the Microsoft Intune Win32 Content Prep Tool

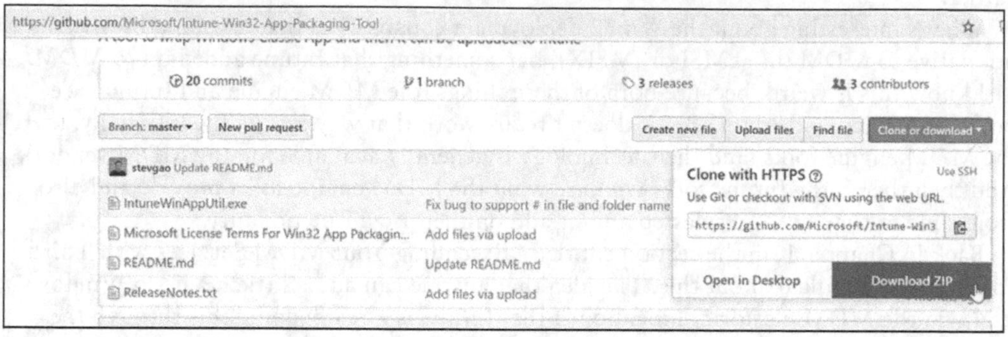

Unpack the contents to your management machine. I'll put mine in
c:\IntuneWin32PackagingApp.

Gathering All the Needed Items in One Place

Earlier, you downloaded Firefox ESR's .EXE (not the Firefox .MSIs).

I'm going to assume on your management machine you have that in c:\FirefoxSetup.

But maybe you also want to make sure all the configuration of that .EXE is exactly to
your liking. If you needed to perform an installation of Firefox ESR again and again by
hand, you might make a .CMD file to do that. Well, let's do that here.

In c:\FirefoxSetup, use Notepad to create a file called Install.cmd. (Careful not to
save the file as .TXT.)

Then, after looking at the Firefox ESR documentation (https://firefox-source-docs
.mozilla.org/browser/installer/windows/installer/FullConfig.html), there's not a
lot I would personally want to change except for maybe one or two things. Maybe I don't
want the Firefox Maintenance Service (also known as the upgrade service) to be installed.
The default is that this will install. And maybe I don't want a Desktop shortcut to be created either; again, the default is that I will see a Desktop shortcut.

In the future, Mozilla is saying these will be nicely made into command-line options,
but for now, we need to create an .INI with the switches we want. (And even if they do get
these into command-line switches, this procedure will likely still work.)

So, the command I would run would be:

```
Firefox Setup 60.3.0esr.exe /S /INI=c:\FirefoxSetup\install.ini
```

Except that's not going to work. Because after this is deployed by MDM,
c:\FirefoxSetup isn't going to exist on the endpoint.

But there's a secret way to say, "Point to my INI file wherever it happens to be unpacked
to." Here's the secret method (and stick with me because it's weird):

```
Firefox Setup 60.3.0esr.exe /S /INI="%~dp0install.ini"
```

So you're reading it right: %~dp0 and then you smash the install.ini filename against it (no spaces) and put it in quotes. %~dp0 is a special variable available within a batch file and will expand to express the drive letter and path in which that batch file is located.

Magic. Total magic.

Okay. Next up, I need to make the install.ini, which describes my desires, namely something that looks like this:

```
[Install]
DesktopShortcut=False
MaintenanceService=False
```

And save it out as c:\FirefoxSetup\install.ini.

The end result will be all three elements in the folder as seen in Figure 6.47.

FIGURE 6.47   Have your setup and your install command in the same folder.

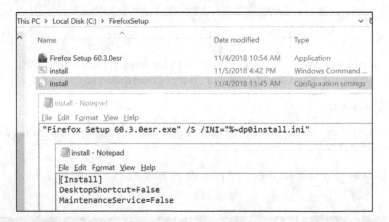

You might want to pretest that you have the install.cmd and install.ini all correct and perfect before continuing. That way, if you've made any mistakes or typos, you know it and can get it out of the way now, before going on. When you precheck the running of it, you should see Firefox installed, the Mozilla Maintenance Service should be *absent* in Add/Remove Programs, and Firefox should not put a shortcut on the Desktop.

You'll also need to know and have handy the product version of your application. You'll see why a little later when we try to "detect" if Firefox is already installed on the machine or not. Get this value by right-clicking over the Firefox.exe itself (not any shortcut) and then check out the product version as seen in Figure 6.48.

FIGURE 6.48   Seeing Firefox installed and getting its file version

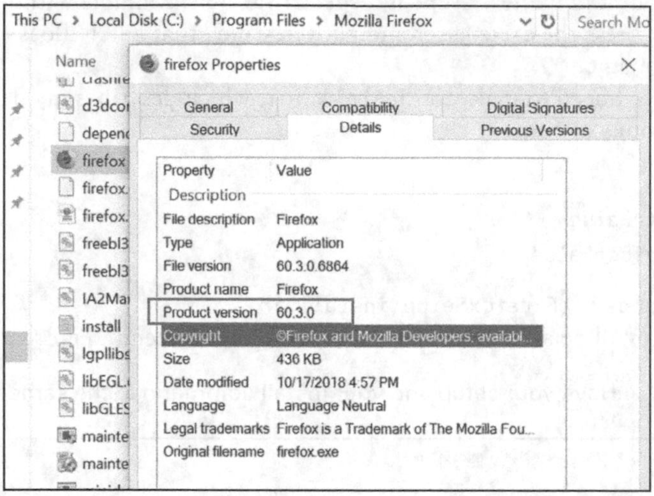

You also need to know the uninstall command for your application (whatever that is). For Firefox, it took me a while to figure out, but the command is

```
"%programfiles%\mozilla firefox\uninstall\helper.exe" -ms
```

And you can see me testing it out in Figure 6.49, and … yep. Sure enough, Firefox was nuked when I did this.

FIGURE 6.49   Pretest the uninstall routine of your app.

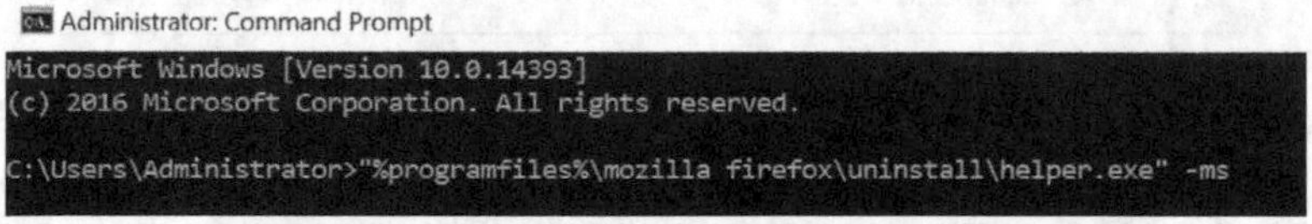

Again, it's best to get all this testing out of the way by hand before moving on.

Preparing the Win32 Application Contents

Now it's time to run the Win32 Content Prep Tool's file, which is named IntuneWinAppUtil.exe. You need to open a command prompt and change the directory to where you unpacked your Win32 tool. Then run it.

When you do, you'll specify the following:

- The source folder, like c:\firefoxsetup
- The setup file, like "Firefox Setup 60.3.0esr.exe"
- The output folder, like c:\firefoxout

You can see this in Figure 6.50.

FIGURE 6.50   Running the Win32 Content Prep Tool

```
Administrator: Command Prompt - IntuneWinAppUtil.exe
C:\IntuneWin32PackagingApp>IntuneWinAppUtil.exe
Please specify the source folder: c:\firefoxsetup\
Please specify the setup file: "Firefox Setup 60.3.0esr.exe"
Please specify the output folder: c:\firefoxout\
```

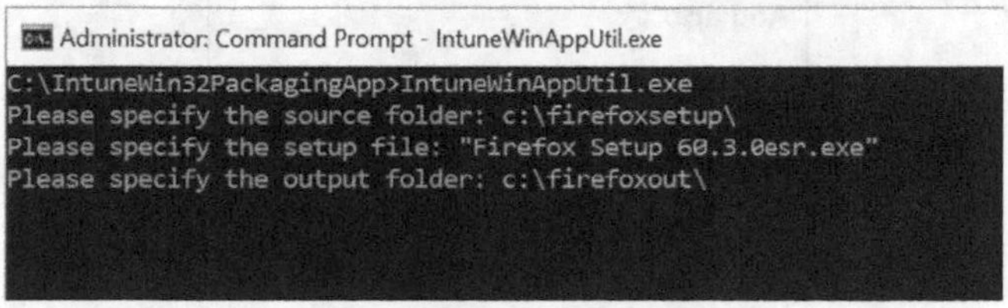

When it's all over, you should see a lot of output fly by, and a nice "Done!!!" message appears as shown in Figure 6.51.

FIGURE 6.51   The Win32 Content Prep Tool finishes.

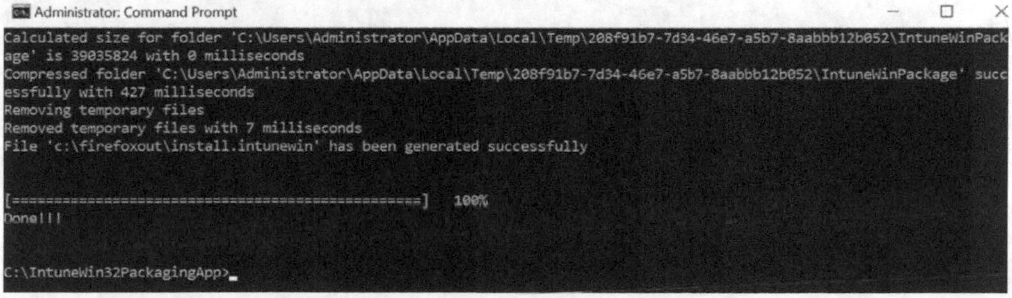

```
Administrator: Command Prompt                                                          —  □  ×
Calculated size for folder 'C:\Users\Administrator\AppData\Local\Temp\208f91b7-7d34-46e7-a5b7-8aabbb12b052\IntuneWinPack
age' is 39035824 with 0 milliseconds
Compressed folder 'C:\Users\Administrator\AppData\Local\Temp\208f91b7-7d34-46e7-a5b7-8aabbb12b052\IntuneWinPackage' succ
essfully with 427 milliseconds
Removing temporary files
Removed temporary files with 7 milliseconds
File 'c:\firefoxout\install.intunewin' has been generated successfully

[================================================]   100%
Done!!!

C:\IntuneWin32PackagingApp>
```

You can see the result of the package in the c:\firefoxout folder, which is a single file called install.intunewin, as shown in Figure 6.52.

FIGURE 6.52   Final result of the Win32 Content Prep Tool

```
Administrator: Command Prompt
C:\IntuneWin32PackagingApp>cd \firefoxout

C:\firefoxout>dir
 Volume in drive C has no label.
 Volume Serial Number is 0444-149D

 Directory of C:\firefoxout

11/06/2018  12:03 PM    <DIR>          .
11/06/2018  12:03 PM    <DIR>          ..
11/05/2018  08:38 PM        39,036,298 Firefox Setup 60.3.0esr.intunewin
               1 File(s)     39,036,298 bytes
               2 Dir(s)  26,455,040,000 bytes free

C:\firefoxout>
```

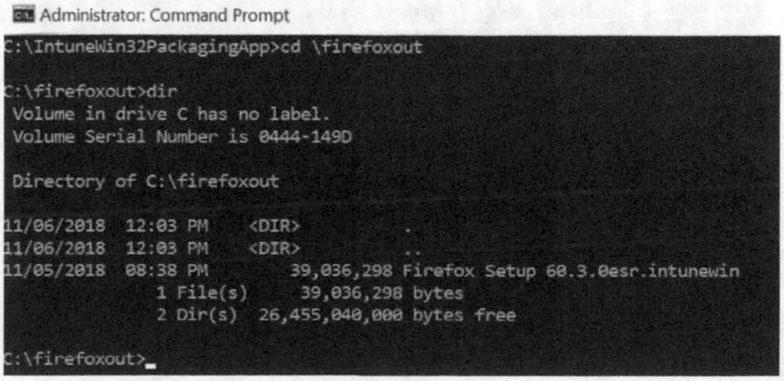

Hang on to this file; you'll use it in a minute.

Add the .intunewin File to Intune

Back in Intune and Client - Apps, once again, click Add. Then within "Add app" you'll select "Windows app (Win32)" as seen in Figure 6.53. Though likely by the time you read this it will not be in preview any longer.

FIGURE 6.53   Select Windows app (Win32) to deploy Win32 apps.

When you do, you'll see an array of items you need to configure, which we'll go over in this section (see Figure 6.54).

FIGURE 6.54   The categories of items you need to configure for Win32 apps

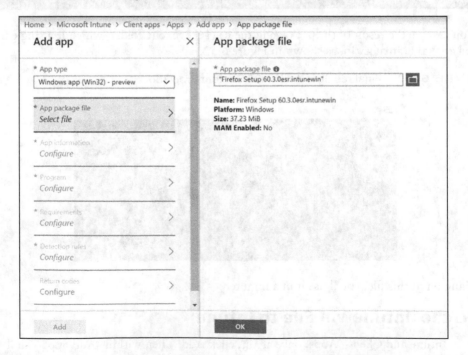

Those items are as follows:

- App package file
- App information
- Program
- Requirements
- Detection rules
- Return codes

App Package File   First things first: Feed Intune your .intunewin file. Click OK and up it goes. The limitation is 8 GB for an uploaded file, which seems reasonably sufficient. Rumor has it that the limit is being increased to 20 GB soon.

App Information (not shown)   Here you mostly just set up the name and description and publisher. Some other information is optional.

Program   You can see these entries in Figure 6.55. This is where you put in your install and uninstall command. I like to put everything in quotes because chances are it will almost always work better. In this example, I'll use the `"install.cmd"` command I created for install and the `"%programfiles%\mozilla firefox\uninstall\helper.exe" -ms` I figured out for uninstall.

FIGURE 6.55   Specify the CMD file you created earlier to install, and the string you discovered would uninstall Firefox.

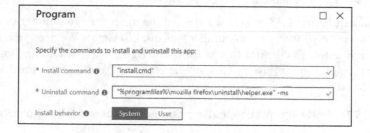

Requirements   Seen in Figure 6.56, most items are self-explanatory and many are optional. But you can specify if, say, a 64-bit package maybe shouldn't run on a 32-bit system. You can also specify a minimum Windows 10 level, like 1607.

FIGURE 6.56 Minimum requirements are "Operating system architecture" and "Minimum operating system."

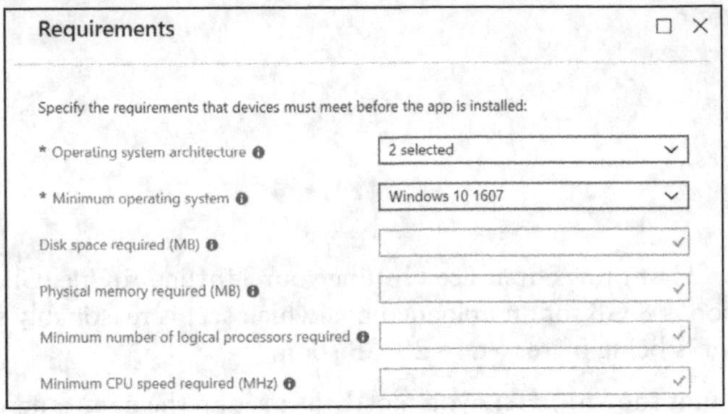

Detection Rules   There are a handful of ways to detect an application, such as if a Registry item exists or a file or folder exists.

Picking the right detection method is important, and you should understand how the version properties will change between different versions of the app. This versioning must be accounted for in the detection method you choose or users might not have their apps updated to newer versions as intended.

For me, it is simply easiest to get the application installed by hand on the machine and poke around to see what would make a good detection rule.

Remember back in Figure 6.48, where we verified the inner version number of Firefox's properties? We saw my inner version number was 60.3.0. Great! We need that tidbit of information right now. You'll enter this as shown in Figure 6.57. Warning: Don't do what I did the first time and (oops!) use Firefox's "File version." You're after "Product version," not "File version"!

FIGURE 6.57 Enter information that is guaranteed to detect your application.

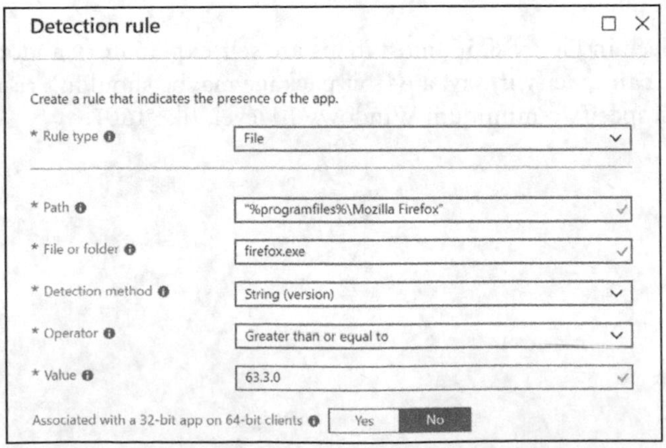

Additionally, since we're using the pure 64-bit version of Firefox, you'll maintain the "Associated with a 32-bit app on 64-bit clients" as No as also seen in Figure 6.57. In short, you only need to flip this switch when you're deploying a 32-bit app on 64-bit machines and not any other combination. (I made a mistake the first time I tried this, so don't do what I did.)

Another useful detection method is MSI product code and knowing a particular MSI package is in fact installed on the machine. That doesn't come into play here, since we're deploying an EXE. But in case you're curious, here are two methods of getting a package's MSI product codes:

- After you have it installed, you can run a one-line PowerShell script to grab all products and all codes. Here's one I tested that worked for me:

```
get-wmiobject Win32_Product |
Format-Table IdentifyingNumber, Name, LocalPackage -AutoSize
```

- Before the product is installed, use a free tool we have on PolicyPak.com/freetools.

Note that you can also go bananas and write your own home-grown detection script. This might be if you needed to run a PowerShell script to let you know, that, yes, indeed, DogFood.ini was present and at line 23 it said "Ruff." But chances are you won't need to craft a detection script like that.

Return Codes   Return codes can be seen in Figure 6.58. This configuration item is pre-packaged with the most common return codes; but if you happen to know if your application might throw a particular value, you can set it up here.

FIGURE 6.58   Return codes

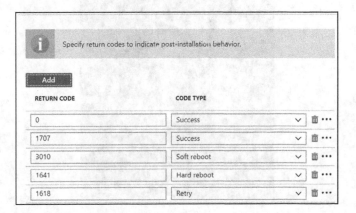

Assign the App and See Results

When I tried this the first time, I made a few mistakes.

Mistake #1 was that I used the file version instead of the (correct) product version.

Mistake #2 was that I flipped the "Associated with a 32-bit app on 64-bit clients" to Yes, which I didn't need to do.

As such, my first time up at bat was a failure.

But yours won't be. If you carefully followed along.

In the Assignments blade of the application, which we configured earlier, make it a Required application that is assigned to all devices (similar to what you see in Figure 6.36).

Now it's time to sync back to Intune and wait for the magic. First the Intune Management Extension will install. Then, Firefox should install reasonably quickly using the Intune Management Extension as the conduit. The result can be seen in Figure 6.59.

FIGURE 6.59   The Microsoft Intune Management Extension and Firefox were installed.

Now, once the Intune Management Extension service is installed (shown in Figure 6.60), it's automatically configured to check once every hour. Or if you restart the service manually on a machine, you're forcing it to check again. As far as I know there are no plans to change the polling period or make it configurable.

FIGURE 6.60   The (now installed) Microsoft Intune Management Extension, which is in charge of Win32 apps and PowerShell scripts

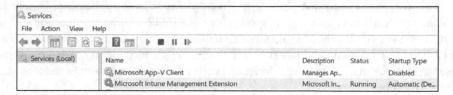

Other Win32 Deployment Examples, Troubleshooting, and Final Thoughts

Getting this to work first time out of the gate can actually be easier than I attempted to do here with my Firefox and .INI file example. To be honest, I used a slightly-harder-than-it-had-to-be example to give you something interesting to try.

If you wanted to, you could deploy single, simple .EXEs or single .MSIs using the wrapper tool.

For a single .EXE, like Acrobat Reader, your install command might be something like "AcroRdrDC.exe" /sAll /rs /l /msi /norestart. And "AcroRdrDC.exe" /Sall / uninstall for the uninstall command as seen in Figure 6.61.

FIGURE 6.61   How to install and uninstall the AcroReader .EXE

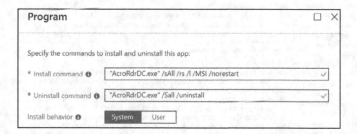

Or if you wanted to use single, simple .MSIs, you would again use the wrapper tool. But for MSIs, remember your install command will be something like what's shown here: You'll use MSIEXEC /I "yourapp.msi" /q for the install command and MSIEXEC /x {GUID} /q for the uninstall command.

Troubleshooting Win32 deployments starts with a single question: Did your machine get the Intune Management Extension Service installed as seen in Figures 6.59 and 6.60? If the service is absent, that means that your deployment of any Win32 applications simply won't work. That's the only bridge into your system for the Win32 deployment method.

Then, if you see the Intune Management Extension, you can assume Intune is at least trying to attempt to download the files. After that, there's a nice log in `c:\ProgramData\Microsoft\IntuneManagementExtension\Logs` called `IntuneManagementExtension.log` (and there could be others).

The log, however, is a little difficult to read unless you use the CMTrace tool (part of the SCCM Client tools, which are found inside any SCCM deployment). What's that? You don't have any SCCM and don't want to have to spin up SCCM just to get this little tool? Well, CMTrace is still part of System Center 2012 R2 Configuration Manager Toolkit and can be downloaded at `https://www.microsoft.com/en-us/download/details.aspx?id=50012`. Details can be found at `https://docs.microsoft.com/sccm/core/support/tools`.

In Figure 6.62, you can see me viewing the `IntuneManagementExtension.log` within CMTrace and also within Notepad.

FIGURE 6.62   The `IntuneManagmentExtension.log` in CMTrace and Notepad

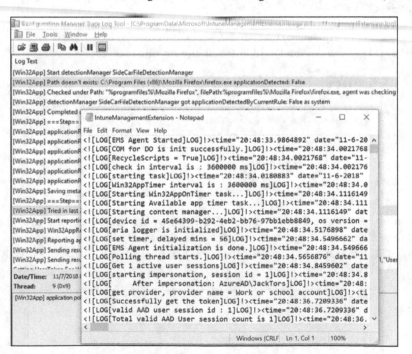

Here are my recommended resources on Win32 deployments:

- Start with the Win32 App Management docs here:
  `https://docs.microsoft.com/en-us/intune/apps-win32-app-management`.

- Continue onward with the Intune Management Extension docs here:
  `https://docs.microsoft.com/en-us/intune/intune-management-extension`.

- If you get in a jam with Win32 and/or Intune Management Extension, a three-part article by MVP Oliver Kieselbach has some excellent information that might help you squiggle out: `https://oliverkieselbach.com/2017/11/29/ deep-dive-microsoft-intune-management-extension-powershell-scripts/` (and his Part 2 and Part 3).

- Another article with Win32 applications and Intune can be found at `http://www.scconfigmgr.com/2018/09/24/ deploy-win32-applications-with-microsoft-intune/`.

- The talk at Ignite 2018 on this subject can be found by going to YouTube and looking for the keyword "BRK3285."

- Additionally, there is a way to pull Win32 application deployment logs back into Intune so you can see from a variety of machines "out in the field" maybe what has gone wrong. For these details (and other application installation troubleshooting steps) check out `https://docs.microsoft.com/en-us/intune/troubleshoot-app-install`.

Deploying Scripts with Your MDM Service

At Ignite 2017, there was a big announcement that Intune could now deploy PowerShell scripts. They touted that this facility would enable you to do the same kinds of work as Group Policy, and you can use it to push the same values that you might do natively with Group Policy.

I see where Microsoft was going with this, but I cannot recommend it.

For me, I wouldn't recommend you use the Intune Management Extension to hand-write scripts to emulate what Group Policy does and push Group Policy (or Group Policy Preferences' buttons). My advice would be to find the corresponding setting in MDM-land if it exists, and if it doesn't, use ADMX-backed policies next, and if it really doesn't exist, then use PolicyPak MDM to deploy all other required Group Policy and Group Policy Preferences settings.

But I am okay with running PowerShell scripts from time to time to, say, clean up a machine, fix a one-time problem, or (what I'm about to show you) deploy software; that makes sense to me.

All the major MDM players have the ability to run PowerShell scripts. It's built into Intune and Workspace ONE. But the MobileIron MDM service has an add-on to deploy PowerShell scripts called MobileIron Bridge.

If your MDM service (whatever it is) doesn't have any script ability, or if you find a limitation in your MDM's ability, then check out the section a little later on PolicyPak scripts, which might help you out a lot.

One interesting way to leverage an MDM service's ability to deploy scripts would be to run a script that literally brings down and installs software from a source on the Internet.

There are a few example scripts (from other MVP smart guys such as Aaron Parker and Eric Haavarstein) that I have found that do this:

- Install latest Notepad++:
  https://xenappblog.com/2018/download-and-install-latest-notepad/

- Install latest Citrix Receiver:
  https://stealthpuppy.com/deploy-citrix-receiver-intune/#.W3I6AOhJFbc

- Install latest Google Chrome Enterprise:
  https://xenappblog.com/2018/
  download-and-install-latest-google-chrome-enterprise/

- Install latest Mozilla Firefox ESR:
  https://xenappblog.com/2018/download-and-install-latest-mozilla-firefox/

- A gaggle of interesting ones at:
  https://github.com/haavarstein/Applications/tree/master/Misc

Sometimes these scripts are called *evergreen* scripts because they are run and always download the latest updated sources.

Deploying Scripts (That Deploy Software) with Intune

On the plus side, this is a unique way to just point a computer toward some application's source and when that computer gets born, or never has the script, then bingo! Those computers will magically just get the latest version of an application! On the minus side, you kind of lose control of testing the latest version of an application and *then* the ability to roll it out.

Additionally, you're at the mercy of the script maker to ensure that script is kept up-to-date, or maybe you are a PowerShell Rockstar and can keep these scripts maintained and up-to-date yourself. But, for me, that would be a challenge, since I'm a "Level 2 PowerShell Guy" and not "Level 9" like these guys. Said another way, if Eric or Aaron got hit by a bus and couldn't (or didn't want to) upgrade those scripts anymore, I would be out of luck.

Last, this PowerShell script deployment method only runs the script once or when the script is updated. So … okay. After you've deployed Firefox and Chrome and Citrix Receiver using this script method, that's it. You've done it one time, but it's not magically always kept up-to-date.

Performing the actual PowerShell script deployment is not hard. And, again, even though this example uses Intune, there are other MDM systems that will run PowerShell scripts.

In Intune, click on Device Configuration ➢ PowerShell scripts. Then Add PowerShell Script. The script will need to be in .PS1 format. Upload and configure it as seen in Figure 6.63. The only choices you have to make are if you want to run the script as System or User and if your script is signed, if you want Intune to run the script run only when signed and the signature is valid. The default of No and No as seen in Figure 6.63 is just fine for a test using a script I recommended earlier.

FIGURE 6.63   Uploading and configuring the Chrome evergreen download script

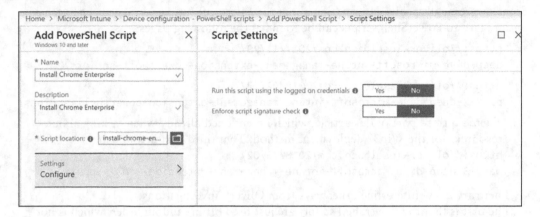

You can see the result of me running the "Install Google Chrome" and "Install Citrix Receiver" PowerShell scripts through Intune in Figure 6.64.

FIGURE 6.64   See the applications installed after Intune deploys the PowerShell scripts.

Troubleshooting the Intune Management Extension

Some awesome deep-dive information about the Microsoft Intune Management Extension with regard to PowerShell scripts can be found at the following pages:

- https://oliverkieselbach.com/2017/11/29/
  deep-dive-microsoft-intune-management-extension-powershell-scripts/

- https://oliverkieselbach.com/2018/02/12/
  part-2-deep-dive-microsoft-intune-management-extension-powershell-scripts/

- There's a third part of this article, which I mentioned already when talking about resources for the Win32 deployment method. That third part is found at https://oliverkieselbach.com/2018/10/02/
  part-3-deep-dive-microsoft-intune-management-extension-win32-apps/.

There are a few interesting takeaways from Oliver's investigations.

The first is that the PowerShell scripts are just fired off in random order, which is not ideal if you want to guarantee some "stacking order." There's also no way to specify when a script will fire off. Oliver has an interesting script-y workaround for it in that article as well.

PowerShell scripts have three attempts before giving up and failing, and then not retrying again. There are two workarounds from this as I see it if your PowerShell script fails, hangs, etc.

- Option 1 would be to fix the script, then kill the profile delivering the original script and then redeploy. That would work since Intune would see it as a new script.

- Option 2 is to twiddle HKLM \ SOFTWARE \ Microsoft \ IntuneManagementExtension \ Policies \ {UserGUID} \ {ScriptGUID} \ DownloadCount and Result. You could set DownloadCount back to 0 and delete the value in Result, leaving it as an empty string. Then when you restart the Intune management service, it should attempt a retry. This second option is recommended during your testing. For instance, let's pretend you had a script that cleaned up the hard drive, but it kept failing over and over again. Okay, well, before you mass roll it out to your 10,000 machines, really make sure it's working on one or two, and if you get into trouble during your testing, you now know how to reset the retry count.

Then you're good to go for your rollout to 10,000 machines.

Limitations with the Intune Management Extension

There are some real limitations with the PowerShell functionality (not just in deploying software, but all around). Here's a list of the current limitations of Intune's PowerShell functionality (which may change over time).

- First, the only script type supported is PowerShell. I *don't* expect this to change over time.

- Scripts are limited to 200 KB. That's not a lot of space if you have a long script.

- Scripts are typically applied and run only once.
    - In Intune, the script attempts to run three times, and if it never succeeds, then that's it.
    - If the script does succeed, it runs one time, and that's it.
    - Scripts are only applied again when the script itself is updated.
- Scripts have no order; they are fired off in random order.
- All logic must be contained within the script. If you want a script to only run on laptops but be on a particular IP range, you have to figure that out *inside* the script.
- Scripts can only call the 32-bit version of PowerShell, so 64-bit cmdlets cannot be used.
- When the script is removed, whatever that script did just "stays around." Maybe that's good, or maybe you want to run something to "undo" or uninstall.

Will Microsoft overcome these limitations? Maybe.

But if you need to overcome these limitations right now, you can check out PolicyPak Scripts, which works alongside Intune or any MDM service to overcome a myriad of problems.

PolicyPak Scripts and Your MDM Service

As you saw, Intune (and other MDM services) have a way to deploy PowerShell scripts. But the limitations might prevent it from being useful when being used day-to-day.

To overcome the in-the-MDM-box limitations, you might want to check out PolicyPak Scripts, which is part of PolicyPak MDM, PolicyPak Group Policy, and PolicyPak Cloud.

When using it alongside an MDM service like Intune, PolicyPak Scripts increases your reach over what can be done with PowerShell natively:

- Scripts can be deployed per user or per computer side.
- Scripts can be .VBS (VisualBasic), JavaScript (.JS), Shell (.BAT or .CMD) or PowerShell.
- Scripts can be applied once, always (every hour), or once again (when retriggered).
- There is no size restriction in the script.
- You can order the scripts.
- It leverages Item Level Targeting (ILT) to detect when conditions are true (instead of you trying to bake it into your script).

The biggest superpower of PolicyPak Scripts is the ability to deploy "On Apply" and "On Revert" scripts. For instance, in Figure 6.65, I'm dropping a shortcut on the Desktop when the script applies.

FIGURE 6.65 PolicyPak Scripts lets you deploy batch, PowerShell, VB Script, or JavaScript type scripts.

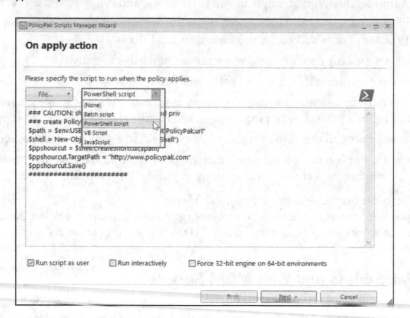

And in Figure 6.66, I'm configuring the same policy to run a script to delete the shortcut when the policy *no longer applies*.

FIGURE 6.66 You can decide what script to run when a policy no longer applies.

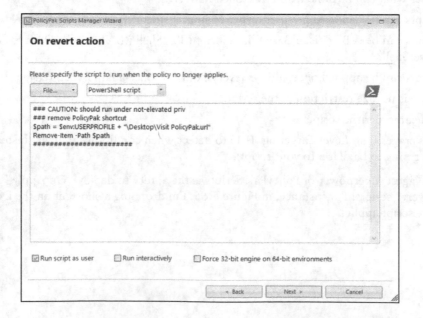

And, the "On Apply" script can be run Always, Once, or Once when forced, as shown in Figure 6.67. These settings are nice depending on your situation, say if users keep deleting your shortcut or make some change you want to always be reapplying.

FIGURE 6.67   When to apply or reapply scripts with PolicyPak Scripts Manager

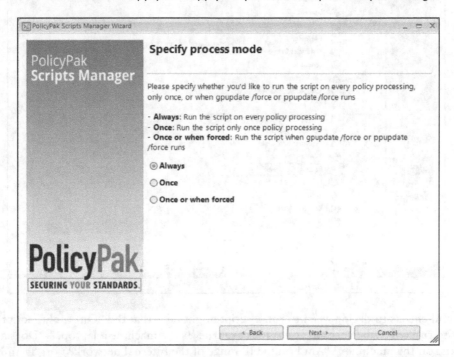

There's a lot more to PolicyPak Scripts Manager. In fact, my favorite feature is the ability to tap into Item Level Targeting to fire off the script when a condition (or multiple conditions) are true. Here's the Item Level Targeting editor built into PolicyPak Scripts (and, also, every other aspect of PolicyPak, by the way).

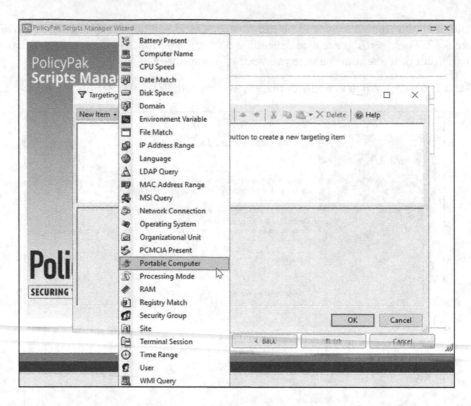

Useful checks to decide when to run a script might be is that the "On Apply" script can be set to run only when certain conditions are true (Is the machine a laptop?" "Does a file exist on the machine?" "Am I on the IP range of the Internal network?" or "Is an MSI application actually already installed on the machine?"). Only then will the "On Apply" script fire off. And if the condition is no longer satisfied, then the "On Revert" script then fires off. You can see a specific demo of PolicyPak Scripts alongside an MDM system at the PolicyPak Script Manager page of https://www.policypak.com/products/scripts-manager.html.

Delivering Other Software and Files with MDM (Using PolicyPak File Delivery Manager)

It's going to be hard not to "show off" too much, but I'll try my best not to brag. And if you want to skip over this discussion because it's about PolicyPak/pay software, that's cool. But it's not cool to miss out!

One of the components of PolicyPak is the PolicyPak File Delivery Manager, or FDM for short.

FDM works with both your on-prem systems via Group Policy and with your MDM system. When used on-prem, you can think of it like "Robocopy meets Group Policy." But I'm not going to talk about that here. If you want to see that in action, check out PolicyPak File Deliver Manager at PolicyPak.com.

But FDM can also be used alongside an MDM service in some really unique ways that the in-MDM delivery methods cannot. Let's explore three interesting scenarios PolicyPak File Delivery Manager can do, that would be not possible using MDM by itself.

Downloading Unusual File Types

It's true that in this chapter we spent time installing software, but that's not the only thing you need to download and get to end computers. Sometimes you might need to get a file—maybe a large file—to your computer population.

Maybe this is a large movie file, a CAD file, or an updated database of contacts or some other structured or unstructured data.

With PolicyPak File Delivery Manager, getting these unusual files to your endpoints is a piece of cake.

You simply stage the file on an HTTP server. The best ones are those that support Content-R and Content-Length headers. For example, Amazon S3 supports these nicely.

You can see an example of this in Figure 6.68.

FIGURE 6.68   PolicyPak File Delivery Manager

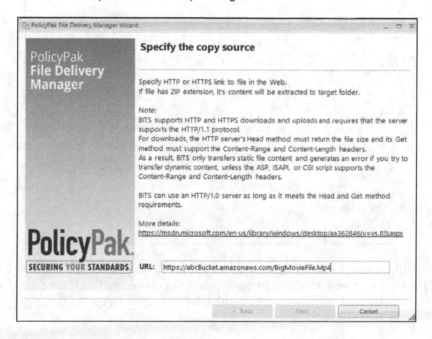

When you use PolicyPak File Delivery Manager with, say, Amazon S3, it will fetch the file and download it using the BITS protocol, which will "drip drip drip" the content from the source to the destination. Even if the person interrupts the transfer, say, by closing the lid on their laptop, then going into a submarine then returning to shore 10 days later ... BITS just says, "The show will go on!" and just keep downloading the file again the next time the Internet is restored.

Learn more about BITS at https://msdn.microsoft.com/en-us/library/ windows/desktop/bb968799(v=vs.85).aspx.

Downloading .EXEs, .MSIs, or Unusual Software, Then Running a Script (and Cleaning Up When You're Done)

After PolicyPak File Delivery Manager has download a file, say, a movie file as in the previous example or an application installer like Notepad++, after the transfer is complete, you can run a process or a script. This is called a Post-Copy action and can be seen in Figure 6.69.

FIGURE 6.69 Performing a PolicyPak File Delivery Manager Post-Copy action

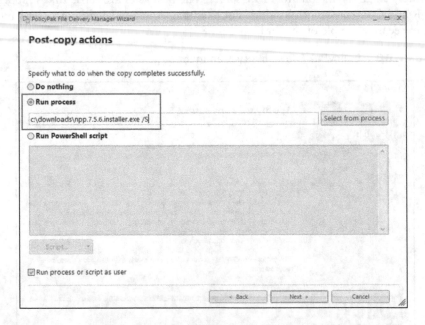

Additionally, when the policy no longer applies, like when you delete the policy from your MDM server, you can then run another process or PowerShell script and also, optionally, delete the files or folders that were downloaded as seen in Figure 6.70.

FIGURE 6.70   Revert action for PolicyPak File Delivery Manager

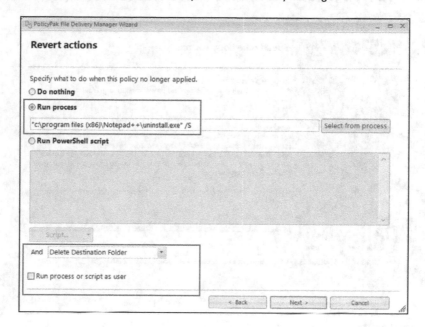

Downloading a ZIP and Automatically Unpacking Its Contents

This last scenario takes a little imagination.

Pretend that Sally in the sales department needed to keep all the sales documents up-to-date and perfectly organized for a whole team of traveling salespeople. Problem is, the sales material is changing all the time. She does a good job keeping it updated, but the salespeople just don't have the time to keep going back and back and back to get updated sales documents.

Well, with PolicyPak File Delivery Manager, you can have Sally stage her sales docs as a ZIP on a cloud service (like Amazon S3 or Azure Blob storage). This ZIP will contain all the sales documents, and Sally will just keep it updated.

Then the ZIP file is automatically downloaded by PolicyPak File Delivery Manager and then unpacked automatically—for example, to a folder on the desktop of all the sales team members. You can see PolicyPak File Delivery Manager using Amazon as a source in Figure 6.71.

FIGURE 6.71   Staging a ZIP file on Amazon S3 for later downloading and unpacking

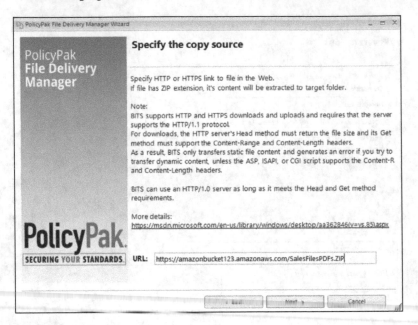

And, because PolicyPak File Delivery Manager is always checking all the time, anytime Sally updates the ZIP, any changes to the files inside the ZIP are automatically updated for all the sales team members. It's magic!

In Figure 6.72, you can see how to specify what to do when files already exist.

FIGURE 6.72   Selecting how to overwrite or replace existing files

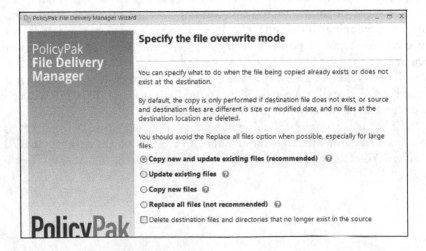

And that's it. Sally's amazing sales ZIP is unpacked and delivered to the whole sales team, old files are updated and overwritten by newer files, and everyone has a great day on the sales team.

Final Thoughts

In this chapter you use MDM to deploy, download, and install the following types of stuff:

- MSIs
- MSIX
- AppX
- Office 365 ProPlus
- Win32 apps
- PowerShell scripts (which downloaded applications)
- Other script types (using PolicyPak Scripts)
- Unusual file types, archives, and applications (using PolicyPak File Delivery Manager)

Tweet me the #1 thing you got out of this chapter @jeremymoskowitz. Use hashtag #mdmbook and say something you liked about this chapter, Chapter 6, "Deploying Software and Scripts."

Chapter 7

Enterprise State Roaming and OneDrive for Business

If you love something, set it free.

Gotta roam, baby, roam.

That's the point of this chapter.

By the time we're done in this chapter, we'll accomplish two main goals:

- We'll enable our users' state to roam with us between devices.
- We'll take our users' existing files and stick them in somewhere. If only you had…one…drive…that you could place things in. That would be amazing.

Then, we can lose our machine in a taxi, drop it on the sidewalk and have one of those annoying Bird scooters run over it. Or have it go overboard in a cruise ship.

It doesn't matter.

 If you want to read about interesting hard drive disasters, check this out:

https://www.itnews.com.au/news/kroll-ontrack-dishes-out-top-ten-data-disasters-161908

Think about it: If your application's state and your user files are in the cloud, and then you replace a machine, that experience (state and files) just comes back.

And, if you're still on Windows 7 (and you know who you are), you can use the same stuff you learn here to get your users' existing documents that are on their local machines up to OneDrive. Then, when the fateful day comes to wipe Windows 7 and install Windows 10 on their machines (manually, or as you will learn in the next chapter, perhaps with Autopilot), the users' files are pre-staged and ready to use immediately in their new Windows 10 world.

OneDrive by itself has some pretty compelling features and benefits once you're there. My favorites:

- **OneDrive files on demand:** Instead of having 100% of the items on the device, the user can have fully searchable placeholder files locally that take up no room on disk. Once a file is opened, it will sync to the local device so that you have a local and cloud version always in sync. You can even choose to have a file always available on the local device if you choose for those times you have no Internet capabilities. Great for mobile and quasi-mobile devices like the Surface Go machines, which have just 64GB of space. I'll show you this a little later in the chapter.

- **File Restore:** Malware sucks. And when users click on an infected file, it then starts to cascade to encrypt all the files on the hard drive and every drive letter, and every "everything" it can touch. OneDrive's File Restore lets users (or you) click to initiate "point in time restore," which will bring the files back from the dead to the time before the disaster. I'll show you this a little later in the chapter.

- **File Previewers:** So if the files are in OneDrive, how does Jane in marketing know what a file looks like? For instance, if Jane sees an .XD file type, can Jane know what the heck is in that file? With OneDrive, there are built-in previewers. That way Jane just clicks on the .XD file and…bingo…it's a wireframe preview of the Adobe XD file (from Adobe XD, a real program she never heard of, `https://helpx.adobe.com/xd/help/faq.html`). But at least she can get the gist of what the file's contents are without having to have Adobe XD preinstalled. Nice. OneDrive currently supports over 400 different file previewers, with more on the way.

- **Walking away from drive maps:** OneDrive is built on SharePoint (as I'll explain a little more in a bit). And as such, Microsoft provides a tool to enable you to suck in existing file shares and spit them out into SharePoint libraries. The goal? No more drive letters, and just use OneDrive to access your files (where there used to be a drive letter).

- There's also some insane, mind-blowing artificial intelligence features in OneDrive. Users can do a general search, say, for the word *school* and any picture with the word *school* in it (clear enough to be interpreted) and any video with the word *school* in it. Just. Wow.

Of course, we have to get it there first, and that's what this chapter is all about. In the next chapter, we'll talk about getting a new machine, and when you do, all the files and state from the cloud will be there, again, like nothing ever happened.

Do me a favor: Don't just jump ahead and try to download or otherwise install and manage the OneDrive client until the time is ready. I want to set up a nice table before you get to sit down and eat there.

If you want to get a good overview of OneDrive's features, head to YouTube and find the Ignite 2018 speech with code BRK2133.

Now, there are going to be some people who say, "I'm already using my Google Drive, Dropbox, Box...or whatever." I would encourage you to at least investigate OneDrive and see if what if offers makes sense for your situation. In fact, you might get unlimited storage for free. Many versions of Office 365 (E3/E5 SKUs) come with unlimited OneDrive storage, so it's definitely worth a gander. That said, if you're dead set on never using OneDrive, you can use a Group Policy found at Computer Configuration ➤ Admin Templates ➤ Windows Components ➤ OneDrive ➤ **Prevent the usage of OneDrive for file storage**, which will prevent OneDrive from being used.

Pregame Setup for This Chapter

We're going to be running pretty fast in this chapter. But in order to do so, we're going to need to do some pregame setup.

I'm going to need you to do these three things now, before we really get going:

- Get your Azure tenant ID.
- Get the OneDrive ADMX files staged properly in Group Policy-land.
- License two users for EM+S E3 or E5 (if not already).
- License two users for Office 365 (and therefore OneDrive).

Let's do all of these things now.

Get Your Azure Tennant ID

The Azure tenant ID is not normally needed, but we do need it for OneDrive.

Back in Azure, click Azure Active Directory. Then under Manage, click Properties. You can see the Directory ID box that holds your Tennant ID in Figure 7.1. Keep this handy as you go through the chapter.

FIGURE 7.1   Getting the Azure Tennant/Directory ID

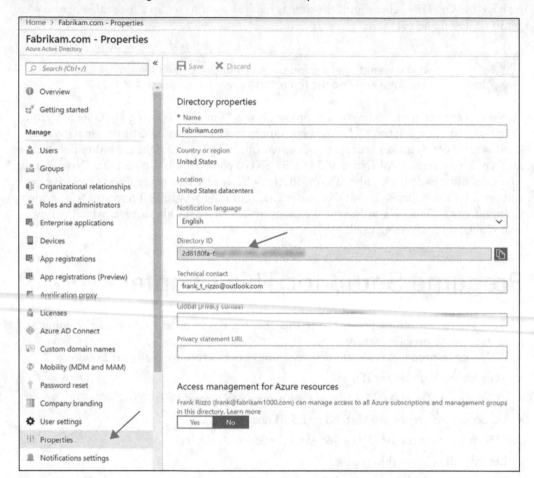

Getting the OneDrive ADMX Files Staged in Group Policy

We'll be covering this in a little bit, but OneDrive can be deployed a handful of ways.

For now, I don't want you to go all gung ho and deploy the OneDrive client yet.

But I do need you to have one machine with the absolute latest OneDrive client, just to pull off some key files.

Much of OneDrive client management is done through Group Policy.

To do this, you'll need to grab the latest OneDrive ADMX files and put them in your Group Policy store: Central Store or Local Store (Central Store recommended).

The latest OneDrive ADMX files are always just installed alongside the OneDrive client (nice touch). So, as I said, on a single, solitary machine, go to https://onedrive.live .com/about/download/ and find the download (or reinstall) for Windows 10. Again, even if you think you have it, just redownload and reinstall it, just so I know you're using the latest OneDrive client version.

Then, once that's done, on a Windows 10 machine, you'll look for the files in `%localappdata%\Microsoft\OneDrive\BuildNumber\adm` (yes, adm and not ADMX for some reason).

Then take a copy of `OneDrive.admx` and `OneDrive.adml` and put them into your Group Policy store (Central or Local).

Now, if you *don't* know what I'm talking about, then I have this big ol' Group Policy book to help you out at `www.MDMandGPanswers.com/book`. Get your signed copy today! (And get one for a friend!)

But, if you want the super quick story, here are two videos I made:

- How to Create a Group Policy Central Store: `www.youtube.com/watch?v=Q4DBdQo4XZs`

- How to update a Central Store (when you get new ADMX files): `www.youtube.com/watch?v=Op7hAvc5a0M`

So if you have a Central Store already, you'll just do what I show in the second video. By the time it's over, you should have your files in the Central Store as seen in Figure 7.2.

FIGURE 7.2   Putting your `OneDrive.admx` and `OneDrive.adml` (not shown) in the Central Store

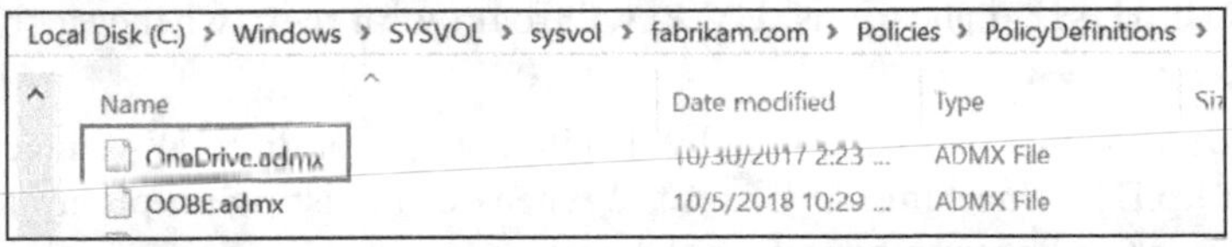

I'll assume you're doing as I ask and you've put the OneDrive ADMX and ADML files into your Central Store.

Getting OneDrive Licensed (with Office 365)

Because OneDrive for Business comes with Office 365, depending on how you got started at the beginning of this book, you may or may not have Office 365. If you don't, and you just want to learn the ropes, then it's gonna cost you.

One Starbucks latte, per user, per month.

So for $5.00 per user per month (paid annually) or $6.00 per month (no commitment), you can tack on Office 365 Business Essentials to your existing plan. Again, if you've already got Office 365 E3 or E5, you've already paid for it and have unlimited storage.

If you're following along in the book and you just want to get the feel for how OneDrive works, then get it for two users to follow along with the examples in the chapter. Here's who to buy them for:

- Any on-prem AD user you like, like EastSalesUser1. Remember, back in Chapter 2, "Set Up Azure AD and MDM," you used Azure AD Connect to take your on-prem AD accounts and sync them up to Azure AD.

- Any purely Azure AD user, like Jack Tors. Remember, Jack was "fully born in the cloud." He doesn't have any on-prem user account at all. And accounts like his, that is, those created purely in Azure AD don't sync backward to on-prem AD. Jack is all cloud, all the way, baby!

If you're unsure which of your accounts might be good candidates, check out Figure 2.49 back in Chapter 2. The plan is that you're about to give Office 365 Business Essentials to one user whose source is Windows Server AD and another license to one user whose source is Azure Active Directory. Again, see Figure 2.49 to remember what I mean.

By the time this is over, we want EastSalesUser1 and Jack Tors to have an Azure and an Office 365 Business Essentials license.

Giving each one of these types of accounts an Azure account and an Office 365 Business essentials license will enable us to explore the following scenarios:

- With EastSalesUser1, you'll be able to pretend to have an old machine (Windows 7 or Windows 10) and give him a new (or newer) Windows 10 machine and have all those files just magically be there for your on-prem population.

- With Jack Tors, you'll be able to pretend to have no on-prem AD at all. And have Jack log on to any purely MDM enrolled machine and get files from anywhere.

- And a third scenario is EastSalesUser1 completely walking away from their on-prem Active Directory, and they still gets their files from anywhere.

- With Jack Tors or EastSalesUser1, key Windows 10 OS settings and data saved in Windows Universal applications (UWP) will roam with them whenever they log onto a new computer.

As a reminder, to start out, EastSalesUser1 will have to log on to DJ++ machines. Again, you set up DJ++ machines in Chapter 2 when your existing on-prem, domain-joined machines used Group Policy to bootstrap themselves into joining Azure and enrolling into MDM.

As another reminder, Jack can only log onto a machine that is MDM enrolled, but not DJ++. Remember, users who are "cloud only" like Jack Tors cannot use DJ++ machines because their account is only in the cloud, and they have no on-prem account to log on to.

As I said, Office 365 Business Essentials is pretty cheap. Once purchased for Jack Tors and EastSalesUser1, there is no downloadable Office software, like Word or Excel, which is fine. We won't need it anyway.

To buy single licenses for these users go to `portal.office.com`. Then in Billing, select Purchase services. Select Office 365 Business Essentials and buy one license, one at a time. One for Jack and one for EastSalesUser1. Note there's a little check box along the way (not shown) called "Automatically assign to all of your users with no licenses." Don't do that during checkout.

Next, back in `portal.office.com` go to Users ➤ Active Users and select Jack Tors. Then select Product Licenses ➤ Edit (not shown) to get to add the Office 365 license, as seen in Figure 7.3.

Repeat the process again for EastSalesUser1, but this time also ensure that you're consuming an E5 license as well as the Office 365 Business Essentials license.

Now, on to configuring Enterprise State Roaming and OneDrive for Business.

FIGURE 7.3   Jack is now licensed for Office 365 and SharePoint (not shown), which means he has OneDrive access. Ensure also that an on-prem (but synchronized) user like EastSalesUser1 (not shown) also gets an E5 and Office 365 Business license.

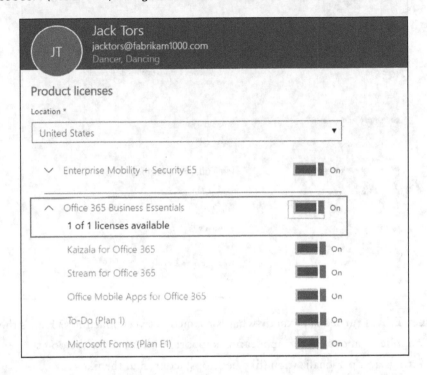

Enterprise State Roaming

It's been there since Windows 8.1. You can see it in Figure 7.4. That is, anyone with a Microsoft account can automatically store settings "in the cloud" and have them automatically come back down on another device that they are logged into. A regular consumer user just goes to Settings ➢ "Sync your settings," and there it is, as seen in Figure 7.4.

But for us, the IT admin, that didn't exist for a while. But it does now, and it's called Enterprise State Roaming, or ESR for short. ESR is pretty darned similar to the consumer service, but as you might expect it has some corporate features. Basically, the service adheres to smart business rules, like keeping your data in the closest Azure data center and, in the case of countries like Germany with stricter data laws, keeping the data entirely within Germany. There's also logging, which you can access if you need to troubleshoot the sync process.

FIGURE 7.4 Consumer sync settings for Windows

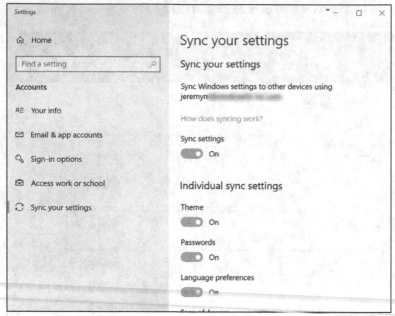

So, when ESR is turned on, exactly what is roamed between machines? Here's the list:

- UWP application data (if the application supports it; some do, some don't)
- OS settings and personalization (like desktops, icons, and the like)
- Accessibility
- Language settings
- Edge browser settings
- Credentials

It's possible, however, that some users could have a consumer Microsoft account and a corporate Azure account and use both accounts on the *same machine*. What? A regular user using your IT department's PC to go to the Windows Consumer Store and download a game or drawing app? See Figure 7.5 for an example of how users could do this.

Well, don't freak out.

As you might expect, first of all, their wallpaper from home with their cat (showing "Hang in there, baby!") won't magically roam to your business PC.

And, any application that isn't from the Windows Store for Business won't roam into the Azure stored data either and then come down to another PC.

ESR is business only.

FIGURE 7.5   Using the Consumer Microsoft Store to add a personal account

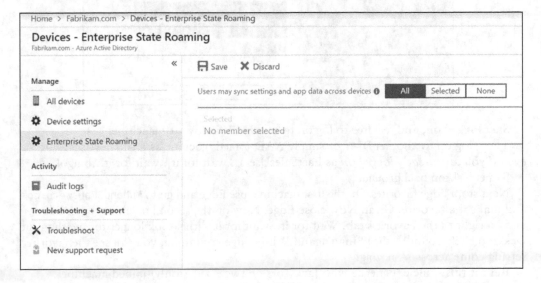

Setting Up Enterprise State Roaming

This will be, hands down, the easiest thing to set up in this book.

In Azure, click Devices ➤ Enterprise State Roaming and select All within "Users may sync settings and app data across devices." You can see this in Figure 7.6.

FIGURE 7.6   Turning on Enterprise State Roaming

You could choose Selected and specify which users would have this. But, I recommend just leaving it set to All and being done.

Click Save and that's it. You've turned it on.

As a quick note, the Windows 10 computers do need to be rebooted, and each user needs to log on again for the magic to occur. Also, if this doesn't work for you right away, wait overnight and try again.

What do you try first? I suggest logging on to your DJ++ machine as EastSalesUser1 and changing your Desktop background to another built-in picture, like what's seen in Figure 7.7.

FIGURE 7.7   Changing your background picture

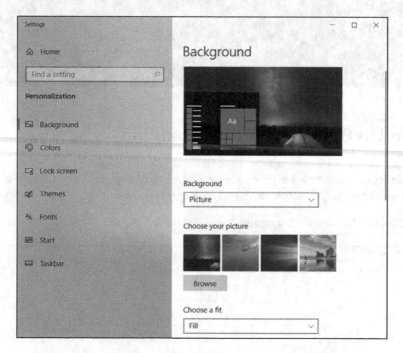

Stay logged on, and feel free to log on to another Windows 10 machine.

Then, log on to another DJ++ or simply AAD-joined machine as EastSalesUser1. Or even if you are *already logged on* as EastSalesUser1…wait for it…wait for it…bingo!

Same desktop background!

Next stop: Edge favorites. On the first machine, use Edge and go to MDMandGPanswers.com and make it a favorite. Great. Now close Edge. Now on the second machine, open Edge and go right to the Favorites tab. Wait for it…wait for it…(this took longer for me than the Desktop background)…then Bingo again! While Edge is running, you can see the favorite setting come across. Amazing!

Repeat this same experience with Jack Tors on two Azure (only)-joined machines. Because Enterprise State Roaming affects all Azure AD users (by default), this just works.

Remember, though, that if you try this with a UWP application, it might or might not magically roam the settings. That's up to the UWP developer to make that call if they want to store and roam the settings data in this way.

The Microsoft docs on Enterprise State Roaming are here (and a troubleshooting guide):

```
https://docs.microsoft.com/en-us/azure/active-directory/devices/
enterprise-state-roaming-enable
```

If you run into trouble, there's a decent troubleshooting guide as well on ESR, which also explains how to turn on logging, here:

```
https://docs.microsoft.com/en-us/azure/active-directory/devices/
enterprise-state-roaming-troubleshooting
```

Last, a good, if not a little older, video about Enterprise State Roaming and another roaming technology, Microsoft UE-V (explained in the sidebar "Other Microsoft Roaming Technologies: Windows UE-V, Roaming Profiles, and fsLogix [Recently Bought by Microsoft]") can be found at www.youtube.com/watch?v=OG58JBMliH8, or search for "Understand settings roaming solutions in Windows."

Other Microsoft Roaming Technologies: Microsoft UE-V, Roaming Profiles, and fsLogix (Recently Bought by Microsoft)

So the next obvious question is, If Enterprise State Roaming is meant to roam the desktop and WUP applications, how do I roam the settings for Win32 apps?

As I write this, there are two official answers, and another one coming soon.

The official answer is to use Microsoft UE-V, or User Experience Virtualization. It is a product that is available for Enterprise paying customers to let the state of the Win32 applications be stored in a share or in the home drive and have those settings come back down as needed when a user roams to another machine.

UE-V isn't super hard to set up, but it's a little tedious getting it working perfectly as expected. It used to be a separate add-in product. Now, the client piece is built into Windows Enterprise and Education and managed with Group Policy. The docs are here:

```
https://docs.microsoft.com/en-us/windows/configuration/ue-v/
uev-for-windows
```

UE-V hasn't been updated in some time, so its progress appears halted, and its lifeline seems dicey as evidenced by this post:

```
https://www.reddit.com/r/sysadmin/comments/8qu07u/ms_may_kill_uev/
```

Another "on thin ice" technology from Microsoft is Roaming Profiles, which I go over in great detail in my book *Group Policy: Fundamentals, Security and the Managed Desktop* in Chapter 9. Maybe you're already using Roaming Profiles and it works reasonably well. But there have been rumors for years that they might eventually kill it off.

If both Roaming Profiles and UE-V are on the potential chopping block, what, then, could replace it?

Well, in December 2018, Microsoft announced the purchase of fsLogix, a company that tries to wrestle the issues of roaming profiles to the ground. The key thing fsLogix does is that it stores the whole profile as a re-attachable VHD (virtual disk) file. This is wholly different than how folks have attempted to solve this in the past. When someone roams from machine to machine, as long as the VHD is available (or cached), then…bingo. Instant roaming desktop.

As I write this, Microsoft has announced support for RDSH (aka Terminal Services) scenarios, VDI scenarios, and in their Windows Virtual Desktop (WVD) service.

Customers can also use fsLogix if they have any RDSH licenses, VDA, or WVD entitlement. What's unclear is if a customer has no RDSH licenses, can they still use the fsLogix technology with their on-prem systems… like normal, boring desktops? Still waiting to see how that shakes out.

The fsLogix technology fixes some key problems inherent with VDI, and could be the successor to Roaming Profiles and perhaps also UE-V. Indeed, they have already said they are definitely going to use fsLogix to replace RDSH's User Profile Disks (UPD) (which will be sunsetted at some future point).

At the time of the fsLogix acquisition, I wrote a blog post which sums up my thoughts at the acquisition time:

```
https://www.policypak.com/pp-blog/
microsofts-acquisition-of-fslogix-is-good-for-cloud-vdi-and-policypak-
customers
```

Note that it could be out-of-date by the time you read this, depending upon what Microsoft keeps or guts from fsLogix's lineup.

OneDrive for Business

Let's get one thing perfectly straight: OneDrive for Business is not OneDrive. Yeah, it can be a little confusing, too. So let's get some clarity:

- **OneDrive Consumer:** The consumer file sharing system. This is for personal files managed by individuals, like your cousin Jimmy who just bought a PC from Best Buy and the files are hanging out in Microsoft's public cloud.
- **OneDrive for Business (ODB):** This is for employee's storage of business files, and it's managed by you in the IT department. It doesn't just handle files, it also handles

SharePoint libraries. This comes with an Office 365 subscription or when you're using SharePoint.

We'll be only, only, and I mean *only*, dealing with OneDrive for Business, often abbreviated ODB.

But man is that a lot to keep typing and saying each time.

So, don't shoot me, but for this chapter, I'm just going to call it OneDrive. And, actually, this is what Microsoft calls it too, unless they are calling out a specific business or consumer feature.

Anyway, let's get on with learning OneDrive. (See what I did there?)

If you're on the fence or maybe not sure about OneDrive, I can recommend a single resource that does a good job setting the stage for OneDrive in the enterprise. If you have an extra minute or two (well, the docs page says 40 minutes, but I think you can do it way faster), give this a quick read before you continue. We'll be hitting some, but not all, of the concepts found on this page.

```
https://docs.microsoft.com/en-us/onedrive/plan-onedrive-enterprise
```

That said, it's perfectly okay if you don't read it. I won't rely on you having read it; it just is a little useful in pre-framing our talk.

So, just to set your expectations, this chapter is not going to be an exhaustive undertaking of all of OneDrive but rather a discussion of the items I think you're going to need to get started the fastest. For instance, I won't be going over any of the following:

- How to roll out or use any OneDrive apps on phones, etc.

- How to roll out or use OneDrive for Macs

- How to get your users trained and/or adopt OneDrive after you roll it out. As a quick tip, end users should go to `https://aka.ms/learnonedrive`, `https://Aka.ms/productivitylibrary`, and `https://docs.microsoft.com/en-us/onedrive/` (in the End-User section) for some OneDrive tutorials once you have it all up and running.

- I'm also not going to go over the older "Groove.exe" sync client, and there could be some unusual cases where you might still use this. If you're using SharePoint 2016 or earlier on-premise, then you will still need to maintain the Groove.exe client.

Earlier, when I asked you to pre-license Office 365 Business Essentials (back at Figure 7.3), what is *not shown* is that OneDrive isn't even listed in the mini-licenses sub-licenses that make up Office 365. (For fun, check out the sub-licenses of what makes up Office 365. What the heck is *Kaizala for Office 365* I didn't know! I had to look it up!)

SharePoint, however, is on the sub-list when that list is exposed; it's just at the bottom. And OneDrive is literally a part of SharePoint. So said another way, when the user is licensed for SharePoint, *that's* what turns on their ability to use OneDrive, which is why you don't see it listed as a sub-license.

To take on OneDrive, we're going to use the following battle plan:

1. We're going to set up the back-end, tenant service side of OneDrive first.

2. We're then going to try to walk away from drive maps. We'll do this by migrating over our server files (that is, old, boring file-based shares). We'll migrate them into

SharePoint Online. I mean OneDrive. I mean SharePoint Online. Whatever, it's the same thing.

3. Then we're going to set up and manage the OneDrive client for our old Windows 7 machines (if you still have any) and our Windows 10 machines. We'll then see the files we migrated in Step 2.

4. We're going to magically move over any on-Windows user files to OneDrive via the magic of *Known Folder Move*.

5. We'll finish up by using Intune to configure the OneDrive client, in case a machine is not also on-prem domain-joined and there's no Group Policy to manage it.

That's the plan. Let's get started.

Managing the OneDrive Tenant

The first thing to do is to get OneDrive configured within your Azure tenant. There are two areas to perform the OneDrive management:

▪ The OneDrive admin center

▪ Managing a specific user

Let's explore both.

Managing OneDrive and SharePoint via Admin Center

For the cloud-side management of OneDrive, you'll want to find it's admin center. Locate it under "Admin centers" ➢ OneDrive as seen in Figure 7.8.

FIGURE 7.8   Locating OneDrive admin center

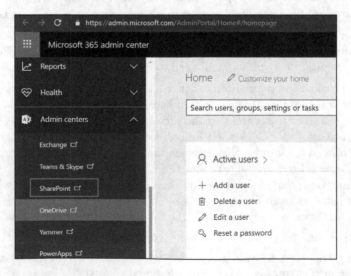

You can also jump to OneDrive's admin console at admin.onedrive.com.

A little later, we'll also use the SharePoint admin, so I'm also pointing it out here in Figure 7.8. And remember, you won't see either SharePoint or OneDrive listed within "Admin centers" unless you've assigned at least one Office 365 license as I did earlier.

Again, nothing to do here just yet; just pointing it out for future reference.

Managing Settings Per-User

The other big place where you can manage OneDrive settings is per-user, as shown in Figure 7.9. You find them inside the Office admin center. For instance, you can change "External sharing," like removing anonymous sharing, say, just from one person.

FIGURE 7.9   The per-user OneDrive settings

Note that if you just purchase your Office 365 Essentials account or light someone up with a new license, you might not see the OneDrive settings right away. For me, these settings appeared overnight.

SharePoint and SharePoint Migration Tool

I know what you're thinking: "When will we get to use OneDrive on Windows 10 already, Moskowitz?" That's coming up. Hang on for a bit.

What I want to talk about next is getting out of the business of mapped drives. Now, it's true that some scenarios still require drive letters. That is, you have an application built back in 2001 or something that "If it doesn't see the Z: drive, it just falls over and dies." Okay, sure I get that; that does exist in the world.

But for the majority of things, you don't strictly need drive letters. Instead, you just point and click your way to get to files. And SharePoint and OneDrive have a nice way of enabling you to take existing file shares (from any flavor of server) and make them accessible via OneDrive.

It's called the SharePoint Migration tool, and it's really easy to use. It enables you to migrate content from on-prem SharePoint 2013 or on-prem file shares to SharePoint Online. And when they're in SharePoint, they're in OneDrive.

First, though, we need to create a dumping ground, I mean, a *SharePoint library* for each existing share we want to migrate away.

Then, after that, we'll also tell your OneDrive machines how to find these spiffy new SharePoint libraries. And we'll use Group Policy and MDM to do it.

Creating a SharePoint Library for Your Existing Content

I don't purport to be a SharePoint expert. But I was able to figure out how to make a new library. In short, start out by being logged in to Azure as Frank, then head over to your default SharePoint site, which will be something like:

```
<yourdomain.SharePoint.com>/SitePages/Home.aspx
```

Mine is:

```
https://fabrikam1000.SharePoint.com/SitePages/Home.aspx
```

Then when you're there, click "Site contents" ➤ New ➤ "Document library" as seen in Figure 7.10.

Give it a name, like ZDrive, YDrive, or any other name you like. Remember, my goal is to replace an existing drive letter, so I'm going to want to use a name that's familiar to my people. You can use whatever name makes sense.

And that's it. You've got a new home for the ZDrive share you're about to copy in.

Migrating an On-Prem File Share to SharePoint

So, I want you to migrate a single file share and get it to SharePoint.

In my example, I'll be migrating \\dc2016\share, which has a gaggle of random things including applications, documents, movies, and so on, and put it right into OneDrive. I mean SharePoint. Arrgh, you get the idea.

FIGURE 7.10   Add a new library before you continue.

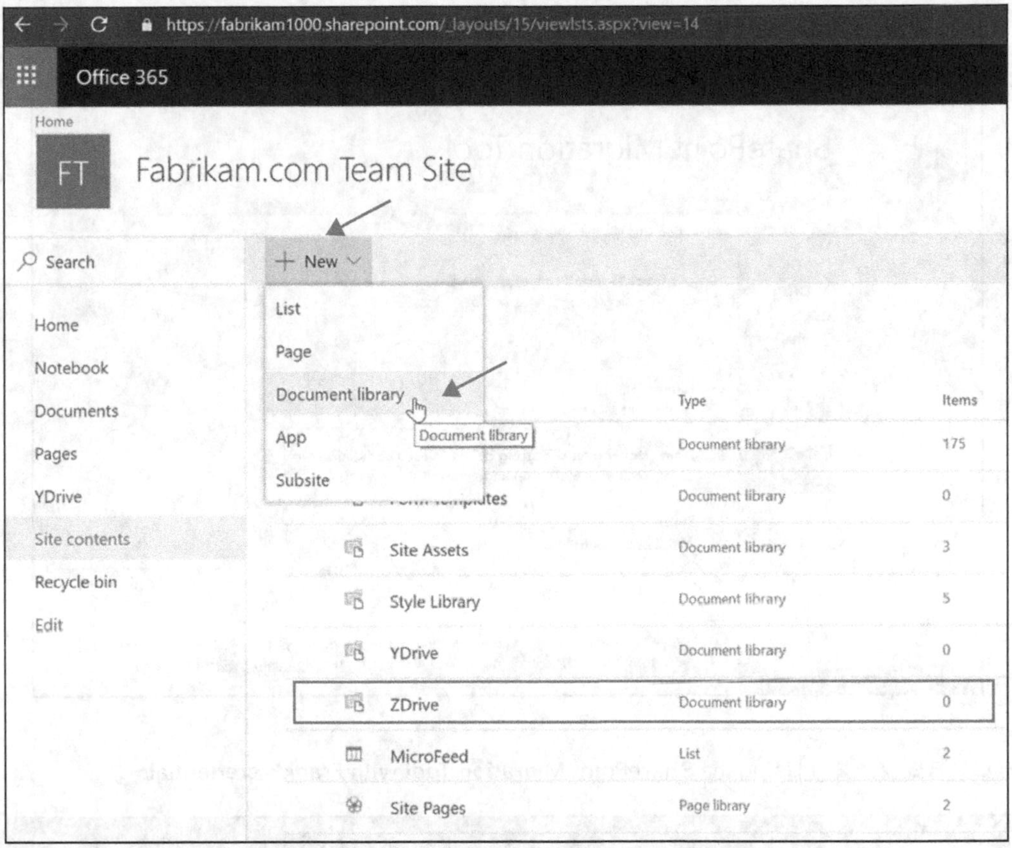

Start out by heading over to this URL for the overview:

```
https://docs.microsoft.com/en-us/SharePointmigration/
migrate-to-SharePoint-online
```

And then there you'll see two more URLs you can use for the program itself:

- Graphical:

```
http://spmtreleasescus.blob.core.windows.net/install/default.htm
```

- PowerShell:

```
https://docs.microsoft.com/en-us/SharePointmigration/
overview-spmt-ps-cmdlets
```

I'll be using the graphical version.

I found that it worked great when running from my Windows 10 administrative station. The download is a small download that then downloads a bigger download. You can see the small download in Figure 7.11, and after it's done and running, you can see me giving the program Frank Rizzo's credentials to kick the whole thing off in Figure 7.12.

FIGURE 7.11 The download of the SharePoint Migration Tool

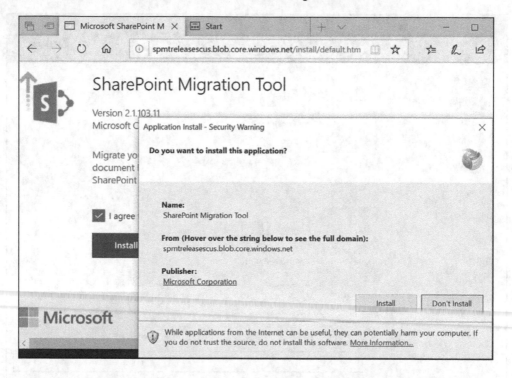

FIGURE 7.12 Using the SharePoint Migration Tool with Frank's credentials

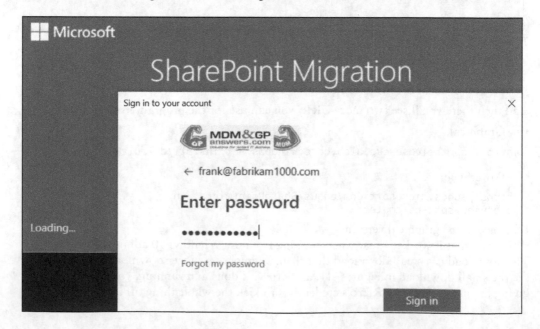

The process is pretty straightforward. Select the content of a file share (as seen in Figure 7.13),

FIGURE 7.13 Using the SharePoint Migration Tool for a whole file share

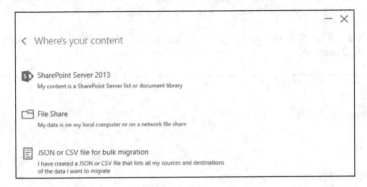

Then, as seen in Figure 7.14, give it the name of your on-prem share like \\dc2016\share.

FIGURE 7.14 Selecting your on-prem share

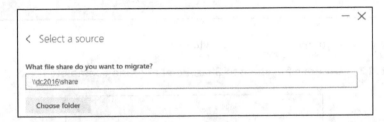

Next, as seen in Figure 7.15, you'll select the SharePoint Online site to migrate your content (which is automatically filled in) and select a document library (just select Documents for most cases).

FIGURE 7.15 Selecting the SharePoint Online site and document library

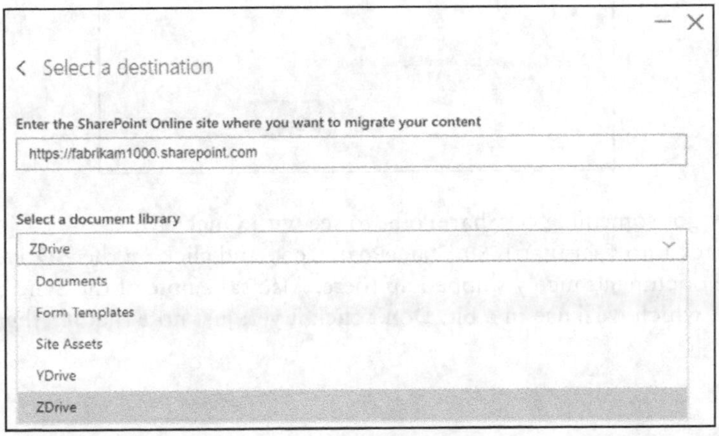

There are some basic and advanced settings if desired (not shown). For instance, you can perform a scan only (which is a kind of verification, instead of actually doing the work) as well as limit which kinds of files are uploaded (say, don't upload .MP3 files).

Once you press Start, you'll see what's in Figure 7.16.

FIGURE 7.16   The SharePoint Migration Tool scans, then copies the files from the source to the destination.

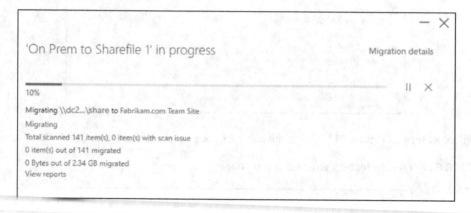

And, when it's all completed, you'll see what's in Figure 7.17.

FIGURE 7.17   On-Prem file share to SharePoint migration completed

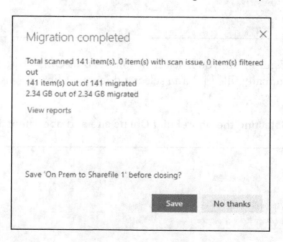

You've now got something on SharePoint to see with OneDrive.

If you go back into fabrikam1000.SharePoint.com and click on the ZDrive site, you should see the documents nicely shipped up there. Also take note of the Sync button, shown in Figure 7.18, which we'll use in a bit. Don't click it yet; just note that it's there.

FIGURE 7.18 Your files have been migrated up using the SharePoint Migration Tool. The Sync button will expose the library ID used a bit later.

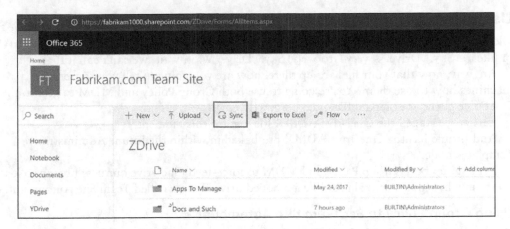

You likely don't need to change anything immediately, but if you wanted to see the permissions on the ZDrive library, select "Site contents," right-click and select Settings (shown in Figure 7.19), then select Permissions for this document library (not shown).

FIGURE 7.19 Right-click over your library and select Settings to set permissions.

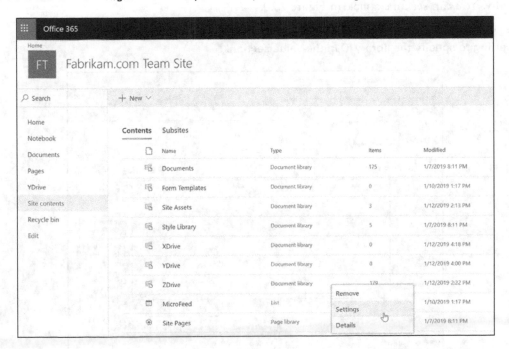

Now, you might be thinking, "This is great, Jeremy, but I don't want 123GB of data coming down and landing onto my machine automatically." In a bit, we'll set up Files

On-Demand to prevent that from happening. (Which is why we're holding off installing the OneDrive client.)

Using Team Site Automount

Okay. You moved one or more on-prem file shares to the sky with a big ol' drive in it. Sort of like a…Sky…Drive. A very Groove(y) Sky…Drive. Wait, wait, we can't call it that.

Anyway, now that your files are up there, how are you going to tell your on-prem machines how to use them? You're going to use both Group Policy and MDM to give to the OneDrive client your tenant ID and a library ID.

Earlier we staged the OneDrive ADMX file just for this moment.

And Intune has the OneDrive ADMX pre-baked in within the Intune Administrative Templates node.

Let's set up both Group Policy and MDM to force-feed OneDrive our new library so it's pretty much, kinda sorta, almost like a mapped drive. This is called Team Site Automount.

Using Group Policy to Set Team Site Automount

The policy setting you're looking for is on both the user and the computer side. Meaning, you can specify that this setting affects computers (and therefore all users upon the computer) or specific users (wherever they happen to roam).

I'm going to be doing this on the computer side, Computer Configuration ➢ Administrative Templates ➢ OneDrive ➢ Configure team site libraries to sync automatically. You can see an example in Figure 7.20.

FIGURE 7.20 Use the **Configure team site libraries to sync automatically** policy setting to specify the library ID in the Value section.

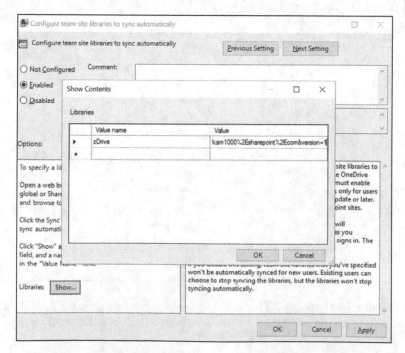

You can see I put in a value name (which is not really used or seen by the user, by the way, but it's nice to match the library name anyway). And I put in a value. A gigantically long string that represents my tenant and library ID. How did I get that?

Well, underneath the Sync button (which we saw earlier in SharePoint's library information), you can click "Copy library ID," as shown in Figure 7.21. And that's it. That's the secret handshake you need for *this library*.

FIGURE 7.21   Grabbing the library ID

The string itself will look something like this:

```
tenantId=2d8180fa%abcde%2D42f5%2Db95c%2abcdeabcdbfd0&siteId=%7B55760d6e%
2D5821%2D41cf%2Dbae1%2D73f1936e5fcf%7D&webId=%7Bba7799e2%2D17dc%2D4247%
2Da10f%2D39b8e2650059%7D&listId=%7B1abcdD%2DCB85%2D433D%2DBD31%
2DABCDF001F7%7D&webUrl=https%3A%2F%2Ffabrikam1000%2ESharePoint%2Ecom&version=1
```

In Group Policy-land, just put one line for each library you want to expose through OneDrive, as seen in Figure 7.22.

FIGURE 7.22   The Registry item that is created for each Team Site Automounted library

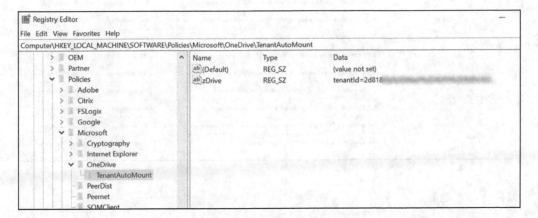

The result of what occurs can be seen in Figure 7.22. That is, a registry item is created at `HKLM\Software\Policies\Microsoft\OneDrive\TennantAutoMount`.

Setting Up Team Site Automount in MDM

Remember that some systems in your world might *never* be domain-joined. As such, they'll never get the OneDrive Group Policy settings.

So, MDM to the rescue. But there's a hitch.

The setting you need is a mere Registry setting on the computer side.

What isn't available today, and would certainly be easiest and likely available by the time you read this, is an Administrative Template item within Intune that would configure Team Site Automount. The Administrative Templates for OneDrive can be seen in Figure 7.23. Indeed, we'll be using some of these a little later. But as you can see, there's nothing (right this second) that correlates to the **Configure team site libraries to sync automatically** setting we saw in Group Policy-land.

FIGURE 7.23   The Intune Administrative Template settings for OneDrive

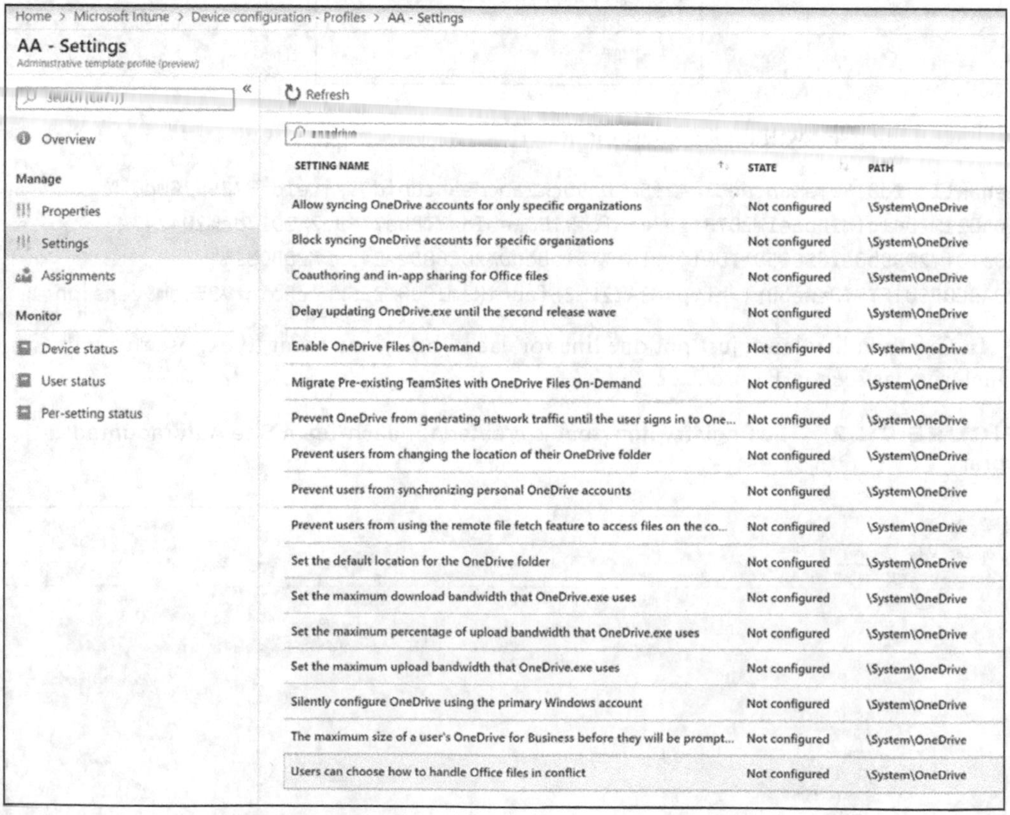

If I'm wrong, and by the time you read this the **Configure team site libraries to sync automatically** setting is still not inside Intune, remember that there are a myriad of ways to get any "normal Registry setting" over to Intune (or any other MDM service). Here are the choices:

- Here's a script you can use to perform the Team Site Automount using any MDM service:

  https://www.cyberdrain.com/
  automatically-mapping-SharePoint-sites-in-the-onedrive-for-business-client/

- You can ingest the OneDrive ADMX and do what you learned in Chapter 3, "MDM Profiles, Policies, and Groups," and ingest the OneDrive ADMX and make custom OMA-URIs. This blog gives all the details:

  https://deploywindows.com/2018/11/05/
  ingest-onedrive-group-policies-manage-settings-in-an-awesome-intune-way/

- You can use PolicyPak Admin Templates or PolicyPak Preferences to make the setting and deliver it with your MDM (more in Chapter 11, "MDM Add-On Tools:Free and Pay").

But as I said, I bet all the Group Policy–based OneDrive settings will make it into Intune's Administrative Templates function, hopefully by the time you read this.

Final Thoughts about Team Site Automount

The point is, OneDrive Team Site Automount works perfectly well on-prem with Group Policy and perfectly well with non-domain-joined machines. When you feed the Windows computer the list of libraries, any kind of computer can use the libraries as drive map replacements.

Nice one, Microsoft.

One little final note here: What if you migrated your content and still need that content to pretend to be a drive letter? As I stated, some applications simply insist on using a drive letter. You can check out the following tool (after you get the basics down with this chapter): OneMapper. I found OneMapper at www.lieben.nu/liebensraum/onedrivemapper/. I didn't try it myself, but the goal would be to help you keep drive letters even when that content is moved using Team Site Automount.

OneDrive Sync Client

The OneDrive storage (and backend service) is only one piece of the marriage.

The other part is the OneDrive Sync Client, which is available for Windows, Mac, Android, and iOS (there's also OneDrive for Xbox, but that's the consumer OneDrive and not OneDrive for business). I'm only going to be going into Windows here, but other platforms can have it installed as well.

Make a change on your Windows machine, and see that change instantly on your iPad. Pretty sweet.

The links for the platforms can be found at `https://onedrive.live.com/about/download/`.

There are other ways that OneDrive can get installed on Windows:

- On Windows 10: OneDrive is just already installed with Windows 10. But it might not be totally up-to-date. If you waited around, OneDrive would auto-update on its own based upon OneDrive's schedule and also its rings (which we'll talk about in a little bit). But I'm going to advise you to get the latest one out there now on your few test machines.

- Click-to-Run Office 2016 and later, ProPlus version and/or deployed via MDM: Any of these methods installs the latest OneDrive client.

- On Windows 7 (if you have any Windows 7 remaining that is), you'll have to get the OneDrive sync client out there. You can use the downloadable version at the link I mentioned earlier.

- A special version for SCCM is available (if you reach out and talk with your Microsoft rep). This version doesn't automatically update and must be manually updated every 60 days or it will stop working. It's recommended only for customers who positively must be hands-on with exactly what version they deploy.

Then for both platforms, you can configure it. Let's handle both of those now. Note also that there is the old Groove.exe client. This is still required if you have SharePoint 2016 or 2013. The modern OneDrive client only supports on prem SharePoint 2019. So you may need one client, or maybe two clients, to do both OneDrive and SharePoint.

OneDrive Client Versions and Rings

As you likely know, Windows, Office, and also OneDrive have "rings." That is, as features get created, they are deployed immediately to the Insiders Ring. Then as features mature, they go to the Production Ring. And finally, features will trickle down to the Enterprise Ring (which is the most conservative). Typically the Enterprise ring is 60 days behind the Production Ring.

You can always see what versions are in what ring at the following URL (shortened to `https://bit.ly/2glxd8Q`):

```
https://support.office.com/en-us/article/
New-OneDrive-sync-client-release-notes-845dcf18-f921-435e-bf28-4e24b95e5fc0
```

An example of what you might see on that page can be seen in Figure 7.24.

You can see what date the next Enterprise Ring will likely be released, which gives you some time to download, test, and make sure all is right in your world before OneDrive is updated to the latest version.

FIGURE 7.24   The OneDrive sync client page expressing the rings

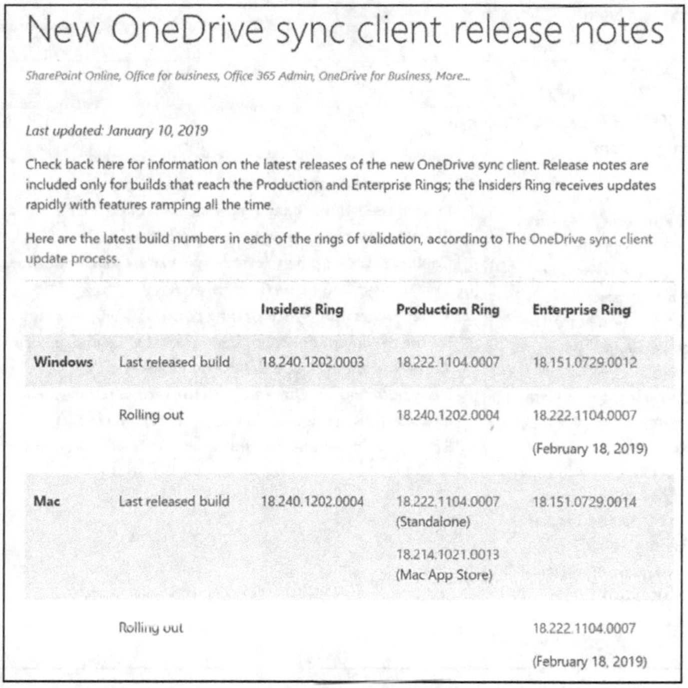

New OneDrive sync client release notes

SharePoint Online, Office for business, Office 365 Admin, OneDrive for Business, More...

Last updated: January 10, 2019

Check back here for information on the latest releases of the new OneDrive sync client. Release notes are included only for builds that reach the Production and Enterprise Rings; the Insiders Ring receives updates rapidly with features ramping all the time.

Here are the latest build numbers in each of the rings of validation, according to The OneDrive sync client update process.

		Insiders Ring	Production Ring	Enterprise Ring
Windows	Last released build	18.240.1202.0003	18.222.1104.0007	18.151.0729.0012
	Rolling out		18.240.1202.0004	18.222.1104.0007
				(February 18, 2019)
Mac	Last released build	18.240.1202.0004	18.222.1104.0007 (Standalone)	18.151.0729.0014
			18.214.1021.0013 (Mac App Store)	
	Rolling out			18.222.1104.0007
				(February 18, 2019)

By default, any OneDrive sync client will try to update itself to the latest Production Ring. The OneDrive sync client is always checking for available updates. It does this once every 24 hours when the OneDrive sync client is running. But it also has a backup plan: There's a Windows 10 scheduled task that also updates the OneDrive sync client (even if OneDrive is shut down and not launched). You can read more about the OneDrive sync client update process with regard to rings here: `https://docs.microsoft.com/en-us/onedrive/sync-client-update-process`.

That said, you might want to use the most conservative ring, the Enterprise Ring, instead of the more consumer-tested, but not necessarily battle-tested, but has more features Production Ring.

To do this for your on-prem systems, you will use the OneDrive ADMX settings we staged earlier. In Figure 7.25 you can see the OneDrive settings on the user-side, at User Configuration ➤ Policies ➤ Administrative Templates ➤ OneDrive. The policy setting you're after is **Delay updating Onedrive.exe until the second release wave**.

The same setting can be configured in Intune via Administrative Templates within Intune, seen back in Figure 7.23. In that screen shot, it's also called **Delay updating OneDrive.exe until the second release wave** and is the fourth policy in the list.

They do the same thing: again, great for when you have clients on-prem with Group Policy and when you have all cloud clients with MDM.

FIGURE 7.25   User-side Group Policy OneDrive settings

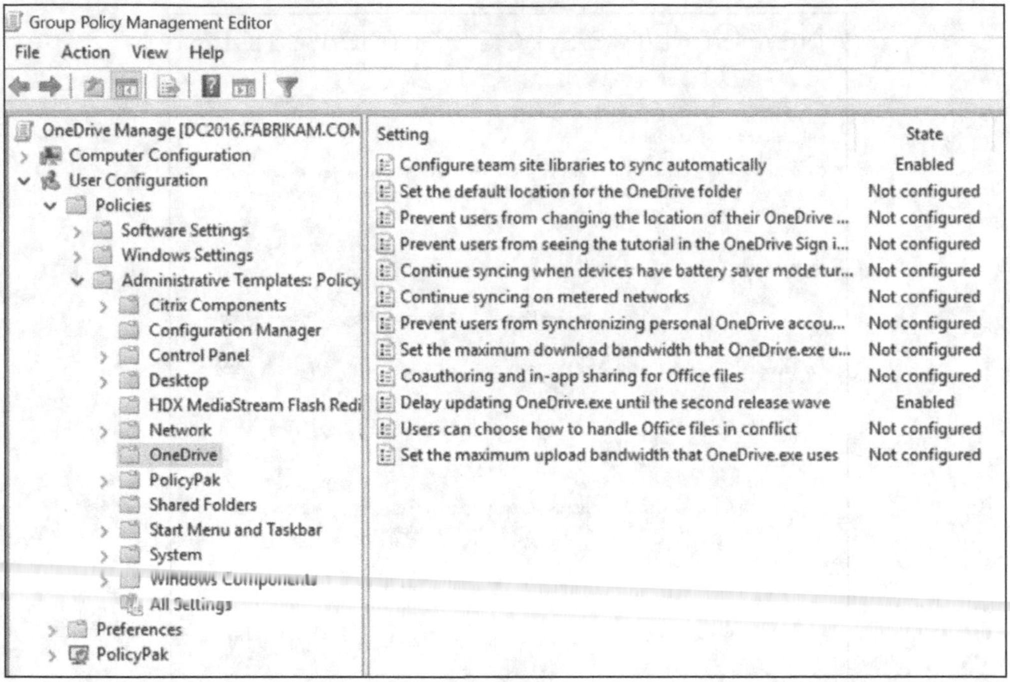

Installing the OneDrive Client on Windows 10

As I said, OneDrive is preinstalled alongside Windows 10 but is always going to be a little on the old side if it's not updated. Remember, the OneDrive client is updated automatically, but also when you install Office Click-to-Run or deploy via MDM, etc.

But I wanted to take a minute for you to see *how* it's installed and talk about an option that I know is coming soon and will certainly be out by the time you read this.

OneDrive for Windows 10 is, by default, always installed per user; which is a little unusual. Being installed per-user means that the entirety of the application lives inside user-controlled space, specifically %appdata%\local\Microsoft\OneDrive. This has advantages and disadvantages. The advantage is that the application can just notice that there's an upgrade available, download it, perform the upgrade, and then the user is back in business. No IT department is needed to perform some kind of upgrade through Intune or SCCM, or whatever. This has the other advantage of not needing admin rights; the software downloads and installs as the user, instead of as the system.

The downside of this per-user model is when multiple people use the same machines, or when the machine is RDS or VDI. The problem here is that now you have a lot of instances of OneDrive, different versions could be installed for different users, and a bunch of other problems ... all using the same core machine.

As such, the OneDrive team announced a "per-machine" installation of OneDrive coming soon for just these cases. It just came out as this book was going to print, so I couldn't test it out beforehand. That being said, the documentation on it can be found at https://docs.microsoft.com/en-us/onedrive/per-machine-installation.

Seems simple enough. Just run OneDriveSetup.exe /allusers and you're off to the races. Instead of each user keeping it up-to-date, OneDrive is kept up-to-date by a scheduled task running as system which is always just checking for updates.

Installing the OneDrive Client on Windows 7 (or Later) by Other Methods

By the time this book hits the shelves (physical or virtual), there will less than a year remaining in Windows 7 support. Buuuut I think there will be a lot of companies still using Windows 7 and just "hoping for the best." So I'm writing this section to help you bootstrap your Windows 7 files into OneDrive so you can then pull it down with Windows 10 when you get there. (Hint: That's the next chapter.)

An incredibly detailed set of directions on how to get OneDrive rolled out to your Windows 7 machines can be found here:

https://social.technet.microsoft.com/wiki/contents/articles/33549
.onedrive-next-generation-sync-client-deployment-guide.aspx.

It might be a little out-of-date, but it should get you to the finish line.

But if you wanted to do the abbreviated version, you really need only to run OneDriveSetup.exe /silent (per-user style install) or OneDriveSetup.exe /allusers (per-machine style install) on new machines and, bingo. It should be there.

Additionally, if want to go with a lightweight deployment mechanism, I always recommend my friends at PDQ.com with their awesome PDQ Deploy software, which would make installation of software like this drop-dead simple.

And, if you don't have any infrastructure, you could use PolicyPak Cloud with the built-in PolicyPak File Deliver Manager to deploy OneDrive for Business to your Windows 7 or 10 machines.

You've got some choices.

Deploying OneDrive Client via MDM (Like Intune)

We already saw back in Chapter 6, "Deploying Software and Scripts," how to deploy Office via Intune. At that time, I asked you to pre-check the OneDrive Desktop client. This is in Figure 6.42.

This sets the stage for when a totally new machine is born into the world and you want to ensure that it gets the latest OneDrive client.

How does a new machine get born into the world? Lots of ways, but you'll see the newest way in the next chapter, with Autopilot. Because you already pre-selected to deploy the OneDrive Desktop client via MDM, when new machines are born, they will immediately start to attempt to get the latest OneDrive client.

Nice job, thinking ahead like that.

As I stated earlier, the OneDrive client is of course also available for iOS, Android, Mac, and the like. You can deploy any of the clients via MDM. For more details on deploying the OneDrive client via Intune for either Windows or alternate platforms, you can check out https://docs.microsoft.com/en-us/onedrive/deploy-intune.

Setting Up Key OneDrive Management Settings via Group Policy and MDM

OneDrive's management through Group Policy and MDM is pretty darned awesome. So awesome, in fact, I cannot go into every darned setting available.

If you wanted to see how many settings there are, and what they do, you can (and should) take some time to pre-read https://Aka.ms/odGPO. Then, after that, here are my initial settings before continuing.

When you're using Group Policy, note that some settings are computer side and others are user-side. Best practice is to use two GPOs (one for user-side stuff and another for computer side stuff). As you follow along, be sure to create and link the GPOs such that the items hit the correct side of your test users and computers.

With that in mind, here are my recommendations of what GPOs and MDM settings to set right away.

OneDrive Silent Account Configuration

So when a user uses the Windows OneDrive client, they have to give it credentials to log on. But that gets old, fast.

Users have to type and re-type in their email (login) and password again and again, as seen in Figure 7.26.

FIGURE 7.26   Manually logging onto OneDrive

Boooring.

Instead, I recommend using OneDrive *Silent Account Configuration*.

For your on-prem systems, it's a Group Policy setting on the computer side. You can see the OneDrive computer-side Group Policy settings in Figure 7.27.

FIGURE 7.27 Computer-side Group Policy settings for OneDrive

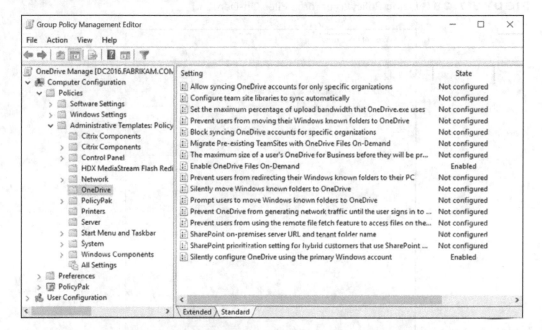

The item you're after is called **Silently configure OneDrive using the primary Windows account.**

When that setting is enabled, the OneDrive client just reads who is logged on and passes that information onward and silently logs Mr. User into OneDrive.

On the MDM side, again, you'll be using the Administrative Template setting with the same name. In Figure 7.23, you can see it third from the bottom, **Silently configure OneDrive using the primary Windows account.**

The docs for this are found at:

https://docs.microsoft.com/en-us/onedrive/use-silent-account-configuration

Note that the documentation also demonstrates a PowerShell script you can use for this, but I only recommend it if you're not using Intune, because the Administrative Template it provides is a better, more straightforward approach.

Turning On Files On-Demand

Instead of syncing every file from OneDrive down to the client, save on disk space and use *Files On-Demand*. The policy setting is called **Enable OneDrive Files On-Demand** and can be seen in Figure 7.27 for Group Policy and Figure 7.23 for Intune.

This is great, because users can then just right-click and download to keep the files they want with them while on the road while not consuming bandwidth for the 96% of files they don't need with them at all times.

This equates to the item in the OneDrive client, shown in Figure 7.28, and is simply forced on when the policy is engaged.

FIGURE 7.28   Using Policy to enforce Files On-Demand

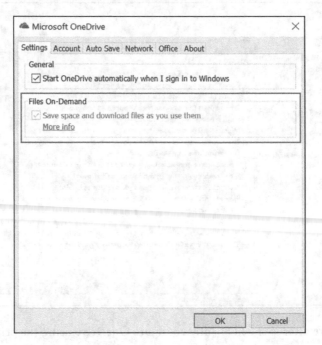

Again: I recommend just turning this on via Group Policy and/or Intune.

For other MDM services, you will have to script this. I found (but didn't test) a user-side and computer-side script to do this here:

```
https://osddeployment.dk/2017/12/18/
how-to-silently-configure-onedrive-for-business-with-intune/
```

Using the OneDrive Client for Windows 10

To accelerate things for this chapter, I already showed you the manual download location for OneDrive for Business (`https://onedrive.live.com/about/en-us/download/`) and you already installed it to get the ADMX files uploaded.

Log on to one of your DJ++ machines as EastSalesUser1, then hand-install the latest OneDrive client. And log on to one of your Azure AD machines as Jack Tors and hand-install the latest OneDrive client.

As EastSalesUser1, run GPUpdate to get the latest computer side GPOs. Then log off and back on as EastSalesUser1, which will get the latest user-side GPOs.

If all went well, some magic occurred:

- OneDrive client automatically logged on as EastSalesUser1@fabrikam1000.com (because his account is being sync'd to Azure AD).

- OneDrive automatically mounted your migrated ZDrive as a SharePoint library.

- OneDrive turned on Files On-Demand.

Alternatively, you could also have the user specifically sync a library of their choice. That user would go to the SharePoint site (usually Fabrikam1000.SharePoint.com) and then find the library and click the Sync button as seen in Figure 7.29.

FIGURE 7.29 How to manually start syncing a SharePoint site

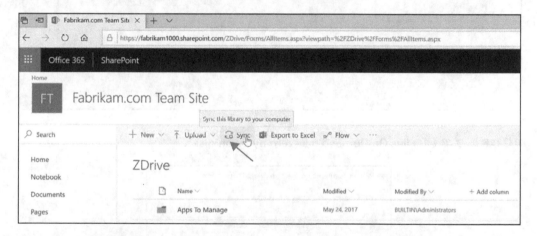

Then, Windows will show a prompt like what's seen here.

After you say yes, OneDrive springs to life and starts to sync that library.

Because we've specified to use Files On-Demand, we can see the difference between a file that is always kept on the device (solid green and checkmark) and one that is available in the cloud (cloud icon.) You can see this in Figure 7.30.

A simple right-click on "Always keep on this device" downloads the needed files to take on the road.

Simple.

Checking out the properties of files in the cloud tells the tale, as seen in Figure 7.31.

FIGURE 7.30   OneDrive Client sync shows files on the device and on demand.

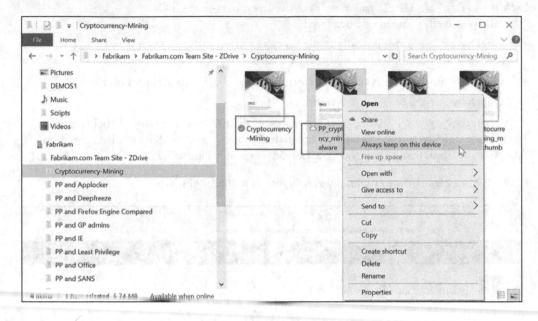

FIGURE 7.31   Files On-Demand take zero bytes on disk.

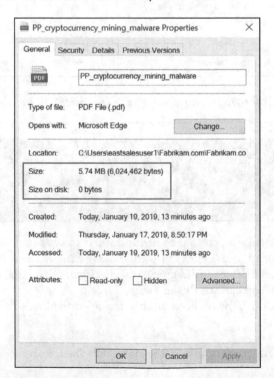

Files that are not downloaded take no disk space.

You can learn more about some of the other OneDrive client settings
(many that have corresponding Group Policy and MDM knobs) at:

https://support.office.com/en-us/article/sync-files-with-
the-onedrive-sync-client-in-windows-615391c4-2bd3-4aae-a42a-
858262e42a49

Saving Space over Time with Storage Sense

Windows 10 1809 and later has a cool feature: Move unused synced files back to cloud
only if not used within a certain amount of days.

To find the setting inside Windows, go to the Windows Settings application, then the
Storage section. Inside, you'll find a section called "Storage sense" as seen here.

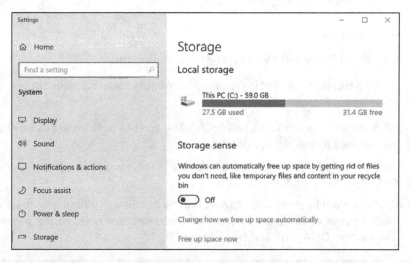

When you click "Change how we free up space automatically," you can see how both
SharePoint and OneDrive can remove content if it's not used in a while.

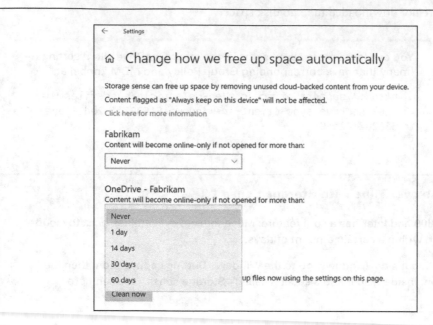

This is a pretty nifty trick.

There are both Group Policy and MDM settings that can set this.

The Group Policy settings are found in Computer Configuration ➢ Administrative Templates ➢ System ➢ Storage Sense.

The MDM CSP that controls this is the Policy CSP. The specific policies are in Storage. You can see all the settings in one place, right here:

```
https://docs.microsoft.com/en-us/windows/client-management/mdm/
policy-csp-storage#storage-policies
```

These are ADMX-backed policies, and I expect that by the time you read this, there will be clickable Administrative Template files in Intune you can click on to configure these. If not, then off to custom OMA-URI land (see Chapter 3).

OneDrive's Magic Trick: Known Folder Move

Previously, we moved existing file shares and made them into SharePoint libraries. That's actually reasonably straightforward because all those files are nicely collected in little piles, ready to be moved.

But files on user's endpoint computers…that's a different story.

Users could have files anywhere on the machine. That's true. And, sorry Mr. User, we cannot scour the hard drive to find all your files that you might have squirreled away anywhere on the hard drive.

But OneDrive's magic trick is an ability called Known Folder Move, or KFM. KFM lets a user (if you want them to) or you (in a controlled or mass-deployed manner) migrate their Documents, Desktop, and Pictures folders to OneDrive.

Why would you do this?

Safety.

Remember the opening posit of the chapter: What happens when someone loses their machine or drops it, rendering it useless? If the most important locations, like Documents, Desktop, and Pictures, are stored on OneDrive, you've closed that hole.

Additionally, if you have any Windows 7 machines that you plan on nuking and later installing Windows 10 on them, this should be very exciting. With the OneDrive sync client installed on your Windows 7 machines, using KFM you'll be able to scoop up your users' most valuable files before you wipe and reload Windows 10.

OneDrive Known Folder Move vs. Folder Redirection

So, in my previous book (*Group Policy: Fundamentals, Security and the Managed Desktop*), I showed how to take various key Windows client folders and, using Folder Redirection, teleport those files to another location on an on-prem server.

Some people have tried to use old-school Group Policy Folder Redirection to teleport those file to OneDrive. I've heard of some successes and some heartaches. By introducing Known Folder Move, Microsoft is saying, "Really, don't use Folder Redirection to teleport files to OneDrive, even if you got it working."

Moreover, Known Folder Move won't work if you have already used Group Policy Folder Redirection to move the Desktop, Documents, or Pictures folder to some other location, like \\server123\Documents\%username%. KFM just cannot grab the files from that location; the files need to be on the client machine.

If you are using Folder Redirection, the documentation says you need to "Remove the Windows Group Policy objects for these folders before you enable the OneDrive Group Policy objects."

Actually, the procedure is a little more (but not a lot more) complicated than that. First note that Redirected Folders (Documents and Pictures go together) and Desktop is a separately redirected folder.

If you're using Folder Redirection, you likely have something similar to what's seen here.

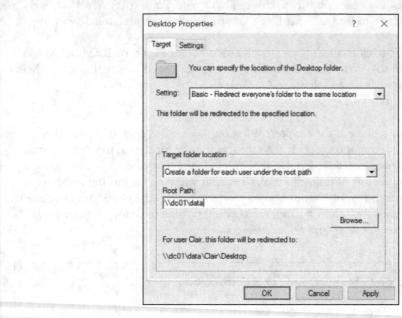

It isn't merely enough to disconnect the GPO's wires and then get on with your Known Folder Move. Instead, you should change it first to redirect back to the user profile location, as seen here.

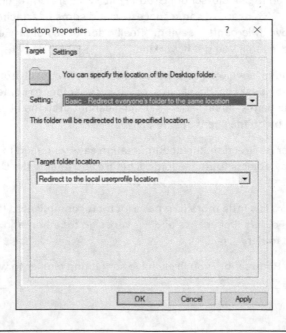

Then, let it bake in for a while until you're reasonably sure your population has gotten the GPO and the work has completed.

In this way, you're backing out of Group Policy-based Folder Redirection.

Then, and only then are you ready to start a OneDrive Known Folder Move.

Manually Performing Known Folder Move (as a User)

By default, an end user can manually perform a Known Folder Move.

If you want to follow along in this chapter, you can look at what's here, but I don't recommend you actually kick off the move.

Inside the OneDrive Sync client's settings within Auto Save, a user can click "Update folders" to start the process, as shown in Figure 7.32.

FIGURE 7.32   This is how an end user could manually initiate a Known Folder Move.

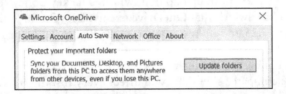

After that, users then simply click "Start protection," as seen in Figure 7.33.

FIGURE 7.33   Manually kicking off a Known Folder Move

Again, I don't recommend you do this now, because I want you to get a feel for doing it with Group Policy.

That said, this can work fine for a handful of users, but it kind of falls apart when you have a lot of them. With lots of users and computers comes at least a little planning.

Getting Ready for KFM by Controlling Bandwidth

Imagine you just turned on Known Folder Move (without buying this useful book full of tips and advice). That would be bad, because then all your computers would send up a billion gigabytes of files all at once to OneDrive.

Don't worry about OneDrive; that system is built like a tank.

I'm worried about *your* network getting overloaded, and you getting 10,000 angry phone calls.

As such you need to plan for the bandwidth you're about to consume. Start out by reading and implementing some of the tips and techniques here: aka.ms/bandwidthplanning.

If you do, you'll get to use one of the least-used features in Group Policy, Quality of Service policy, which can prioritize packets over one another. Beyond that, you can also use OneDrive to specify the maximum upload bandwidth. The key policy setting is named **Set the maximum upload bandwidth that OneDrive.exe uses**. In Group Policy on the user side, it can be seen in Figure 7.25 and on the computer side Figure 7.27. For Intune, you can see it in Figure 7.23.

Because in Group Policy, this setting can be set on either the user or computer side, I recommend using the computer side. This will affect every instance of OneDrive on the computer and will therefore keep things more consistent.

Once it's enabled, the default value is 70%, meaning that 70% of the bandwidth will be used for pushing OneDrive files from Desktop, Documents, and Pictures up to OneDrive.

Remember, you don't have to go whole hog with KVM right away. You can use Group Policy and scope what you're about to do to some computers, then further roll it out to more computers as you're ready and confident that it's working as expected.

Setting Up the Policies for KFM (Group Policy and MDM)

After you've set the stage for bandwidth use and got those policies out the door (via Group Policy or MDM), you're ready to specify the KFM style. The two styles are Prompted or Silent.

Prompted means that users see what you saw earlier in Figure 7.33. Every time OneDrive starts, they get the offer. And they can choose to kick it off or to ignore it.

Silent means just what you'd expect. No prompts; just do it.

Here we'll see how to perform the work with Group Policy for your on-prem machines and for your cloud-only machines with MDM.

Performing a Known Folder Move with Group Policy

The Group Policy setting for a prompted KFM is named **Prompt users to move Windows known folders to OneDrive**. The setting itself can be seen in Figure 7.34. In order to make it work, you need to drop in the tenant ID we acquired all the way back at the beginning of the chapter.

FIGURE 7.34 To perform a prompted Known Folder Move, drop your tenant ID into this policy setting.

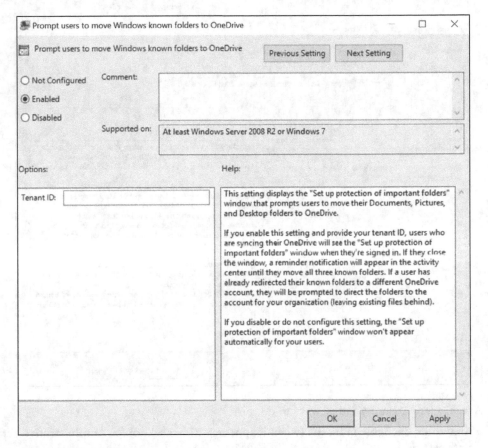

Alternatively, to perform a silent move, you can use the policy setting called **Silently move Windows known folders to OneDrive** as seen in Figure 7.35.

As in the previous setting, you'll need to drop your tenant ID into the policy setting before it will work.

Performing a Known Folder Move with MDM

As of this moment, there is not an easy clickable method via Administrative Templates in Intune. The general gist, however, to configure a Known Folder Move with MDM would be to configure the Registry items using your MDM service.

FIGURE 7.35 To perform a silent Known Folder Move, drop your tenant ID into this policy setting.

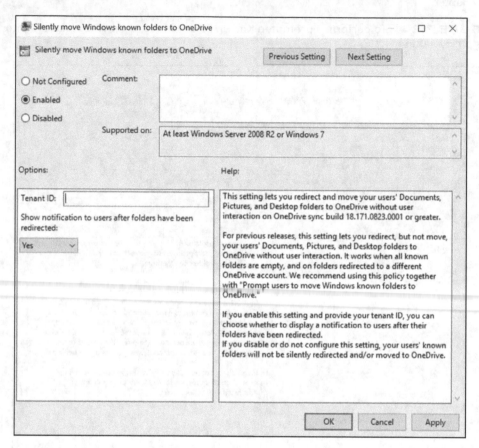

Again, there are a myriad of ways to do this:

- Something clickable in Intune (when it appears). Either a knob or Administrative Template setting

- Ingesting the ADMX template (which we talked about in Chapter 2) and using that to configure the setting. The basic directions for that are found at:

  https://tech.nicolonsky.ch/onedrive-known-folder-move-ms-intune/

- Using a PowerShell script to perform the Registry settings with your MDM service. Two scripts I found for that can be found at:

  https://gallery.technet.microsoft.com/scriptcenter/
  Onedrive-Known-Folder-Move-dfcea689

```
https://osddeployment.dk/2018/07/06/
how-to-deploy-onedrive-known-folder-move-with-intune/
```

- Using PolicyPak MDM to export an Admin Template or make a Group Policy Preferences Registry item and deliver it using your MDM. (More in Chapter 11.)

I expect that by the time you read this, there will be an Administrative Template setting in Intune. So be on the lookout for that.

Seeing Known Folder Move Work

Again, the easiest way to see this work is to run GPUpdate on the client machine to get the latest computer-side settings. Then log off and back on to get the latest user-side settings. This has the added benefit of automatically restarting the OneDrive sync client, which will automatically pick up the new Group Policy settings.

The result will be what you see in Figure 7.36.

FIGURE 7.36   Silent Known Folder Move working

When KFM is done, you can see the change to icons like what's seen in in Figure 7.37. Because we're using Files On-Demand, items are not guaranteed to be there unless they are right-clicked to "Always keep on this device" as I did with, say, this PDF just hanging out on the Desktop, also seen in Figure 7.37. There's a little green circle; it's hard to see, but it's there.

Documents and pictures will act similarly.

FIGURE 7.37   Items on the Desktop are silently moved to OneDrive.

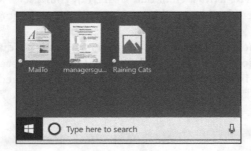

Now you're prepared anytime this machine needs to be replaced.

The user's files are nicely stored on OneDrive and anything that happens to the machine really doesn't matter, including a malware attack (explored in a bit).

One more spit-and-polish thing I think is a good idea here. When this is over, the user could undo what you did. In Figure 7.38, you can see what the user can do by default. That is, they can click "Stop protecting" on any of the three KFM locations. You can use the policy **Prevent users from redirecting their Windows known folders to their PC** (in Group Policy-land).

FIGURE 7.38   Use the **Prevent users from redirecting their Windows known folders to their PC** policy setting (not shown) to gray out the "Stop protecting" links.

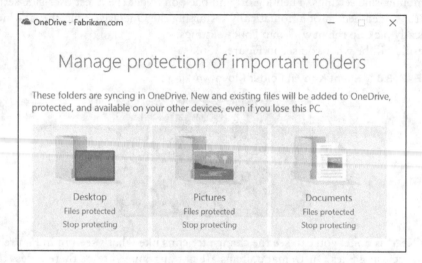

Files Restore (from Malware or User Error)

Malware sucks. Cryptomalware is worse.

And when it hits, it just goes bananas and tries to read and encrypt every file the user has access to (and also drive letters, etc.). But, by having your users' files protected in OneDrive, you get the benefit of being able to use OneDrive to perform a point-in-time restore.

A user would go to their OneDrive location, which is a little bit different than the SharePoint URL we explored earlier. A user's personal OneDrive location would be something like https://fabrikam1000-my.SharePoint.com/. Once logged on, they simply click the gear icon, click "Restore your OneDrive" as seen in Figure 7.39. and follow the prompts.

FIGURE 7.39   How a user can manually restore their own OneDrive

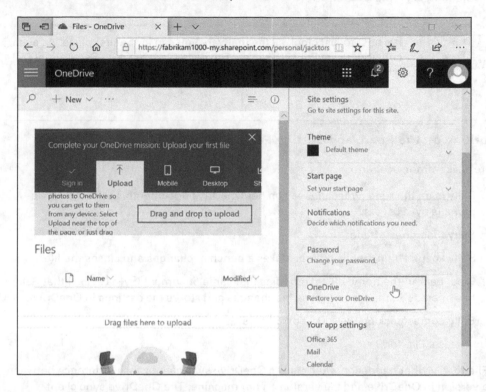

Then a user can pick a day, like Yesterday (as seen in Figure 7.40) or a specific number of days ago. And...bingo. Instant restore.

FIGURE 7.40   Pick a day ago or a custom date to restore to.

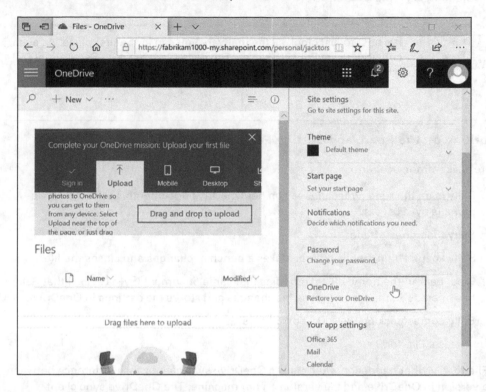

Take that, cryptomalware!!

 It's best to just block all the malware you can in the first place. As such, consider using PolicyPak Least Privilege Manager with SecureRun(TM) which does a heck of a good job here.

Working on the Road, and Getting Forked Files

Here's a common scenario:

- Sally is on the road, working away on her OneDrive documents. Let's say the file-name is myFile.txt.

- Sally then goes offline.

- Sally keeps editing while offline. Makes a bunch of changes and closes the file.

- Fred, back in the home office, modifies that same document (myFile.txt) that Sally has open. Fred makes and saves his changes and stores the settings in OneDrive.

- Sally comes back online and…Forkin' files!

So, what is a File *fork*?

A File fork is what happened when Sally's OneDrive sync client saw a difference between the version in OneDrive and the version on her machine. The OneDrive sync client shouldn't overwrite the cloud version, and it shouldn't get blown away by the different copy on OneDrive.

So what happens in this case is the following:

- Fred's copy "wins." The OneDrive file is the "source of truth" in this universe.

- Sally's file "loses." Sally's file gets renamed to myFile-COMPUTER1.txt.

- Because that file is newly created by the OneDrive sync client, it gets sent up to the OneDrive service.

Result? Sally's OneDrive gets myFile.txt (from Fred, actually), and a new file, myFile-Computer1.txt, will be seen locally on Sally's computer and also in OneDrive.

Now, if you see this happen, that's what likely occurred.

Note that Office 2016 and later is a little special and has the ability to merge changes or keep both copies (fork) as seen here.

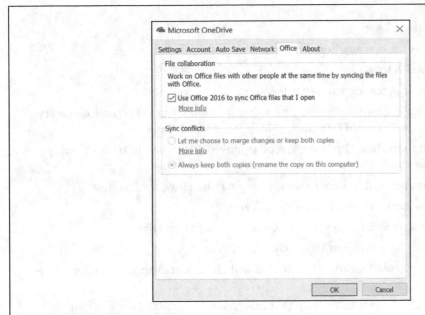

You can change this behavior for Office 2016 and later with the policy setting **Users can choose how to handle Office files in conflict**.

Final Thoughts

You can't take it with you when your PC's dead.

But you can store it nicely in the cloud: your settings and your files.

And that's what we did with Enterprise State Roaming and OneDrive.

We accomplished a lot with OneDrive in this chapter, but alas, there's a bunch of stuff I *couldn't* cover in the OneDrive section. Most of what I didn't cover is in the OneDrive Admin Center (admin.onedrive.com). In there, you'll find lots more to explore, like setting up auditing, Data Loss Prevention (DLP), retention policies, alerts, and more.

In case you want more on OneDrive, some additional resources (with self-describing URLs) are listed here:

- docs.com/OneDrive

- https://docs.microsoft.com/en-us/onedrive/plan-onedrive-enterprise

- aka.ms/ODAdminDocs for administrative guidance.

- aka.ms/onedriveblog

- aka.ms/OnPremSync

- aka.ms/UninstallGroove

- aka.ms/KFMFaq
- aka.ms/FilesOnDemandMac
- aka.ms/productivitylibrary (for end users)

Here are two special resources:

- OneDrive.uservoice.com for voting for features
- The OneDrive blog for interesting and up-to-date materials. https://techcommunity .microsoft.com/t5/Microsoft-OneDrive-Blog/bg-p/OneDriveBlog.

If you want to watch the best OneDrive videos at Ignite 2018, I would recommend typing in the session codes at YouTube:

- **THR2142:** What you need to know about managing OneDrive for Business
- **BRK3099:** Microsoft OneDrive Deployment deep dive
- **THR4009:** Microsoft OneDrive Sync Fundamentals and Deep Dive
- **BRK2131:** Driving Adoption and Usage with OneDrive
- **BRK2126:** How to build OneDrive habits that will make users happier and more productive

Now, you're (reasonably) safe to go drop that machine in a (virtual) lake and ship the user a brand-new computer...in the next chapter...With Autopilot.

Before you do that, tweet me @jeremymoskowitz with the hashtag #mdmbook and let me know what you learned in Chapter 7!

Chapter 8

Rollouts and Refreshes with Configuration Designer and Autopilot

At this point in the book, you've got a pretty nice layer cake:

- You're enrolled in MDM, which gets you the ability to remotely manage the machine.

- You've got computers automatically putting themselves into dynamic groups.

- You've got applications of all kinds downloading automatically.

- You've got scripts running when needed.

- You're using MDM to deliver the in-box policies for Windows and some applications.

- You've got users' data stored nicely in OneDrive.

Everything is going great.

Until…Jack leaves his PC in the back of a taxi on the way to the airport.

Crap.

Now what?

The way I see it, there are four scenarios:

Scenario 1 After Jack lands, let Jack run to the electronics store and buy his own machine.

Scenario 2 After Jack lands, he can go into a nearby branch office that your company has, and someone there can just give him a machine (which, conveniently, already has Windows 10 on it).

Scenario 3 You can drop-ship a new, but unconfigured, PC to Jack (which you happen to have in your office). He'll get it the next day.

Scenario 4: You can work with an OEM partner like Dell, Lenovo, and others to drop-ship a new machine to Jack.

In all cases, Jack's new machine will have to be configured to your corporate standards. Of course we want to configure as much as possible to be automated.

There are a few more scenarios to contemplate along the way; for instance, if Jack leaves the company and you want to give Jack's perfectly good computer to someone else. How can you quickly clean up the Jack-specific stuff and get it ready for Tom? And, yet another thing to consider: Jack's perfectly good machine just ups and dies. Well, the hard drive does.

For all of the above scenarios, we'll be using two methods to do as much automation as possible in this chapter: the Windows Configuration Designer (WCD) and Autopilot.

The goals of both of these technologies is ostensibly the same: Instead of wiping and reloading a machine with a perfectly good operating system already on it, you get to use what the OEM shipped in the box. Then get close to your desired configuration goals… faster.

This ends up being way faster than wiping and reloading, plus avoiding all the pre-game time to stage the "perfect golden image."

Windows Configuration Designer

So let's pretend we have scenario 1 first. That is, Jack lost his laptop, and he just has to go to Best Buy or gets a new laptop from Amazon or otherwise acquires a new machine.

This machine likely already has Windows 10 on it, but maybe not the right *version* of Windows 10. For instance, Pro and not Enterprise.

And, we definitely want Jack to be up and running right away. Having someone rip and replace the image that came on the machine from the manufacturer is super time consuming, that's for sure. Yes, you could argue that ripping and replacing will get rid of "bloatware" and unnecessary items, but you can already do that when you buy PCs with the "signature" edition. Signature edition PCs come liberated without the bloatware and cruft of old. But with what we'll do together, you can also blow the unwanted junk off the machine.

You can learn more about these Signature edition machines here:

https://www.microsoft.com/en-us/store/b/pcsignatureedition

And here:

https://www.laptopmag.com/articles/
microsoft-signature-edition-windows-10-analysis

But even then, it could be argued that the PC as it comes from the factory is often the best from a performance perspective: You'll get the fastest speeds and the best battery life if you don't mess too much with what came in the box.

Get WCD from the Windows Store

How do we take an existing PC with Windows 10 already on it and transform it to our will? Get Wicked! Well, it's really called Windows Configuration Designer, or WCD, but sometimes I've heard it pronounced *wicked*.

WCD comes in two forms:

- Part of the Windows ADK (Assessment and Deployment Kit)
- Downloadable in the Windows Store as a Store app

In this book, we'll use the Windows Store app. Why? Well, it's always kept up-to-date and it's a lot easier to install, that's for sure.

Well why would you ever need the ADK version then? Only if you needed to go backward and teach an older machine, say, a Windows 1803 or 1709 or 1703 or similar machine, how to be reconfigured.

If you use the Windows Store WCD, it's always up-to-date, lockstep with whatever the most current version of Windows is. You can acquire WCD on your management station. Just head over to the Windows Store and search for it, and then get it as shown in Figure 8.1.

FIGURE 8.1   Getting the Windows Store version of the WCD

What Can You Do with WCD? (And What Shouldn't You Do with WCD?)

In this scenario, where Jack gets a new Windows machine, it has to be the latest version of Windows to work with what we'll do here with the Windows Store WCD. If Jack is handed an older Windows machine, he has to get it upgraded to the latest version of Windows (using Windows's auto-update) before the Windows Store WCD will reconfigure it to your liking.

But then after that, what can you do with WCD? Here are some big wins:

- Install Win32 applications.
- Enroll device in Active Directory.
- Join Azure AD.
- Add certificates.
- Change product versions.
- Specify Wi-Fi parameters.
- Email profiles.
- Run PowerShell scripts.
- Configure "Always on VPN" client.
- Remove OEM bloatware.

Can you do *everything* that you could do if you were using an imaging process? No not everything, but a lot of things—typically the most important things.

I wouldn't recommend you try to configure anything you're *also* going to be dictating through MDM, like policies or certificates. But I could see a world where maybe you need to provision some items to be guaranteed right away, or items that are somehow particular to these machines and not something that would come down from MDM.

And that's the point of the WCD.

WCD Example

In this example using WCD, we'll install an application Jack needs right away as well as remove any bloatware, also known by the more "politicially correct" name of *pre-installed software*.

Start out by running WCD and then selecting "Provision desktop devices," the first tile in the upper-left corner as seen in Figure 8.2. As you can see, there are a lot of other things the WCD can do, like provision HoloLens and Surface Hubs, but we'll just skip over all that stuff.

FIGURE 8.2   WCD main screen enabling you to perform provisioning tasks

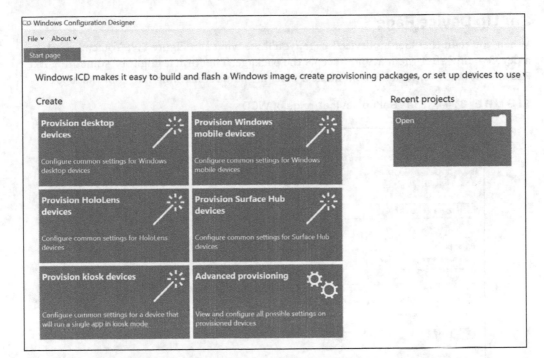

In Figure 8.3 you'll see the steps you'll take before a provision file, known as a .PPKG file is finalized. I'm going to demonstrate some, but not all, of these steps. Note also that at the bottom the page (not shown), there's a way for you to "Switch to advanced editor," which we'll talk about a little later.

FIGURE 8.3   The WCD navigation for "Provision desktop devices"

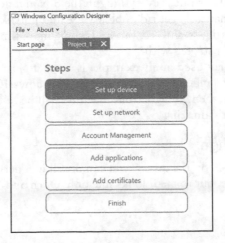

Let's go through each major page, one by one (briefly).

Set Up Device Page

When you're in the "Set up device" page, you'll see what's in Figure 8.4. You can specify a device name after the machine accepts the package. The format might be something like Fabrikam%RAND:4%, which would make a machine name something like Fabrikam0001.

FIGURE 8.4   The "Set up device" page of WCD

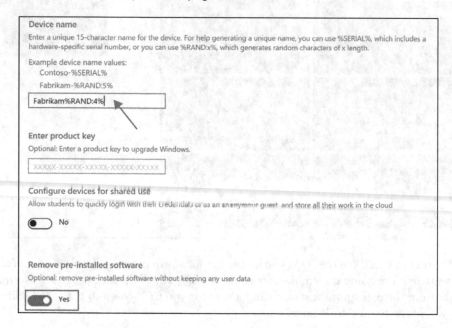

Additionally, my favorite feature is on this page, the "Remove pre-installed software" switch, which will remove darn near everything in the box and do a Windows reset. In other words, it will automatically get rid of bloatware and junk someone might have had in the box and make it spring-fresh! Yes, this adds some more time, but who wouldn't want the cleanest machine to get started with?

Also on this page, but not used in my example, is a way to just throw in a product key for your enterprise, and if a machine starts out life as Windows 10 Pro and you put in a key for Enterprise or Business, then…bingo. Your machine will be re-born as that machine type when this is all over. That's amazing.

Set Up Network Page

If you know you have Wi-Fi on the target, you can prefill in a network SSID to connect to. I didn't try this end to end, but to me it looks like only Open and WPA2 Personal password types are supported.

You can also click this to Off, which will ensure that you must use hardwired Ethernet to continue.

Account Management Page

The Account Management page can be seen in Figure 8.5. On this page you'll select if the machine should enroll into on-prem Active Directory (provided you also have a VPN connection), enroll in Azure AD (which we'll set up), or just have a local admin. I'll select Enroll in Azure AD. You'll also set a Bulk Token Expiry date, which is how long you will allow this package to enroll machines. Maybe you want to set this for 30 or 90 days, or even maybe 10 years in the future. It's your choice. Note that as far as I know, you cannot revoke an enrollment token once it's baked into the .PPKG file. But each time you create a token, it creates an account in AAD that corresponds with that token. If you can figure out which account is used to create that token, just delete that account and that would effectively deactivate the token.

In Figure 8.5, you can see my success after providing Frank Rizzo's Azure admin credentials and setting the date into the future.

FIGURE 8.5   Result of supplying credentials and creating a bulk token

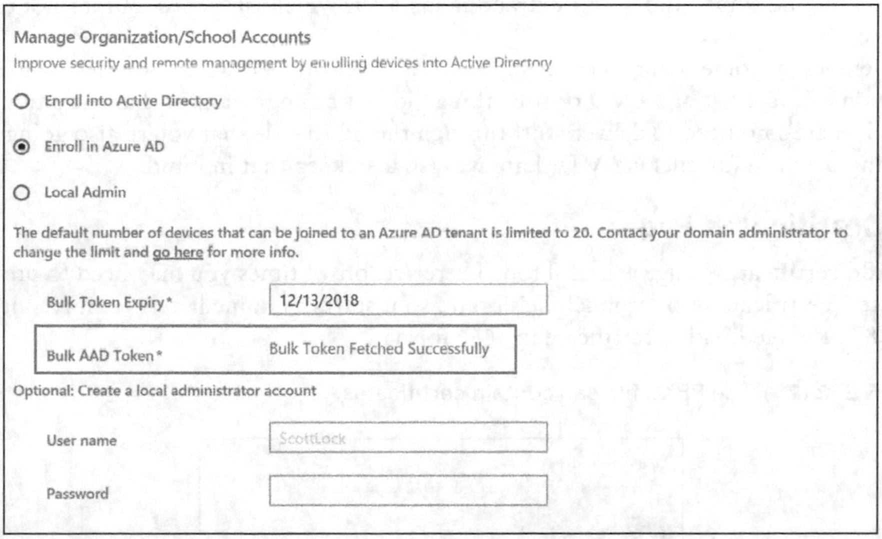

Add Applications Page

The "Add applications" page, seen in Figure 8.6, is useful if you have some package that might not be deployed automatically through MDM. In this example, I'm adding PuTTY (www.putty.org), a common networking application. After selecting it, the command-line arguments are nicely already put in for me, a nice touch.

FIGURE 8.6   Adding applications through the WCD

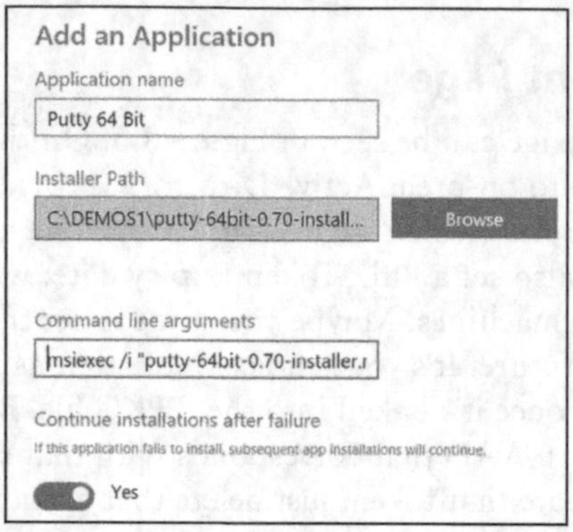

Note that the actual application itself is embedded into the .PPKG file. So the more applications you add, the bigger and badder this file gets. Note that there is a catch with this: you can only have one file for each app, along with a command line to install that one file. So if you have an installer that consists of multiple files, you'll have to bundle those that are utilizing some kind of self-extracting installer, which isn't hard, but it's not really fun either.

Remember, at some point you're going to have to get this .PPKG file over to the user, usually on a USB stick or a DVD or something. So just be cognizant of that. Additionally, as I said, there's no need to deliver stuff through the .PPKG file that you're also going to be deploying over the Internet via MDM anyway, so also keep that in mind.

Add Certificates Page

The "Add certificates" page is useful too. There are lots of times you may need to pre-populate a certificate into the machine's brain, so it starts to immediately trust resources. In Figure 8.7, I'm feeding it a certificate in .CER format.

FIGURE 8.7   The PPKG file can contain certificates.

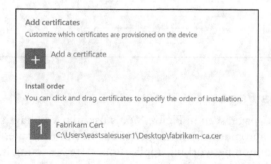

You can click Finish and see a review of the .PPKG file before you save. You can optionally protect the package with a password, which isn't a bad idea, but for this example, I'm not going to.

The Advanced Editor

Additionally, I noted earlier that there is the Advanced editor within the WCD (which I won't be using, but did want to show you). You can see this in Figure 8.8.

FIGURE 8.8   WCD advanced configuration options

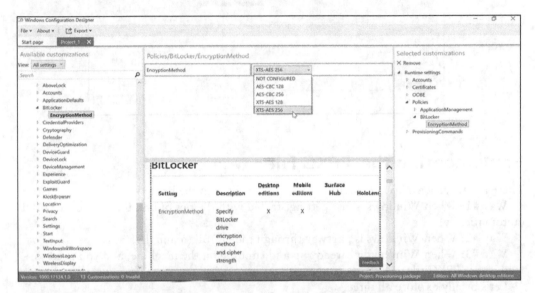

The WCD Advanced pane opens up even more possibilities of knobs and things to do. Some are pretty awesome and important, like turning on BitLocker, DeviceGuard, and Defender. And some are just fun, like Desktop background and other look-and-feel items (that could be covered in MDM-land).

I have two warnings about the advanced editor though:

1. The Simple editor we've been using then becomes unavailable for the same .PPKG file. That is, going forward, if you use the Advanced editor for the advanced stuff, you cannot use the Simple editor again.

2. When you save your packages out using the Advanced editor, you need to expressly specify that you are an IT admin and not an OEM or other vendor type. You can see this in Figure 8.9. You'll also need to update the Version number in case you make any updates later, or else existing machines will ignore any files (with the same version) they've seen before.

FIGURE 8.9   Exporting packages in the Advanced view requires you to specify that you're an IT admin and specify the version.

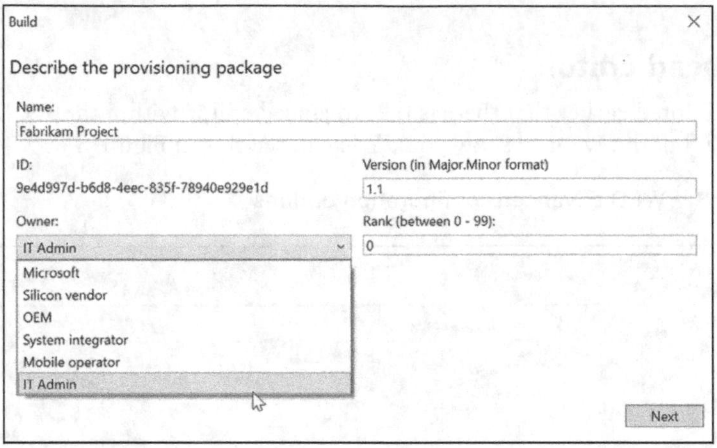

Implementing the .PPKG File

There are three ways to get the .PPKG file implemented to the box

Way #1: When Windows is just getting started with the out of box Experience, or OOBE (automatically)

Way #2: When Windows is partway through the OOBE (manually)

Way #3: When Windows is already up and running on the machine, and you need to feed it the .PPKG file

Let's briefly explore all three.

Implementing the .PPKG File Automatically during OOBE

Back to Jack. Remember Jack? He just went to Best Buy and bought a new laptop. And you've got him a USB stick with the .PPKG file.

All Jack has to do is put in the USB stick with the .PPKG file in the machine and turn on the machine when it starts the first time.

That's it.

When he uses the USB stick, Windows OOBE will open the .PPKG file and just ask him if he wants to set up the device (not shown in any screen shot). Jack simply says yes, and then…Jack gets some coffee while Windows does its thing.

Implementing the .PPKG File Manually during OOBE

What if Jack already turned on the machine because he couldn't wait a second longer? But he didn't know all the answers, and now Windows is not quite ready but still in the OOBE. In this case, Windows started to take care of some initial housekeeping items and Jack missed the window to get the OOBE to see the USB stick automatically and start to use it.

No problem. Tell Jack to hit the Windows key five times. Then it will wake up and see the USB stick with the .PPKG file on it. Jack then says yes to use the file, and Jack will see what's in Figure 8.10.

FIGURE 8.10   The .PPKG file is consumed during OOBE.

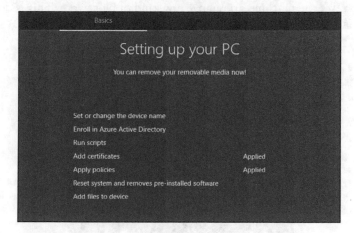

Implementing the .PPKG File after Windows Is Already on the Machine

What if Jack didn't know you were going to send him a USB stick with a .PPKG file and finished OOBE and now Windows is running? Or, similarly, what if Jack was handed a machine from the supply closet, with Windows already running?

In this case, Jack will need to feed Windows the .PPKG file on the USB stick. It's as simple as double-clicking on the .PPKG file. The person doing it will need local admin rights, but that's all there is to it. When they double-click on the file, they'll get what's in Figure 8.11.

FIGURE 8.11   Selecting the .PPKG file after Windows is running

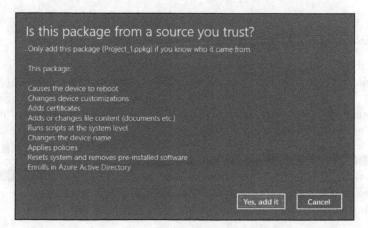

Results from Using a .PPKG File

When the .PPKG file runs (from any of the aforementioned techniques), the final result is the same. In my WCD example, I made a .PPKG file where I wanted the following things to occur:

- I wanted to reset the machine, to remove any kind of bloatware. This is done and seen when the machine is reset, as seen below.

- I wanted to join Azure AD and auto-enroll in to MDM and download all my policies. This is done, but not shown.
- I wanted the machine to get the name Fabrikam*Number*. This is done, but not shown.
- I wanted to install a special application, PuTTY, right away. This is done, and shown in Figure 8.12.
- I wanted to put a special certificate on the machine, right away. This is done, but not shown.

Final Thoughts about WCD

I like WCD. I think it's a big step forward in provisioning a machine without having to rip and replace what's already on the machine in order to make it immediately useful for "the next guy."

WCD's Simple editor gets the job done for the basics, and the Advanced editor has a lot of awesome configuration options in there as well.

As I said a few times already, I wouldn't try to do things in WCD that you're *also* going to do with MDM. Just pick one method. And if you can pick the MDM method, then I would just do that, because it's more policy-based than WCD. In other words, remember that WCD is a one-time action, where MDM is about setting the settings you'll get *now*, plus the ongoing settings and policies you want people to get *tomorrow*.

FIGURE 8.12 PuTTY is installed via the .PPKG file, before the rest of the items come down from MDM.

The official docs on WCD can be found here:

`https://docs.microsoft.com/en-us/windows/configuration/`
`provisioning-packages/provisioning-install-icd`

And a good YouTube video on the subject can be found by searching for "BRK3393."

Autopilot

Autopilot is getting a lot of buzz. Like if you ask 100 admins why MDM is a "cool thing," almost all of them would say, "Autopilot!" But then ask an IT admin how Autopilot changes the game, you might get a variety of stories.

Here's the point of Autopilot: Instead of taking a nice, brand-new machine from the factory and ghosting it, MDT-ing it, or otherwise nuking it to overwrite it with your "unique snowflake" image, you can stop all that madness.

You can take the device right from the manufacturer and transform it immediately into something ready for productive use. G'bye wipe and reload, and hello immediately useful.

As a bonus, Autopilot enables you to pre-answer the questions that would occur when the machine is started up for the first time and runs the OOBE. The user needs only to specify the language and keyboard, connect to Ethernet or Wi-Fi, and provide their credentials.

Then the machine is enrolled into your MDM service, like Intune, and…a machine with the operating system, your customizations, policies, and your installed applications is ready to rock.

Just drop-ship the machine, turn it on, wait a little bit. And bingo. New machine, let's get to work!

Autopilot is a cloud-based service, run by Microsoft, that stores hardware IDs (more in a minute). When a machine turns on for the first time and is registered in your Autopilot, something magical happens. Autopilot will dictate a few final setup instructions, reducing the interaction by the end user to a few, or even zero, clicks before the machine is ready to be used by the end user.

So, let me break down what Autopilot is in simple terms as seen in Figure 8.13.

FIGURE 8.13   The Autopilot infrastructure

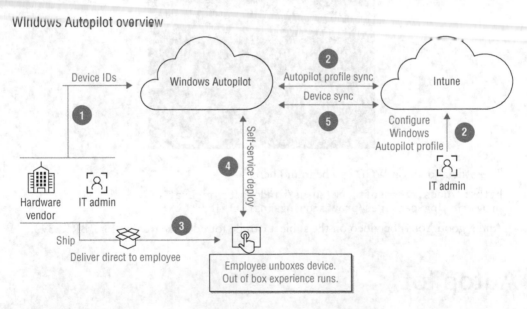

Windows Autopilot overview

1. A Windows 10 device has a unique hardware identifier (also known as a hardware hash). I'll just call this the hardware ID. If you own and want to then manage the device, you (or an OEM hardware vendor or IT service provider) would pre-stuff that hardware ID into the Autopilot service. (I'll explain later how to do that.) A Windows machine gets shipped to an end user. The Windows 10 machine can be delivered directly from an OEM like Lenovo, HP, or Dell, or you can do the work yourself on existing machines (after a little preparation).

2. The admin configures the Autopilot profile for machines. This tells the computer how to act when it first starts up.

3. The machine gets shipped from the OEM (or possibly by you) to the end user.

4. User gets the new machine, opens it up, turns it on, and connects it to a network. The machine contacts the Windows Autopilot service. When Windows 10 starts outs in the OOBE as we already talked about, it asks the servers at the Microsoft mothership if the machine's hardware ID is pre-enrolled (registered) in your Azure AD tenant. Specifically, your Azure AD tenant and not, say, someone else's Azure AD tenant.

5. If the machine's hardware ID is detected in Autopilot, the machine enrolls into your Azure Active Directory (AAD).

If you have enabled automatic enrollment to an MDM service (say, Intune) after AAD enrollment, your device will be enrolled to Intune.

Then after a while, it gets all the stuff Mr. or Ms. User needs to be productive: apps, policies, scripts, Windows updates, Windows features, and so on from the MDM service.

And, the beauty of Autopilot is that when the machine is done enrolling into MDM, the end user can be just a standard end user and *not* an administrator (it is configurable if you'd like it to be a local admin). If you'll remember back in Chapter 2, "Set Up Azure AD and MDM," when we hand-enrolled a machine to MDM via the out of box experience, the person doing the enrollment became a local admin. And likewise, also in Chapter 2, when we hand-enrolled a machine to MDM via the "Set up a work or school account" option, that person also became a local admin.

Not good. You don't want that.

Autopilot nicely tidies up this "local admin" problem for us when a user gets a new computer. Or, if for some strange reason you want your user to have admin rights after you drop a machine into their lap, you can also do that with Autopilot.

That's the basic summary of Autopilot for new device deployment.

But Autopilot is also useful *after* the device is deployed.

Autopilot also has hooks to remotely reset a device, which we'll also explore later. This is super handy when it comes to resetting a machine to basically wipe it down to the studs. Then, next time it connects during the (now) "born again" out of box experience, it then connects back to Autopilot, reregisters in MDM, and once again the computer then gets all the stuff Mr. or Ms. User needs to be productive: apps, policies, scripts, Windows updates, Windows features, and so on. All of that configuration just drops onto the device, and, oh yeah, all their documents are happy and secure in OneDrive because you did that already.

Autopilot does have some prerequisites. And if you're following along in the book examples, you've already got them. But to put a fine point on it, Autopilot will work with the following subscriptions. You only need one:

- Microsoft 365 Business

- Microsoft 365 F1

- Microsoft 365 E3

- Microsoft 365 E5

- Enterprise Mobility + Security E3
- Enterprise Mobility + Security E5
- Azure Active Directory Premium P1 or P2 and Intune or another MDM service
- Intune for Education Subscriptions
- Microsoft 365 Academic A1, A3, or A5 subscriptions

More could also be available by the time you read this. You can see this list at:

`https://docs.microsoft.com/en-us/windows/deployment/windows-Autopilot/windows-Autopilot-requirements-licensing`

Why these subscriptions? Well, first you need MDM auto-enrollment after AAD enrollment, which is an AAD Premium feature. I said right in Chapter 2, before you decided on what to buy (or even what to investigate), that auto-enrollment was a "must-have." The second reason is that you get custom branding; that is, using your own company name, company logos, custom help text, and so on; we'll explore this a bit later.

Also, normally it doesn't make any sense to buy AAD Premium and Intune separately, because Enterprise Mobility + Security E3 is cheaper than AAD Premium and Intune.

Getting Devices Registered into Autopilot

The first and most important step in Autopilot is to get devices' Hardware IDs tucked away inside your Autopilot. Not some other guy's Autopilot instance.

Yours.

That way when your machines turn on, they wake up, see their hardware ID in your Autopilot, and get your directives.

The easiest way to get devices registered into your Autopilot is to have an OEM do it for you or have the OEMs give you a list of devices you're about to buy in a CSV file. Participating OEMs include Dell, HP, Lenovo, Microsoft (Surface devices), Toshiba, Panasonic, and Acer. Check the list of participating manufacturers at `http://aka.ms/WindowsAutopilot`.

Basically, there's some magic under the hood where, when you buy a slew of new machines, and tell them your Azure AD tenant name (e.g., `fabrikam1000.onmicrosoft.com`) and tenant ID (your Azure GUID). There is an approval process that you have to go through for each OEM, which enables them to add devices on your behalf. After that, they will then auto-plunk the hardware IDs of the machines you're about to buy directly into your Autopilot service. Or, you can opt to have them give you a list of the devices in a CSV file, which you can upload yourself.

Additionally, you can work with the OEMs to start out with the most stripped-down Windows possible, free from as much bloatware as possible to make this go well.

I haven't done this myself, so I cannot speak to the process. I suspect it's a little different for each vendor. And if you buy a gaggle of machines from an OEM vendor, I'm sure you'll get nice, white-glove service for getting those hardware IDs into your Autopilot.

Beyond the idea of OEMs automatically putting hardware IDs into your Autopilot service, there are other ways you can place them into your Autopilot service. Indeed, there are multiple portals for defining where Autopilot hardware IDs can be stored. Four portals, in fact, where hardware IDs can be stored. Why four? Let's check each one out.

Microsoft Store for Business   This was the original place Autopilot hardware IDs were stored. This is still valid, but it's only needed if you use an MDM provider other than Intune.

Microsoft Intune   Intune has an Autopilot blade where you can just put in your IDs. This is where we'll be doing our registrations in this chapter.

Partner Center   You might partner with a reseller or integrator who sells you hardware and needs to add devices on your behalf. I'm not going to worry too much about this portal in this chapter, but you should know it exists. There's a good write-up on this here if this is your scenario:

```
https://osddeployment.dk/2017/07/07/
how-to-use-windows-Autopilot-from-microsoft-partner-center-csp/
```

Microsoft 365 Business   This is for small and medium-size businesses, usually fewer than 300 seats. Organizations with this subscription can partake in the fun as well.

As I said, Autopilot is really is its own service, but there's a place inside Intune to manage it. The fastest way to get there inside Intune is Device enrollment ➤ Windows Enrollment, where you can then see a section entitled Windows Autopilot Deployment Program, as seen in Figure 8.14.

FIGURE 8.14   The Autopilot section within Windows Intune

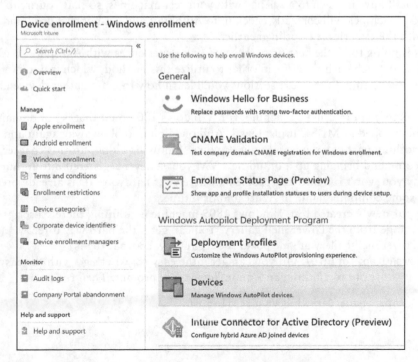

In the next few sections, we'll spend time within these areas (in the following order):

- Devices
- Deployment profiles
- Enrollment status page (often abbreviated ESP)
- Intune Connector for Active Directory

You're welcome to poke around for a second, but I recommend holding off configuring anything until we're ready to do so.

Manually Getting a Hardware ID into Autopilot

What we'll do in this section is an excellent "walk before you run" with Autopilot. We'll grab one machine's hardware ID and put it into Autopilot.

We'll use a PowerShell script running upon an existing, "up and running" Windows 10 machine (1703 or higher). The script outputs a CSV file that we'll then have Autopilot consume.

Why would you want to do this with an "up and running" Windows 10 machine? Well, normally you wouldn't. Remember, the core scenario of Autopilot is "you buy a bunch of machines from Dell or Lenovo and then ship them to your end users."

But you're going to need to pre-flight-test Autopilot so you know it's working perfectly. So when you get the ID of a test system or two or three, you can then keep trying and retrying. Nuking the box, and restarting the out of box experience. Try and try again until you know you've got it right.

Then you'll have it down to a science with your test machines, so that your real "bulk purchased" machines will correctly check in to Autopilot and get bootstrapped and get started with the experience I outlined earlier.

So this is going to be the best first steps and first experiences with Autopilot. But you would have to touch each machine in order to utilize this method, which is not handy...not at all. But don't panic. In the next sections you'll learn how to mass-gather device hardware IDs.

In this example, I'm using a machine with Windows 1809 on it that is not domain-joined, not enrolled in MDM. It just exists. And one I plan to blow away again and again, so it has nothing particularly useful on it. If you're following along, for this chapter, I highly recommend bringing up a brand-new VM you've never registered into Intune before. In this way you won't run into any problems where your hardware ID is already preassigned to some computer name in Azure and/or Intune.

Once your newly created test Windows 1809 machine is running, there's a script we can leverage from the PowerShell gallery. You can get it the hard way directly from the PowerShell gallery at www.powershellgallery.com/packages/ Get-WindowsAutopilotInfo/. Or, you can get it the easy way. Let's go with the easy way.

To use it, start out by running an Admin PowerShell prompt. Then run:

```
Install-Script -name Get-WindowsAutopilotInfo
```

Say yes to any prompts (see Figure 8.15).

FIGURE 8.15   Running the Get-WindowsAutopilotInfo PowerShell script

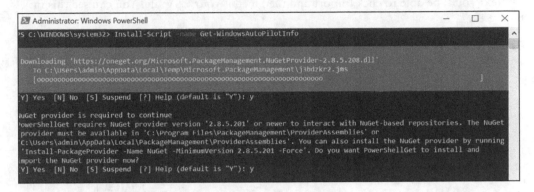

When done, you're almost ready to use the script. You'll need to tell Windows it's A-OK to run scripts. Then run the script and save the hardware ID as a CSV file someplace handy.

```
Set-ExecutionPolicy Unrestricted
Get-WindowsAutopilotInfo -outputfile c:\out1.csv
```

Then open the file with Notepad, as shown in Figure 8.16, to check it out.

FIGURE 8.16   Examining an Autopilot hardware ID

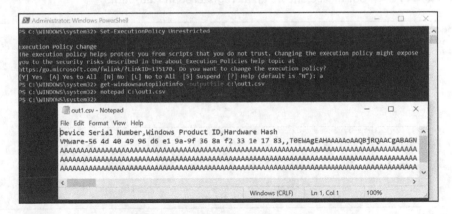

Get this file over to your management station and keep it handy. In the next step, you'll upload the CSV file into Autopilot (through the Intune console).

Uploading Your Device CSV File into Autopilot

Back in the screen shown in Figure 8.14, look for, and then click upon the Devices category.

Next you'll be able to click Import and then feed it your CSV file. You can see this in Figure 8.17.

FIGURE 8.17   Feed Autopilot your CSV file.

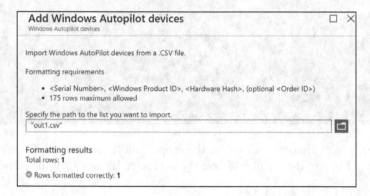

In this example I'm feeding one hardware ID, but you can feed it up to 175 IDs at a time. Then sit back and wait. This process takes a while to complete

When done it will look similar to what's seen in Figure 8.18.

FIGURE 8.18   Your device shows up as registered in Autopilot.

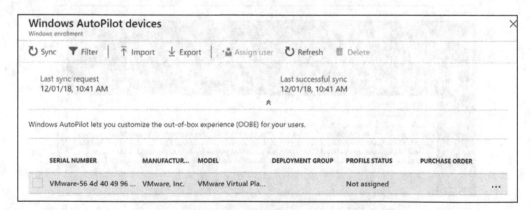

You can come back here in a bit to verify that the hardware ID is A-OK.

In the meantime, you can continue onward and make your Intune Autopilot profile. Before I forget, here are some more resources about getting the hardware ID manually:

```
https://blogs.technet.microsoft.com/mniehaus/2017/12/12/
gathering-windows-Autopilot-hardware-details-from-existing-machines/
```

```
https://docs.microsoft.com/en-us/windows/deployment/windows-Autopilot/
add-devices#collecting-the-hardware-id-from-existing-devices-using-powershell
```

Windows Subscription Activation

When you buy a palate of machines from Dell or Lenovo or whomever, they might not ship you Windows 10 Enterprise. Instead, they might sell you Windows 10 Pro, which you'll then drop-ship to your end users.

But, wait! You don't want to use Windows 10 Pro; you want to use Windows 10 Enterprise. What are you going to do?

Windows Subscription Activation to the rescue!

You assign a Windows 10 E3 or E5 license in Azure AD to a user or a group of users. Then, when the user logs on, it immediately transforms the machine from Windows Pro to Windows Enterprise...bingo...just like that. And, yes, every time a user touches another machine, re-bingo. He would just keep transforming every Pro machine he touches to Enterprise.

Learn more about Windows Subscription Activation at https://docs.microsoft.com/en-us/windows/deployment/windows-10-enterprise-subscription-activation.

Edition Upgrade and S Mode Switch

You might be familiar with Windows 10 in S Mode. We talked about this ever-so-briefly in Chapter 1. Windows 10 in S mode is a way you can buy a machine that will be very secure (hence, the *S*) and only trust applications downloaded and purchased via the Windows Store, and not those attempted to be installed on the machine like a Win32 app.

This is great, until you run into some showstopper where, at least on some machines, it turns out you do need to have, say, Windows 10 Pro or Enterprise instead. This can happen if your application is absent from the Windows Store, or needs a driver to drive some kind of unusual hardware. As I stated in Chapter 1, a one-way upgrade path is possible from Windows S to Windows Pro or Enterprise.

And, you can do this with Intune to one or more machines.

You do this with an Edition Upgrade Profile, as seen here.

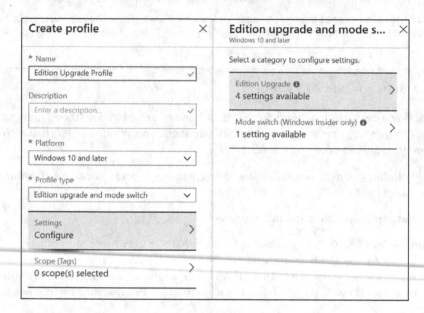

Then, you select the version (seen here) and give it a key (not shown).

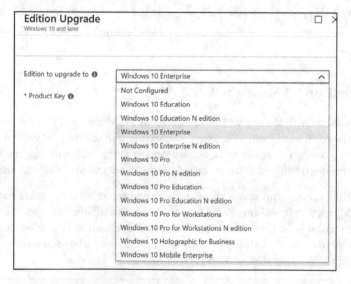

Finally, you can specify to No Configuration, "Keep in S mode," or Switch.

Mode switch (Windows Insider only)
Windows 10 and later

Once a device has been switched out of S mode, it can only be put back into S mode by factory re-setting the device.

Learn more about Windows S mode.

Switch out of S mode: ⊕

| No Configuration ⌃ |
| No Configuration |
| Keep in S mode |
| Switch |

Note that the Windows S Mode switch only works for Windows 10 1809 and later.

Remember though, this really is a one-way trip. If you wish to go backward again to Windows 10 in S mode, you need to format the hard drive and reinstall Windows 10 in S mode.

For more information on edition upgrades and switching away from Windows 10 S mode, see `https://docs.microsoft.com/en-us/intune/edition-upgrade-configure-windows 10`.

Creating Groups for Your Autopilot Machines

Remember the idea of creating groups back from Chapter 3, "MDM Profiles, Policies, and Groups"?

Well, they're about to come in really handy here. (And don't worry if you cannot remember anything about them, or if you skipped it. We'll do it together here.)

In short, the idea is that you will need to have your computers plunked into groups (manually or dynamically). That way, in the next big thing we do together (when we set up Autopilot deployment profiles), you can have different profiles (potentially) hit different groups.

But here's the thing: You don't have computers you can put into groups.

You appear to have an amorphous blob of uploaded hardware IDs, which, ultimately, are just a gaggle of serial numbers that are registered in Autopilot. Technically, what's really happening is that each of these machines really does have an Azure AD object for each imported device. But those Azure AD objects are named using the device serial number (since there is nothing better to use for a name at that point).

What's next? You need to get these serial numbers into groups! You need a serial number to group converter! Do not despair.

As a refresher, you can create two kinds of groups:

- Assigned groups (where you can cherry-pick specific serial numbers)
- Dynamic groups (where you can automatically sweep in Autopilot serial numbers)

Creating an Assigned Group for Autopilot

Creating an assigned group is the quickest way to get started.

But I recommend you read through this section and the next section, because ultimately you might want to just create and use dynamic groups.

If you want to create an assigned group, go back to the Azure Active Directory console and create an assigned group and pick one or more serial numbers, as seen in Figure 8.19. I'm calling my group Autopilot Assigned.

FIGURE 8.19   You can make a direct assignment to Autopilot serial numbers.

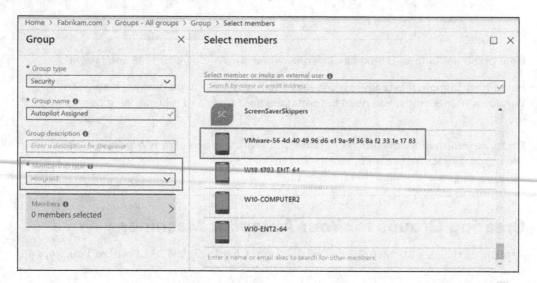

As you can see in Figure 8.19, you can assign and click upon very specific serial numbers, which adds them to a group. And then (a little later) you'll associate this group to a profile.

Note that after the machine is used for Autopilot, magically the display of the machine will change from the serial number to the assigned computer name.

This tripped me up the first time.

So, if you *don't* see serial numbers here after you uploaded the hardware IDs to Autopilot, chances are you already enrolled the system into Intune, and the amorphous blob in Autopilot (which has the computer's serial number embedded within it) has already been converted into a real computer name. As a little side note, to be honest, discovering which computer names have come from *what* serial numbers is really, really hard. I expect this to change in the future.

Creating Dynamic Groups for Autopilot

Alternatively, you might want to just sweep 100% of Autopilot devices into one big ol' group, to manage en masse. You likely don't want to do this in the real world, but this is a good exercise to get you up and going right away.

To do this, you'll use Azure AD groups and create a Dynamic Device group as seen in Figure 8.20.

FIGURE 8.20   Creating a dynamic group for all Autopilot devices

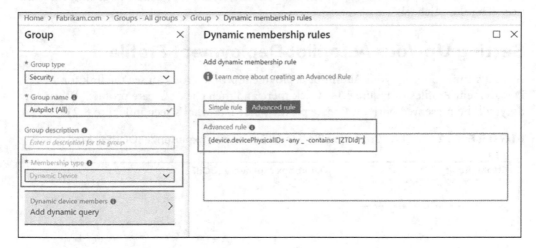

The secret sauce to sweep all Autopilot devices in is:

```
(device.devicePhysicalIDs -any _ -contains "[ZTDId]")
```

In case you're having a little trouble reading this, after the -any there's a space, an underscore, another space, then the -contains.

You can see me use this dynamic query in Figure 8.20.

You can also have queries specific to the PurchaseOrder:

```
(device.devicePhysicalIds -any _ -eq "[PurchaseOrderID]:24601")
```

Same idea here with the syntax. After -any, add a space, an underscore then another space before the -eq.

You can also make a query which discovers computers by OrderID. OrderID is a generic field you can use for, say, expressing Sales machines versus Marketing machines versus Human Resources machines. If you decide to use the OrderID field, your query might be something like this:

```
(device.devicePhysicalIDs -any _ -eq "[OrderID]:Marketing")
```

Later on, if you follow all the examples in this chapter, you'll be using this exact query in a different way; to automatically sweep in machines that will have no human interaction (also called self-deploying machines). So, stay tuned for that.

I made mention about the weird syntax in the preceding examples with the -any, the space, then an underscore, then another space before the -eq. The unusual syntax means to enumerate all the values for that property. The devicePhysicalIDs property is a multi-valued property and, as such, the unusual syntax.

A good blog entry on dynamic groups with Autopilot can be found at Using:

```
https://blogs.technet.microsoft.com/mniehaus/2018/06/13/
Autopilot-profile-assignment-using-intune/
```

And, I also got a little help from the man himself, Michael Niehaus, to get this information. Thanks Michael!

Setting Up Your Autopilot Deployment Profile

Next it's time to set up your Autopilot deployment profile. You can see the link for Deployment Profiles in Figure 8.14. Click there and then click "Create profile." When you do you'll be presented with the Create profile blade like what's seen in Figure 8.21.

FIGURE 8.21 The "Create profile" and "Out-of-box experience (OOBE)" blades

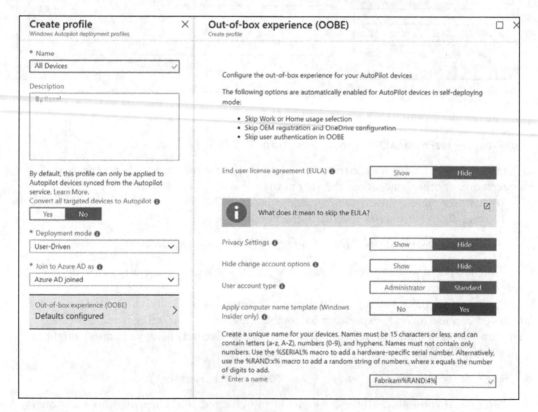

Here's the items you will see in the "Create profile" blade:

- Name: Anything you like
- Description: Optional

- "Convert all targeted devices to Autopilot": This is a one-time, one-way switch that will take existing Windows 10 (1709 and later) devices and send their IDs to Autopilot on your behalf. For now, leave this set to No. You manually uploaded the CSV file with the hardware ID, so you should be okay.

- "Deployment mode": Can be User-Driven or Self-Deploying. We'll do User-Driven in this first attempt. We'll do Self-Deploying later in the chapter.

- "Join to Azure AD as": Can be Azure AD joined or Hybrid Azure AD Joined. We'll do Azure AD joined in this first attempt.

In the OOBE blade, also seen in Figure 8.21, you'll be able to do the following:

- "End user license agreement (EULA)": Show or Hide

- Privacy Settings: Show or Hide

- "Hide change account options": Show or Hide

- "User account type": Administrator or Standard

- "Apply computer name template": No or Yes

As you can see in Figure 8.21, I've decided to hide everything, make the user a Standard user and give a name in the format resulting in something like Fabrikam2898. Click Save (not shown) before continuing.

The next and last stop before trying this out is to marry up your Autopilot profile with a group that you want to target. Click Assignments and pick one of the device groups you created earlier. I'm going to pick my Autopilot (All) group, which will always have every Autopilot device (see Figure 8.22).

FIGURE 8.22   Make the Autopilot profile assignment to an Azure AD group.

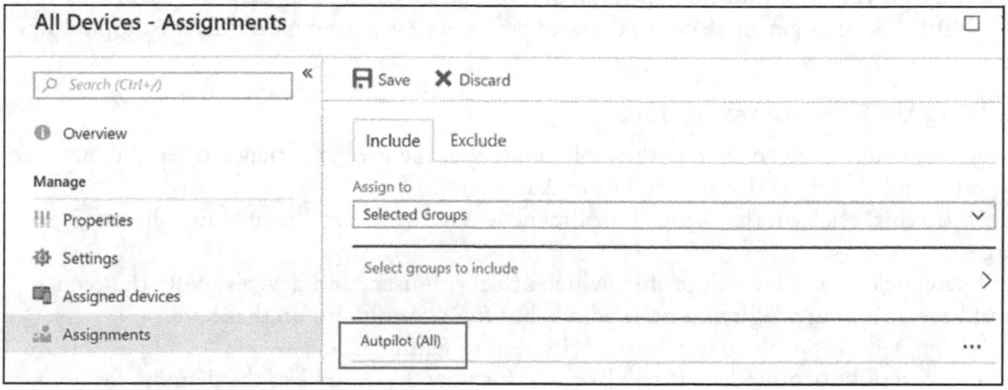

For good measure you can click "Assigned devices" and see which devices should get this profile, as seen in Figure 8.23.

FIGURE 8.23   See which devices will get the Autopilot profile you created.

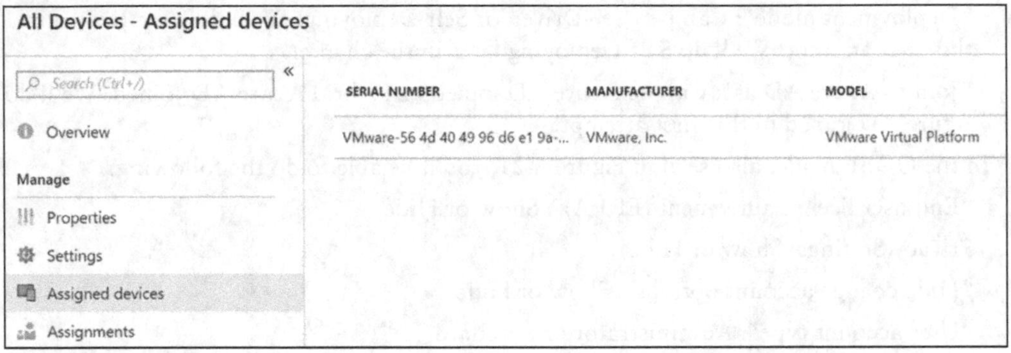

I'm sure you're ready to nuke a machine and get started with testing our Autopilot. Don't.

Don't do it yet.

Just,,,don't.

I recommend you continue onward, and I'll tell you when to hit the "nuke button."

Setting Up Enrollment Options and Setting Up Branding

At this point you can dictate more of the Autopilot user experience via the enrollment options and (optionally) the Azure AD branding.

Both of these hone and craft the look and feel and user experience when users kick off the OOBE. So let's get these out of the way before we even attempt our first Autopilot dry run.

Setting Up Enrollment Options

In Intune you'll want to express the look and feel of the user experience when the machine is getting all its brains downloaded from Autopilot.

To do this, click on the Device Enrollment ➤ Windows enrollment ➤ Enrollment Status Page.

Then click on the Default profile, which affects all users and devices. Note that you could create a new profile and be selective, but I'm not going to do that here.

In the Default profile, select Settings, as seen in Figure 8.24.

You can poke around here if you like, but for now, I would keep the defaults for your initial test flight. You can make it such that the machine waits for certain conditions to be true before releasing control to the end users to start working. Those options are seen in Figure 8.25, but again, I don't recommend you turn them on right now.

FIGURE 8.24   The default "All users and all devices" settings, which I recommend you use in the chapter

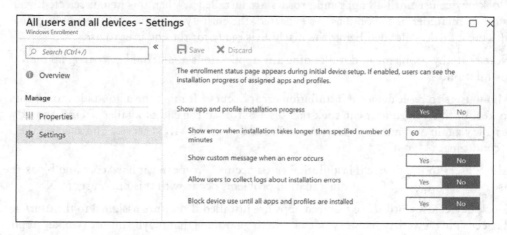

FIGURE 8.25   Additional enrollment options (which I don't recommend for the chapter, but useful in real deployments)

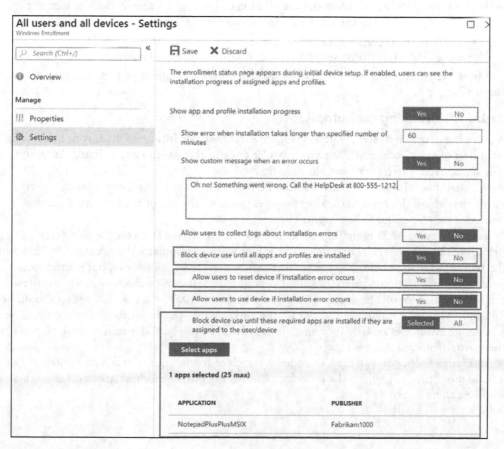

Let's take a look at some of the policies seen in Figure 8.25.

Block device use until all apps and profiles are installed   When this item is selected, you get the remainder of the options. As expected, the entirety of all the applications and profiles must be downloaded before the machine is ready for the end user to use.

Note that any problems in downloading any applications at all could also hang up the installation.

Allow users to reset device if installation error occurs   It might be a good idea to set this to Yes. In this way, a user can click the Reset button at the end of a failed OOBE and at least try again and maybe contact Autopilot and then the MDM service and succeed the second time.

Allow users to use device if installation error occurs   You can get hard core and block the use of the Windows PC if any installation problems occur with this option set to No.

Block device use until these required apps are installed if they are assigned to the user/device   This is a nifty feature you can use to guarantee that maybe one or two key applications are installed first on the machine and then control is released to the user. And then, later, in the background, the other nonessential applications are installed. This gets the user to work more quickly and defers the installation of lesser-used applications to a later time. You can learn more about this particular nuanced feature here:

```
https://blogs.technet.microsoft.com/mniehaus/2018/12/00/
blocking-for-app-installation-using-enrollment-status-page/
```

There are some other settings here as well, but again, I suggest you use the defaults as seen in Figure 8.24.

Azure AD Branding for Autopilot

A completely optional step, which is neither Autopilot-nor Intune-related, is to update the branding of your Azure AD. But when you're done in this area, users utilizing Autopilot will see a visual difference from the defaults.

We call this "the warm fuzzies" in the IT business. Users really like this stuff. They know they're on the right track after they get the machine out of the box; it's a gentle reminder they're going to be alright.

To get to Azure AD branding, click Azure ➤ Azure Active Directory ➤ Company Branding. There are really two fields you might want to populate: the square logo field and the rectangular logo field. The square one can be seen in various areas, but it's the rectangular logo field that you pretty much must populate. Self-deploy mode actually requires the rectangular logo! The square logo should be 240×240. The rectangular logo should be 280×60. Also, you might need to tweak and tinker with your logos to reduce the size. Use a tool like Paint.Net or GIMP or Snag-It to reduce the physical size and on-disk size to get these small enough to be accepted.

In Figure 8.26, you can see I've added a bunch of logos, square and rectangular. If I took a little more time, I could make it perfect, but for my purposes, these are good enough and we'll see them later.

FIGURE 8.26   Configuring Azure AD branding, which you'll see in Autopilot

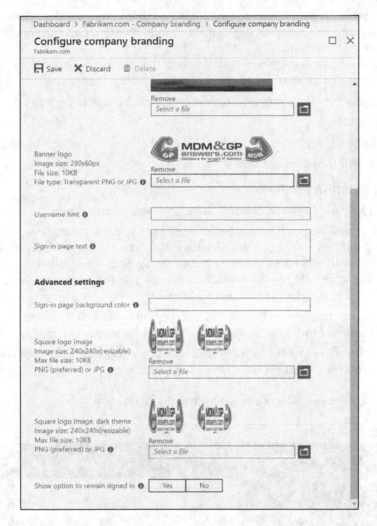

Additionally, beyond the use of branding for Autopilot, branding has a handful of other functions. For instance, from this point onward, when people go to log on to, say, the Azure portal (like Frank Rizzo), they'll also see these graphics to let them know they're on the right track.

A great and detailed blog entry about which branding elements will appear in Autopilot as well as other areas of Azure can be found at:

```
https://blogs.technet.microsoft.com/mniehaus/2017/12/22/
windows-Autopilot-azure-ad-branding/
```

Final Preparation for Autopilot: Reset, Sysprep, or Reinstallation

At this point, you now have one hardware ID in Autopilot. You have set up an Assigned or Dynamic group and the Autopilot deployment profile. You've set up enrollment options and optional Azure AD branding.

Now you need to get a machine ripped down to the (almost) bare metal and start the out of box experience. There are three main ways to accomplish that goal:

- Sysprep a machine (not recommended; but we'll go through it anyway).
- Reset a machine.
- Reinstall a machine.

    Let's explore all those options here.

Sysprep an Existing Machine

Now, you've likely used Sysprep before, but here are some quick notes:

- Sysprep can now be run 99 times before the whole Windows image needs to be replaced. So if you're using a virtualized machine (say, VMware Workstation or Hyper-V), I recommend you take a snapshot before the Sysprep. Then tell Sysprep to perform a Shutdown option. Then take another snapshot when the machine is powered down. (Then you'll be ready to test and retest Autopilot.)

- The Generalize flag seen in Figure 8.27 can be problematic. If you have any down-loaded Windows Store apps, you have to uninstall them first before this will work.

- If Sysprep just doesn't want to cooperate, then don't spend an hour on it. Just move on. As I said, there are other ways to flatten a machine.

FIGURE 8.27   Using Sysprep to get back to the OOBE

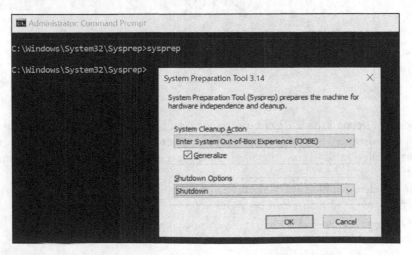

Some quick side notes if Sysprep just doesn't want to work for you:

- Try rebooting the Windows 10 PC; then try Sysprep again.

- You can try the steps in this article, which is kind of like a Sysprep "mind erase."

```
https://www.wintips.org/
fix-sysprep-fatal-error-dwret-31-machine-invalid-state-couldnt-update-
recorded-state/
```

Resetting the PC

You can use the "Reset this PC" feature in the Settings application to initiate a full PC reset. This takes longer than Sysprep, but you can do it an unlimited amount of times. You can see the button to kick this off in Figure 8.28.

FIGURE 8.28 Click "Get started" to reset this PC and provide admin credentials; then follow the prompts.

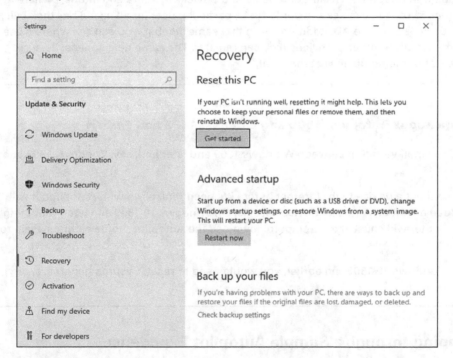

Reinstalling Windows on the PC

If neither Sysprep nor "Reset the PC" is to your liking, you can always just reinstall Windows 10 1809 or later on the same machine or virtual machine (wiping out what's there and literally just reinstalling Windows 10).

Remember, the hardware ID is the same no matter how Windows OOBE gets launched. A Windows Reset, Sysprep, or fresh Windows 10 install will do the trick.

Once you've decided on a method, you can make a strategic snapshot (if you're using VMware Workstation or Hyper-V) after the machine is reset and just before OOBE is about to start. This will come in handy as you try and retry Autopilot settings.

Make Sure Your Users Have Rights to Join Azure AD

Before we get started, the user (and any user) you want to perform this experience must have the right to join devices to Azure AD. In my example, I'll be using Jack Tors, a regular user (and not an admin like Frank Rizzo).

So, if Autopilot isn't working for you as you give it credentials to join Azure AD, check out the sidebar in Chapter 2, "Restricting Users and Devices in Azure and Intune," where in the screen shot, you can see and verify that a particular user (or all users) has the ability to join devices to Azure AD. Additionally, in that same sidebar, you can see where a user has a maximum number of devices they can register. The same deal applies: Be sure they're not bumping up against that limit.

Gotcha about Autopilot (1809 and Later vs. 1803 and Earlier)

There's a small variation between Windows 1809 and later and, say, Windows 1803 and earlier.

If you connect a device to the Internet before it's been registered with Autopilot, it will download a "not an Autopilot device" profile. On Windows 10 1809 and later, rebooting the computer will cause it to attempt to download the Autopilot profile settings again to succeed.

But on Windows 10 1803 and earlier, you would need to reset, Sysprep generalize, or reimage again.

Stepping through a Sample Autopilot Experience

The first three screens after the OOBE starts are not that interesting, and as of this writing, in user-deployed mode, you cannot turn them off. Those initial screens are as follows:

- Pick your region.
- Pick your keyboard layout.
- Pick your second keyboard layout.

Booooring. So I'm not going to show them.

The interesting stuff happens immediately after that where, if you're paying close attention and can catch it, you'll see a very, very brief "Connecting to Microsoft." This is the Autopilot handshake. After that, a reboot occurs to provide the computer with its new name.

Then you'll know you got it all right when you see a screen similar to Figure 8.29. You'll see your company name and company logo (mine is super-duper small—sorry).

FIGURE 8.29   You can see Autopilot is working when you see your company's custom welcome.

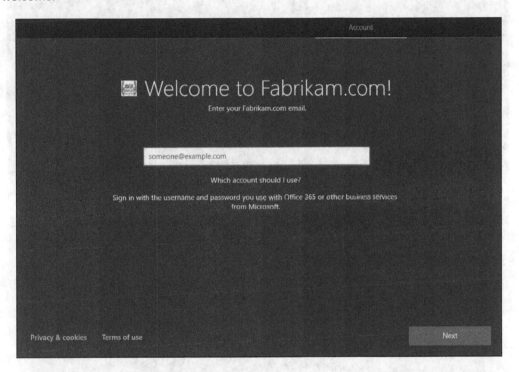

Then, give it the credentials for Jack Tors. As you'll remember, he is not an admin, just a standard user. You'll see Autopilot do its thing (Figure 8.30). If you'd like to also, you can expand the categories by clicking "Show details" and see some more details (Figure 8.31).

The final results of Autopilot are…a beautiful new Desktop:

- You should see your OneDrive data in place.

- You should see your deployed applications from Chapter 6, "Deploying Software and Scripts," in place (like VLC Media Player).

- You should have your policies in place. For example, when you open Edge, you should have your desired tabs always open.

FIGURE 8.30   Waiting for Autopilot to finish configuring the machine

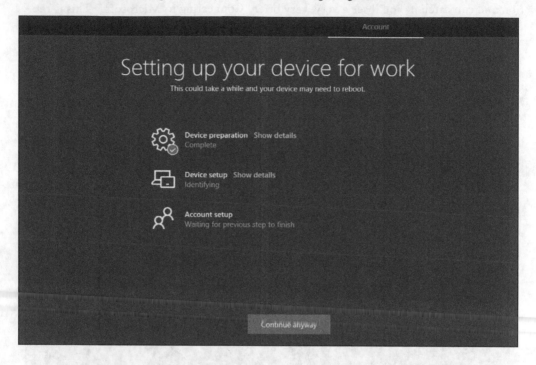

FIGURE 8.31   Autopilot details expanded

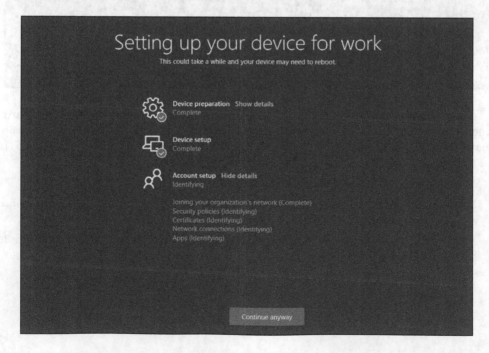

And, remember what happens if this machine needs to get reset?

It just gets reset and it's back in business.

Note for fun that you may want to go back into Azure AD Groups and see that the groups you created, which originally only showed serial numbers instead of computer names, will now show the actual computer name, like Fabrikam7542.

Automatically Harvesting Hardware IDs into Autopilot

Okay: Autopilot is working; life is good.

But remember, you've already got machines out in the field enrolled in Intune. And those machines' hardware IDs are not in Autopilot.

I'll tell you what not to do: Don't run around from machine to machine to collect those IDs with the PowerShell script we created earlier. That's crazy.

Instead, you're going to *harvest* those IDs. I wish I came up with this term, but I didn't. I've heard Microsoft use the term *harvest* a few times and I like it.

Here's the gist: You'll link an Autopilot profile to an existing Azure AD group that contains computers. Or you'll link an Autopilot profile to a dynamic Azure AD group that meets specific criteria (you'll see what I mean in a moment). But before you do this linking, you'll flip a special switch in the Autopilot profile to say "Harvest the IDs of the machines in the Azure AD group if they're not already in Autopilot (and, of course, running Windows 1703 and later)."

Let's first take a look at a group we created back in Chapter 2, the dynamic group where the word *Computer* is in the name. You can see it in Figure 8.32.

FIGURE 8.32   Seeing your existing dynamic group

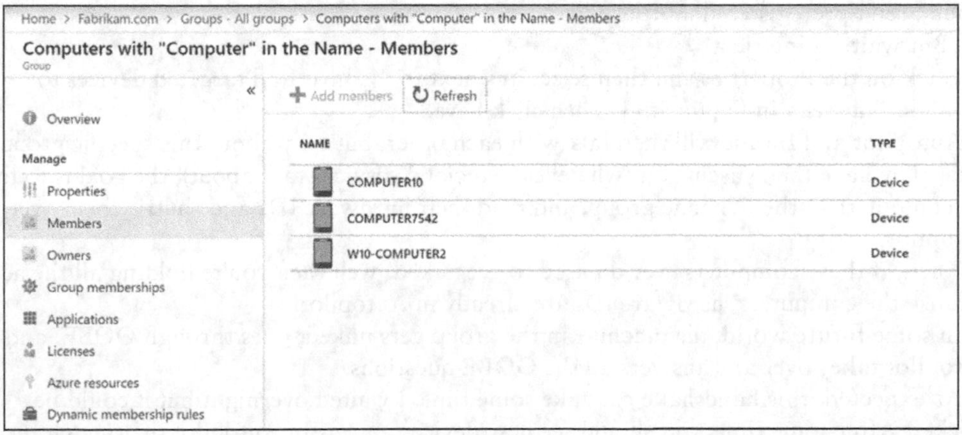

For me:

- Computer10 is one I joined to on-prem AD and used Group Policy to auto-enroll in MDM.
- W10-Computer2 is one I enrolled directly to Azure AD and Intune.
- Computer7542 is the one that got born from Autopilot after I uploaded only the hardware ID and let Autopilot complete the installation.

Next, let's go back to the Autopilot profile. That would be Intune ➤ Device enrollment ➤ Windows Enrollment ➤ Windows Autopilot deployment Profiles and then the device profile you created earlier.

Inside Assignments, in addition to the Autopilot (All) group you targeted earlier, also add in the "Computers with 'Computer' in the Name" group, as seen in Figure 8.33, and click Save.

FIGURE 8.33   Assigning Autopilot to the "Computers with 'Computer' in the Name" group

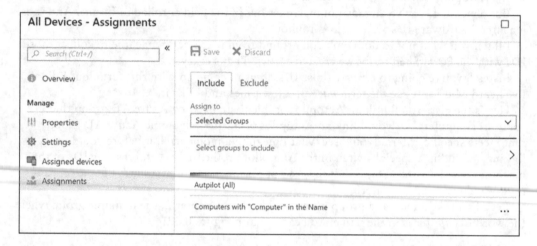

"But wait!" you think to yourself. "This can never work! Those devices in the other group aren't preregistered in Autopilot."

"But wait!" I interject!

Click on the Properties and then select Yes next to "Convert all targeted devices to Autopilot" as seen in Figure 8.34. Then click Save.

Autopilot and Intune will then talk with each other, but only about this specific group. After they have their discussion (whatever two cloud services talk about), the goal is to take the computers in the dynamic group, and read their hardware IDs and shuttle them over to Autopilot.

Then, if these computers ever do need to get nuked, well then you're holding all the aces, because the computers' hardware IDs are already in Autopilot!

In some future world, the machine in the group gets nuked, goes through OOBE, and Autopilot takes over and answers all the OOBE questions.

As expected, this handshake can take some time. I waited overnight but it could be quicker. After some time, you should see new devices appear in Autopilot that match the criteria. In my case, computers with *Computer* in the name are those that are enrolled in my Intune MDM.

After a sync and a refresh in the "Windows Autopilot devices" blade, you can see the results in Figure 8.35.

FIGURE 8.34 Converting targeting devices for Autopilot.

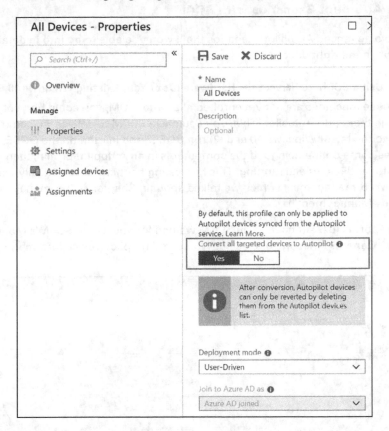

FIGURE 8.35 Seeing newly imported devices in Autopilot

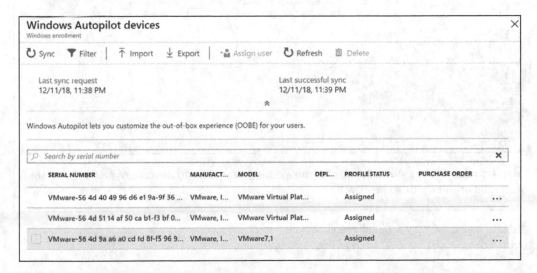

Advanced Autopilot Scenarios with SCCM

There are two advanced Autopilot scenarios that I won't be able to go into in detail, but I can point you in the right direction.

Scenario #1: Using SCCM to Harvest the Hardware IDs of Your Existing Windows 10 Fleet

So even if these machines are not yet enrolled at all into MDM, you could harvest the IDs and pre-stage them into Autopilot. Then you could use SCCM to deliver the commands to (1) upgrade to the latest Windows 10 and (2) run OOBE. And in running the OOBE, when the machines come online...bingo. If the computer is in an Autopilot profile, then it just uses Autopilot and it's off and running. This harvesting happens automatically when you enable SCCM co-management (which we talked about in Chapter 4, "Co-management and Co-Policy Management").

Basically a report is just sitting there in SCCM waiting for you. Go to SCCM's Monitoring ➤ Hardware - General ➤ Reports and select Windows Autopilot Device Information.

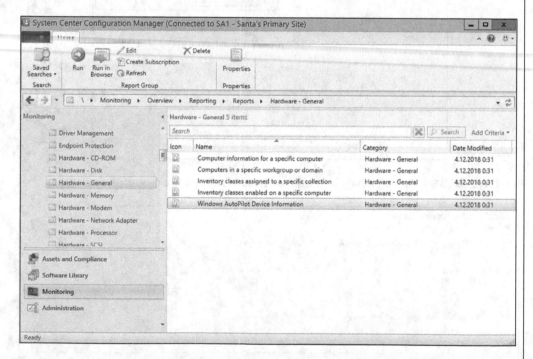

Then you can see the Autopilot IDs for the existing Windows 10 devices (which maybe are or maybe aren't enrolled in MDM).

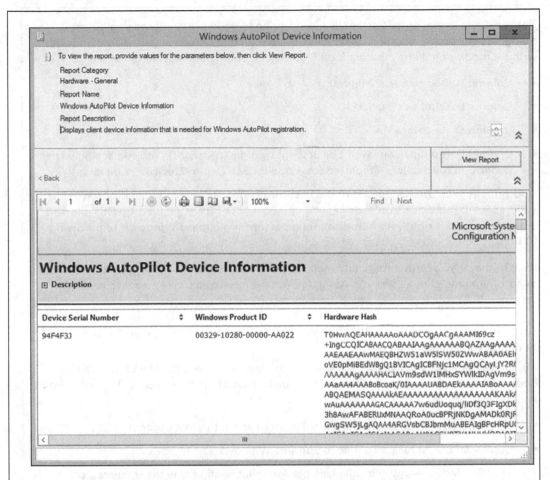

You can export the device information from SCCM and get a resultant CSV file.

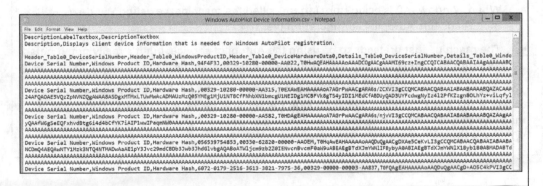

That said, the actual output of the CSV file is going to need a little massaging before going into Autopilot. Because the CSV has more than four columns, you cannot import it without modifying it and cleaning it up first to get just the data that Autopilot wants:

- Column A: Device Serial Number

- Column B: Windows Product ID

- Column C: Hardware Hash

- Column D: (optional, and won't be present by default) OrderID (You can see how I use OrderID in the section "Preparing for Autopilot Self Deploy Devices" a bit later.)

Additionally, you also need to trim the first three lines; as you can see, those are not valid as well. But when you're done, you can take your nicely cleaned-up CSV file and you can upload it right into Autopilot, thus performing a mass Windows 10 hardware ID harvest.

It's a bummer you cannot magically grab IDs from existing Windows 7 machines and then export them and shove them into Autopilot, but the next scenario is meant to help with that.

Scenario #2: Using a Tool, Like SCCM, to Migrate from Windows 7 to 10, then Triggering Autopilot via Configuration File

So, the sad fact is that Windows 7 doesn't have magic hardware IDs like Windows 10 does, so a little extra magic has to occur. Actually, a lot of magic. Here are the basic steps and ideas:

- Generate an Autopilot configuration file (more about this in a second).

- Deploy an SCCM task sequence to upgrade Windows 7 to 10.

- That SCCM task sequence will place the Autopilot config file in the right magical place on the "Not yet born" Windows 10 machine.

- When Windows 10 is being born (after it killed the machine's existing Windows 7), it then reads this Autopilot configuration file.

- The machine just pretends to be using the Autopilot service, but it's really not. It gets its Autopilot directives from this Autopilot configuration file.

The machine knows which Azure AD tenant to use from the configuration file and grabs that information, but remember: Autopilot (the service) never, ever had this particular machine's hardware ID (because it was running Windows 7 and being upgraded to Windows 10).

You might wonder, what is this Autopilot configuration file? Well, it's basically a representation of the same Autopilot profile information, but dumped out as a text file in JSON format.

So again, when this Windows 7 to Windows 10 upgrade happens, Windows 10 doesn't look at the Autopilot service for a hardware ID (which would then normally connect it to an Autopilot profile). Instead, the machine just looks inside *itself* at this Autopilot configuration file, and…bingo.

Autopilot…without using the Autopilot *service*.

Then, once the machine is actually enrolled in MDM, you can use what you learned earlier to trap machines enrolled in MDM and write their Windows 10 hardware IDs back into Autopilot (permanently).

The best way to understand and see this scenario is simply by seeing a demo of it. There were two demos of this at Ignite 2018. Look for BRK3015 (then start at the 45 minute mark until about 60 minutes). The second demo is at BRK3018 around the 59 minute mark.

The official docs on this are at:

```
https://docs.microsoft.com/en-us/windows/deployment/windows-Autopilot/
existing-devices and https://docs.microsoft.com/en-us/sccm/core/
get-started/includes/1810/1358333
```

A blog entry here:

```
https://blogs.technet.microsoft.com/mniehaus/2018/12/17/
revisiting-windows-Autopilot-for-existing-devices/
```

Two excellent walkthroughs are at:

```
https://techcommunity.microsoft.com/t5/Windows-IT-Pro-Blog/
Upgrade-Windows-7-using-Windows-Autopilot-in-Configuration/ba-p/267747
```

and

```
https://www.petervanderwoude.nl/post/
offline-windows-Autopilot-deployment-profile/.
```

Note that you don't necessarily have to be using SCCM to do this Windows 7 to 10 and Autopilot via file magic. You should be able to use anything that's able to perform a task sequence and nuke the machine, install Windows 10, and copy a single file down. That's all that's required.

Autopilot: Resets, Retire, Wipes, and Fresh Starts

Machines. Slow down. Over. Time.

My favorite term for this is *Winrot*. Hey, it's made it into the Urban Dictionary (www.urbandictionary.com/define.php?term=Winrot), so it has to be a thing, right?

And you can implement various kinds of resets to bring the machine back to ground-level state and then have it re-get all the stuff from your MDM service. There are other reasons you might want to reset a computer. The most common one is resetting classrooms at the end of the semester or when you give students loaner computers and you have no idea what they did with them. Then when the semester or summer break is over, you can just initiate a mass reset against the machine, and bingo: fresh installs.

Additionally, machines might get lost. Sally left her laptop in the back of the Uber again!?? Time to just "Nuke it from the sky!!"

So in the following sections, we'll check out "Resets, Retire, Wipe, and "Fresh Starts."

Autopilot Resets: Local Reset and Remote Reset

The two Autopilot Reset types are local reset, and remote reset.

Both reset types have the same gist and provide the same benefits. Here are the basics of what occurs:

- All the apps, settings, and personal files are nuked. If it's not on a network or external disk, it's nuked.

- The Azure AD join and MDM enrollment are preserved and reused. In other words, when this process is over, you're not going to see another phantom record in either AD or MDM.

- If you happened to apply a provisioning package using the Configuration Designer, those settings are maintained.

- Language and keyboard settings are maintained.

- Wi-Fi settings are maintained with any pre-known and stored passwords.

Local Autopilot Reset   This doesn't perform a full OOBE reset. What this will do is discard all the apps, and data. It will also preserve the MDM enrollment, Azure AD join, and the languages.

This is awesome in school scenarios where you just want to nuke a machine from the dirty work of those mischievous kids and return a machine back to a baseline.

Then it will connect back to MDM and get anything new to reload and or download.

But you might also want to walk up to a machine and perform this local reset. This is initiated by the keystroke Windows+Ctrl+R at the login screen, except that it won't work unless it's first enabled by MDM.

In Intune, you'll find the setting called Automatic Redeployment under "Device restrictions" ➢ General, as seen here. (Don't forget to associate a profile to a computer group.)

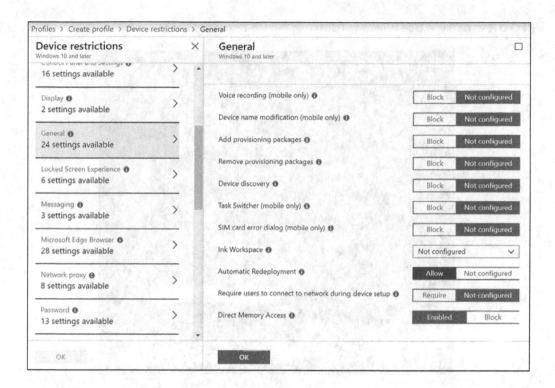

 TIP This is really setting the PolicyCsp, namely PolicyCSP/CredentialProviders/ DisableAutomaticReDeploymentCredentials, and setting it to 1. You may need this information for troubleshooting or if your MDM service is not Intune and you need to set this up by hand.

Then to try this out: At the login screen, press Windows+Ctrl+R. Then when you give it admin credentials (local or Azure), as seen in Figure 8.36, the machine will immediately start to reset.

Remote Autopilot Reset   Another choice is to nuke a machine, or multiple machines from your cozy console, all from afar using the Internet.

Just for a moment, you can feel like Dr. Evil.

So, how do you do it? Use Intune's Devices ➤ "All devices" and click on the device. Select More and then find Autopilot Reset as seen noted with (1) in Figure 8.37.

FIGURE 8.36 Use Windows+Ctrl+R at the login screen to start a reset there.

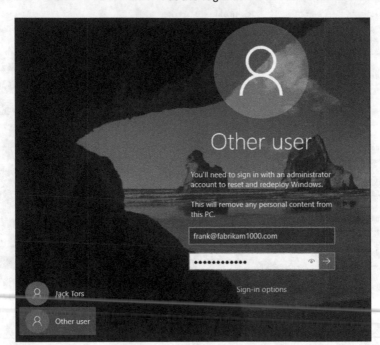

FIGURE 8.37 The different kinds of wipes and resets in Intune

Note that Autopilot Reset requires Windows 1809 or later; if you see this option grayed out, that means the machine is not likely Windows 1809 or later.

When you remotely reset a PC, you'll get a notification that's it been initiated, like this:

Then, on the endpoint, the end user will get a message like this:

The machine will restart in 45 minutes and be totally reset again and rejoin Autopilot.

The end user doesn't get the out of box experience (OOBE); it's just ready to go because it maintains its MDM enrollment.

Then when the machine is done, end users see the normal login page. But before you press Ctrl+Alt+Del, in verrrrry small letters, you'll see "Success! Windows is set up and ready to go." If you squint, you'll see what's seen here.

Retiring a PC

The Retire button can be seen in Figure 8.37 noted with (2).

Retiring a PC basically removes it from Intune. This doesn't perform a wipe of the PC. You just won't see it in Intune anymore because you're not managing it anymore. Any MDM policies on the machine are removed; some settings will peel back, others may stick. Software that is on the machine will usually stick around. The user's personal data that is stored on the device is maintained.

Wiping a PC (Previously Known as *Factory Reset*)

The Wipe button can be seen in Figure 8.37 noted with (3).

The MDM Wipe feature has two methods: Retain enrollment state and user account... nor not. I'll call this Wipe + Retain and Wipe-Retain to keep it simple.

In both cases the wipe will remove user accounts, user data, user-installed apps, and OEM-installed apps and reset the operating system to the default.

Wipe + Retain will maintain Intune enrollment.

Wipe-Retain will remove Intune enrollment (but it could be reenrolled if the device's hardware ID is in Autopilot).

The docs on this function are at https://docs.microsoft.com/en-us/intune/ devices-wipe.

MDM Fresh Start (aka Clean PC)

The Fresh Start button can be seen in Figure 8.37 noted with (4).

This is a way to mini-nuke a machine, but not fully. You can see Fresh Start in Intune's Devices ➤ "All devices."

Fresh Start (also known as Clean PC) will remove any Win32 or UWP applications on the machine and upgrade them to the latest version of Windows. The device can be told to preserve (or nuke) the user's data.

And, if you choose *not* to preserve the user's data, you're actually un-enrolling it from Azure AD and your MDM service as well, so be careful using this feature.

Only if the device is established in Autopilot will it magically reconnect and still be managed by MDM.

When you log back in, you can see an HTML document on the Desktop called "Removed apps," which express which applications were in fact, cleaned off.

A good blog entry with a lot of nice screenshots about Clean PC can be found at

```
https://osddeployment.dk/2017/05/13/
windows-10-1703-cleanpc-csp-with-intune-1704/
```

If your head is spinning from all the options, please take a look at Table 8.1. That said, it's good to pre-try your Wipe, Reset, or Fresh Start option and make sure you get the expected result in the test lab, before your real emergency is nipping at your heels.

TABLE 8.1   Windows Wipe, Reset and Fresh Start (Clean PC) options

Option	Description	Intune Action
Wipe	Original, wipe and reapply OEM provisioning packages	Wipe
Wipe but keep provisioning data	Original, wipe and reapply user/IT and OEM provisioning packages	Wipe
Wipe protected	Same as wipe, but with protections to prevent it from being stopped	Wipe
Wipe retaining user data	Same as wipe, but retains user data	Wipe (retain)
Autopilot Reset	Wipe, keep provisioning packages, AAD join, MDM enrollment, OOBE settings, some Wi-Fi connections	Autopilot reset
Clean PC without retaining data	Wipe, discard provisioning packages	Fresh start
Clean PC retaining user data	Wipe, discard provisioning packages, retain user data	Fresh start

Linking a Specific User to a Specific Hardware ID

One little Autopilot magic trick is to marry a particular user to a particular hardware ID or multiple hardware IDs, as seen in the example in Figure 8.38.

FIGURE 8.38   How to marry a user to a specific hardware ID

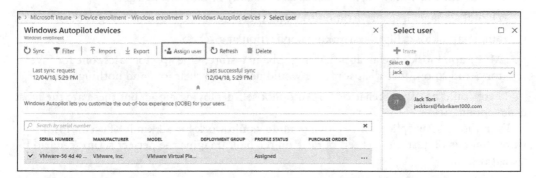

What this doesn't do is reduce those initial boring screens like Region, Keyboard, and so on. Maybe in the future there will be a way to do that, but it's not available right now.

But look what does happen. In Figure 8.39, you can see that once you've married a user to a hardware ID, only that user (in this case, Jack Tors) can log on to this machine initially.

FIGURE 8.39   The result when a machine starts up with Autopilot and a user is married to a hardware ID

Autopilot Self-Deploying Mode

Another very interesting and useful Autopilot scenario is called *self-deploying mode*. Self-deploying mode is mostly meant for the times when you don't have a specific user on the device. There could be multiple anonymous users. Or the scenario in which you have maybe no users at all. The following kinds of devices usually fit into this category:

- Digital signage, like airport monitors and those signs outside of meeting rooms
- Single-app kiosk, like a test-taking application at a school
- Multi-app kiosk, like an app that might be in a store. One app for sales, one for inventory, and so on. Just what someone would need to do their job, and nothing else.

There could be other scenarios for Autopilot self-deploying mode, but these are the most usual candidates.

Even though Autopilot self-deploying mode would work for all kinds of scenarios, I want to focus on just one to keep our eye on the ball. Imagine the perfect setup scenario for a digital sign:

- It gets shipped from the manufacturer.
- A facilities worker unboxes and mounts the thing onto the wall.
- The worker plugs it into Ethernet.
- The worker turns it on, and then does absolutely nothing.
- The machine then shows a single app, like an airport flight board, meeting room information, or interactive application.

In other words: you didn't have to fly to Podunk, Iowa, to click next-next-next on Windows and configure one stinkin' app just to stand up one lousy digital sign. So this is awesome. But in these cases there are two problems that Microsoft had to overcome:

1. These machines might not have any keyboards or mice, so literally all the answers to the OOBE questions have to be pre-populated in Autopilot profiles.
   - This issue (no keyboard) is reasonably easy to overcome. The profiles for Autopilot self-deploying mode handily deal with all the OOBE questions.
2. Remember, there is no user on the machine (and again, maybe no keyboards to even do this even if you wanted to specify a user). Therefore, an alternative mechanism was needed to do the authentication.
   - This issue (no user) is a little thornier to deal with. So since you aren't using a user to authenticate the box to Azure, the box has to authenticate itself. And it does this with a very secure mechanism. But how? Normally, as a user you would use a username and password (or similar password replacement credential).
   - A computer doesn't really have a password. So what can you use?
   - You use a computer's TPM 2.0 chip of course!

The TPM 2.0 chip is used when Autopilot needs to prove that the device is not an imposter (it uses TPM attestation). And once the TPM has a handshake with Autopilot, then and only then is it allowed to join the organization's AAD tenant without providing any credentials. Remember the hardware ID? The TPM identifying information is embedded inside it, and then that's used for device matching.

Now a quick note here: If you want to try out these steps all the way through, you're welcome to. But know that it will fail (by design) if you use any virtual machine type, like Hyper-V or VMware Workstation, even though those virtual machines use (virtual) TPM 2.0 chips. This is a "by-design" limitation in Autopilot self-deploy.

Said another way, you'll have to crack open a laptop or PC—yes, a real actual laptop or PC with a TPM 2.0 chip—to test this all the way though. For this test, you'll want to have Windows 10 1809 or later preinstalled and then verify that the TPM 2.0 chip is ready.

Note that not all machines with a TPM chip come with TPM 2.0 chips or even properly-ready TPM 2.0 chips. First of all, many machines come with TPM 1.2. Some can be upgraded to TPM 2.0, with a lot of work. Trust me, I tried it and couldn't make a Lenovo T430 TPM 1.2 chip upgrade to TPM TPM 2.0. And, also, as a side note, some TPM 2.0 chips don't support TPM attestation *at all*. Some have attestation disabled by default,. And yet others must be flash-upgraded to support it. I found this out the hard way with a Lenovo V330 that has a TPM 2.0 chip but then wouldn't play ball until I flash upgraded it. Then, bingo...TPM 2.0, which properly showed it was ready for attestation.

You can see this in the Settings app within Windows Security, in the Security processor details section as seen in Figure 8.40.

FIGURE 8.40 Autopilot self-deploying mode requires a TPM 2.0 chip which is capable of attestation.

Also, if you really want no screens of questions at all, then this is best used with Ethernet connectivity. When you do use Ethernet, this kind of deployment from Autopilot really is *zero touch*. On the other hand, if at setup time you have no hardwired Ethernet and therefore you must pick a Wi-Fi network, you are then prompted to do so, and thus a keyboard and mouse are required.

Turning Off Warnings for Self-Deployed Devices

Positively everyone in IT has seen it: Some poor machine at the airport, train station, or other public place prompting for an update, or otherwise begging to be put out of its misery and rebooted after it got some Windows update. Here's an example my friend Matt sent me showing a helpless Windows 7 machine sitting at the Department of Motor Vehicles in Delaware. (Don't *your* friends send you pictures of goofed-up Windows computers?)

Starting in Windows 1809, there is a Group Policy setting and an MDM setting you can use to squelch these messages. In Group Policy-land, the setting is found in Computer Configuration ➢ Policies ➢ Admin Templates ➢ Windows Components ➢ Windows Update ➢ **Display options for update notifications**. Once it's enabled, you can further specify to disable all notifications, including or excluding restart warnings.

The same setting is available via ADMX-backed MDM policy. It's in the Policy CSP and called Update/UpdateNotificationLevel. You might have to make a custom OMA-URI for it (as described in Chapter 3, in the section titled "Custom URIs for Any PolicyCSP Items without a GUI").

One note about using this setting: Once it's set, you really don't get notified about updates or that a reboot is required. You will need to use other Group Policy or MDM settings to specify Windows Update settings that specify "Active Hours" such that the computer can reboot itself when no one is there.

The Group Policy setting for that, in case you're curious, is found at Computer Configuration ➤ Policies ➤ Admin Templates ➤ Windows Components ➤ Windows Update ➤ **Turn off auto-restart for updates during active hours**. And the ADMX-backed MDM setting is called Update/ActiveHoursEnd.

Preparing for Autopilot Self-Deploy Devices

In the real world, you would likely buy a gaggle of machines and then have them shipped where you need for them to be. And as I explained in the section "Creating Dynamic Groups for Autopilot," hardware IDs can be associated with an order ID, which in turn you can use as a generic tag for similar devices (Sales machines, Marketing machines, and so on).

Additionally, when you buy machines from Dell or Lenovo, and so on, you could get the OrderID (or the PurchaseOrderID) fields pre-populated.

Well, for this test, you won't be ordering anything, but you will pretend to buy and deploy a machine where the OrderID field is pre-populated. The OrderID will be like a tag we use to know, "Okay, these machines are all our self-deploy machines."

To do this, you'll need to acquire the hardware ID and get it into CSV format as we did earlier in the section "Manually Getting a Hardware ID into Autopilot." Then, before you upload to Autopilot, I want to show you how to add an OrderID as if you were buying 100 of these systems with the OrderID pre-populated.

If you look at the CSV file for this machine, you'll see the following items (which represent columns):

```
Device Serial Number,Windows Product ID,Hardware Hash
```

I want you to add a column so it looks like this instead:

```
Device Serial Number,Windows Product ID,Hardware Hash,OrderID
```

Then, at the very end of the CSV file, add in a comma and enter in a bogus OrderID. In my example, I just put in ORDER1.

Then I uploaded the file to Autopilot. The result can be seen in Figure 8.41. Note that this screen shot shows a virtual machine's ID uploaded, which won't work in real life. So remember, Autopilot self-deploying mode only works for real machines.

FIGURE 8.41 The OrderID is seen in the Deployment Group field in Autopilot.

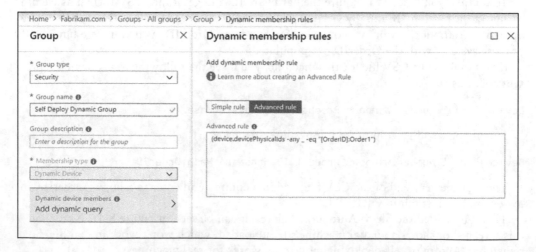

Next stop is to create a dynamic membership rule to sweep in all the machines with the ORDER1 tag into one place. The advanced dynamic membership rule would be this, and it's seen in Figure 8.42. I've called my group "Self Deploy Dynamic Group."

```
(device.devicePhysicalIds -any _ -eq "[OrderID]:Order1")
```

FIGURE 8.42 Creating a dynamic group to capture a specific OrderID (ORDER1 in this case)

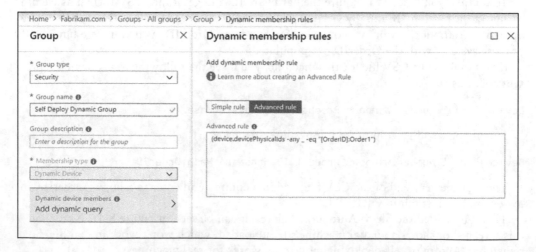

You might not want to continue until you can see that your device automatically shows up in the dynamic group as seen in the Members section. When the group membership goes from 0 to 1, you're ready to continue.

Next stop is to create a profile, similar to what we did earlier. This time though, we'll specify the deployment mode as Self-Deploying, as seen in Figure 8.43.

FIGURE 8.43   Select Self-Deploying as the deployment mode within the profile.

The settings of the profile are reasonably self-explanatory and can be seen in Figure 8.44. Of course, you want this to be as optimal as possible, pre-answering all the questions you can, as seen in Figure 8.44.

Next, you'll assign the profile to the group you created just before, as shown in Figure 8.45. This then marries the Autopilot profile to the Self Deploy Dynamic Group.

FIGURE 8.44   Pre-answering the OOBE questions for self-deploying devices

FIGURE 8.45   Specifying the dynamic group to which the Autopilot profile will apply

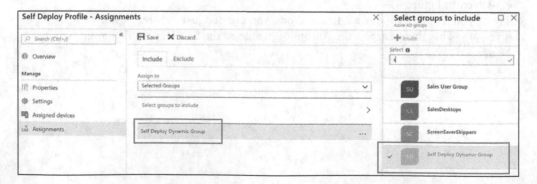

One more thing: You don't want the general "catchall" Autopilot profile we created in the first part of the chapter to collide with the self-deploying profile for these specialized machines. As such, you can (and should) go back into your original Autopilot profile (which was called All Devices - Assignments) and *exclude* your newly created dynamic group.

In Figure 8.46, you can see the first Autopilot profile, and where I've clicked on the Exclude tab and selected Self Deploy Dynamic Group, thus keeping the user-driven and the self-deploy worlds separate.

FIGURE 8.46   Specifically excluding the self-deploy devices from the user-driven devices

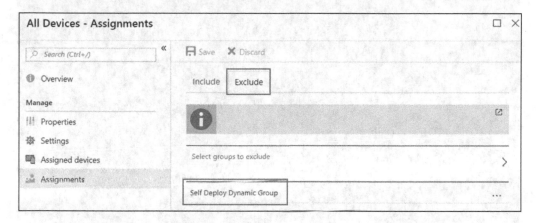

Testing Self-Deploying Autopilot Devices

Testing a device like this is similar to the testing we did earlier. You'll need to nuke the machine via reset, Sysprep, reinstall, or maybe you took a snapshot before OOBE started.

When OOBE starts, you'll see something like the screen in Figure 8.47.

And with that, you've accomplished the goal: A device self-enrolling device to Autopilot.

Remember, if you get 95% of the way through, and this catches fire, chances are there is some problem with the TPM 2.0 chip (not ready, not initialized, and so on).

Remember again, the machine you're testing on might not have the "right" TPM chips at all. Many, many devices are using TPM 1.2 chips. And those are simply the wrong kind and won't work. And what's more, just because a chip is labeled as a TPM 2.0 chip doesn't mean it performs the attestation part of the equation, which is necessary for the handshake to occur. When I tested this on a few laptops with TPM 2.0 chips, I got 95% through with the process only to realize the laptops didn't have the *right kind* of TPM 2.0 chips. The attestation simply didn't work as expected. Frustrating! If you get this far, and it's not working, again, try to flash-upgrade your TPM chip to get it to support attestation. In these cases, go back to the screen in Figure 8.40 on an example machine and reinspect: Do I have TPM 2.0? Does it support attestation? Am I using a real machine and not a VM?

FIGURE 8.47   Autopilot asks no questions to self-deploy machines when Ethernet is used.

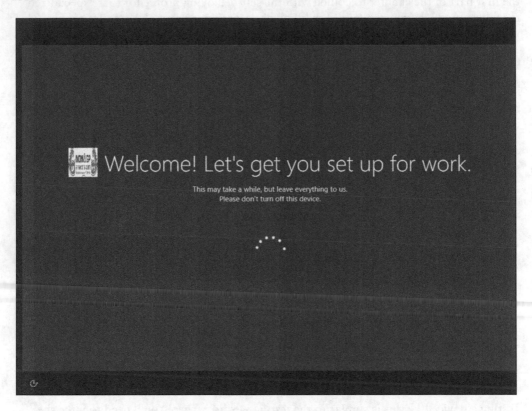

The official docs on Autopilot with self-deploy devices are at:

`https://docs.microsoft.com/en-us/windows/deployment/windows-Autopilot/`
`self-deploying`

And a good blog is found at:

`https://www.petervanderwoude.nl/post/windows-Autopilot-self-deploying-mode/`

Bonus Points: Making Self-Deploying Kiosk Machines

So having machines that self-deploy is pretty nifty. But it's what you do with it that counts. Two good options for self-deploying kiosk machines would be:

- Anything that uses a webpage (airline display at the airport, stock ticker, etc.)
- A specific application you want to lock users into using

If you're going to use a web page, you want to use what's called Edge Kiosk mode. This is a pretty involved topic that has a lot of particulars and options. It's just too many pages, so you'll have to check this out yourself here:

```
https://docs.microsoft.com/en-us/microsoft-edge/
deploy/microsoft-edge-kiosk-mode-deploy#use-microsoft-intune-or-other-mdm-service
```

The second option I mentioned would be to use an application from the Windows Store. Well, not the Windows Consumer Store, no no. You'll have to pre-stage that app in your Windows Store for Business as we did back in Chapter 6.

In a moment, I'll give you a URL for the lash-up of how to do that. But note that this blog entry is a bit out-of-date. It recommends using the *Kiosk browser application*, which is downloadable from the Consumer Windows store (and, of course, which you could then stage in your Windows Store for Business).

But there's another choice as well.

As I said two paragraphs ago, Edge (now) comes with its own Kiosk modes, which opens up some enhanced scenarios like multi-tab, printing, and more. It's somewhat more complicated to set up than the Kiosk browser application found in the Windows Store.

But if you wanted to set up a simple web page to show on your kiosk, the Kiosk browser application still works and is a perfectly fine choice.

So, if you want to, you can follow these directions and pick…well, any application from the Windows Consumer Store and get it into your Windows Store for Business, then tell that self-deploying machine to run that Windows app. Here's some handy URLs:

```
https://blogs.technet.microsoft.com/mniehaus/2018/06/07/
deploying-a-kiosk-using-windows-Autopilot/
```

```
https://docs.microsoft.com/en-us/microsoft-edge/deploy/
microsoft-edge-kiosk-mode-deploy
```

```
https://www.petervanderwoude.nl/post/
single-full-screen-kiosk-browser-app-in-kiosk-mode/
```

Additionally, a good speech on this topic can be found at YouTube by searching for BRK3016 for a talk titled, "Shared Devices for Kiosk and Firstline workers (with Windows 10 and Intune)" and THR3003 for a talk entitled "Specialized device deployments for Windows 10 with Microsoft Intune."

Autopilot Hybrid Azure AD Join

There's one final Autopilot scenario I want to set up with you.

For me, this functionality underscores that Microsoft gets that many organizations will want to do many things with cloud and also maintain (at least for some period of time) a foot in the on-prem world.

Back in Chapter 4, we bootstrapped our already Active Directory-joined, on-prem machines (using Group Policy) to auto-enroll themselves into MDM.

Now, in this section, you'll kind of do the reverse.

That is, you'll tell a totally fresh machine, one that is new in the box, or one that has maybe been reset, to enroll in MDM (using Autopilot) and then, also magically, join your on-prem Active Directory.

How is this done? With a little help from some friends, of course.

Let's start with understanding the flow of how this is going to work. Refer to Figure 8.48 as I explain all the steps.

FIGURE 8.48 Flow diagram of Hybrid Azure AD Join

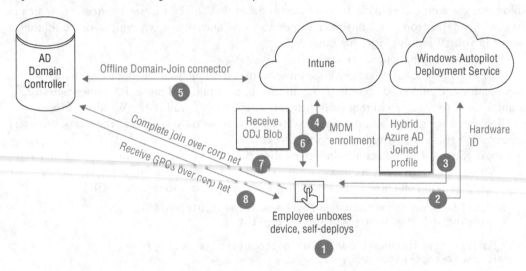

Hybrid Azure AD Join through Windows Autopilot

1. A new machine shows up at the user's door.

2. As a machine starts up OOBE, it will contact the Autopilot service. (You've done this like 18 times now.)

3. The profile type is a new special Autopilot type called "Hybrid Azure AD Joined, which we'll investigate in this section.

4. Device enrolls into MDM, in this case Intune.

5. Intune then reaches out to your on-prem AD with a new thing called the Offline Domain Join connector, or ODJ connector, which we'll also investigate in this section.

6. Intune then pushes down a thing called an Offline Domain Join Blob, or ODJ blob; yet another thing we'll investigate in this section.

7. The computer does the join using the ODJ blob.

8. You are now joined and can get, say, Group Policy or other on-prem or AD specific stuff.

Let's get this set up, and you can see it working for yourself.

What Is an ODJ Blob?

How can you join a machine if the machine isn't connected (right now) to the LAN such that the computer can be joined by a technicion?

The truth is, you can't. But you can do the next best thing.

So this idea has existed for a long time in on-prem AD-land (since Windows 7 to be precise) and it's called Offline Doman Join, or ODJ for short.

With ODJ you can create a reservation for a computer in Active Directory. Then you can tell a computer to consume that reservation.

It's easy to try yourself, just to get the hang of what's about to go on automtically in a few minutes when we add Intune to the mix. On any AD-joined machine at all, run the following command to reserve the space for the "not yet joined" computer named `testjoin01`:

```
djoin /provision /domain fabrikam.com /machine testjoin01 /savefile provision.txt
```

This is the output file, `provision.txt`, which is technically known as an ODJ blob, and you can just check it out in Notepad. You can see the command and the file in Figure 8.49.

FIGURE 8.49 Creating and inspecting an Offline Domain Join (ODJ) blob

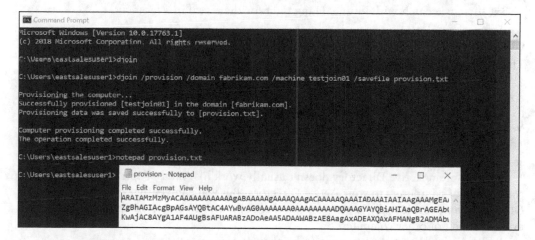

Then go over to a machine that is not domain-joined but is on the same network as your Active Directory. And, of course, get your ODJ blob file over there. Then, using an elevated command prompt, let's claim the reservation. Use the following command:

```
djoin /requestodj /loadfile provision.txt /windowspath c:\windows /localos
```

You can see the command run in Figure 8.50.

FIGURE 8.50   Performing a by-hand domain-join with an ODJ blob

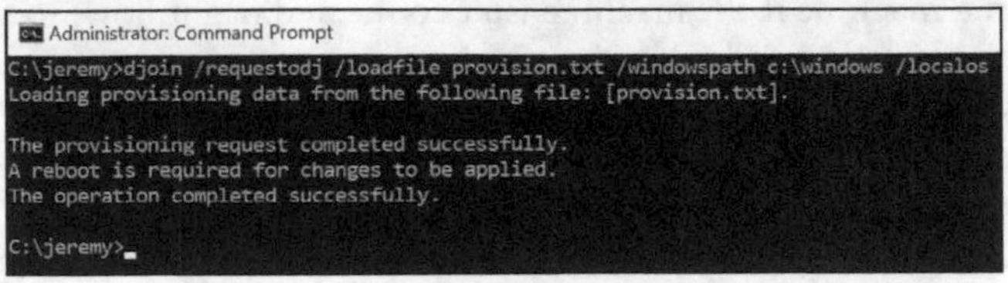

After the client reboots, the first time the client can make contact to on-prem Active Directory, they sync up and magic happens: The machine is now really domain-joined.

The full docs on Offline Domain Join can be found here (but you won't really need them for what we're going to do):

```
https://docs.microsoft.com/en-us/previous-versions/windows/it-pro/
windows-server-2008-R2-and-2008/dd392267(v=ws.10)
```

The takeaway here is that Intune is going to do all the hard work to make the reservation and the ODJ blob for you, then download it and apply it on a target machine, thus joining a computer to Active Directory automatically.

But there is a catch with Intune. Hang tight for the reveal in a moment.

Preparing Active Directory for Hybrid Azure AD Join

There's a little pregame setup involved in Hybrid Azure AD Join.

One of the optional steps in Chapter 2 was to set up AAD synchronization using the Azure AD Connect tool. If you didn't do this, and want to get your on-prem AD married to your Azure AD, then you can flip back to Chapter 2 and see the section titled "Syncing Your On-Prem AD to Azure AD Automatically."

Then, after that, you need to first tell your on-prem Active Directory that it's A-OK for some *computer* on your network to add *other computers* to your domain.

Your on-prem Active Directory doesn't usually work like that; *people* usually do the joining of computers to your Active Directory. But you can gently explain to Active Directory that, yes, it really is okay for another *computer* to create computer records and do the joining of other computers.

Really Active Directory, it's going to be okay.

To teach Active Directory about this, you'll delegate the ability to create computer objects as well as manage their properties and permissions. In most Active Directories, the place where new computers magically show up when joined is the Computers container (and yes, I did mean container...it is not an OU).

This is typically where you'd start your delegation. It is possible that this is not your default location (this is changeable via the old and crusty (but it still works) command redircmp). If you're unsure if the Computers folder is where computers appear when you join one to Active Directory, then just join one. Then find it. Once you know your default location, right-click over it and select Delegate Control as seen in Figure 8.51.

FIGURE 8.51 Delegate Control over your known default location. If it's not the Computers folder, then be sure to do it on your redirected location.

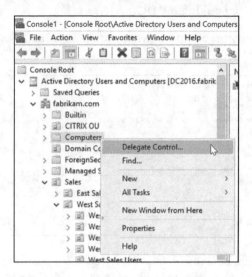

Then once inside the Delegation of Control Wizard, you need to change the view such that it lets you look for computers. (Again, this is unusual for Active Directory, so the default is that it doesn't show you computers.) In the screen shown in Figure 8.52, you'll click Object Types and then click to check on Computers.

FIGURE 8.52 Enable Computers as an Object Type.

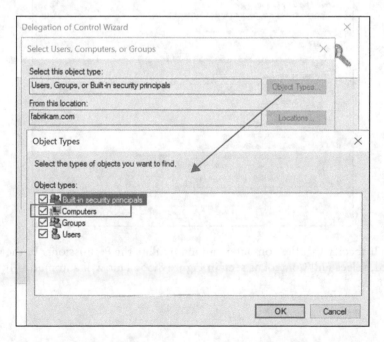

Then, as seen in Figure 8.53, search for the computer name where you plan to install the Intune Connector for Active Directory. This can be a Domain Controller or member server within Active Directory. I'm picking my DC.

FIGURE 8.53   Specify the computer where you plan to install the Intune Connector for Active Directory.

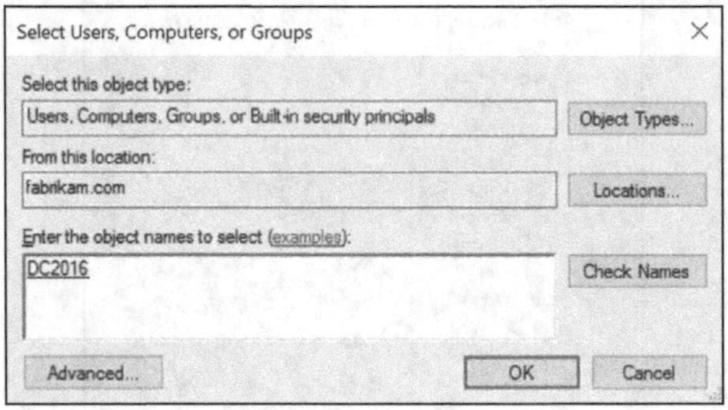

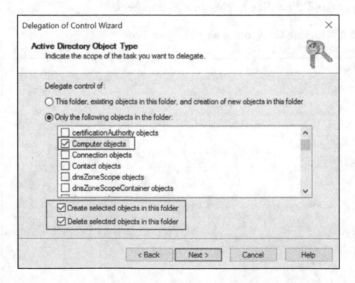

Then, in the Delegation of Control Wizard, select "Computer objects" as seen in Figure 8.54 along with "Create selected objects in this folder" and "Delete selected objects in this folder" and click Next.

FIGURE 8.54   Specify that the computer can perform the selected delegated items.

Last, you'll specify that the computer can manipulate the Permissions. In the next page of the wizard, select Full Control as seen in Figure 8.55. This will automatically check every other box.

FIGURE 8.55   Select Full Control on the Permission page.

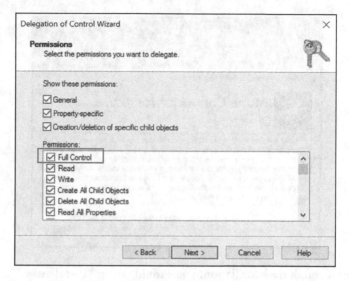

The final page is a review from the wizard. Click Finish and you're all set.

Installing the Intune Connector for Active Directory

Now, let's flip back to Intune. This is where you're going to find and then download the Intune Connector for Active Directory. Head over to Intune ➢ Device Enrollment ➢ Windows Enrollment ➢ Intune Connector for Active Directory. Then click the link in Step 2 as seen in Figure 8.56.

FIGURE 8.56   Downloading the Intune Connector for Active Directory

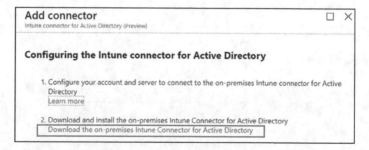

Back on your on-prem server, it's time to install it. You can do this upon a DC or a member server. It's a simple MSI and doesn't take very long. You can see the MSI and opening screen in Figure 8.57.

FIGURE 8.57   Installing the Intune Connector for Active Directory

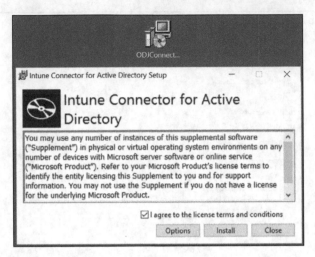

After clicking through the installation, you should see an "Installation Successfully Completed" message (not shown) and a "Configure now" button (also not shown). Also, if needed there is a Start Menu item if you need to re access it.

Simply click the Sign In button (seen in Figure 8.58), and then give it the credentials for the main Global Azure Administrator, Frank Rizzo (who also needs an Intune license for this to work). When it's all done, you should see what's seen in Figure 8.58.

FIGURE 8.58   After you give the Global Admin's credentials, you will get a success message from the connector.

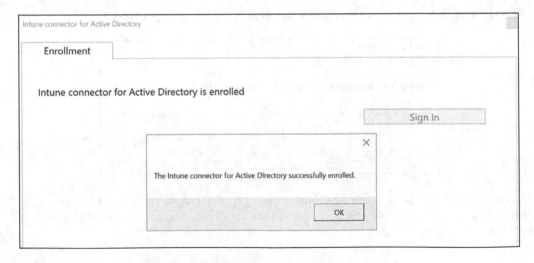

At this point we're almost ready to try this out.

Verifying the Installation of the Intune Connector for Active Directory

Once you've installed the Intune Connector, as we just did, you can take a moment to look inside Windows's Services and see that it's present and running. It's called the Intune ODJConnector Service and can be seen in Figure 8.59.

FIGURE 8.59   Inspecting the Intune ODJConnector Service

You can also see logs for the ODJConnector Service on this same machine. You would look in Windows's Event Viewer ➤ Applications and Services Logs then ODJ Connector Service as seen in Figure 8.60.

You can see interesting event logs from the ODJ Connector Service, like the one in Figure 8.61, in case you need to do any troubleshooting.

Finally, back in Intune, you should (eventually) see the computer you're using notated as performing a sync, as seen in Figure 8.62. This took about 10 minutes for me, and the Refresh button didn't actually refresh it for me. I had to press F5 to refresh to the actual page.

FIGURE 8.60   Finding the ODJ Service event log

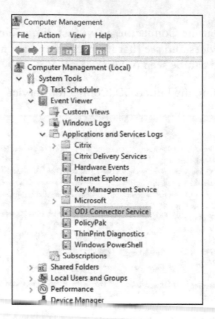

FIGURE 8.61   An event log item from the ODJ Connector Service

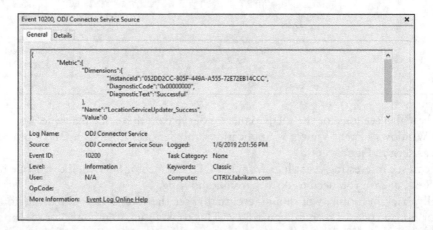

FIGURE 8.62   The Intune Connector should show you the connection, if it's active, and last sync time.

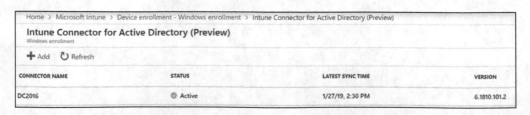

Note that you can have multiple connectors if you anticipate a huge onslaught of computers attempting to do this. For instance, if you were doing a company-wide refresh and expected everyone to get new computers within the same few days, you might want multiple connectors to shoulder the load. Note that at this time, there's no way to delete a connector. You would simply uninstall the on-prem component you installed a little earlier, and the Intune Connector pane will realize the sync time has not updated and will stop attempting to use the connector.

Create and Use an Autopilot Hybrid AD Join Profile

Next, you'll create a Windows Autopilot profile specifically for machines for which you wish to perform an MDM enrollment *and* the on-prem Active Directory join. In Intune ➤ Device Enrollment ➤ Windows Enrollment ➤ Windows Autopilot deployment profiles, you'll create a new profile. Then, as shown in Figure 8.63, you'll select User-Driven and "Hybrid Azure AD joined."

FIGURE 8.63 You can select User-Driven and "Hybrid Azure AD joined" to enroll in both MDM and on-Prem Active Directory at the same time.

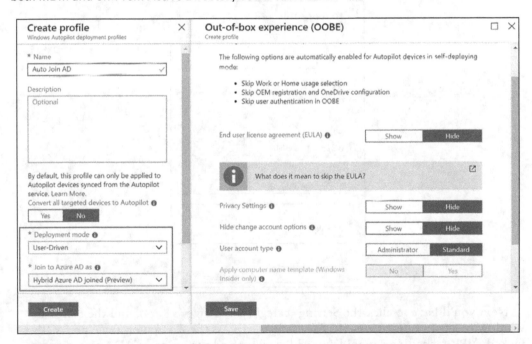

 In this scenario, we're applying the ODJ scenario to all machines. If you wanted to go the extra mile, you could assign Autopilot profiles by exception with Include and Exclude groups. The basic gist can be found here:

https://blogs.technet.microsoft.com/mniehaus/2018/12/30/assigning-Autopilot-profiles-by-exception/

A little warning about the field "Apply computer name template," which is seen grayed out in Figure 8.63. It's possible to save, then come back to this field and try to use this to auto-name the computer. Do not attempt to use it. There's another place for that, which is right around the corner, in the Domain Join profile.

Create and Use a Domain Join Device Profile

Creating the Autopilot piece of the profile is only a part of it.

There's a second part. It's called the Domain Join profile. This is back in Intune's device configuration, something you've done a few times now. Head over to Intune ➤ Device Configuration ➤ Profiles and then "Create profile."

Put in a name of your choice, like Offline Domain Join Policy, and for Platform, pick "Windows 10 and later," and finally, select Domain Join in "Profile type," as shown in Figure 8.64.

FIGURE 8.64   Create a Domain Join profile to tell the machine how to connect to your Active Directory.

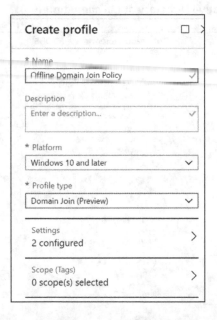

Next you'll have to click the Settings category (see Figure 8.64), and the resultant window is shown in Figure 8.65. The settings express the Computer name prefix (I've picked DJPP-, meaning Domain-Joined Plus Plus) and the on-prem AD domain name, Fabrikam.com.

FIGURE 8.65   The Domain Join settings for the device configuration profile

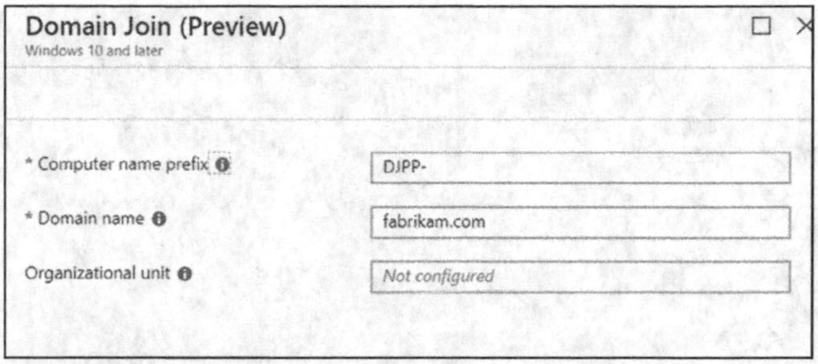

I'm leaving "Organizational unit" blank because I'm using the Computers folder as the drop-in point after they join on-prem AD.

And with that, you're ready to test!

Performing Your Hybrid AD Join

So, earlier I said there was a catch to using the ODJ blobs with Intune.

The catch is that the machine must actually be available with "line of sight" connectivity to a Domain Controller to complete the ODJ blob to Active Directory handshake. If that Windows 10 machine cannot see the DC, the handshake doesn't happen, and the Autopilot process doesn't complete.

So practically this cannot be done just "over the air," say at Starbucks or via VPN connection (because there isn't one yet). If I had to guess, this might be something that I could foresee changing in the future, but that's not the story as I write this.

So before you start your test, be sure your machine has access to the Internet (for Intune enrollment) and to the DC for Active Directory joining. Before you roll back your snapshot, reset the machine, or reinstall Windows, you can do two itty-bitty little tests to give yourself the best chance of this working.

Test 1: Ping the DC by NETBIOS and fully qualified DNS names.

Test 2: Map a share (net use) from the Windows client to Domain Controller (and also to the machine running the Intune connector).

By testing the connectivity on your test system, you're ensuring that you really do have line of sight from your endpoint to the DC.

Okay. Now if you created a snapshot of your Autopilot machine before it started OOBE, then reset to that or otherwise nuke the machine such that OOBE is restarted.

OOBE will start, and you will give it credentials like EastSalesUser1@fabrikam1000.com, one of your on-prem accounts that is auto synchronized to Azure AD.

When you do, it won't look a lot different than usual, but if you interact with the setup page, you can see what's in Figure 8.66.

FIGURE 8.66 You can see that you've joined Active Directory here.

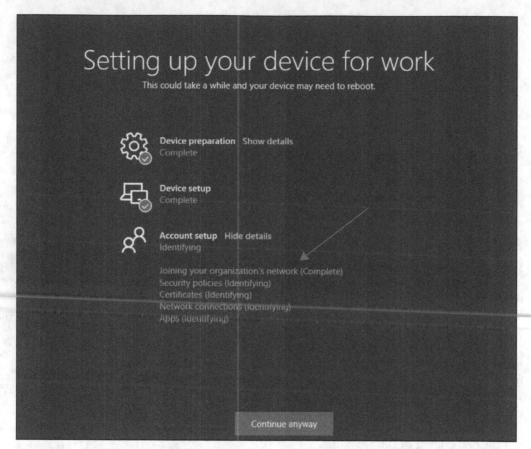

The next time you start the machine, you should be able to log on as any Active Directory user (like EastSalesUser1) but not any "only born in the cloud" Azure Active Directory user (like Jack Tors). The usual screen can be seen in Figure 8.67.

At this point your computer will go through some gyrations getting set up and trying to make connection to your MDM service to enroll.

The computer then downloads any new policies and software from MDM, as you've seen before. Then, you have a happy full Desktop as you expect for EastSalesUser1.

Back in on-prem AD, you should see your computer show up in the Computers folder, as seen in Figure 8.68.

FIGURE 8.67   With Hybrid joined Windows 10 machines, you must log on with an on-prem Active Directory account; an Azure AD account won't work.

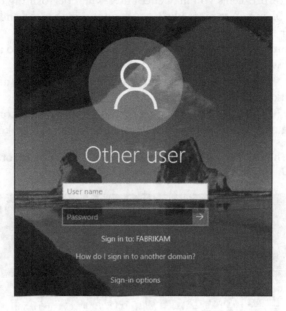

FIGURE 8.68   Computers appear in the Computers folder after they join Active Directory.

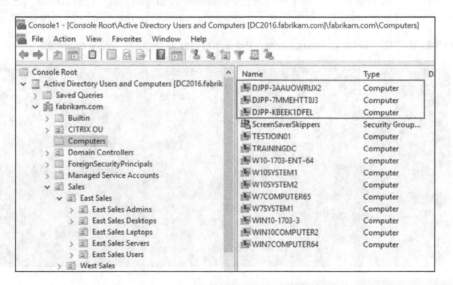

Troubleshooting Hybrid AD Join

There are a handful of problems you may encounter when performing the Hybrid AD Join. The number one problem you're most likely to encounter is that the endpoint cannot reach a Domain Controller to perform the final handshake.

Again: The endpoint computer needs "line of sight" connectivity to a Domain Controller—right now, right during OOBE. It cannot happen later.

When this occurs, the machine keeps trying for about 30 minutes, and then you'll see an 80070774 message like the one in Figure 8.69.

I also got the 80070774 when I failed to realize I needed a device configuration profile; I thought just having the Autopilot profile was enough. It isn't. So make sure you have both.

FIGURE 8.69   The 80070774 message means the computer cannot complete the ODJ handshake with a DC.

The other common occurrence is that the machine is already MDM enrolled. When this happens, you'll see a similar, but different error message, like the one in Figure 8.70.

FIGURE 8.70   Error message when the computer is already MDM enrolled

If you want to check out the docs on Windows Autopilot Hybrid AD Join, the official docs can be found at:

```
https://docs.microsoft.com/en-us/intune/windows-Autopilot-hybrid
```

And the blog from the man himself can be found at:

```
https://blogs.technet.microsoft.com/mniehaus/2018/11/22/
trying-out-windows-Autopilot-user-driven-hybrid-azure-ad-join/
```

A good third-party MVP post on this subject can be found at:

```
https://www.petervanderwoude.nl/post/
hybrid-azure-ad-join-with-windows-Autopilot/
```

Final Thoughts on Hybrid AD Join

You might think that someone like Jack Tors, who is born "only in the cloud," could magically use the machine we just utilized with the Hybrid AD Join.

But that's not how it works.

Devices can only be joined to one or the other: either to Active Directory or Azure Active Directory.

If the computer is joined to Active Directory, the device can *also* register with Azure AD to get that Hybrid Azure AD Join state. Again, this happens via the Azure AD Connect you set up in Chapter 2. When using a hybrid AD-joined computer, a user still always signs on with their on-prem AD credentials. And when they do, they will simply also get their on-prem Kerberos token plus an Azure AD token. The Azure AD token enables single sign-on to AAD-protected resources and additional benefits.

Conversely, if the computer is joined strictly to Azure Active Directory (and not to on-prem Active Directory), the user must sign in with cloud-only Azure AD credentials and can thus access cloud-based resources. But if Windows sees that there is an AD Domain Controller available, my understanding is that it also gets a Kerberos ticket, which it can use to access on-prem resources.

So, the summary here is as follows:

- AD-joined computers can access on-prem resources but still get access to cloud resources.
- AAD-joined computers can naturally access cloud services but still get to on-prem resources.

Amazing how that works.

If you want to read more about this magic trick, here are the write-ups for that:

```
https://docs.microsoft.com/en-us/azure/active-directory/devices/
azuread-join-sso
```

```
https://blogs.technet.microsoft.com/mniehaus/2018/01/19/
afraid-of-windows-10-with-azure-ad-join-try-it-out-part-1/
```

```
https://blogs.technet.microsoft.com/mniehaus/2018/02/21/
afraid-of-windows-10-with-azure-ad-join-try-it-out-part-2/
```

Autopilot White Glove

So far in all the scenarios we've seen, the gist is the same: New PC is born from the factory. The machine comes with all it needs for Windows to be happy. But it has no applications, settings, or policies. All of that stuff comes down after Autopilot has done its thing and Intune kicks in and downloads those pieces from the Internet.

Okay, great. But what if you have 900MB of applications to install?

That could take … a long time. Especially when you ship laptops to field offices or unusual remote places with slow Internet connectivity.

As we saw earlier, one of the options is to block the user from being productive until all (or some) applications are downloaded from the cloud. Or, you can enable them to trod ahead, wondering where the applications are.

Maybe there's a third choice.

There is, and it's called Autopilot White Glove.

The idea of White Glove is that after the machine is born, it's physically intercepted before it gets to the end user. This interception can be done by the IT department, partners, or the OEM itself (before it leaves the premises and goes onto the loading dock).

Now instead of the user opening up the box, connecting to Autopilot, and waiting two hundred years for apps to install, that portion of the work has been pre-performed. In the end, the user gets the same experience we've already talked about, except it's just faster, because the long, boring parts have already been pre-done (mostly) by someone else.

Now the process looks like this:

Another bonus for using White Glove is around the Hybrid Azure AD Join function we explored in the last section. It removes one of the big, big problems with that scenario: If a user was drop-shipped a new PC from the manufacturer and then, say, tried to do Autopilot at Starbucks, how could he join his on-prem AD domain? Answer: He could not. With White Glove though, because the machine is provisioned, then intercepted, this is a perfect time to join it to an on-prem AD before shipping it back out to users. Of course, this means that in all likelihood you have to be the one intercepting the machine (and not your OEM), then making sure it has line-of-sight ability to join your on-prem AD. And, when the user receives the machine, they will also need line of sight to an on-prem DC in order to log on to on-prem AD.

White Glove is available in Windows 10 1903 and later.

To use White Glove, you already need to understand and use either the user-driven and Hybrid Azure AD scenarios we set up earlier. It works alongside those and is just another check box to enable the scenario.

White Glove has some requirements:

- Like the Autopilot "self-deploying" scenario, it uses the same attestation handshake. That means it needs a TPM 2.0 chip, and one that supports attestation.
- White Glove requires physical hardware and will not work on virtual machines.
- The machine must have physical Ethernet connectivity during the White Glove process. Wi-Fi cannot be used because otherwise it would have to prompt the user to select a language, locale, and keyboard, something that can only be chosen by the final end user.

To set up White Glove, you will need to set up an item in the deployment profile called, "Allow White Glove OOBE" (not shown.).

When the machine is intercepted after being provisioned and turned on, it begins to go through the normal Windows Autopilot routine and looks to see if it's hardware hash is registered in a tenant...your tenant. If for some reason the machine isn't intercepted, that's fine. Things just work normally. But upon the desired interception, the operator (again, that's you, or your OEM or partner) would press the Windows key five times, then select Windows Autopilot provisioning as seen in Figure 8.71.

FIGURE 8.71   Autopilot provisioning after OOBE starts and the Windows key is pressed five times

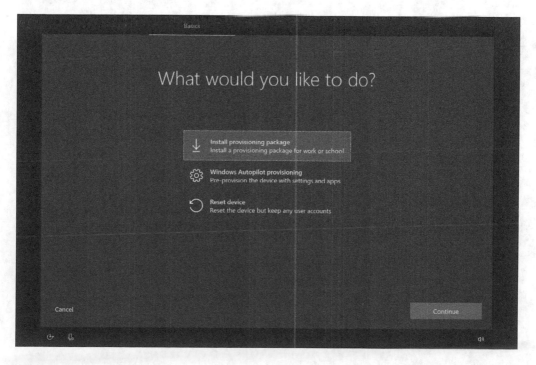

At this point, the machine can be looked up via a QR code shown on the screen (sorry, no screen shot to show you). And then the operator clicks Provision and the long and boring download starts.

Success? You get a nifty green screen and see a button to click labeled Reseal which will shut the device down. Time to get it to FedEx, DHL, or "inter-office mail it" to that end user.

Fail? A red status screen appears with the problem details. You can grab logs and/or restart the process and hope the next attempt goes better.

Remember, too, this intercept point is the perfect opportunity for the machine to perform the hybrid domain join, which absolutely must have direct connectivity to a Domain Controller. Of course, you'll need some way to get those on-prem AD creds to your users, or maybe they already have them.

The official docs on White Glove can be found at `https://docs.microsoft.com/en-us/windows/deployment/windows-autopilot/white-glove`.

Final Autopilot Resources

Clearly Microsoft is investing a lot in Autopilot. It's a big, big deal and a nice game changer and articulates a bunch of scenarios that cannot be done with on-prem infrastructure alone.

If you want to see some of this in action, let me recommend some videos. An awesome two-part talk on Autopilot was at Ignite 2018. Go to YouTube and watch BRK3014 and BRK3015.

Autopilot may be a moving target for the next few years. That said, here's what I plan to do to keep up-to-date on Autopilot.

The documentation is found here:

`https://docs.microsoft.com/en-us/intune/enrollment-Autopilot`

But for generally staying up-to-date in Autopilot happenings, I recommend subscribing to Mike Niehaus's blog, which has an RSS feed (if you're into that sort of thing).

`https://blogs.technet.microsoft.com/mniehaus/`

And, of course, I'll keep you up-to-date as fast as I can at MDMandGPanswers.com.

Now that you made it all the way through this chapter, tweet me @jeremymoskowitz and let me know what you learned in Chapter 8 with hastag #mdmbook. Thanks !

Chapter 9

Windows 10 Health and Happiness: Servicing, Readiness, Analytics, and Compliance

Ultimately, keeping Windows healthy and happy is up to you.

Part of keeping windows healthy is keeping Windows (and Office and OneDrive) up-to-date. We'll start there. That's called *servicing*.

Then, we'll use some tools to survey our on-prem-land and assess our readiness to jump to the next version of Office. We'll use tools like the Office 365 Readiness Toolkit and assess our posture regarding our Desktop applications (using the App Health Analyzer).

We'll take a look at the cloud service called Desktop Analytics to help gain knowledge across our whole kingdom for rolling out Windows and Office upgrades.

Windows, Office, and OneDrive as a Service

When I first heard the term *Windows as a Service*, I thought to myself, "Well, this must mean that we each pay $6.25 a month or something and Windows will keep working, month after month."

I was wrong; but the basic idea is sort of correct.

Windows will keep *upgrading*.

If you don't know what I'm talking about, Microsoft has changed its upgrade cadence from previous versions of Windows.

Remember when you installed XP and then didn't touch it except for patches for 10 years? Those days are basically over.

Now with Windows 10, under most circumstances you will need to ensure that Windows can get updated or else it falls out of support. To be clear, that machine with "old Windows 10" will not just up and stop working (as I thought would happen if I stopped paying my $6.25 a month). It just falls out of support.

So exactly what versions of Windows are supported for how long?

This is a super tricky answer. So before I expose that nugget, let me first explain Microsoft's battle plans. Before I go into those battle plans, let me start by saying that in the modern world, there is no WSUS server to manage your patches or updates. Instead, as you'll see in the following sections, you simply tell each component, via MDM or via Group Policy, what "ring" they're going to be on. And the client downloads and does the work itself. Don't panic. You can still get some insights into the process, and we'll cover that in this chapter as well.

I'll start with servicing Windows and pepper in some servicing for Office 365.

Servicing Windows

The whole topic of keeping Windows up-to-date with new releases, and also up-to-date for general health, is called Windows Servicing.

Here's what we'll learn together:

- **Windows Features:** What are they, and how often they come out (and which one you should pick).

- **Windows Patching:** How often these come out, and what to do if you miss one

- How to stay ahead of the curve to know what's coming next

Let's explore these now.

Understanding Feature Updates, Release Cadence, and Names

The general goal is to release two big bangs of Windows 10 per year. These releases are targeted for March and another for September. Maybe they make those exact months, maybe they don't. And, from time to time, expect some hiccups, like Windows 1809 rollout (meaning 2018, 9th month, or October). So this release started to go out the door in October, but was halted because of some breakage of machines during upgrades. Then it finally rolled out in January of 2019. And it's still called the Windows 1809 release!

So this is why there are all these versions of Windows 10. Year and month are smashed together. So you have releases with names like these:

- 1607

- 1703

- 1709

- 1803

- 1809
- 1903

And so on.

That said, Microsoft also seems to be switching gears a little bit and referencing build names with different monikers. Names like 19H1, 19H2, and 20H1 are different and represent more of a release *time frame*. I think this is because of what happened with build 1809, which was released, then pulled, then released again. If they maintained the name 1809, it would refer to the original release *date* instead of a release's *time frame*. That being said, as I write this, the final name of Windows 1903 appears to be... Windows 1903, and not Windows 19H1.

There is also still other names for Windows.

You might have seen these names. These names are like RS3, RS4, RS5, and so on.

RS? Does that stand for ReleaSe or something? No, it stands for *Red Stone*.

Red Stone? What the heck is that? Something inside the game *Minecraft* actually, which I don't claim to really know anything about. The name Red Stone for releases is sort of just like a "pet name" for the release and is not official, but you may see it in some documents that express the features of a build before it is released.

Great! A star is born! With this new star comes new features. Security features, look and feel features, and so on. Microsoft used to call these *upgrades*. But the term they've landed on now is *feature updates*.

Now how long does a feature update live?

Again: this is the tricky part. See Table 9.1 for the answer.

TABLE 9.1 Longer servicing for Windows 10 Enterprise and Education editions

Products	March Targeted Releases	September Targeted Releases
Windows 10 Enterprise	18 Months	30 Months
Windows 10 Education	18 Months	30 Months
Windows 10 Pro	18 Months	18 Months
Windows 10 Home	18 Months	18 Months
Office 365 ProPlus	18 Months	18 Months

All currently supported feature updates of Windows 10 Enterprise and Education editions 1607, 1703, 1709, and 1803 will be supported for 30 months after release date.

The March (H1) release is destined to live shorter than the September (H2) releases. Why the seemingly disparate support cycles?

So it's a little counterintuitive, but the idea is that some customers do want to perform a feature update twice a year, and other customers don't want to perform a feature update twice a year. If you deploy the September build, you only have to do a forced feature update every two and a half years (30 months). But, if you're gung ho and want to get all the features out there (security, look and feel, and so on), then you're already upgrading twice a year anyway, so the March build dies in 18 months. And it won't matter, because you're already doing twice-a-year feature updates!

Said another way, it enables customers who want to stay the most current (and take advantage of these features) to do so, but it also enables customers who want to defer feature updates for a while. If you're still getting your feet wet with Windows 10, the smart thing to do would be to use a build released in the September time frame, which gives you the longest runway to require an upgrade. Once you've got your groove down, you can then do two-times-a-year upgrading with the March and the September builds.

There is one piece of fine print in Table 9.1 if you look closely. That is, the 30 month life span for Windows is only offered for Enterprise and Education and not Professional. And, the 30 month life span is only offered for the H2 version for those customers.

So, said another way:

- Enterprise and Education can pick 18-month or 30-month cycles.

- Enterprise and Education can pick H1 or H2 releases. If they choose the H2 release, they are opting in to the 30-month cycle.

- If a customer is using Windows 10 Professional, they have to keep upgrading it every 10 months to stay in support

 One lens to look through here would be time versus money. You could say, "Well, it's more expensive (in labor costs) for our company, which uses Windows 10 Professional, to keep upgrading every 18 months." So by encouraging an organization to spend money on Enterprise or Education, one argument is that there is money spent on Enterprise but saved in ongoing Windows 10 upgrade labor costs (18 months of Professional versus 30 months of Enterprise).

If you want to read the official announcement on this cadence change, you can check it out here:

https://www.microsoft.com/en-us/microsoft-365/blog/2018/09/06/helping-customers-shift-to-a-modern-desktop/.

If you want to see all the items Microsoft has pumped into Windows 10 since its release, you can see a "change log" for each release:

https://docs.microsoft.com/en-us/windows/whats-new/

The servicing details in the Release Information page are here:

https://docs.microsoft.com/en-us/windows/windows-10/release-information

There is an interesting demonstration graphic I saw in a slide deck, and I found a copy on the Internet showing how with each release, a *lot* of new features are added. Hopefully this link is still live by the time you see this, but note that it's always going to be out-of-date. Anyway, it's a nice graphical representation of what's new and improved, and again, you can maybe see it here: https://imgur.com/nhftbo9.

But, what's also true is that at some point, you will have to upgrade. You cannot lollygag as you did with Windows XP. That's the deal. That is, unless you deploy Windows 10 LTSC. See the sidebar for more information.

Another handy link to know is the "Windows lifecycle fact sheet," which explains all the currently supported builds, their birthday (aka, date of availability) and their death day (end of service), which are different for Home and Pro SKUs versus Enterprise and Education SKUs.

That very helpful link (also useful for server information as well) is found at:

https://support.microsoft.com/en-us/help/13853/windows-lifecycle-fact-sheet

---

Windows 10 LTSC

So Windows is born, and it lives for 18 or 30 months.

That is, unless it's Windows 10 LTSC. LTSC stands for *Long-Term Servicing Channel*. LTSC is pretty much just like regular Windows 10, but not quite exactly.

First, Windows 10 LTSC is meant to be used for MRI machines, cash machines, point-of-sale machines, security camera machines, and other kinds of "appliance" types of computing scenarios. In other words, you set up Windows 10, you chuck your single-purpose-built software on there, and then you don't have to think about it.

For 10 years. Literally. 10 years.

New versions of Windows 10 LTSC come out every three years or so.

Wow! If this is so great, why doesn't everyone just use it?

Well, some people do, and they may or may not be using it correctly. The reason that Windows 10 LTSC isn't for everyone is that "constantly updated" Office 365 ProPlus is not supported on Windows 10 LTSC, though Office 2019 is supported. And LTSC doesn't have Microsoft Edge, the new browser.

Additionally, and something that can really throw people off their guard, is that LTSC is actually tied to what's called the "silicon level" of the hardware. The idea is that if you're using a particular version of LTSC, then that same version of LTSC might not work on some new modern Intel chips that haven't been born yet! This means that if you use LTSC and build your "perfect golden image machine" and then buy some new whizzbang desktops or laptops, Windows might just decide not to work at all! Crazy!

So LTSC does have its merits—again, mostly for these single-purpose machines that have no particular users upon them. MRI machines, cash machines, and so on are the most obvious kinds of machines for this usage. But there are some more subtle reasons to use LTSC. For more information and to see if LTSC might be a good choice, here are two places to go:

Blog: https://techcommunity.microsoft.com/t5/Windows-IT-Pro-Blog/ LTSC-What-is-it-and-when-should-it-be-used/ba-p/293181

Video: Pros and Cons of LTSC in the Enterprise. Find it on YouTube and search for code THR3006.

Understanding Windows Patching Cadence (Quality Updates)

This is a little easier to understand than the feature update cadence.

Every supported Windows 10 version has one big Quality Update (that is, patches for bugs and such) every month. This is called Quality Tuesday, or sometimes Patch Tuesday.

Quality updates are simple: Every month, you get a fix-er-up (and no new features).

What happens if your Windows 10 laptop is offline and in a desk drawer somewhere for six months? No problem. When it connects and checks for updates, Windows 10 just downloads the latest Quality Update, which is cumulative. That means every bugfix you missed for six months just comes down and is applied. Nice.

There's a little more to what happens underneath the hood inside the mother ship at Microsoft. Specifically, there is a second Quality Update that's available as a preview two weeks after the regular monthly Quality Tuesday update has gone out the door. Windows will not install these automatically, but an end user can request it by checking for an update and then agreeing to install the update.

There are also out-of-band updates, which you can think of as "emergency fixes" that will be blasted down, only as needed. Of course, Microsoft wants to minimize these kinds of updates because they are not really scheduled.

And, typically, any kind of Quality Update will reboot the machine when it's over (outside of the active hours; more on that later). And no one wants more reboots than necessary.

If you want read more about it check these two fascinating blog entries:

```
https://blogs.windows.com/windowsexperience/2018/12/10/
windows-monthly-security-and-quality-updates-overview
```

```
https://techcommunity.microsoft.com/t5/Windows-IT-Pro-Blog/
Windows-10-update-servicing-cadence/ba-p/222376
```

The Windows Insider Program for Business

As a little curveball to what we just talked about, there's also the Windows Insider Program for Business. The point of the Windows Insider for Business program is to give you previews to features you might need to plan for and roll out.

For instance, as I was originally writing this chapter, the Windows Insider build just released the Windows Sandbox feature, which is like a mini virtual machine that you can throw away if you're doing small-scale tests. Then, this feature ended up shipping in Windows 10 1903.

The point is you can at least preview these upcoming proposed features now, before they get rolled up and finally released into the Semi-Annual Channel. And you can make good decisions about rolling this out, and/or making a training program for end users if you think there's something useful in it.

 To see the Group Policy, MDM, and SCCM settings to configure a machine to use Insider builds, see `https://Aka.ms/manage-builds`.

Servicing Office

Windows and Office are like cousins. They're similar, but each kind of has its own style. But of course they play well together. As such, Office 365 ProPlus has its own deployment cadence. Here's the general gist.

Monthly Channel   Bleeding edge with all the newest features.

Semi-Annual Channel   Twice-a-year updates, usually January and July. This is the mainstream channel that most customers should shoot for. The Semi-Annual Channel feature upgrades will live for 18 months before their support expires.

Semi-Annual Channel (Targeted)   Also twice-a-year updates, but with features rolled in from the monthly channel. These updates are March and September. The idea is that you can hand this build over to your testers to verify your macros, and unusual Office integrations don't explode when you eventually upgrade to the next Semi-Annual Channel (which releases in January and July). The Semi-Annual Channel (Targeted) upgrades only live for four months because they're not meant for everyone, just your testers. Therefore, in practice, only the latest release of Semi-Annual Channel (Targeted) is supported.

If you want the overview of the update channels from Microsoft, here's their take:

```
https://docs.microsoft.com/en-us/deployoffice/
overview-of-update-channels-for-office-365-proplus
```

Additionally, if you want to see how much improvement each consecutive version of Office 365 gets, you can see this link:

```
https://docs.microsoft.com/en-us/officeupdates/
update-history-office365-proplus-by-date
```

 Unrelated but worth a mention is the stand-alone version of Office 2019 and its support. Its support date ends on 10/14/2025.

Reducing the Network Impact of Feature and Quality Updates

What you don't want is 10,000 of your on-prem machines asking for quality updates from Microsoft at the same time. And you really, really don't want 10,000 of your on-prem machines asking for feature updates from Microsoft at the same time.

That would 'asplode your on-prem network.

The good news is that Microsoft thought of that.

For both feature and quality updates, a Windows machine may download the full update. But it could also download the *express* update. An express update is similar to the full update but contains only the changes to the files that actually need to get updated, not the full files.

The result is the same. Whenever it's possible to use the express updates, Windows does, saving bandwidth. A lot of it.

Additionally, if the Windows machine doing an update sees other Windows on the same network, it will use peer-to-peer caching. The idea is that Sally in Accounting already downloaded the latest Windows update at 2.5GB. But the other nine people in Accounting haven't yet. Those nine computers will ask, "Hey, does any other computer on this network have that big ol' update yet?" Sally's machine will say, "Yes, I do!" And the nine computers pull from Sally's machine on the LAN instead of eating up all the bandwidth to request the sources from Microsoft.

This is called Windows 10 Delivery Optimization.

And it works with Windows 10, Office ProPlus 365, driver downloads, and Windows Store content. And it's managed with either Group Policy or MDM.

To be honest, if you literally do nothing at all, then Delivery Optimization is pretty well good to go. As I said, its default behavior is to pull from the other computers on your local LAN. You can do all sorts of crazy things if you want to, like hand-picking a private group that computers should pull from (even if they're on different LANs). There are also some configurations to optimize bandwidth utilizations and such.

If you want to manually configure Delivery Optimization with Intune, there's a device profile for it like what's seen here.

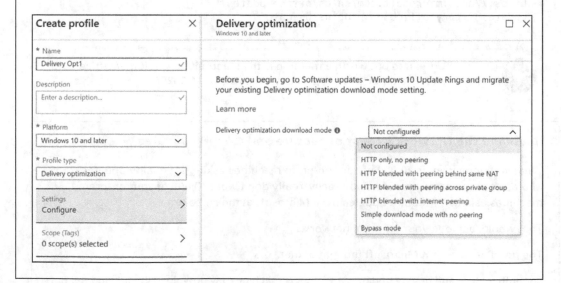

If you wanted to learn how to manage Delivery Optimization here are my favorite resources:

```
https://docs.microsoft.com/en-us/windows/deployment/update/
waas-delivery-optimization
```

```
https://docs.microsoft.com/en-us/intune/delivery-optimization-windows
```

```
https://docs.microsoft.com/en-us/windows/deployment/update/
waas-optimize-windows-10-updates
```

Another good resource is to search YouTube for BRK3019, which is a Delivery Optimization deep dive.

There's also an extra-neat add-on that can help consume *more* bandwidth. Wait, wait. Why on earth would I want to consume more bandwidth? Well, actually, you want to consume only *unused* bandwidth. The idea is that you can intelligently download updates (and other things) using the bandwidth that is otherwise going unused (and stop downloading when the bandwidth is needed). You can learn more about this protocol, with the unusual name LEDBAT (Low Extra Delay Background Transfer) with some demos here:

```
https://blogs.technet.microsoft.com/networking/2018/07/25/ledbat/
```

And you can keep up-to-date with the LEDBAT Networking Blog:

```
https://blogs.technet.microsoft.com/networking/category/
windows-transports/ledbat/
```

Servicing OneDrive (Revisited)

As a reminder, OneDrive also gets frequent updates as expressed in Chapter 7, "Enterprise State Roaming and OneDrive for Business."

Again, as features get created for the OneDrive client, they are deployed immediately to the Insiders Ring. Then, as features mature, they go to the Production Ring. And finally, features will trickle down to the Enterprise Ring (which is the most conservative). Typically the Enterprise Ring is 60 days behind the Production Ring.

You can see the current state of affairs at the following link, that is, what the OneDrive version is for the Insiders, Production, and Enterprise Ring: `https://bit.ly/2glxd8Q`.

Making Your Own Rings for Windows, Office, and OneDrive

Flights, rings, channels, releases, cadences.

Man, it can be a lot to try to wrap your head around.

So use the information in Table 9.2.

The top and bottom rows will give you the guidance as to when to use a particular build. And the rows for Windows, Office, and OneDrive explain the program names to help you get there.

TABLE 9.2   Guidance on when to use a particular build

	Plan and Develop	Validate	Broad Deployment
Purpose	Early evaluation of new features	Validate before broad deployment.	Production Deployment
Release cadence	–	Target March and September	As fast as safe
Windows	Windows Insider Program for Business	Semi-Annual Channel	Semi-Annual Channel
Office	Monthly	Semi-Annual Channel (Targeted)	Semi-Annual Channel
OneDrive	OneDrive Insider	Production Ring	Enterprise Ring
Audience	IT Pros and developers who need to evaluate new features	Representative sample of production devices derived from M365 analytics	All remaining production devices

So, let's be clear on two points.

Point #1: Each piece of Microsoft tech (Windows, Office, and OneDrive) seems to have its own vocabulary for the same thing. Windows has *channels*, and Office has *channels* as well. But Office has *targeted channels*, where Windows does not. And OneDrive has rings. Honestly, these are all the same thing.

Point #2: Your goal is to make what I call "business rings." A business ring is something that only you can do for your company. The goal of business rings is to make little, well, rings where you can test the latest downloads and guide in each piece of tech for landing on all your endpoints in a controlled fashion. For instance, here's a good scenario and rule of thumb (that is not exactly right for everyone, but should be reasonable for most companies).

- One percent of your company (or less), like developers' test machines, and IT staff test machines that mimic production machines, should get the following:
    - Windows Insider Program for Business builds
    - Monthly Office 365 ProPlus builds
    - OneDrive Insider Ring builds
- Five percent of real users (IT staff and "friends of the family" who are "reasonable people when things don't go perfectly") should get the following:
    - The Windows 10 H1 or H2 release immediately after it's available (within the first 30 days)
    - Monthly Office 365 ProPlus monthly builds
    - OneDrive Production Ring builds

- Fifteen percent of your company (who might also have something go wrong, and shouldn't throw bricks at you) should get the following:
  - OneDrive Production Ring builds
  - Windows Semi-Annual Channel builds. That is, this cohort gets both the March (H1) and the September (H2) release.
  - Office Semi-Annual Targeted Channel for Office 365 ProPlus builds
- Eighty percent of your company should get:
  - OneDrive Enterprise Ring builds
  - Windows Semi-Annual Channel builds from September only (H2)
  - Office Semi-Annual Channel for Office 365 ProPlus builds

I realize the math adds up to 101%, but hopefully you can see what I'm doing here. You'll be spreading the upgrade risk across the company in an easy-to-deal-with manner. And moreover, you'll learn something—a big something—up front.

Here are two examples.

For instance, let's say it's January and 5% of your company is using the monthly Office 365 ProPlus build. Then, oops! Your wacky Outlook plug-in stops working! Don't panic. At least now you know, and you have a few months to get it handled before the March Office Semi-Annual Targeted Channel for Office 365 ProPlus should be consumed by the next 15% of the company.

Here's another example. Let's say it's April and that 15% cohort (explained above) at your company consumed the Windows Semi-Annual Channel build back in March. And now, oddly, some specific Brand X laptops are displaying text upside down. And in your testing, you find that if you roll back to the previous Windows, the problem goes away. (Again, a totally fictitious example.) Okay then! You have until this September, or maybe next September, to figure this out. Remember, the September builds have a 30-month life span for Enterprise and Education customers.

There is a slight downside to the picture and math I've just put before you. If you have some March and some September builds of Windows in your environment, that could mean some additional costs. For instance, if, say, your antivirus vendor isn't able to keep up with the pace, then that's going to be a potential problem with that 15% cohort I'm suggesting you upgrade with every Windows upgrade.

You could also argue that the Windows Insider builds are simply not production ready for use, by anyone. I think that's the case sometimes, but not all the time. And this is why I recommended keeping it on the machines your developers do their testing with, and with the IT team wherein they are mimicking a future production environment.

The point is to be able to predict the future, which is always coming up faster than you realize.

So, I already covered how to configure "who should get what version of OneDrive" when I talked about its Group Policy and ADMX settings in the OneDrive chapter (Chapter 7: "Enterprise State Roaming and OneDrive for Business"), so I'm not going to re–go over it here. See the section "OneDrive Client Versions and Rings" in Chapter 7 for details. But since I didn't yet cover Windows or Office upgrade settings, let's do that now.

Windows Update for Business

So, again, in the brave new world, there is no WSUS server. Instead, you're simply controlling the delay—the "when" these machines will eventually be installing updates and upgrades.

The way I like to explain it to people sometimes is like this: Think of your smartphone. Your smartphone has updates. But it doesn't let you pick which mini-updates or micro-updates to install. You have to consume the whole update on your smartphone. And you *will* eventually consume it. You can say, "Not now" or "Update my phone tonight while I'm sleeping." And if for some reason the update doesn't kick in as expected, you will eventually have to consume that update. Oh yes, *you will consume that update* on your smartphone. All of it.

That's exactly the same idea of what Windows 10 has in mind for you. The goal is not to control which mini-updates or micro-updates you consume on Windows 10. The only knobs and dials you have are for tuning in the "when" you will eventually consume these updates.

These settings to manage the "when" you will consume updates for Windows 10 are called Windows Update for Business, or WUfB. (It's pronounced *WOOF-bee*, and no that isn't a joke. That's really how you say the abbreviation out loud.)

So WUfB settings live in both Group Policy and MDM land. And the gist is the same, and both sets of settings configure the exact same places in the Registry on the endpoint. Ultimately, machines that are managed traditionally using Group Policy or SCCM and machines that are managed by MDM are downloading updates from the same place: the Windows Update Service.

See Figure 9.1 for what I mean.

FIGURE 9.1   How both traditional and modern devices use the same Windows Update Service.

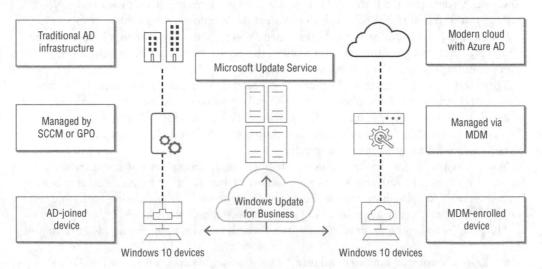

In short, you need to teach your computers what ring they belong to, where each ring contains some properties. The basic properties are as follows:

- Which servicing channel:
  - Semi-Annual: meaning March (H1) or September (H2)
  - Windows Insider - Fast

- - Windows Insider - Slow
  - Release Windows Insider
- Number of days to defer getting a Quality Update (more on this in a second)
- Number of days to defer getting a Feature update (more on this in a second)
- Active Hours: That is, when Windows shouldn't reboot after an update
- Feature Update Uninstall period: Number of days to keep the previous version of Windows on the machine and available for rollback

There are a few more knobs and settings, but those are the most important ones.

In Group Policy-land, you would go to Computer Configuration ➤ Policies ➤ Administrative Templates ➤ Windows Components ➤ Windows Update ➤ Windows Update for Business. The settings are all in there. For a "walk-through" of the WUfB settings for Group Policy, see:

https://docs.microsoft.com/en-us/windows/deployment/update/waas-wufb-group-policy#configure-windows-update-for-business-in-windows-10-version-1607

In MDM-land, you use a special configuration profile. Find it in Intune ➤ Software Updates ➤ Windows 10 Update Rings. Then create a profile as seen in Figure 9.2.

FIGURE 9.2   Setting up WUfB policies in Intune

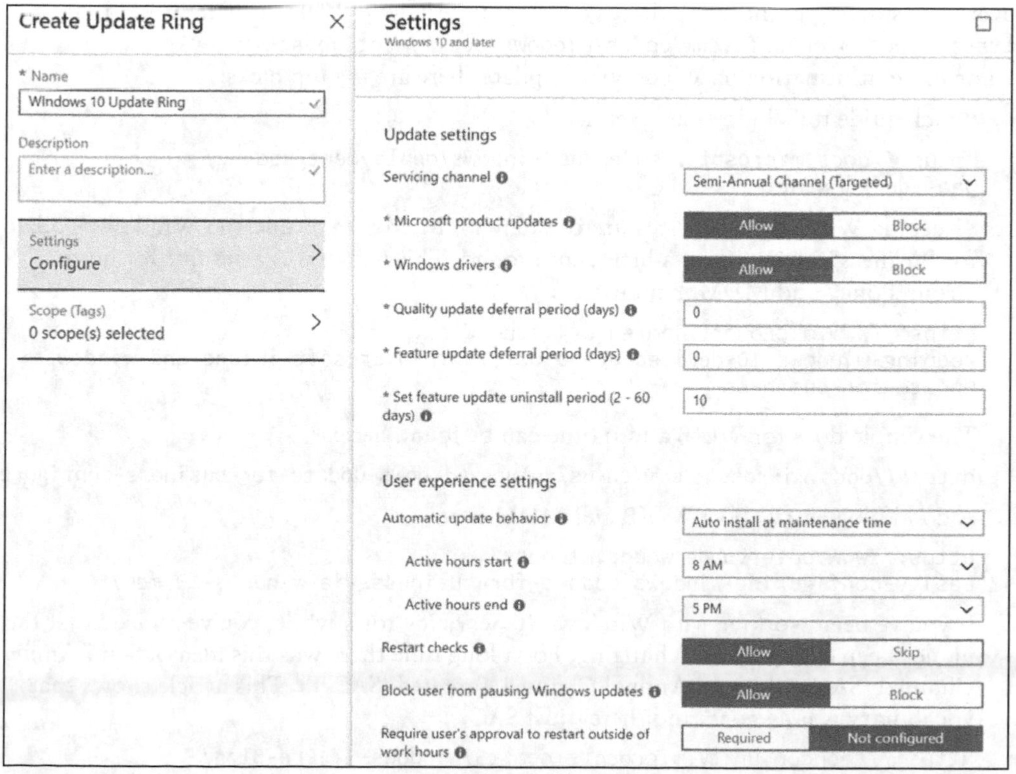

Save when finished (not shown). Then select Assignments and assign to a group of computers, like the group Computers with "Computer" in the Name that you created earlier, as shown in Figure 9.3.

FIGURE 9.3   Assigning a Windows 10 update ring to a group of computers

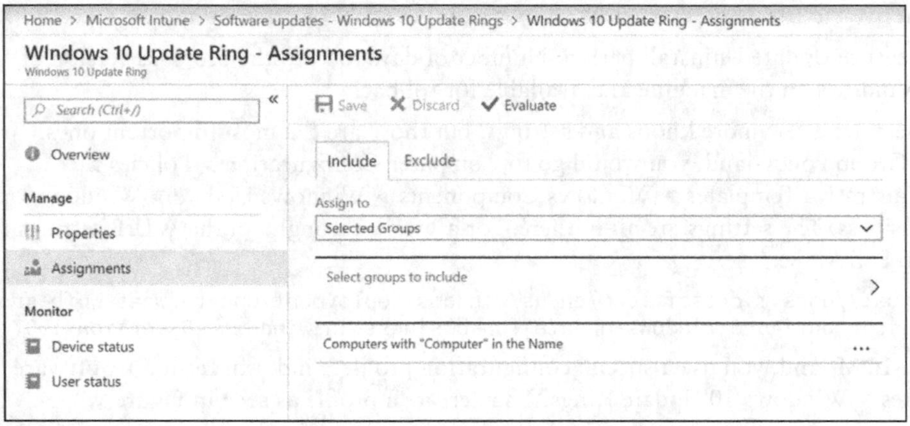

These are the basics, but it's possible you have some unusual scenario or need I didn't cover. The starting point for all things on keeping Windows 10 up-to-date would be `https://docs.microsoft.com/en-us/windows/deployment/update/`.

For more information on Windows 10 updates here are my top picks:

- Quick guide to Windows as a service:

  ```
  https://docs.microsoft.com/en-us/windows/deployment/update/
  waas-quick-start
  ```

- "Keeping Windows 10 devices up-to-date with Microsoft Intune and Windows Update for Business" is the title of a little gem I found. This material is awesome for both Group Policy and MDM. Find it at:

  ```
  https://www.microsoft.com/en-us/itshowcase/
  keeping-windows-10-devices-up-to-date-with-microsoft-intune-and-windows-
  update-for-business
  ```

- The simple docs for WUfB and Intune can be found here:

  ```
  https://docs.microsoft.com/en-us/intune/windows-update-for-business-configure
  ```

- A good blog entry about WUfB and MDM is at:

  ```
  https://www.petervanderwoude.nl/post/
  easily-configuring-windows-update-for-business-via-windows-10-mdm/
  ```

- If you've been working with Windows 10 Servicing for a while, you've noticed that the names keep changing and changing. For a long time there was this idea of Semi-Annual Channel (SAC) and Semi-Annual Channel Targeted (SAC-T). This article shows that vocabulary is now gone, and there's just SAC:

  ```
  https://techcommunity.microsoft.com/t5/Windows-IT-Pro-Blog/
  Windows-Update-for-Business-and-the-retirement-of-SAC-T/ba-p/339523
  ```

- Detailed rollout guidance and official documentation can be found here:

  `https://docs.microsoft.com/en-us/windows/deployment/update/index`

But, to summarize, your goal is to use Group Policy or MDM (and really, pick just one, and not both) to express to gaggles of machines which servicing channel those computers should use when performing an auto-upgrade and how many days to delay getting an update, the active hours, and that's it.

Office 365 Channel Control Using Administrative Templates

Similar to using WUfB settings to control which computers will get what channel of Windows, you will be doing something analogous for Office 365 ProPlus.

The settings are found in both Group Policy-land and MDM-land (again).

In Group Policy-land, they are found when you update your Group Policy store (local or Central Store) to have the latest Office ADMX files. (At last check the URL was `www.microsoft.com/en-us/download/details.aspx?id=49030`, but I would search within the page for "Administrative Template files (ADMX/ADML) and Office Customization Tool for Office 365 ProPlus, Office 2019, and Office 2016." After updating the store, the Office policies you want are at Computer Configuration ➤ Policies ➤ Admin Templates ➤ Microsoft Office 2016 (Machine) ➤ Updates. The key Group Policy setting is **Update Channel** as seen in Figure 9.4.

FIGURE 9.4   The Office **Update Channel** Group Policy setting

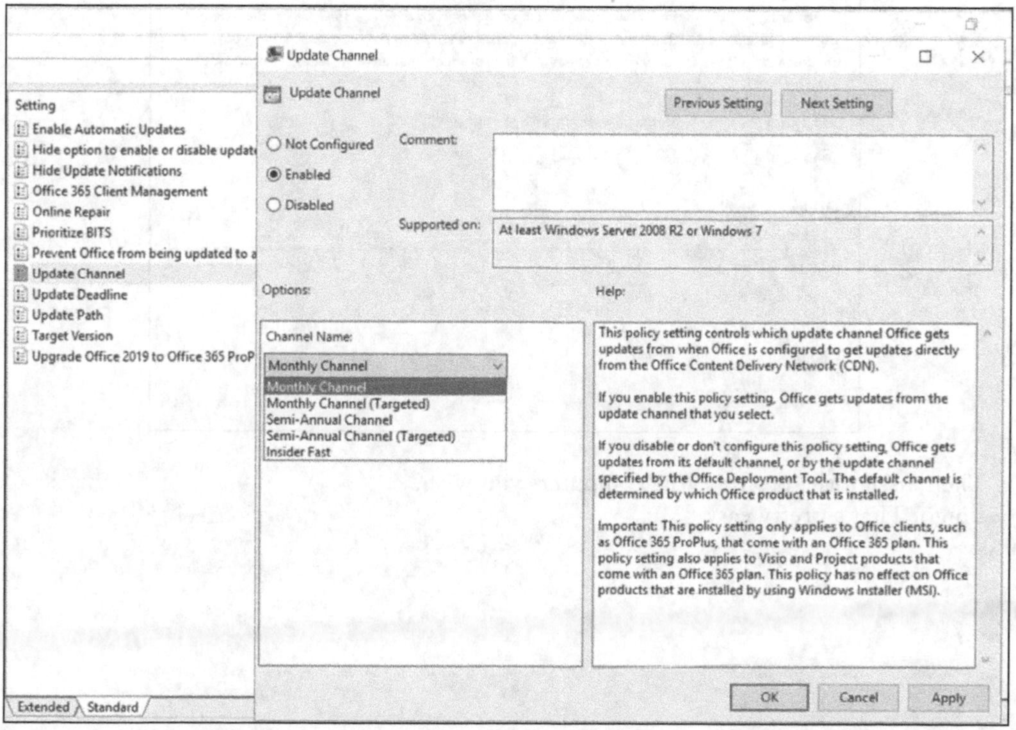

There are others, which are nicely documented here:

https://docs.microsoft.com/en-us/deployoffice/
configure-update-settings-for-office-365-proplus

In MDM-land, these are configured as ADMX-backed policy settings. In Intune, these same settings are found in the Administrative Templates section. which makes it handy. So, no custom URIs to have to figure out. To start, go to Intune ➤ Device Configuration Profiles ➤ Create Profile. Then give it a name, select the platform as Windows 10 and later, and for Profile, select the Administrative Templates profile type.

Then in the Settings, find and select the policy named **Update Channel**. You can see the MDM Administrative Template setting as seen in Figure 9.5.

FIGURE 9.5 The Intune Administrative Template setting

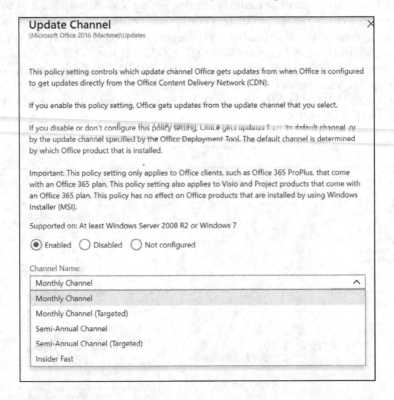

Then, assign the profile to the computers you wish.

Bingo. That's pretty easy.

A good blog entry with some troubleshooting steps on managing Office settings via Intune Administrative Templates settings can be found at:

```
https://www.petervanderwoude.nl/post/
easily-controlling-the-office-update-channel-by-using-administrative-templates/
```

Office and Application Readiness

Windows 10's overall compatibility with previous versions of Windows is unparalleled. It's pretty rare that I talk with someone and they say, "Well, I have this old Windows XP application and the darn thing refuses to launch on Windows 10." It does happen, but it's rare. Here are the two most common things I hear in this arena:

- "My system-y software (antivirus, security software, or VPN software) doesn't want to work on Windows 10."
- "I tried to launch this ol' BrainScan 12.0 app as a Standard User (from a vendor not in business anymore) and it's prompting me for UAC credentials."

Yes, that's true; these are the things that can happen reasonably often.

 To overcome UAC prompts for troublesome applications, check out PolicyPak Least Privilege Manager at www.policypak.com/products/least-privilege-manager.html. It works with Group Policy or MDM. (We'll explore PolicyPak Least Privilege Manager a little bit in the next two chapters, but not a whole lot.)

But Windows 10, on the whole, is pretty darned compatible once the application is launching. And Microsoft is putting its money where its mouth is. If you have over 500 computers, the idea is that you can tap into Microsoft's resources to overcome desktop compatibility issues with the Desktop App Assure program. You can read more about it here, from my friend, the AppCompat guy himself, Chris Jackson:

```
https://techcommunity.microsoft.com/t5/Windows-IT-Pro-Blog/
What-is-Desktop-App-Assure/ba-p/270232
```

Another interesting resource to check out is readyforwindows.com, where you can type in the name of your product and see if your pet application is listed and recognized as "Supported on Windows 10."

That said, I wanted to go over two tools to help you get ready for Office 365 and also Windows 10. And, hey, maybe you're already using Office 365 and Windows 10.

That's cool. Run these tools anyway and gain some insights.

Let's start with Office and then backtrack to applications.

Office 365 Readiness Toolkit

The Office 365 Readiness Toolkit's job is to run on one machine (by hand) or on multiple machines (via script) and return back a nice spreadsheet of what documents have VBA macros and Office plug-ins that need attention.

Why would you need to know these items? Because you might already have an army of machines with the old MSI-based version of Office and want to switch to Office 365 ProPlus with its (different) click-to-run installer. You're going to need to know if what you use today is going to work tomorrow with the newer style versions of Office.

The full docs on the Office 365 Readiness Toolkit are here:

```
https://docs.microsoft.com/en-us/DeployOffice/
use-the-readiness-toolkit-to-assess-application-compatibility-for-office-365-pro
```

And the actual download for the toolkit is at:

```
https://www.microsoft.com/en-us/download/details.aspx?id=55983
```

But I'm just going to do a quick breeze-by of the tool. As I said, you can run it by hand on one machine and gain some quick insights. That's what I did on my own personal machine to see what my own story looked like. In the real world, you would run the script version to acquire details across multiple machines.

In Figure 9.6, you can see what happens when you run the Readiness Toolkit.

FIGURE 9.6 Running the Office Readiness Toolkit

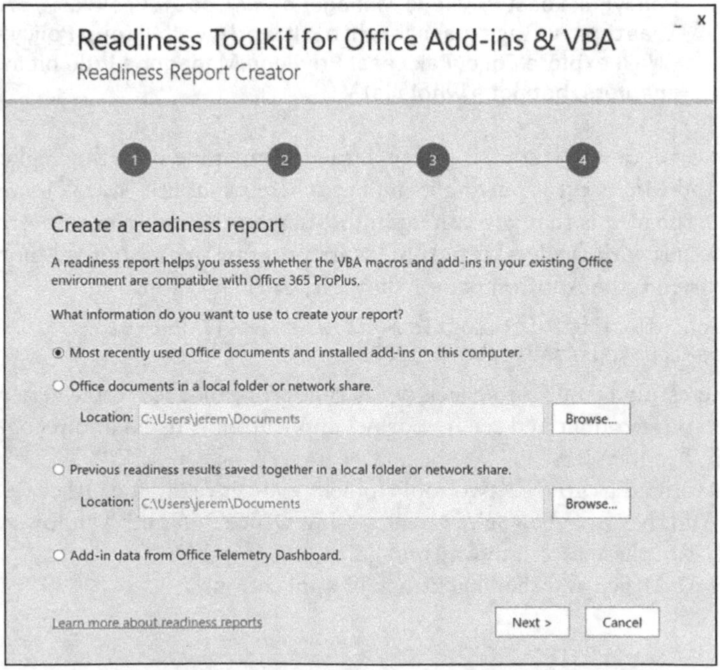

Then, you'll select your report location as seen in Figure 9.7.

FIGURE 9.7 Choosing your report location and some other options

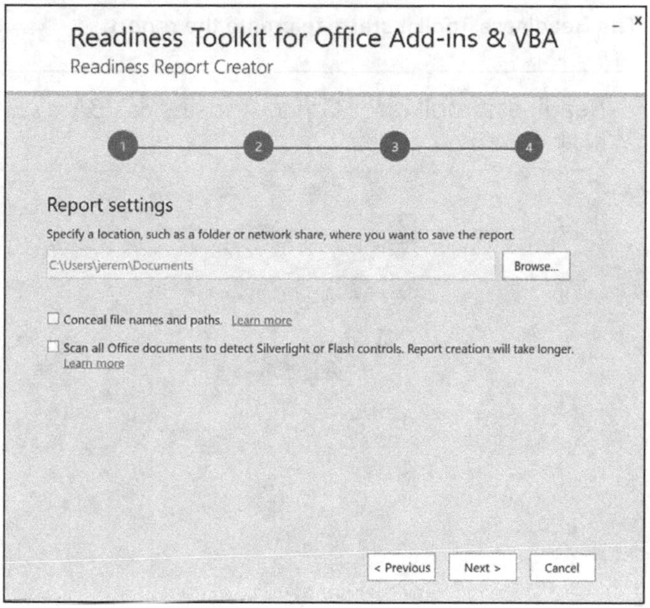

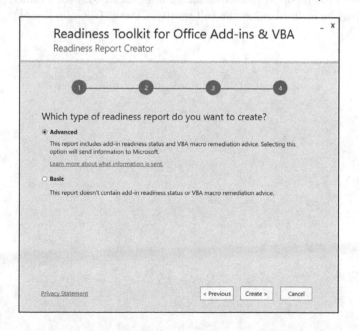

The next screen is seen in Figure 9.8. Here, in order to get the most useful data, you need to ask Microsoft if the add-ins or macros you have are going to be problematic. The tool can only tell you results if you opt-in to share your discovery with Microsoft.

FIGURE 9.8 Advanced reports send data to Microsoft to evaluate your machine's data.

Then the tool goes to work, as seen in Figure 9.9.

FIGURE 9.9   The Readiness Toolkit starts to create the report.

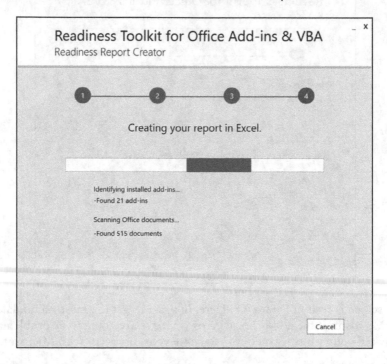

When it's over, the report appears in Excel, and ironically, it uses a bunch of macros itself, which must be enabled to see the full results. Classic. Click on Enable Content as seen in Figure 9.10.

FIGURE 9.10   Click Enable Content to display your report.

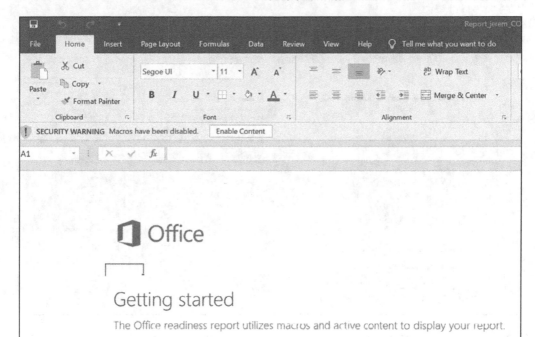

Finally, the Excel spreadsheet will reveal a plethora of information about VBA and add-in details. These are all in tabs at the bottom of Excel (not shown). One nifty report, the add-in readiness report, can be seen in Figure 9.11.

FIGURE 9.11 The add-in readiness report

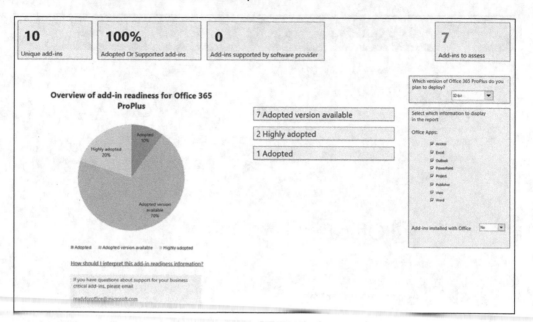

Here you can see if the plug-ins you're using (or that I'm using in this case) are Adopted or Highly adopted . Adopted means that these plug-ins are being used within other organizations, mostly without issues. Highly adopted means that many thousands of computers or more are using these plug-ins, mostly without issues.

In neither case of Adopted or Highly adopted does it mean that the add-in is supported for use with Office 365 ProPlus, but it seems to be working out anyway. There are some other statuses as well, such as "Supported version available" and "Contact Software Provider." These are all in the docs I alluded to earlier.

So this report in Figure 9.11 is meant to give you an indicator of whether you need to find an update or start to scout for an alternative.

App Health Analyzer

Wouldn't it be great to have a quick application readiness report to know if some application might do weird things when moving from Windows 7 to 10 or when moving from some older version of Windows 10 to a newer version of Windows 10 (as you will need to do a lot now)?

Well, you do run a tool called the App Health Analyzer (with the adorable acronym Aha!), which can be run on one system (interactively) or on a gaggle of systems, via script. Then it can saw through all the applications on the machine and discover unusual items that may prevent or block nice rolling Windows and Office updates. It can discover the following unusual items:

- Java dependency
- VB6 dependency

- UAC violations
- Non-DPI awareness
- 16 bit binaries
- UI access
- Driver dependency
- OS version violations
- Framework dependency (.NET, VC++, Silverlight)

An example output of App Health Analyzer can be seen in Figure 9.12.

FIGURE 9.12   Using App Health Analyzer on one machine in interactive mode

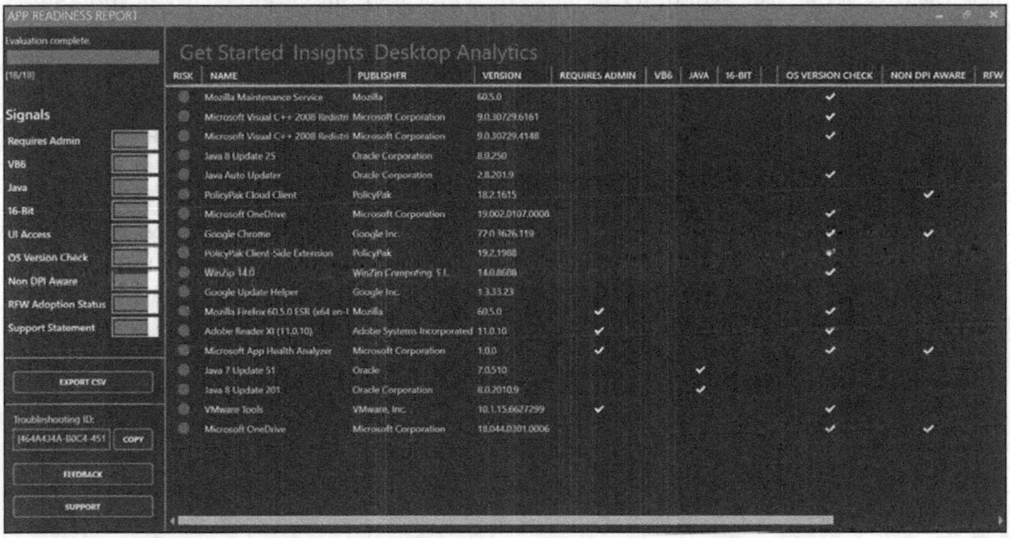

Additionally, the App Health Analyzer can be run en masse on all your machines. Then, you'll feed this detailed information upward into Desktop Analytics, which we'll explore in the next section. This should be ready to go by the time you read this book, and the en-masse setup directions to acquire data from lots of machines at once.

For more information on the App Health Analyzer, search on YouTube for THR3092 for an Ignite 2018 speech from Deepam Dubey and Aniket Sapre.

Desktop Analytics

If you decide this "cloud thing" isn't for you (or isn't for you yet) and you decide to keep using on-prem for some foreseeable future, I would still encourage you to investigate Desktop Analytics, or DA for short.

DA's job is to help you look into the past, present, and future with regard to Windows and Office. It's like a big crystal ball to help you seek insights into what is going on right now and, if you decided to make a possible move or Windows or Office upgrade, what the likely outcome of that upgrade would be.

So it tells you your current posture, and it helps you "look before you leap."

As I write this, Desktop Analytics isn't quite ready yet, but I got an inside sneak peek to what is coming, and I want to share with you the reasons you should investigate it when it's available.

Desktop Analytics is the next generation of something called Windows Analytics. But it's been renamed because it does more than just Windows, including Office.

Introduction to Desktop Analytics

DA's job is to learn about your world: your Windows, your apps, and your Office. And once it learns about your world, it can make recommendations about what you *should* do. That's pretty powerful stuff.

DA doesn't actually do the work. DA informs you on how you *would* do the work. With DA you get insights.

So, what *does* the work? SCCM (at first) or Intune (future plans) actually performs the work.

The secret is in *deployment plans*. Deployment plans is the "future" part of the crystal ball. As you can see As you can see below, when you create a deployment plan, you pick the product you want to jump to. Office and Windows are supported and maybe others in the future. Then, say, for Office, you pick the proposed version. Again, in the graphic below, you can see "Office 365 clients, version 1808."

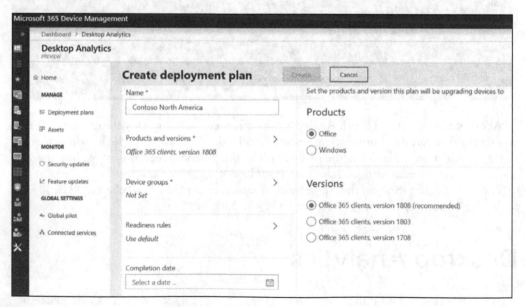

Then after the proposed version, it's time to Prepare, Pilot, and Deploy. Let's understand that part next.

Prepare, Pilot, and Deploy Phases

A deploy plan has three phases:

- Prepare
- Pilot
- Deploy

The Prepare phase enables you to review specific assets, like Office add-ins, and determine if those assets are critical, important, or not important. You also specify a set of potential pilot devices, which you'll use in the next step.

The Pilot phase is where you're doing an actual rollout, but to your pilot group, not everyone. The goal is to find stuff that is breaking during your upgrade so you can know how to fix them for the next step when you actually go full bore and deploy.

The Deploy phase is when you go to do the rest of your machines. As you might expect, the goal is to pre-find all the problems in the pilot group before Deploy happens. But even during the Deploy phase, some problems could occur.

Final Thoughts on Desktop Analytics

Remember that Desktop Analytics is the next generation of Windows analytics. If you already set up Windows Analytics, then you're in a good place and there should be a migration path available (maybe) by the time you read this. If not, I recommend holding off with deploying Windows Analytics and then nicely deploying Desktop Analytics when it's all ready to rock.

DA should connect to both SCCM (at first) and Intune and Azure (pretty soon thereafter). I don't know the plans about other MDM services though. The basic gist is that you'll marry up DA with your Azure tenant so it can know about your Azure groups and it will also install an Azure "microservice."

The final documentation on DA isn't available as I write this, but again, its predecessor Windows Analytics is found here:

```
https://docs.microsoft.com/en-us/windows/deployment/update/
windows-analytics-get-started
```

Additionally, you might want to see Microsoft's vision on Desktop Analytics, which you can find by searching YouTube for Ignite 2018 session code BRK2417 or BRK2417R. Another useful talk is "Windows 10 and Microsoft Office 365 ProPlus lifecycle and servicing update," Ignite session code BRK3039.

Device Compliance and Health Attestation

You should welcome a call to the help desk from a screaming user.

Why?

Because when you have Device Compliance turned on, you could, if you wanted to, automatically restrict access to your Azure AD when devices don't meet some minimum compliance bar.

For instance, BitLocker could somehow get dislodged and disabled, or Windows Defender or other antivirus software could be turned off, and so on. You wouldn't want those systems traipsing around un-fixed. Additionally, you could establish a minimum bar of "Acceptable Windows 10." So if someone finds some old laptop stuck in a drawer with Windows 10 on it, from 8 years ago, then don't permit it to get on your network.

In all these cases, the remediation would be reasonably straightforward: Correct the offending conditions, and you're back in business.

Establishing a Windows 10 compliance policy is pretty easy, and that's what this section is about.

All the items in this discussion are in Intune in the "Device compliance" section, as seen in Figure 9.13.

FIGURE 9.13   The "Device compliance" section is on the left, but Intune's default Status values shows the status of compliant devices on the right.

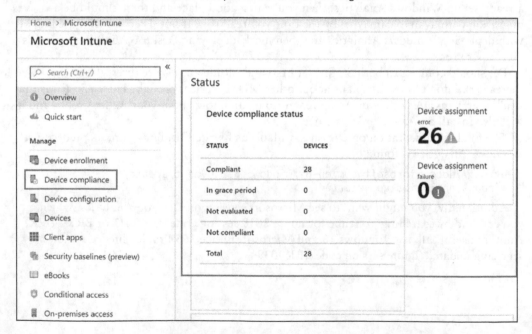

Now this section is about *compliance* and *attestation*.

Compliance generally means reporting on these values. You'll see the values nicely rolled up into reports and upon things you can click through.

Attestation generally means a technical interlock that determines if a value is actually true or not. Does a Windows 10 machine have BitLocker upon it? Is an iOS device jailbroken? These questions are answered by attestation, which interrogates the machine and makes a determination about its state, and returns a True or False value.

With that, let's check out Compliance Policy.

Getting Started with Compliance Policy

To set up a Compliance Policy, there are a few steps.

First, you need to decide a device's default state.

Then you need to set up some definitions about what compliance looks like and/or take some actions.

Finally, you can send some alerts out to noncompliant users.

Compliant or Not Compliant by Default

The first decision you have to make is, "If I have zero compliance policies, is a device still compliant?" That's a little tricky because you could argue that zero compliance policies could mean something fishy is going on (like an evil admin removing all compliance policies).

Because of that, I recommend you start off by setting "Mark devices with no compliance policy assigned as" to Not Compliant, which is a change from the default. To get there, use Intune ➤ Device Compliance ➤ Compliance policy settings, select the first item, and change it to Not Compliant as seen here.

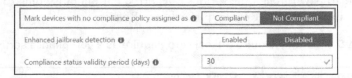

Creating a Compliance Policy

In this example, I'm going to say, "If a computer doesn't have BitLocker enabled, then it is out of compliance." Now, we haven't set up BitLocker in the book (yet), and as such, all computers joined (if you followed along) should not have BitLocker yet enabled. And, therefore, all Window 10 computers should be noncompliant once the policy is set up and enabled.

Then, in Chapter 10. we will set up BitLocker automatically, and at that point, you're welcome to see if those machines tip from Not Compliant back to Compliant. But you're also welcome to hand-enable BitLocker on a device and see the device tip from Not Compliant back to Compliant.

If you don't want to do this particular exercise, you could also make a compliance policy that, say, alerts you when the Windows Firewall is disabled. I'll show you how to do both here, one at a time.

For the "Computer does not have BitLocker" policy, click on Device ➤ Policies and then click Create Policy. Give the policy a name as seen in Figure 9.14.

FIGURE 9.14   Creating a device compliance policy

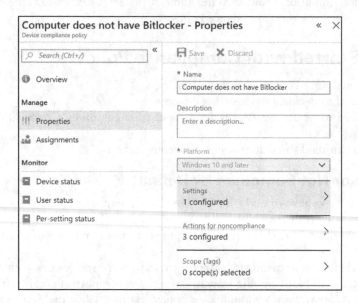

Then, while in Settings, you can see the categories, as seen in Figure 9.15 on the left. You're welcome to paw through the various categories, but I'm only going to set one setting, as seen in Figure 9.15, Require BitLocker to Require.

FIGURE 9.15   Setting Require BitLocker to Require as a compliance setting

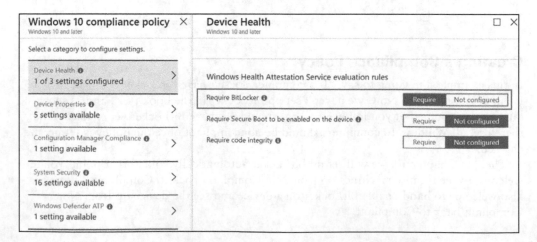

Save the policy out, and back in the screen in Figure 9.14, select Assignments and assign the policy to a computer group, like "Computers with 'Computer' in the Name."

Alternatively or additionally, if you want to create a device compliance policy for when the Firewall is not enabled, create another policy and give it a name like "Computer Does not Have Firewall Enabled." Then in the properties, within System Security, specify Firewall as Require as seen in Figure 9.16.

FIGURE 9.16   Creating a device compliance policy to check for the Windows Firewall to be on.

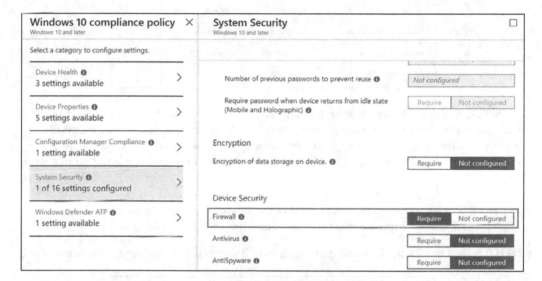

Save this policy as well.

At this point, assign only one (and not both) of these profiles to your "Computers with 'Computer' in the name" group.

Now you have two, unrelated compliance policies for future use: one that checks for BitLocker and another that checks for Firewall enablement as seen in Figure 9.17. And only one of these policies is active. In Figure 9.17, you can see these two policies and only my "Computer does not have BitLocker" compliance policy is assigned.

FIGURE 9.17   Seeing your two policies (and having only one enabled).

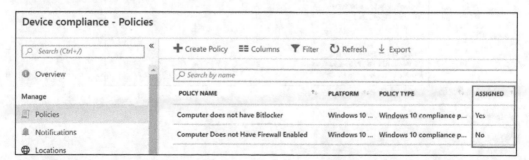

If you want to, you can go back into one or both compliance policies and experiment with the "Actions for noncompliance" section seen in Figure 9.14. Then you can add action as seen in Figure 9.18.

FIGURE 9.18   Selecting one or many actions for noncompliance

ACTION	SCHEDULE	MESSAGE TEMPLATE	
Actions Specify the sequence of actions on noncompliant devices			☐
+ Add			
Mark device noncompliant	Immediately		...
Send email to end user	Immediately	Alert Email1	...
Remotely lock the noncompliant...	Immediately		...

In short, you can "Mark device noncompliant," which just shows you in reports that the device is noncompliant within Intune. You can "Send email to end user," which uses a template to express what is wrong (more in a moment). Also note that "Remotely lock the noncompliant device" is not supported for Windows 10 desktop and is a bit of a red herring here.

In Figure 9.19, you can see a test email that I got about 10 to 15 minutes after the device was detected as noncompliant. Note that it doesn't express which requirement is out of compliance; it simply expresses that the machine is out of compliance.

FIGURE 9.19   Example email that a user gets if you select to deliver an email template

From: Microsoft Intune Notification <IntuneNotificationService@microsoft.com>
Sent: ▮▮▮▮▮▮▮▮▮▮▮▮▮▮▮▮▮▮▮
To: ▮▮▮▮▮▮▮▮▮▮▮▮▮▮▮▮▮▮▮
Subject: Your device is incompliant

Hi,

Unfortunately, your device is not compliant to our company's policy. Our requirements are:
- At least Windows 10 1803
- Bitlocker is enabled

Best wishes,

Device details
OS Version: 10.0.17763.253
Model: Virtual Machine

Result of Compliance Policy

Back in the Overview pane of Device compliance, some magic should start to happen. And if it doesn't, you can click Sync Report (not shown) on the Overview pane to refresh the data; note that for me it took a while for it to actually update and return results.

When it does, here's an example result of what you should see.

First you'll see an overall compliance status overview.

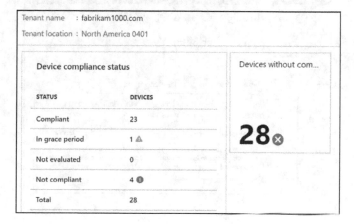

Scrolling down, you'll see the compliance policy or policies you assigned and how many devices are compliant versus noncompliant.

Policy compliance		
POLICY	**COMPLIANT DEVICES**	**NONCOMPLIANT DEVICES**
Computer doess not have Bitlocker	0	1
Compliance Policy OS Too Old	2	0

Then, you can also see which individual settings are not hitting the devices; that is, which ones register as noncompliant devices.

Setting compliance		
SETTING	**PLATFORM**	**NONCOMPLIANT DEVICES**
Has a compliance policy assigned	All	9
Require BitLocker	Windows 10 and later	1
Is active	All	0
Enrolled user exists	All	0
Minimum OS version	Windows 10 and later	0

A client can also see their state of affairs inside the Company Portal app (which we deployed back in Chapter 6). After clicking to run the application, the user can look at their own machine's status and see something similar to Figure 9.20.

FIGURE 9.20   The end user's view of the problem while using the Company Portal app

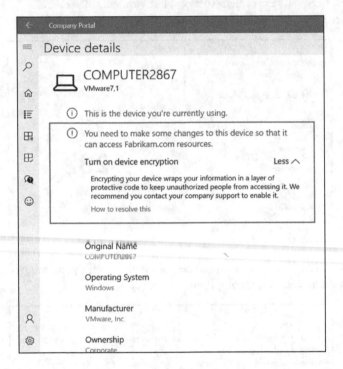

When Does Device Attestation Take Effect?

I found this out the hard way, but even if you turn on BitLocker and then sync with MDM 200 times, you won't see a device tip from noncompliant to compliant.

The answer, my friends, is found in this article:

```
https://techcommunity.microsoft.com/t5/Intune-Customer-Success/
Support-Tip-Using-Device-Health-Attestation-Settings-as-Part-of/
bc-p/287335
```

Good news: You don't have to read it. Short story: Ya gotta reboot!

Device attestation for BitLocker only happens after the device is rebooted and then syncs back up with Intune. Only then will you start to see machines go from noncompliant to compliant. In Figure 9.21, you'll see two computers: COMPUTER2867 and COMPUTER10. COMPUTER2867 has a TPM and has BitLocker enabled…but hasn't been rebooted yet. COMPUTER10 has no TPM chip and isn't a good candidate to use BitLocker.

FIGURE 9.21   A tale of two computers: COMPUTER2867 and COMPUTER10

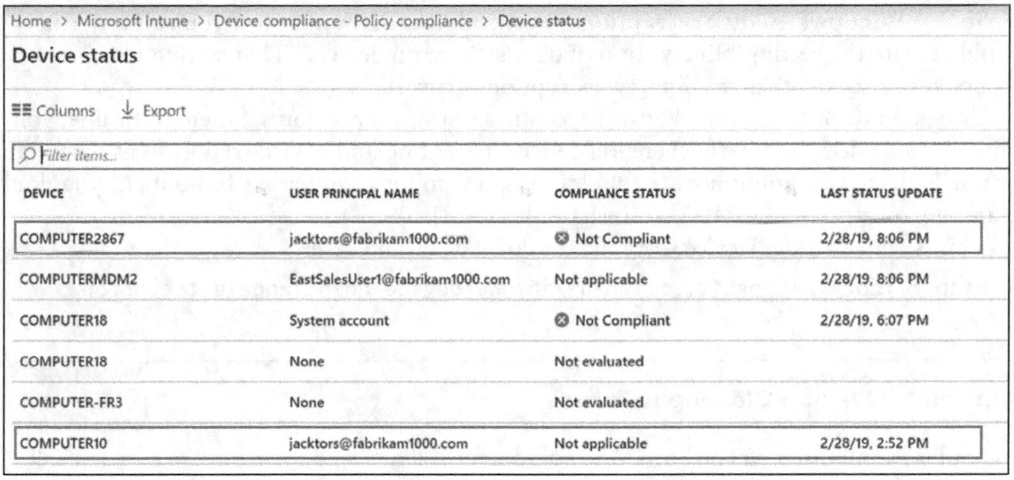

Home > Microsoft Intune > Device compliance - Policy compliance > Device status

Device status

≣≣ Columns   ↓ Export

🔎 Filter items...

DEVICE	USER PRINCIPAL NAME	COMPLIANCE STATUS	LAST STATUS UPDATE
COMPUTER2867	jacktors@fabrikam1000.com	⊗ Not Compliant	2/28/19, 8:06 PM
COMPUTERMDM2	EastSalesUser1@fabrikam1000.com	Not applicable	2/28/19, 8:06 PM
COMPUTER18	System account	⊗ Not Compliant	2/28/19, 6:07 PM
COMPUTER18	None	Not evaluated	
COMPUTER-FR3	None	Not evaluated	
COMPUTER10	jacktors@fabrikam1000.com	Not applicable	2/28/19, 2:52 PM

Only after rebooting Computer2867 (then waiting for the details to change), did this computer flip to compliant as seen in Figure 9.22.

FIGURE 9.22   Checking device compliance status

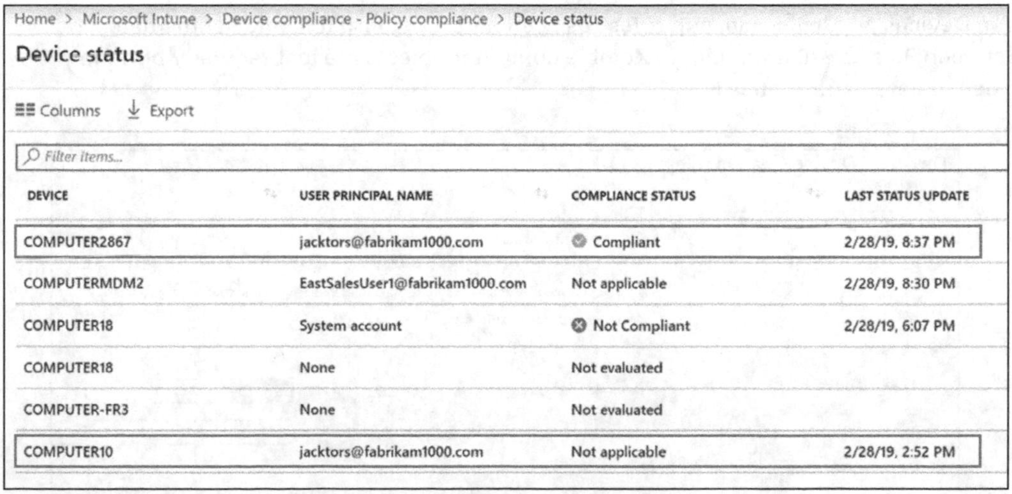

Home > Microsoft Intune > Device compliance - Policy compliance > Device status

Device status

≣≣ Columns   ↓ Export

🔎 Filter items...

DEVICE	USER PRINCIPAL NAME	COMPLIANCE STATUS	LAST STATUS UPDATE
COMPUTER2867	jacktors@fabrikam1000.com	✅ Compliant	2/28/19, 8:37 PM
COMPUTERMDM2	EastSalesUser1@fabrikam1000.com	Not applicable	2/28/19, 8:30 PM
COMPUTER18	System account	⊗ Not Compliant	2/28/19, 6:07 PM
COMPUTER18	None	Not evaluated	
COMPUTER-FR3	None	Not evaluated	
COMPUTER10	jacktors@fabrikam1000.com	Not applicable	2/28/19, 2:52 PM

But Computer10 is merely "Not applicable" and is thus considered compliant. It seems weird: The absence of being able to set the value will mean the device will always appear compliant. Why is that?

Well, here's an example not related to Windows 10. Imagine that some settings are only available for iOS99 (which doesn't exist; I'm just making it up). But then that setting doesn't exist at all for iOS98. It's not reasonable to flag every iOS98 and earlier device as noncompliant if there's no way to get them compliant…ever.

So, for Windows 10 disk encryption, in general, there's another test you can try. You could require the setting "Encryption of data storage on device." That setting requires BitLocker or some other third-party encryption software.

Unrelated to BitLocker, and onward to other settings, once you set them in Intune, you will see some delay between when you deliver the setting and devices report in as compliant or not. Indeed, you might not see the setting show up for a whopping 10 hours (if you don't manually instantiate the MDM refresh on the client).

This is stated in the Device Compliance docs for Intune here:

https://docs.microsoft.com/en-us/intune/device-compliance-get-started

Automatic Device Cleanup in Intune

Over time, computers will be born. And computers will die. And their zombie corpses will live on to haunt you in every report and everywhere you click within Intune.

Bury those zombies. Or put a stake in those zombies. Or whatever the kids are doing nowadays to kill zombies.

Anyway, it's easy!

Use Devices ➤ "Device cleanup rules" as seen here. Just turn it in and set the date between 90 and 270 and…bingo. Zombie computer objects are just regularly buried…I mean, deleted automatically.

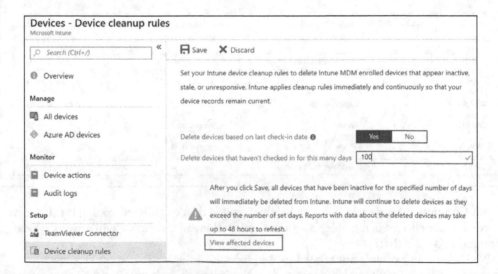

A good blog entry on this can be found at:

https://osddeployment.dk/2018/07/08/automatic-device-cleanup-in-intune/

Final Thoughts on Windows Health and Happiness

Your happiness is under your control.

Microsoft is giving you the tools to keep Windows healthy and happy. That's what this chapter is all about.

Keep Windows and Office updated; don't fall behind. Desktop Analytics can help you make your plans to know what to shoot for during each rollout.

Know your posture with Device Compliance and Health Attestation.

Tweet me @jeremymoskowitz and use the hashtag #mdmbook to tell the world something you learned in this chapter.

And in the next chapter, when we tackle a bunch of Windows 10 security topics alongside modern management, we'll also intersect between device compliance and some security features like conditional access.

So, stay tuned and see you in the next chapter.

Chapter

10

Security with Baselines, BitLocker, AppLocker, and Conditional Access

The topic of Windows 10 security in a modern, managed world of MDM and Azure could be a whole book in itself. I cannot promise I'll sit down and write a whole book on the subject, but if one comes out by me or someone I trust, I'll let you know through MDMandGPanswers.com.

But until that time, you should at least implement some initial "base hits."

Remember, your Windows 10 machine is out there, always on the go, and/or it's hybrid-joined and using on-prem AD and Azure AD. Now make sure your Windows 10 doesn't go under attack. Or if it does go under attack, at least give that machine the best chance of defenses you can! And if the defenses fall, you should be able to detect the breach and disable access to company resources until the problem is remediated.

In this chapter, we'll be putting to work some layers of "tried and true" security technologies, delivered by your MDM service.

What I'm not going to show you is anything like magic fairy dust or unusual "level 11" security technology that would perplex an alien. I simply cannot make this book weigh 17 pounds and go into every Azure, Windows 10, and EM+S security feature.

I just can't.

What we can do, though, as a reasonable goal is to just put on a handful of key security items that will work reasonably well to repel the most common kinds of attacks.

In this chapter, we'll learn how to use the following "old school" items, but with our MDM "new school" twist:

- **Security Baselines:** Predefined advice from Microsoft to change the operating system behavior to increase security.

- **BitLocker:** Full disk encryption, so when Jack leaves his laptop in the back of a taxi (see Chapter 7, "Enterprise State Roaming and OneDrive for Business"), it's nigh impossible to get to the data on that hard drive.

- **AppLocker (and/or PolicyPak Least Privilege Manager):** Prevents users from running applications they shouldn't

- **Conditional Access:** Based upon compliance and attestation (which we tackled in the previous chapter) to actually block access to resources

Could we be adding to what we're doing here? Surely. Just Bingle (Bing or Google) for "Windows security tools" and get a feel for just how many hits that gets. (It was, not a joke, 720 million hits when I did it.)

But by implementing these reasonable security items, you will be ahead of the curve for the majority of common attacks and prevent a mountain of generalized "bad stuff" from occurring.

Let's get started.

Security Baselines

You might be familiar with the term *security baselines* from the traditional management sense. Security baselines are, quite simply, "good advice" from Microsoft to ensure that Windows 10's settings are set up to defend from the most common attacks.

Security baselines are a smorgasbord of settings, served up all at once. They're recommended to be consumed all at once, but if you do, like a real smorgasbord, you'll get an upset tummy, er...I mean, computer.

Security baselines come in two forms: predefined advice in the form of Group Policy Objects that you can consume and use on-prem and, now, predefined advice you can use inside an MDM service like Intune, as in Figure 10.1.

In the following sections, we're just going to get a taste of the idea of the baseline itself. The baseline's guts contain dozens of settings, none of which I plan to go into. Indeed, I wouldn't wholesale recommend you just say, "Let's deploy this thing as is!" as that could implement some breaking changes in real life. For this book and your test lab examples, though, it's reasonably safe to deploy a test baseline to get a feel for how it operates. But, again, in the real world, you would examine each entry and ask, "Does this apply to me, and will this help make me more secure (and not break anything)?"

Also, related to Security baselines is the Security Configuration Framework. The Security Configuration Framework is a subset of the advice in the baselines that can be used for specific machines. The basic idea is to plunk the most important security settings on the right kinds of boxes. Got a "regular user box"? Lay down Level 5 framework. Got an admin station which could be potentially used for evil on your network? Lay down the Level 1 framework. Got something in between? That's Levels 2-4.

FIGURE 10.1   Finding "Security baselines" in the Microsoft Intune navigation menu

My pal Chris Jackson at Microsoft is heading up this effort. You can read more about it here. This is a work in progress, and as such there is no Security Configuration Framework entries in Intune (or other MDM systems) yet. But it's worth to get to know this project and get a feel for where it's going:

```
https://www.microsoft.com/security/blog/2019/04/11/
introducing-the-security-configuration-framework-a-
prioritized-guide-to-hardening-windows-10/
```

Creating Your Security Baselines in Intune

Once you are in the "Security baselines" section, click the baseline that you are interested in on the right side. In Figure 10.2, that would be "Preview: MDM Security Baseline for October 2018." By the time you read this, there would doubtless be others as they are upgraded and made available each time a new Windows is born (usually with a little, but not a lot of, delay).

FIGURE 10.2   New MDM Security baselines are born with each new Windows 10.

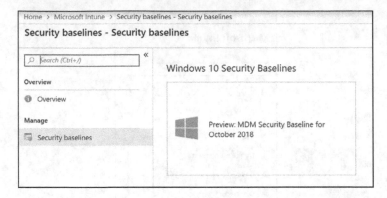

Once you click upon the baseline you want, then you can create a profile, as seen in Figure 10.3. Start out by just giving it a name and optional description. The Platform and Baseline fields are grayed out and automatically filled in for you.

FIGURE 10.3   Creating your baseline and giving it a name and optional description

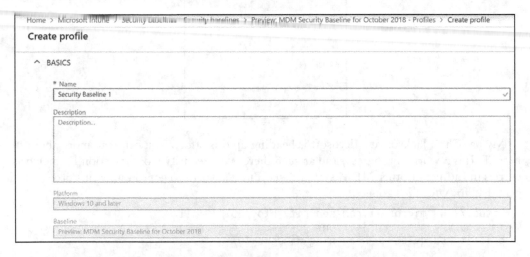

Then at this point, you can paw through each of the settings, and there could be a lot of them. Again, the more you leave on, the more secure you are. The more you undo (from Yes to Not Configured), the less secure you are, but the less annoyed your users are. And, for clarity, I'm not saying you shouldn't make something less secure to make it less annoying.

In Figure 10.4, I'm leaving most settings but changing the Block Password Manager setting just for fun.

You can click on the little (i) item next to each setting to get a feel for what it is. Or you can go to the docs to see the actual settings and their defaults with some reasoning around why you might want to configure a setting: https://docs.microsoft.com/en-us/intune/security-baseline-settings-windows.

When done, click Create, also seen in Figure 10.4, to save the baseline.

FIGURE 10.4   You can keep all or change any baseline setting, as seen here.

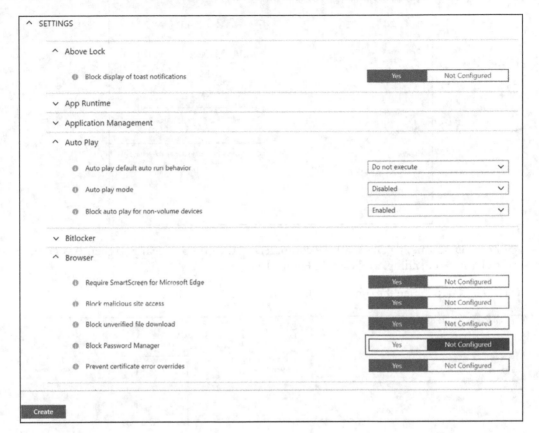

Assigning Your Security Baseline to a Group

Next is assigning your baseline to get it applied.

Click into the newly created profile that contains the baseline. Then click Assignments. You cannot specify just one user or computer. You must specify a group. In real life, I would suggest creating a group of test computers first. That way, when you roll this out, you can get some feedback from your team that, "Yep, you didn't break anything!"

But for my examples, I'm going to use the group we used earlier called "Computers with 'Computer' in the Name." In Figure 10.5, I've selected that group.

FIGURE 10.5   Assigning a security baseline to a group

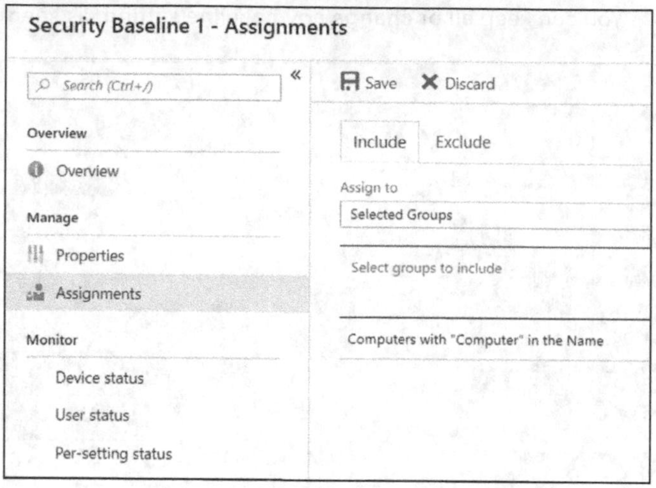

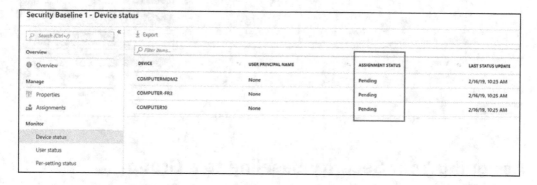

When you do this, you'll see all the computers in the group appear and their Assignment Status change to Pending, as shown in Figure 10.6.

FIGURE 10.6   See the computers lined up to get the baseline

When you do this, you'll see all the computers in the group appear and their Assignment Status change to Pending, as shown in Figure 10.6.

At this point you can just wait, or force a refresh.

Syncing Your Client to Get the Baseline

The fastest way to force a refresh would be to go to the client and sync like you've seen before, as seen in Figure 10.7 (again, this is in the Settings app ➢ Access work or School).

After syncing, you should see a myriad of CSP settings light up, asseen in Figure 10.7. Each category is poking the CSP, and the basic MDM client report shows you what you poked.

FIGURE 10.7   After you Sync with MDM, which delivers a baseline

Now you can take a quick test and see for yourself that you made a difference.

Testing Your Baseline

Many of the security baselines settings are hard to see or hard to immediately test. But there are a few that you can. Perhaps the easiest would be to see if you've actually enabled SmartScreen for Edge, which you saw earlier in Figure 10.4. If you look closely, one setting in Figure 10.4 that you've turned on is called "Require SmartScreen for Microsoft Edge."

SmartScreen's job is to, um…smartly screen out bad stuff when users attempt to download and/or run stuff. Okay then. Let's see it in action.

Use Edge to try to browse to, then download the following (safe, but pretending to be evil) file: `https://secure.eicar.org/eicar.com.txt`.

If you've not heard of the EICAR standard, the general gist is that these are known safe, but pretending-to-be-evil files that will be honored by security and antivirus programs. This way you can use test files without having to use a real virus or malware to light up your tests. Learn more about EICAR at `https://en.wikipedia.org/wiki/EICAR_test_file`.

In Figure 10.8, we can see that Edge honors SmartScreen and prevents the pretending-to-be-evil file from being downloaded.

FIGURE 10.8   See that Edge has been configured to honor SmartScreen via the security baselines.

Reporting and Monitoring Baselines

Right now, the reporting in the "Security baselines" section is a work in progress. As of this writing, you can see the Monitor section within your baseline, as seen in Figure 10.9.

FIGURE 10.9   The Monitor section within a baseline

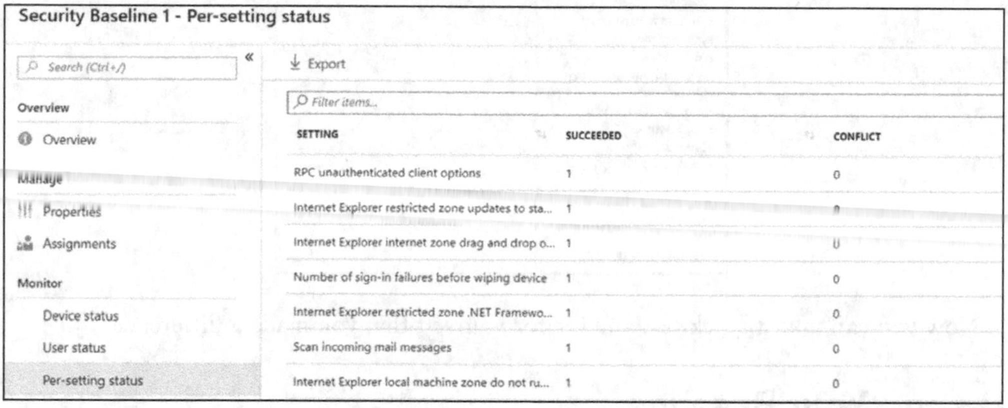

Security Baseline 1 - Per-setting status

SETTING	SUCCEEDED	CONFLICT
RPC unauthenticated client options	1	0
Internet Explorer restricted zone updates to sta...	1	0
Internet Explorer internet zone drag and drop o...	1	0
Number of sign-in failures before wiping device	1	0
Internet Explorer restricted zone .NET Framewo...	1	0
Scan incoming mail messages	1	0
Internet Explorer local machine zone do not ru...	1	0

(Sidebar menu items: Search (Ctrl+/), Overview — Overview, Manage — Properties, Assignments, Monitor — Device status, User status, Per-setting status; Export; Filter items...)

I expect this monitoring and reporting section to get better soon.

But right now, you can see "Device status," "User status," and "Per-setting status." The first two just tell you if the baseline at all has been delivered to a User or Computer group. The last report, "Per-setting status." tells you if the setting you wished to apply actually got applied. There's also a column called Conflict. The Conflict column is designed to tell you when there's a collision between a device configuration profile and a baseline profile. Then you can tweak or remove the setting from one of the profiles.

The next logical questions of course are, Which profile should you tweak, and which profile should win? The answers are that you should go back and unwind the conflicting settings in the device configuration profile and use the setting within the baseline profile. This is a recommendation directly from the PM, Joey Glocke, when this feature was announced. But it makes sense to me, and I basically agree.

You can see both the announcement of this feature and the comment from Joey Glocke in the blog article here:

```
https://techcommunity.microsoft.com/t5/Enterprise-Mobility-Security/
Microsoft-Intune-introduces-MDM-Security-Baselines-to-secure-the/ba-p/313442
```

Other resources:

- The official docs on Windows 10 Security Baselines with Intune can be found at:
  `https://docs.microsoft.com/en-us/intune/security-baselines`

- Some more details on monitoring, reporting and troubleshooting can be found here:
  `https://docs.microsoft.com/en-us/intune/security-baselines-monitor`

- The Group Policy–based version of the security baselines can be found at:
  `https://docs.microsoft.com/en-us/windows/security/threat-protection/security-compliance-toolkit-10`

- A good blog entry with a walk-through and showing a conflict (and how to resolve it) can be found at:
  `https://osddeployment.dk/2019/01/27/start-using-intune-security-baseline/`

VMware Workspace ONE and Security Baselines

Microsoft Intune isn't the only MDM solution with baselines.

VMware Workspace ONE also has baselines. To see them as a Workspace ONE customer, go to Devices ➤ Profiles & Resources ➤ Baselines as seen here.

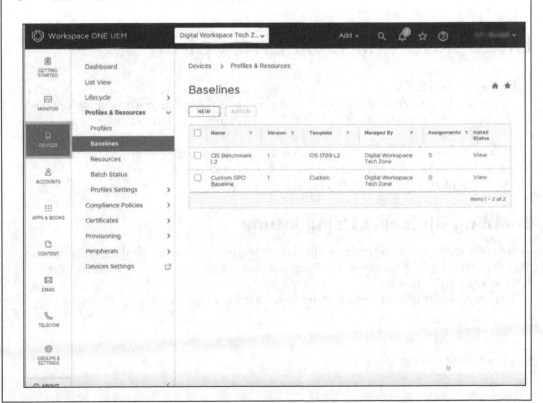

Then you can use CIS benchmarks or a custom baseline.

CIS benchmarks are similar, but not exactly equal to what Microsoft is doing with its baselines. Some might say the CIS benchmarks are even more hard core.

You can also upload your own custom baseline, but doing so is a little cumbersome. The basic process is that you use the Microsoft LGPO tool (from the Security Compliance Toolkit) to suck out the policies of an existing machine's local Group Policy store and store it as a ZIP.

Then, to perform the application of the policy, VMware Workspace ONE will drop the ZIP on the machine and "play back" the policy using, again, LGPO. LGPO must live in %ProgramData%\Airwatch\LGPO (how you get it there is up to you).

Note that this VMware Workspace ONE facility doesn't have any way to do Group Policy Preferences or any easy way to make an update to your ZIP without first going back to the source machine, re-sucking out its brains, re-making the ZIP, and re-pushing it back out to machines.

That said, a video on the process can be found at https://youtu.be/B5VzzhH0r20 from the one-minute mark to about the six-minute mark.

BitLocker: Full Disk Encryption

BitLocker: Just do it.

Of course, BitLocker is full disk encryption so that if the bad guys get your laptop, it's impossible for them to see what's on it. The laptop is a few hundred to a few thousand dollars; the data on that laptop is priceless.

What's interesting about BitLocker is that it's configured with Intune, but it's really Azure that does the work and where the final keys are stored.

There are a few ways to force BitLocker to be on.

Enabling BitLocker Using Intune

There are a variety of ways to turn BitLocker on while using Intune. Well, actually, Intune does the "turning on," but the real enforcement is through Azure (as are the BitLocker keys). More on this in a bit.

The variety of ways you could turn on BitLocker are as follows:

- Intune's device profiles
- Alongside Autopilot
- PowerShell and deploying a script

Let's explore each of these options.

Before we do though, we need to talk about the idea of a device owner. A device owner is the person who first enrolled the device into Azure (which then gets auto-enrolled into MDM). Maybe that person to enroll the device was Frank Rizzo, your global admin, after a machine was up and running with Windows (and enrolled later). Maybe that person was Jack Tors, who enrolled the machine alongside the OOBE pages with Autopilot.

In Azure ➢ Devices, you can see the owner of each machine, as seen in Figure 10.10.

FIGURE 10.10   Using Azure AD to see the device owner

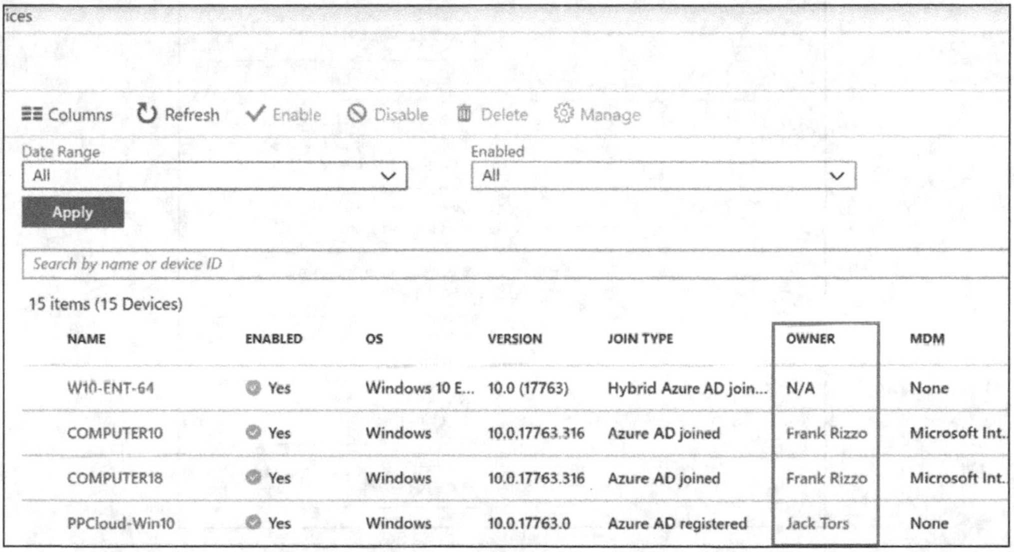

That idea of the device owner—the first person to register the device in Azure and MDM—is going to be a key thing. So keep that in the back of your brain as we continue.

Enabling BitLocker via Intune Device Configuration Profiles

Here's one way to turn BitLocker on. Note that these steps require Windows 1809 or later to work as expected.

Start out by going to Intune ➢ "Device configuration" ➢ Profiles. Then create a new profile with type of "Endpoint protection" as seen in Figure 10.11. Then click into Windows Encryption policies.

FIGURE 10.11   How to turn on BitLocker for a device

Then, there's a huge array of settings inside. The only one strictly required to make this work is seen in Figure 10.12—namely, setting "Encrypt devices" to Required. But if that's the only setting you select, then BitLocker will only activate and start to encrypt when a local admin is on the box, and not a standard user. To adjust for this, select Block for "Warning for other disk encryption," which gives you the ability to select Allow for "Allow standard users to enable encryption during Azure AD Join." That policy name itself is a little misleading, because (I tested it) it works after the machine is Azure AD joined, not necessarily during or "at the moment of" Azure AD Join as the name implies. Maybe a better name would have been "Allow standard users to enable encryption when Machine is Azure AD Joined."

I'm also a fan of the following two settings: "Save BitLocker recovery information to Azure Active Directory" and "Store recovery information in Azure Active Directory before enabling BitLocker" (both seen in Figure 10.13). For me, I like the idea that the keys are escrowed (or saved on the computer's behalf). And I like the idea that encryption won't even start until I know the keys are up there in the cloud somewhere. (More on this in a bit.) But I can also see the logic in not forcing this, at the sake of just ensuring that all machines "out there in the wild" are encrypted, even if there's some problem getting the recovery keys stored in Azure AD.

Another pretty good idea would be to Block the "Write access to fixed data-drive not protected by BitLocker" (which is not shown).

When this is all set up, and saved, you can assign it to a group. For my example, I've created a group with a single test machine, but if your lab is small enough, you can also try to assign the profile to All Devices (not recommended in real life, but should be okay here).

FIGURE 10.12 Enabling BitLocker encryption for the main drive and enabling standard users to encrypt the drive

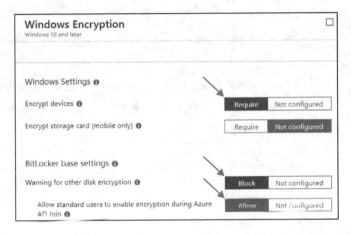

FIGURE 10.13 Forcing BitLocker encryption for removable drives and storing the recovery information to Azure AD

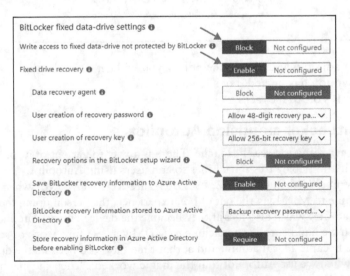

Then, as you might expect, sync with Intune.

What happens next?

Well then, it depends on who you *are*. More specifically who you are logged in as—a standard user or a local admin—when you get the policy.

If you are a standard user when you get the policy, a whole lot of *nothing at all appears to happen*. But in reality, underneath the hood, BitLocker encryption is kicked off and doing its thing as seen in Figure 10.14.

FIGURE 10.14   No indication BitLocker has started for a Standard User, but the drive begins encryption

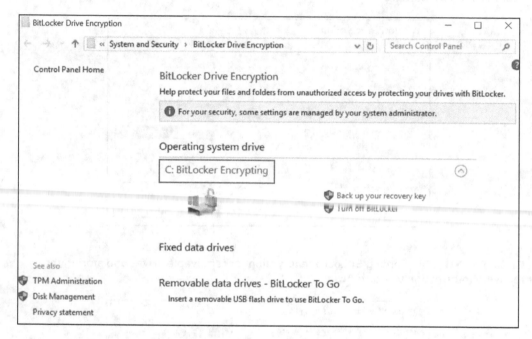

If you are an admin when you get the policy, you will get a simple pop-up notice that BitLocker encryption has started (not shown).

At this point it's off to the races.

Enabling BitLocker alongside Autopilot

This device owner thing is a real headache. There is a way to get out of it, but you have to think it through and deploy fresh machines to end users using Autopilot.

If you'll remember back in Chapter 2, "Set Up Azure AD and MDM," when we hand-enrolled a machine to MDM via the out of box experience, the person doing the enrollment became a local admin, which also meant they became the device owner. And likewise, also in Chapter 2, when we hand-enrolled a machine to MDM via "Set up a work or school account," that person also became a local admin, and at that time they also became the device owner.

It was only when we use Autopilot that the magic worked: When the machine was done enrolling into MDM via Autopilot, the end user was just a standard user on the box, and... *they* became the device owner.

So, when possible, using Autopilot to do your rollouts has a big advantage when you also roll out BitLocker at the same time. The end user on the box becomes the owner, and they can see their own BitLocker recovery keys in their portal information page (more on this in a bit in the "BitLocker Key Recovery and Management" section).

Now, there are two types of BitLocker-capable devices in the world:

- Hardware Security Test Interface (HSTI) and/or InstantGo capable
- Non-HSTI/Non-InstantGo capable

Newer hardware is HTSI/InstantGo; older hardware and virtual machines are Non-HSTI/InstantGo.

Depending on your target machine, you have to set up BitLocker settings a little differently.

Note that if you followed along in the Autopilot chapter (Chapter 8, "Rollouts and Refreshes with Configuration Designer and Autopilot"), then you might have various Autopilot Deployment profiles. I recommend for now to un-assign all profiles except the All Devices profile before continuing, which will perform the basic user-driven experience. That way you won't get into any hot water with conflicting Autopilot profiles or unusual or complex Autopilot scenarios. Remember also that this should work with virtual machines, if the virtual machine has a virtual TPM 2.0 chip.

Windows Autopilot deployment profiles				
Windows enrollment				
+ Create profile				
Windows Autopilot deployment profiles lets you customize the out-of-box experience for your devices. Learn More.				
NAME	**DESCRIPTION**	**JOIN TYPE**	**ASSIGNED**	
Auto Join AD		Hybrid Azure AD joine...	No	...
Self Deploy Profile		Azure AD joined	No	...
All Devices		Azure AD joined	Yes	...

BitLocker for Non-HTSI/Non-InstantGo Capable

This scenario is pretty simple.

Just assign BitLocker test profile you created earlier to your Autopilot (All) group.

The BitLocker test profile is set to turn on disk encryption as soon as it can and escrow the keys.

Because the person enrolling the machine for the first time in Autopilot will be a standard user like Jack Tors...bingo. Jack logs on with Autopilot, he enrolls the machine to Azure AD and Intune MDM, and BitLocker encrypts the machine.

Jack becomes the device owner, and all is right in the world.

A quick side note if you're testing this with VMware Workstation and are using a vTPM 2.0 chip and aren't on real hardware. For me, Autopilot wouldn't kick in unless the vTPM chip was removed, then re-added. Specifically, I was able to add the vTPM chip after Autopilot discovered the machine and rebooted it after the rename. At that point I shut down the virtual machine and added in the vTPM chip. Only then would Autopilot be bootstrapped, see the machine, see the vTPM, and continue onward without incident.

Again, you shouldn't need to do any of those gyrations in the real world with real TPM hardware. And maybe it "just works" for you with VMware Workstation as well and I just experienced something weird that moment.

BitLocker for HTSI/InstantGo Capable

These kinds of machines will automatically begin to perform BitLocker encryption as soon as they are joined to Azure AD. Wow.

If you want some details on InstantGo and the automatic BitLocker-ing when joining Azure AD, check out:

```
https://blogs.technet.microsoft.com/home_is_where_i_lay_my_head/2016/03/14/
automatic-BitLocker-on-windows-10-during-azure-ad-join/
```

Here's the key takeaway though; it's weird, so stick with me. Ironically, your Windows Encryption settings in the Intune profile need to be set to "Not configured" for "Encrypt devices," as seen in Figure 10.15.

There are two blog articles that gave me the formula here:

```
https://osddeployment.dk/2018/11/18/
how-to-delivering-BitLocker-policy-to-
Autopilot-devices-to-set-256-bit-encryption/
```

```
https://techcommunity.microsoft.com/t5/Microsoft-Intune/
BitLocker-Encryption-Policy-for-Autopilot-Devices-Windows-10/td-p/291187
```

Let me break it down though a lens based upon what you've already set up in the book:

- Do *not* recycle the device profile with BitLocker settings you created earlier. Instead, create a brand-new Windows 10 device profile with "Endpoint protection" policy settings. (The MVPs from the blog have reported that the settings will not work if applied when using an existing profile! But I didn't try that.)

- In the "Windows Encryption" settings pane, this is weird: Leave the "Encrypt devices" setting to "Not configured." This is a critical step! See this in Figure 10.15.

- Do select "Warning for other disk encryption" to Block and "Allow standard users to enable encryption during Azure AD Join" to Allow.

- Do other settings on the page that you wish.

- Create a new Azure AD group for Autopilot or use an old one. I'm going to assign my new BitLocker with Autopilot profile to my Autopilot (All) group from Chapter 8, "Rollouts and Refreshes with Configuration Designer and Autopilot," which will hit every Autopilot device.

- Make sure that the Windows 10 ESP (Enrollment Status Page) is enabled for all Autopilot devices. This is the default as we set it up (and you can see an example of the Windows 10 EST seen way back in Figure 8.31 if you want to double-check what I mean.

FIGURE 10.15 For hardware with HTSI/InstantGo, do not select to perform encryption; that happens automatically.

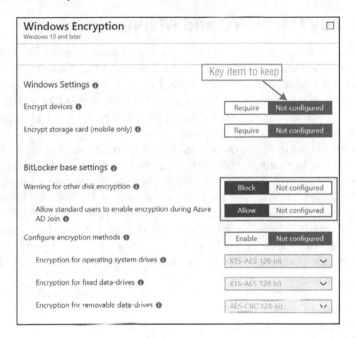

Now, get reset or otherwise get an "already registered machine in Autopilot" to kick off and start the OOBE process.

Enabling BitLocker via PowerShell Script

There is an alternate method to enabling BitLocker, which I did not try out but looks promising. And, this method also works if for some reason you are using a version of Windows 10 earlier than 1809. There is a jankier method to kick off BitLocker when only a standard user is available.

Basically, you use the PowerShell scripting method to twiddle BitLocker as SYSTEM, and the user is none the wiser.

I wouldn't recommend doing it this way unless you absolutely had to, but the details and script to do it are here.

But you would seem to get the added benefit that the standard user would see their own keys in their profile instead of the keys of the device owner. Here are two blog entries that express this method:

```
https://blogs.technet.microsoft.com/showmewindows/2018/01/18/how-to-
enable-BitLocker-and-escrow-the-keys-to-azure-ad-when-using-Autopilot-for-
standard-users/
```

```
https://blogs.technet.microsoft.com/home_is_where_i_lay_my_head/2017/06/07/
hardware-independent-automatic-BitLocker-encryption-using-aadmdm/
```

Again: I didn't try these out, so use at your own risk.

BitLocker Key Recovery and Management

BitLocker has an itchy trigger finger. In fact, just merely putting in media (like a bootable USB stick) at boot time can often make BitLocker say, "Whoaaaaa there...what shenanigans are you trying to pull?" And present the user with the foreboding BitLocker recovery key screen. (Of course, just removing the bootable media like a DVD or USB stick and then rebooting the machine typically makes the problem go away.) But other things can make BitLocker think someone was tampering with it.

As such, your users (well, device owners in this case) might need to retrieve their BitLocker keys. They can do this by visiting https://myapps.microsoft.com and logging in with their AAD credentials and selecting their profile. When they do they can see all their machines and any that have BitLocker enabled, and the keys can be retrieved as seen in Figure 10.16.

But note that only the person who originally enrolled the machine, also known as the device owner, can read the keys. So if Frank enrolled a machine but Jack uses it every day, then, well, this isn't an ideal story for Jack. But on the other hand, if Jack's machine was deployed via Autopilot, and Jack is both a standard user on the machine and the device owner, then...glory day!

Using some other machine (any machine with a web browser), Jack can see his own BitLocker keys via the myapps.microsoft.com page, clicking on Profile and finding the computer with the BitLocker screen. And he's out of the woods!

FIGURE 10.16   How a user recovers his BitLocker keys

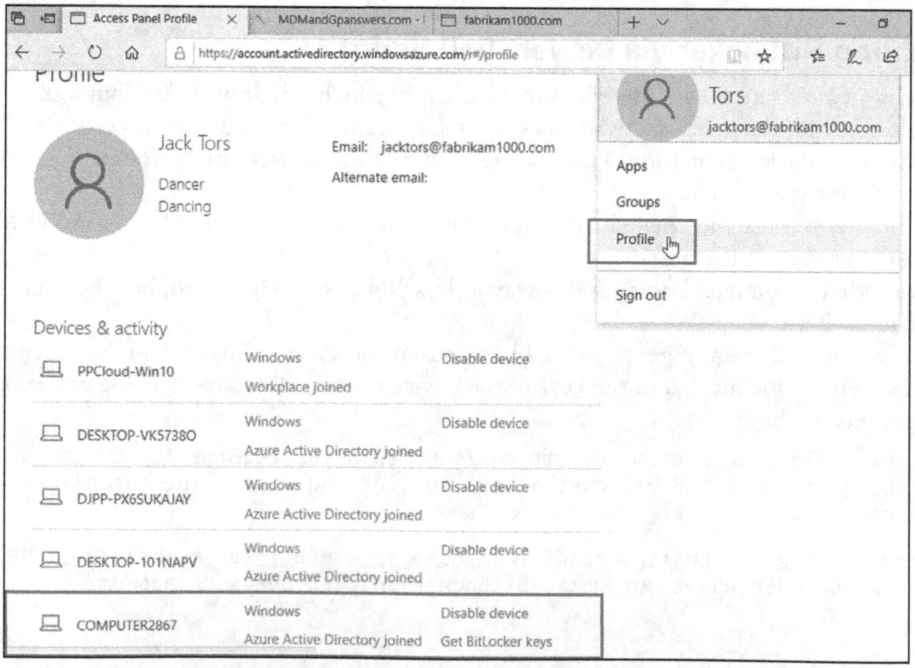

As I said, though, this is problematic if the daily user is not the device owner. I have some ideas in a bit to help you get out of this jam. Let's explore in these next sections how a user could recover his keys even if he is not the device owner.

How Admins Can Read Out BitLocker Keys over the Phone

Jack Tors is freaking out because he has the BitLocker blue screen, right before a meeting. And he doesn't have his recovery key on him, and he's nowhere near another computer to recover his own keys.

So he calls you up. What are you going to do?

You're going to look up his computer, in this case, COMPUTER15, in Azure Active Directory ➤ Devices and click upon it. At the bottom of the page, as seen in Figure 10.17, you'll find the drive identifier (BitLocker Key ID) and the BitLocker Recovery Key. Microsoft also announced that BitLocker recovery keys will be part of the Intune portal, so be on the lookout for those changes soon.

Just read those (what feels like) 823 digits to Jack, and his machine should boot.

FIGURE 10.17 Using Azure AD to discover the BitLocker recovery key

Of course, you likely have more than just *you* as the IT admin at the company and might want to delegate the ability to get back BitLocker keys to other trusted admins at your company. For that, you'll use Azure's Administrator Roles function. I realize this could be a topic in and of itself, but we'll have to keep it short here. You can learn how to delegate IT admin roles to other admins at these three links:

```
https://docs.microsoft.com/en-us/azure/active-directory/users-groups-roles/
directory-assign-admin-roles and use portal.microsoft.com
```

```
https://docs.microsoft.com/en-us/azure/active-directory/users-groups-roles/
directory-manage-roles-portal
```

```
https://docs.microsoft.com/en-us/azure/billing/
billing-add-change-azure-subscription-administrator
```

In this way, the roles of Global Administrator, Helpdesk Administrator, Security Administrator, Security Reader, Intune Service Administrator, and Cloud Device Administrator can see a device's BitLocker key from `portal.microsoft.com`.

Using Automation and PowerShell to Get the BitLocker Key

Additionally, it's possible to use PowerShell with Azure's API get BitLocker keys and export them somewhere else, like an on-prem or Azure SQL database or SharePoint. You can do this en masse, so you won't have to click the machines one by one to find each key.

Maybe you just want to have a backup somewhere so there's just not one record of the key in the universe that is Azure only.

Here is an example PowerShell script to help you scoop up the existing BitLocker keys and get them into the format of your choice:

```
https://pwsh.nl/2018/10/26/
retrieving-BitLocker-keys-from-azure-ad-with-powershell/
```

Enabling Standard Users to Manage Their Own BitLocker Keys and Settings Locally

One of the issues I hear about BitLocker is that all of its functions are restricted to local admins. So if a user wanted to be able to use the "Back up your recovery key" setting seen in Figure 10.14 and he wasn't a local admin, he would be blocked by a UAC prompt. This always seemed a little unfair to me as I could see where some users should be able to maintain a copy of their own backup keys.

There is, however, a way to overcome this challenge, say, if you wanted standard end users to be able to save their recovery keys to USB sticks, print them, and so on. To do this, you'll need a way to elevate the application in question. In this case, it's the BitLocker Back Up Recovery Key wizard, also known as `BitLockerWizardElev.exe` for its actual executable name.

You'll need a (pay) tool like PolicyPak MDM (more on this in the final chapter). But the general idea is that using a tool like PolicyPak Least Privilege Manager (part of PolicyPak MDM), you can specify which application(s) you need to run elevated, as seen in Figure 10.18. Then you export your setting(s) and deploy them using MDM. (Again, more on this next chapter.)

The upshot is what you see in Figure 10.18, a rule to overcome the UAC challenge, and the result of success can be seen in Figure 10.19, where the user can back up their own recovery key, say to a file on a USB stick if they wanted.

FIGURE 10.18   Using PolicyPak Least Privilege Manager to make a rule to enable standard users to run the BitLocker Backup Recovery Key wizard

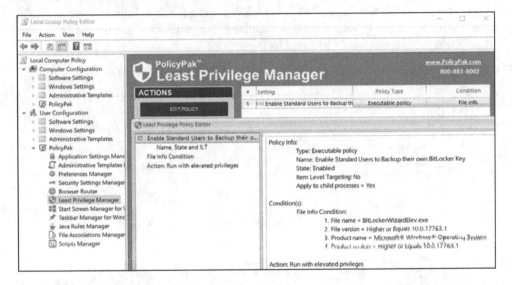

FIGURE 10.19   Standard users cannot back up their own BitLocker keys. But using PolicyPak MDM with PolicyPak Least Privilege Manager, you can overcome UAC prompts for standard users to enable scenarios like this.

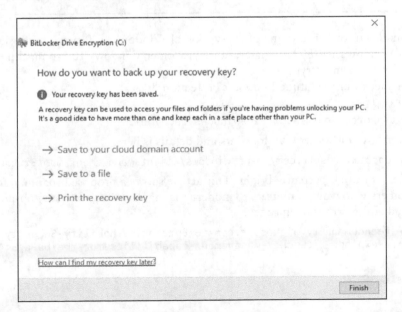

BitLocker Final Thoughts and Additional Resources

If during your testing, you're not finding that BitLocker is automatically starting as expected, maybe you're doing what I did, which was, I (oops) left a DVD in the computer; well, the virtual machine's "fake DVD" drive with an ISO file actually. When you do this, BitLocker won't start until the DVD is removed and the computer is rebooted as expressed in the event log, specifically in the BitLocker - API's event log as seen in Figure 10.20.

Remember, when you're logged on as a standard user, BitLocker has no indications at all; it's all silent. Silent success and silent fail.

FIGURE 10.20   Don't leave a DVD in the drive or BitLocker will fail to start.

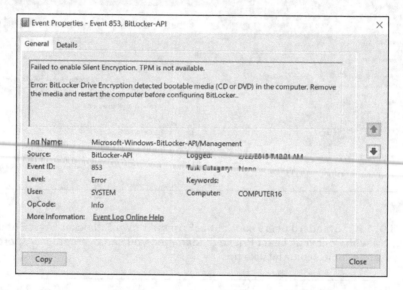

Additionally, automatic starting of encryption of Windows 10 Pro machines should only occur with Windows 10 1809 and later; otherwise older Windows 10 Pro machines will not automatically perform encryption.

You can check out the Intune Endpoint Protection docs at

```
https://docs.microsoft.com/en-us/intune/
endpoint-protection-windows-10#windows-encryption
```

The lower-level BitLocker CSP for hints and details is here:

```
https://docs.microsoft.com/en-us/windows/client-management/mdm/BitLocker-csp
```

BitLocker's future is currently bright. This article shows a proposed roadmap for on-prem customers who want to migrate to modern management (or, even stay on-prem). It's worth a read and worth staying tuned:

```
https://techcommunity.microsoft.com/t5/Enterprise-Mobility-Security/
Microsoft-expands-BitLocker-management-capabilities-for-the/ba-p/544329
```

Application Whitelisting with AppLocker or PolicyPak Least Privilege Manager

The idea of whitelisting is that only sanctioned applications will run. Only stuff we know and are trusting will run. Everything else, bam! Denied!

AppLocker as a whitelisting solution has been around for a long time, since Windows 7. But Applocker with Group Policy only works with Windows 10 Enterprise and Education editions. With MDM, AppLocker also works with Windows 10 Pro, which is a nice little bonus. AppLocker is reasonably powerful, and getting it set up in Intune or another MDM service isn't too, too hard, but it's not click-click easy as you might expect. It requires a custom OMA-URI, which we'll explore in a bit.

And, since AppLocker is not the right tool for everyone, I wanted to express an alternative solution: PolicyPak Least Privilege Manager, which can perform AppLocker-like duties, and a bunch more. Indeed, we already saw PolicyPak Least Privilege Manager in the previous section when we talked about process elevation and overcoming UAC prompts, which is something AppLocker can't do, and isn't trying to do.

But now we'll start off with taking some on-prem AppLocker rules and converting them to use with Intune.

Then after that, we'll explore PolicyPak Least Privilege Manager to perform AppLocker-like whitelisting.

Using AppLocker for Whitelisting

The first part of using AppLocker involves opening up the Group Policy Editor and doing some small-scale tests. Time to get a copy of the green Group Policy book, (www.MDMandGPanswers.com/book) and follow the directions in the chapter, "Implementing Security with Group Policy," to create some initial AppLocker rules.

What's that? No time? Don't have the book? (Or, heaven forbid, you don't *want* the book?) Well, I'll cut to the chase and give you a crash course example to get you bootstrapped. But, in truth, I go into 500 level detail in the Group Policy book on AppLocker, so I'm not going to repeat all those details here.

Creating Local Group Policy AppLocker Rules

As a local admin of a Windows 10 machine, run GPedit.msc. Then navigate to Computer Configuration ➢ Windows Settings ➢ Security Settings ➢ Application Control Policies ➢ AppLocker.

Right-click over the AppLocker node and select Properties. For this example, select only Executable Rules and verify that "Enforce rules" is selected (as seen in Figure 10.21) and click OK.

Then right-click in the white space and select to Create Default Rules as seen in Figure 10.22. The default rules are there to help prevent you from blowing your foot off while using AppLocker, so they're recommended for first tests.

FIGURE 10.21   Using AppLocker to dictate what item types to block

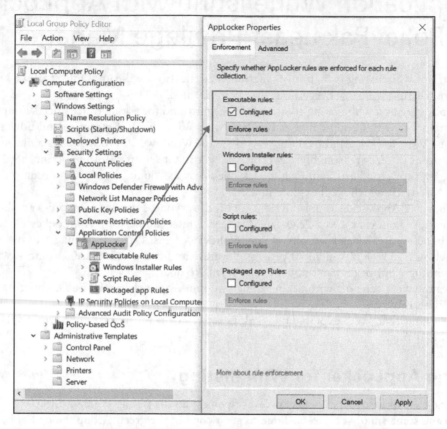

FIGURE 10.22   Create the AppLocker default rules.

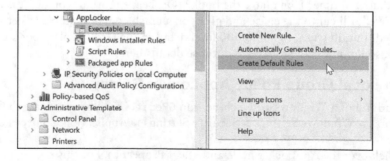

Let's keep it simple and stop here with making the rules. For everything else at this point, you would have to create an Allow rule which opens up AppLocker to permit items to run. So this is a pretty strong configuration and a perfectly good first test.

To export these rules, right-click the AppLocker node and select Export Policy as seen in Figure 10.23.

FIGURE 10.23   Exporting the AppLocker policy

Keep that newly generated exported XML file handy; you'll need it in Intune in a bit.

Performing Small-Scale/Local AppLocker Testing

Now, I recommend that you can do a small-scale and local test by downloading an executable that should be prevented by AppLocker. I recommend you download Chrome Portable, which is a no-need-to-install-anything version of Chrome from https:// portableapps.com/apps/internet/google_chrome_portable. You do need to unpack it first. Give it a quick test run before we turn on AppLocker locally.

Next, you should turn on the Application Identity service (which you'll need to do as an admin like Frank Rizzo) and then wait a few minutes for it to kick in. (It takes around two or three minutes after you turn the service on.)

Note that there is a weird thing where you may not be able to use the MMC snap-in to set the AppLocker's AppID service to work as Automatic. You can, however, use the elevated command line:

```
sc.exe config appidsvc start=auto
```

which works fine.

Then, as a standard user, try to run that Chrome Portable again. You should get what you see in Figure 10.24. Don't continue until you get AppLocker working in a small scale, local test before trying to bring it to Intune.

FIGURE 10.24   Preventing applications that are not sanctioned via AppLocker. Note that the Application Identity service must be running for a few minutes before AppLocker kicks in the first time.

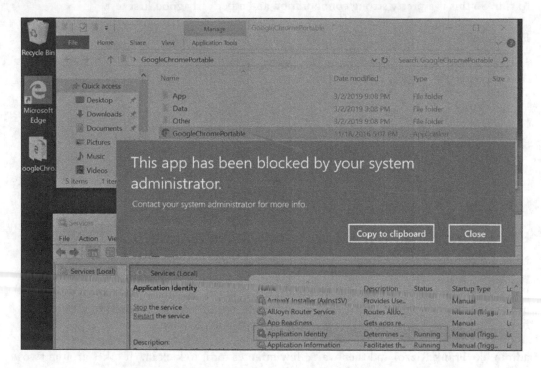

Using Your AppLocker Rule with Intune

Next stop: Intune.

Well, not exactly. First we have to examine the export and trim the file. Then we'll jump into Intune and give it the nicely trimmed AppLocker XML file.

Trimming the AppLocker XML

Let's examine the output of the AppLocker export. You'll see a screen shot of my XML as viewed from Notepad++ (so you'll see line numbers on the left). What's weird about AppLocker is that you're not just going to take the XML you exported as is and slam it into Intune. That won't work! You need to carefully find the beginning and end of the category type; in our example, Executable Rules. So in Figure 10.25, you can see a line around exactly what to copy and paste into Intune (in a moment).

FIGURE 10.25   Isolating the parts of AppLocker to use with Intune

```
1  <AppLockerPolicy Version="1">
2    <RuleCollection Type="Exe" EnforcementMode="Enabled">
3      <FilePathRule Id="921cc481-6e17-4653-8f75-050b80acca20" Name="(Default Rule) All files located in the
       Program Files folder" Description="Allows members of the Everyone group to run applications that are
       located in the Program Files folder." UserOrGroupSid="S-1-1-0" Action="Allow">
4        <Conditions>
5          <FilePathCondition Path="%PROGRAMFILES%\*" />
6        </Conditions>
7      </FilePathRule>
8      <FilePathRule Id="a61c8b2c-a319-4cd0-9690-d2177cad7b51" Name="(Default Rule) All files located in the
       Windows folder" Description="Allows members of the Everyone group to run applications that are located
       in the Windows folder." UserOrGroupSid="S-1-1-0" Action="Allow">
9        <Conditions>
10         <FilePathCondition Path="%WINDIR%\*" />
11       </Conditions>
12     </FilePathRule>
13     <FilePathRule Id="fd686d83-a829-4351-8ff4-27c7de5755d2" Name="(Default Rule) All files" Description=
       "Allows members of the local Administrators group to run all applications." UserOrGroupSid=
       "S-1-5-32-544" Action="Allow">
14       <Conditions>
15         <FilePathCondition Path="*" />
16       </Conditions>
17     </FilePathRule>
18   </RuleCollection>
19   <RuleCollection Type="Msi" EnforcementMode="NotConfigured" />
20   <RuleCollection Type="Script" EnforcementMode="NotConfigured" />
21   <RuleCollection Type="Dll" EnforcementMode="NotConfigured" />
22   <RuleCollection Type="Appx" EnforcementMode="NotConfigured" />
23  </AppLockerPolicy>
```

Adding the AppLocker XML Segment to Intune

Now it's time to create the custom OMA-URI to poke the AppLocker CSP. Create a new profile as seen in Figure 10.26, and select Custom for "Profile type."

FIGURE 10.26   Creating a Custom profile type

Then, for the AppLocker settings, you'll give it the following:

- A name: Can be anything

- OMA-URI: Must be ./Vendor/MSFT/AppLocker/ApplicationLaunchRestrictions/ {anything unique at all}/EXE/Policy (more on this in a second)

- Data type: String

- Value: The highlighted segment from Figure 10.25

The OMA-URI needs a little explanation. First, it needs to be spelled and exactly case sensitive as I've shown it. Then, after that, where I've written "anything unique at all," you will put some value in there that makes sense to you. You can use a GUID you make up, or a name, or whatever. In Figure 10.27, you can see my unique value is Basics01 to match with my name.

FIGURE 10.27   Paste in your trimmed AppLocker snippet into the Value field. The highlighted section must be a unique value not used again, which is required for proper removal of AppLocker policies.

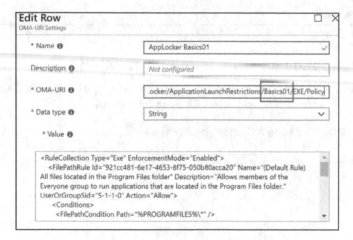

Click Save on each pane to save your changes and finally create the profile. Last, assign it to your favorite group, like "Computers with 'Computer' in the Name."

Before you sync your settings, on a target computer, pre-stage the Chrome Portable again so you know you have something that's blocked. Once done, sync a computer to Intune and let's see what happens when you try to run Chrome.

You should see what's in Figure 10.28, where AppLocker has blocked Chrome Portable. And, if you wanted to check out the Application Identity service as a local admin, you'll see that's automatically enabled when we give AppLocker the directions through the AppLocker CSP and Intune.

FIGURE 10.28   Result of AppLocker getting directions via Intune. Note how the Application Identity service is automatically enabled when data is delivered to the AppLocker CSP.

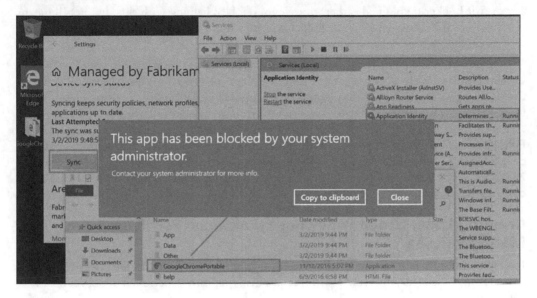

A great blog entry on AppLocker and Intune can be found at:

```
https://blogs.technet.microsoft.com/matt_hinsons_manageability_
blog/2018/08/21/blocking-apps-with-intune-and-AppLocker-csp/
```

Additionally, not exactly related, but a Microsoft sanctioned add-on to AppLocker from my buddy at Microsoft, Aaron Margosis, can help you automatically generate more rules with tighter controls and get better AppLocker reporting. It's got the cutesy-poo name AaronLocker; a name given to this toolset by my other Microsoft pal Chris Jackson, the AppCompat guy. Anyway, if you're already invested in AppLocker and want to make it sing and dance a little stronger than it normally does, it's worth a look. Find out more at `https://blogs.msdn.microsoft.com/aaron_margosis/tag/aaronlocker/`.

PolicyPak Least Privilege Manager for Whitelisting

As I said in the introduction to this section, AppLocker is great, and if you're already invested in it and it's working great, then, yay!

But AppLocker just isn't for everyone.

AppLocker cannot do some magic tricks that some people want AppLocker to do.

Here are some of those things that people "wish" AppLocker could do:

- Specify user- and computer-side policies. AppLocker only works on the computer side, and you can then only filter by user or group, which is not really the same thing.

- You want to specify "when" AppLocker policies will open and close the doors; say, run Application XYZ when it's a laptop, or run Application ABC when I'm on this IP range, and so on.

- You want AppLocker to have less "babysitting" and fewer rules. Said another way, you want whitelisting to be "one-click" and engaged to stop the bad guys and limit how often you re-create rules. With AppLocker, you're constantly setting up rules. AaronLocker (explained earlier) does a good job of helping with this, but it still means that you'll have to generate the golden machine and then rerun the AppLocker tool, or rerun the AaronLocker scripts for your new configuration.

Additionally, as I said, and showed earlier, AppLocker has no means to try to overcome UAC prompts and elevate applications that won't run as a standard user. Nor will it elevate the user to get to portions of the operating system, like updating drivers or managing their network cards, or enable standard users to uninstall sanctioned software.

All of these items are nicely addressed by PolicyPak Least Privilege Manager, part of PolicyPak MDM. We'll be going into the nuts and bolts of PolicyPak MDM in the next chapter. But I hope you'll permit me to talk ever so briefly about PolicyPak Least Privilege Manager in the context of putting the smackdown on applications à la AppLocker and contrast them each a little bit.

Creating Local Group Policy PolicyPak Least Privilege Manager Rules

PolicyPak Least Privilege Manager's whitelisting ability starts with an idea called PolicyPak SecureRun™. SecureRun™ starts with the premise that only sanctioned people can run software.

So instead of dealing with the messy business of "good locations" versus "bad locations" like AppLocker thinks, PolicyPak SecureRun™ is all about the "who." In Figure 10.29, you simply turn on PolicyPak SecureRun™ and the default "good guys" are allowed to run anything they want. This would be local admins, SYSTEM, and installers.

FIGURE 10.29   Using PolicyPak Least Privilege Manager SecureRun™ to perform whitelisting

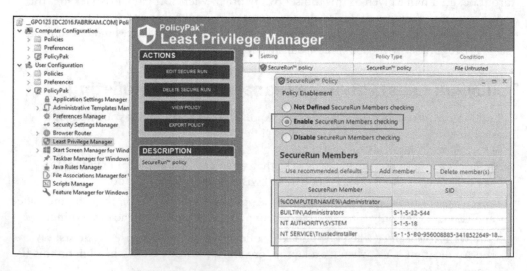

The final result ensures that only the good guys (like you) can install software on your Windows 10 machines. And once the good guys have installed that software, it's then permitted to run by anyone. And if you're not on the "good guy" list, then you must be a bad guy, and therefore you're blocked from running software.

The secret here is in how every NTFS file has an owner that's set when the file is created. Here are two easy-to-follow examples to show you how:

Example one: Deploying software with Intune:

- Use Intune to install DogFoodMaker 12 via MSI or MSIX or any other method you learned in Chapter 6, "Deploying Software and Scripts." Usually SYSTEM does the work and therefore owns the files it installs.

- When any standard user like Jack goes to run DogFoodMaker 12, it operates as expected and SYSTEM is the owner of the installed files, Jack is A-OK to run the files.

- When Jack goes to the Internet to be naughty and download a game, a browser, or other application, Jack is the file owner of that downloaded file as he downloads it.

- Jack tries to run the recently downloaded application, but...he isn't on the "good guy" list, and...is blocked in his tracks.

- But Jack can still run anything installed properly via Intune (or SCCM, etc.).

Example two: Sometimes needing to install software locally:

- Imagine the computer has two people who regularly log on: teacher and student.

- The teacher is on the SecureRun™ list as the "good guy." The student is not.

- The teacher can then go out to the Internet and download and run software if needed. And if that software needs local admin rights to be fully installed, you can make a rule with PolicyPak Least Privilege Manager to overcome that UAC prompt.

- The software is installed by the teacher and therefore the teacher becomes the owner of the files.

- Once the software is installed, the teacher logs off.

- When the student logs on, the software runs, because the teacher nicely installed the software, and in doing so, wrote the files and is is the owner of those files. And, the teacher is on the "good guy" list.

So lots of people love PolicyPak SecureRun™ because it automatically blocks the following types of files:

- .MSIs

- .EXEs

- .JAR (Java files)

- .PS1 (PowerShell scripts)

- .BAT

- .CMD

- .JS

- .JSE
- .VBS
- .VBE
- .PS1

To do PolicyPak SecureRun™ justice, you have to check out the videos. If you had a minute to check it out, here are the three best links:

```
https://www.policypak.com/video/
stop-cryptolocker-and-other-unknown-
zero-day-attacks-with-policypak-secureruntm.html
```

```
https://www.policypak.com/video/
policypak-application-control-with-pp-least-privilege-manager.html
```

```
https://www.policypak.com/video/
policypak-mdm-using-least-privilege-managers-securerun-feature.html
```

More about PolicyPak MDM, in general, like how to install it, create rules, and get them uploaded to MDM, will be in the next chapter.

Conditional Access

In the previous chapter, we used Intune's compliance policy to describe what compliance looks like. Does a machine need to have BitLocker enabled? Does a machine need to have a Firewall enabled? Does a machine need to be a specific version of Windows or higher?

These questions are just that: questions. If you wanted to do something when the questions are not what you expect, that's conditional access, and that's part of Azure.

Conditional access has a bunch of moving parts, as expressed in Figure 10.30.

FIGURE 10.30   Windows 10 with internal and external security components

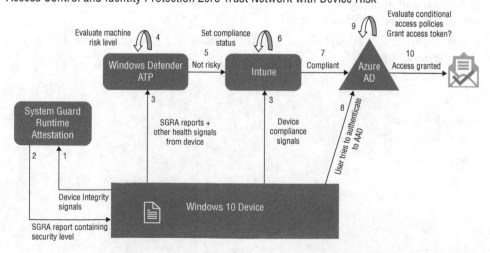

1 and 2. Windows 10 itself will check in with the System Guard Runtime Attestation (SGRA) to see if anything is not up to your desired standards.

3 and 4. SGRA (optionally) hooks into Windows Defender ATP, an add-on security product (explained later in the chapter). This product can add signals of heath and/or risky behavior. Part of the risk level is evaluated here.

5. If the machine is not found to be risky, it's then evaluated by your Intune compliance policies (which we explored in the previous chapter).

6. The compliance status is "Compliant" or "Noncompliant" based upon all the policies you set.

7. If the status is Compliant, the machine is able to get access to Azure AD resources, like Office 365, and/or any other Azure AD connected resources. If the status is Noncompliant, the resources you dictate are blocked.

Let's see how to set up Azure conditional access now.

Setting Up Azure Conditional Access

The first part of Azure conditional access isn't in Azure at all.

It's in Intune. And I'm going to expect that you already created one or two Intune compliance policies in the previous chapter. In the previous chapter, you should have Intune compliance policies as follows:

- Computer does not have BitLocker on.
- Computer does not have firewall enabled.

Once you have that all set up, it's time to turn on the thumbscrews and connect Intune's compliance policies to Azure's conditional access.

In Azure, click Conditional Access, as seen in Figure 10.31.

FIGURE 10.31   Kicking off Azure conditional access

On the Conditional Access page, click New Policy to get started. Then, as seen in Figure 10.32, add your first conditional access policy with a name like "Azure Cond Access Policy 1."

FIGURE 10.32 Creating a conditional access Policy

In the conditional access policy, you'll see the following sections:

- Users and groups
- Cloud apps
- Conditions
- Grant
- Session

We'll be exploring each of these sections here.

Remember the point of conditional access: If the criteria you set up in Intune isn't adhered to, then Azure will do the dirty work of making life hard for the user.

Assignments: Users and Groups, Cloud Apps, and Conditions

In "Users and groups," you need to specify exactly who will have to adhere to the first policy you create.

I recommend that you specify a very specific, singular user, like Jack Tors for your first go-round. You can see me adding Jack Tors in Figure 10.33 as the singular user. It's a little too easy to have an access policy that blocks All Users, and ... oh <faceplant> ! You just locked yourself, the admin, out of Azure and Intune.

For a firsthand account of getting locked out like this (and the road to recovery) check out https://www.itpromentor.com/ conditional-access-misadventures/.

FIGURE 10.33 Use Jack Tors as your single user to have the policy apply to.

Note that the conditional access policy also lets you attempt to target some special groups like "All guest users" (which includes people from other Azure tenants) and "Directory roles," where you can, say, have all the help desk and admins require two-factor authentication for login.

Next, you'll click into the "Cloud apps" section. This is where you dictate which application to block. This is weird because as you can see in Figure 10.34, you're in the Include tab. So you're *including* the items you want to *block*.

Pick Office 365 Exchange Online, which prevents access to web services items like Office. And you may also pick Office 365 SharePoint Online, which would block access to web services items like SharePoint and OneDrive. In Figure 10.34, I've selected both of these, but you're welcome to test with just one.

FIGURE 10.34 Picking the cloud apps to block when noncompliance is detected

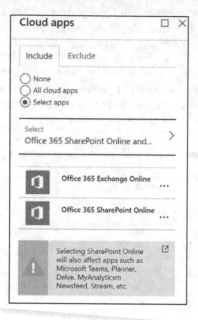

Then in Conditions, you'll pick when this is going to apply. To keep it simple, click in "Client apps," select Configure, then leave all the defaults, as shown in Figure 10.35. In our test example, we'll be putting the smackdown on the browser but leaving all the defaults for good measure.

FIGURE 10.35 Expressing which client apps will adhere to this policy

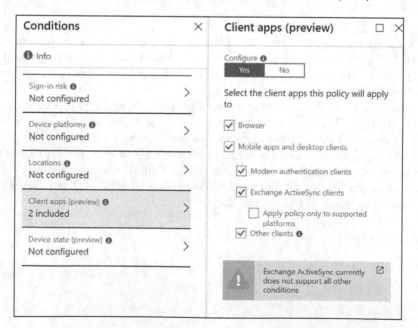

Access Controls: Grant and Session

The next major section is "Access controls," which contains Grant and Session (seen in Figure 10.36).

The Grant settings are seen in Figure 10.36 and also are counterintuitive.

The "Block access" setting in this context basically means "do nothing."

It's "Grant access" that then gets wired up to the thing you want to force the user to adhere to. We're saying that when the machine is not compliant, we want to block access. Therefore, the right check box is "Require device to be marked as compliant."

Additionally, you need to select what to do if multiple items are selected in the "Grant access" category. We're only selecting one, so it doesn't really matter. But for good measure, select "Require one of the selected controls."

So, by the time this is over, you can read it like, "If the machine is marked as noncompliant, then block access."

Again, maybe it's just me, but I found this whole Grant page totally turned around for the way my brain operates.

FIGURE 10.36   Specifying why a machine should be considered for blocking

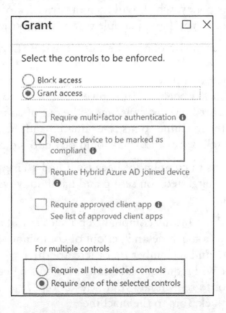

The last block is called "Session controls," and is not used in this example. Session controls can give signals back to cloud applications to perform what's known as a "Limited Access Experience." This varies from app to app. But, for instance, in Outlook Web, you will be blocked from downloading attachments until the conditional access is satisfied. A starting page for it can be found here:

```
https://docs.microsoft.com/en-us/azure/active-directory/conditional-access/
controls#session-controls
```

And an example on how to use it with Outlook and Exchange online can be found here:

```
https://techcommunity.microsoft.com/t5/Outlook-Blog/
Conditional-Access-in-Outlook-on-the-web-for-Exchange-Online/ba-p/267069.
```

Finally, when done, click Create (not shown).

The result of the policy creation can be seen in Figure 10.37.

FIGURE 10.37 Your Azure conditional access policy

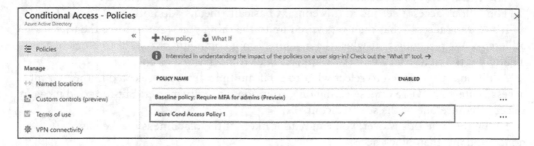

Testing Azure Conditional Access Policy

You need to tip the apple cart. That is, you need to get out of compliance such that you'll trigger Intune's compliance policy, which will then in turn kick off the Azure conditional access policy. The way I see it, you have a couple of ways to do that.

Way #1: If your machine was in compliance because it had BitLocker enabled Remember the Intune profile that turned on BitLocker? You had it set to "Computers with 'Computer' in the Name." First, set that such that it's not hitting any machines anymore. Then, on, say, one machine that was BitLocker enabled, fully revert out of BitLocker. Note that for me, merely "Suspending BitLocker" did not cause me to be out of compliance. After you fully disable BitLocker, reboot the machine so it's re-evaluated and the attestation is rerun. Then the data will make it back to Azure, and you should be out of compliance.

Way #2: If your machine was in compliance because it had a Firewall enabled The other Intune compliance policy I suggested you set up and had handy was one that tested if the firewall was enabled or not.

Make sure only one of these Intune compliance policies is still assigned (and not both). Then, log on as Jack Tors to a machine and get out of compliance (turn off BitLocker or fully disable the firewall, and remember that there are three parts of the Windows Firewall). Either procedure will require local admin rights (use Frank@fabrikam1000.com) to do the deed. Then reboot to re-evaluate your attestation of either compliance stance.

At this point, log on as Jack Tors to the machine.

Before you continue, though, in Intune, pre-verify that yes, indeed, your machine is now officially out of compliance, as seen in Figure 10.38.

FIGURE 10.38   Verifying that the machine is out of compliance

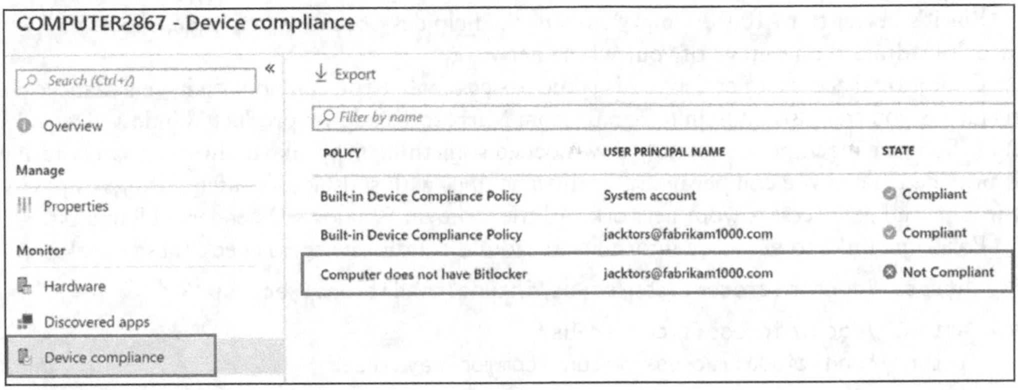

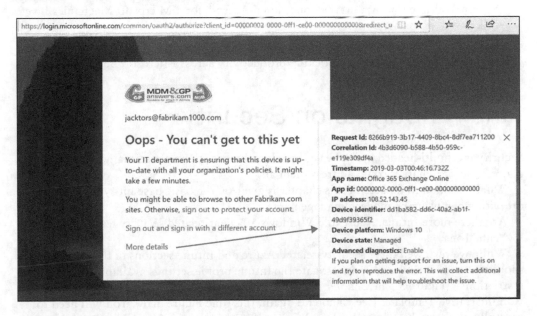

COMPUTER2867 - Device compliance

POLICY	USER PRINCIPAL NAME	STATE
Built-in Device Compliance Policy	System account	✓ Compliant
Built-in Device Compliance Policy	jacktors@fabrikam1000.com	✓ Compliant
Computer does not have Bitlocker	jacktors@fabrikam1000.com	✗ Not Compliant

Now, as Jack, use Edge to go to office.microsoft.com after you're logged in (to get to Outlook) or onedrive.microsoft.com to get to OneDrive. If you're logged in successfully, and all the credentials are being passed correctly, because you blocked (one or both) services, you'll get what you see in Figure 10.39.

FIGURE 10.39   What the user sees when conditional access blocks resources

Now, I realize a user seeing what's in Figure 10.39 definitely means a very angry call to the help desk.

But it's better than 10,000 angry calls to the help desk because of a huge, successful attack leading to an outage of your whole network.

Conditional access is neat, and this is the basics of what you can do with it. In advanced scenarios you can also hook in to signals from Microsoft's add-on product Windows Defender ATP. So if the machine has recently downloaded something fishy, like malware, a safety rating is provided. Then you can permit, say, only machines with satisfactory safety ratings to pass through and get access to your network. A little more on Windows Defender ATP in a bit.

For some links to get more information around condition access check these out:

- https://docs.microsoft.com/en-us/intune/conditional-access
- https://docs.microsoft.com/en-us/intune/conditional-access-intune-common-ways-use
- Troubleshooting why users might get the block notification (and you didn't intend it): https://docs.microsoft.com/en-us/azure/active-directory/user-help/user-help-device-remediation
- https://techcommunity.microsoft.com/t5/Azure-Active-Directory-Identity/New-enhanced-access-controls-in-Azure-AD-Tenant-Restrictions-is/ba-p/245194
- Search Youtube for "Azure AD Conditional Access" for a Microsoft Mechanics Live! talk
- Search YouTube for BRK3241 for "Enable Azure Active Directory Conditional Access to secure user access while unlocking productivity across Microsoft 365."

Final Thoughts on Security

Security is a multi-headed hydra beast, by which I mean, there are so many heads to address, no one chapter could address them all.

What I wanted to do here in this chapter is give you the basic base hits you would start off with when utilizing modern management.

Are there more Intune, Azure and Windows 10 client-related security features?
Yeah. Tons.

While we reviewed these security-related Azure and Intune sections in the book, you should take some time and re-investigate the Intune profile settings available in "Device restrictions" (Figure 3.5 in Chapter 3), "Endpoint protection" (Figure 10.11), and Administrative Templates (see Chapter 3 again, this time Figure 3.16). You will need to carefully go through each setting to ask yourself, "Is this setting something I should use to make my world more secure?"

But you'll have to jump off here from this starting point and investigate a fuller complement of security features to produce the full picture. Here are some resources to start your journey. But note that your journey to keep protecting and protecting again is basically endless.

Security Features within each version of Windows 10   If you're ever lost about which features are in what Windows 10 Product (Home, Pro, Enterprise), you can check out the link below. Whenever new Windows 10 ships with new security features, you should be able to see them on this list and if your version of Windows has it: `https://www .microsoft.com/en-us/windowsforbusiness/compare`.

Getting Started with Windows 10 Security Features   This is a good starting page about Microsoft's documentation of Windows 10 security features: `https://docs.microsoft .com/en-us/windows/security/index`.

General Overviews   On YouTube, find the video named "Microsoft 365 security – Everything you need to know in 8-minutes." Get a 30,000-foot understanding of some of the extras you can do, like identity-based and location-based detection. (That is, if someone logs on from the USA and Sweden at the same time, chances are that's a hacker doing some evil.) Learn about Office Message encryption, Office Data Governance, and a whole lot more. Just eight minutes!

Also, many good security overviews can be found at the Microsoft Mechanics YouTube playlist at `aka.ms/MechanicsM365Security` if you just want to hole up on a winter's day and watch a million security videos and scare yourself to death.

IT Roadmap and Assessment   If you want to try to "get there from here" to increase your security, check out `https://transform.microsoft.com/itroadmap#!/itroadmap/welcome`. The general idea is that you express your goals and the tool will spit out the (very high level) steps you would need to get there. See an example in Figure 10.40.

FIGURE 10.40   Use the IT Roadmap to help you plan out future ways to get more secure.

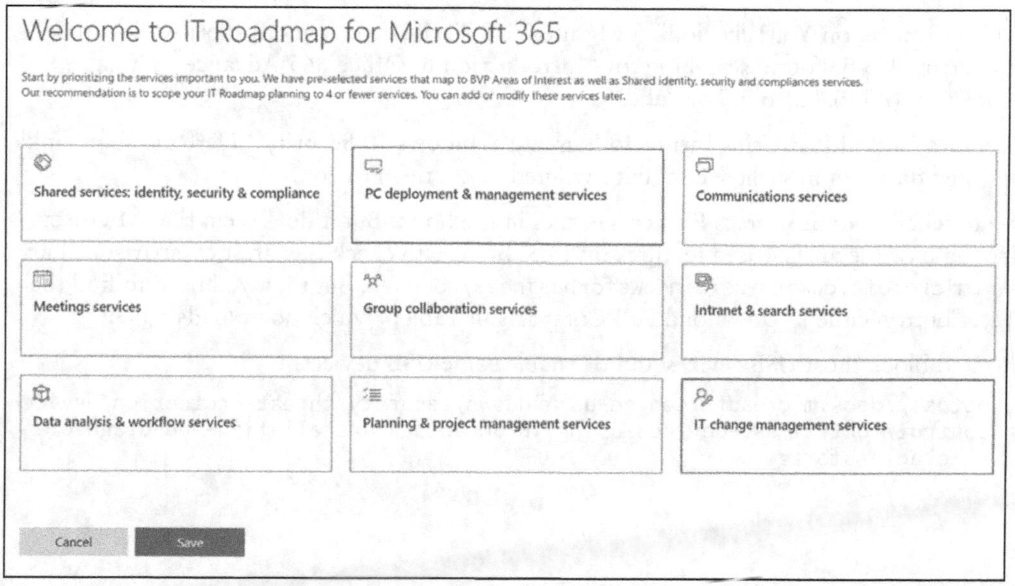

Protection.office.com   This is part of Azure and Office. This section has a whole universe around data loss prevention, data governance, threat management, and data privacy. Additionally, this is where you would set up settings to dial in the details for anti-phishing, anti-spam, DMIK (email protection), and anti-malware. These protections are built into your subscription.

Windows Defender Exploit Guard   Windows Defender Exploit Guard was born out of the Enhanced Mitigation Experience Toolkit (EMET) and is now baked into Windows 10. If you want to put the smackdown on evil applications of a myriad of kinds, you can check out the original details at:

```
https://www.microsoft.com/security/blog/2017/10/23/
windows-defender-exploit-guard-reduce-the-attack-surface-
against-next-generation-malware/
```

Windows Defender ATP   Windows Defender ATP is a whole add-on suite of security tools that hooks into Intune and Azure for an additional fee. You must first be licensed for Microsoft 365 E5. Windows Defender ATP isn't just for Windows; Mac and Linux can also participate here.

Windows Defender ATP's goal is to give you the full anatomy of an attack. Plus when you're using it, you (along with other Windows Defender ATP customers) are sharing signals about what the bad guys are probing for. And if your Windows 10 computer goes into "risky" status, you can trigger it to be noncompliant until you hunt down the problem.

Additionally, Windows Defender ATP adds another whole universe of anti-phishing, anti-spam, and anti-malware beyond what's already provided in in the Protection.office.com page.

The official start page is www.microsoft.com/en-us/WindowsForBusiness/windows-atp.

To learn more, on YouTube, look for Ignite 2018 THR2065. A good, short walk-through video can also be found searching for "Introduction to Office 365 Advanced Threat Protection (ATP)." also in YouTube.

Random Good Ideas Using Intune to Increase Windows 10 Security   Here are some links that just didn't fit anywhere else, but I wanted to get them to you.

We touched upon E3 versus E5 items earlier in the book. But it does seem that Microsoft is driving more security-based features into E5. Be sure to check the latest comparison chart www.microsoft.com/en-us/windowsforbusiness/compare. But then you need to find the secret button called "Download Full Comparison Table," which downloads a PDF.

How to block most USB devices and/or enable some USB devices:

```
https://docs.microsoft.com/en-us/windows/security/threat-protection/device-
control/control-usb-devices-using-intune#block-installation-and-usage-of-
removable-storage
```

How to turn on Windows Defender Application Guard (WDAG). WDAG provides a way, with Edge, to have a little "throw away Hyper-V pool" for when users download evil stuff and run it. Instead of causing harm to your system, the changes are just thrown away. Good step-by-steps are here:

```
https://albertneef.wordpress.com/2018/05/03/
part-5-configure-microsoft-intune-windows-defender-application-guard/
```

Windows Defender is now very good antivirus software. If you stopped using it in years past, give it another shake. The score has increased wildly over the last few years. See:

```
https://www.av-test.org/en/antivirus/business-windows-client/manufacturer/
microsoft/
```

Step-by-step guide to configuring Windows 10 security with Intune by Amy Babinchak, MVP, who just crushes it with this easy-to-follow list: `http://techgenix.com/ intune-windows-10-security/`.

I could give you 80 more items to check out, I want to keep it short and wrap it up. I'll give you more advice at `MDMandGPanswers.com` when you sign up for my weekly newsletter.

What did you learn how to do in this chapter? Use the hashtag #mdmbook to shout out and tell me @jeremymoskowitz what you learned in Chapter 10. I love hearing your "A-ha!" moments!

See you in the next chapter where we talk about third-party tools to enhance and augment your MDM environment.

Chapter

11

MDM Add-On Tools: Free and Pay

In your journey, be it to go totally in-cloud or work in hybrid for the foreseeable future, you're going to need a backpack of tools that can help aid you along the way.

In this chapter, I'll be covering some free and pay tools (in no particular order, actually). Here are some of the tools that can be used alongside your MDM deployment:

- Intune's Company Portal app
- Microsoft Graph and the Graph Explorer
- PolicyPak On-Prem Edition and PolicyPak MDM Edition
- Miscellaneous scripts and interesting "Things I Found on the Internet"

Let's check it all out together!

Company Portal App

Almost everything in this discussion, I can attribute to the awesome article by Scott Duff from Microsoft about the Company Portal app.

We've rolled out the Company Portal app back in Chapter 6, "Deploying Software and Scripts," and used it a few times. If you'll remember, first we used the Company Portal App to see what applications we had available (again Chapter 6). This enables users to grab applications directly from the Microsoft Store for Business that you set up, made available by Intune. And in a little while we'll see how to make applications "Available for Enrolled devices" which makes acquiring those applications optional.

That said, there's a bunch more things you can do with the Company Portal. And, indeed, before you try these out you might want to set up the branding on the company portal (aka, the look and feel).

Setting Up Company Portal Branding

To set up the Company Portal branding, inside Intune, click Client apps ➤ Branding and customization. You'll be able to then specify company logo graphics and what users should see when they ask for help. In Figure 11.1, I filled in some items using my MDMandGPanswers.com logo.

FIGURE 11.1   Setting up the Company Portal branding

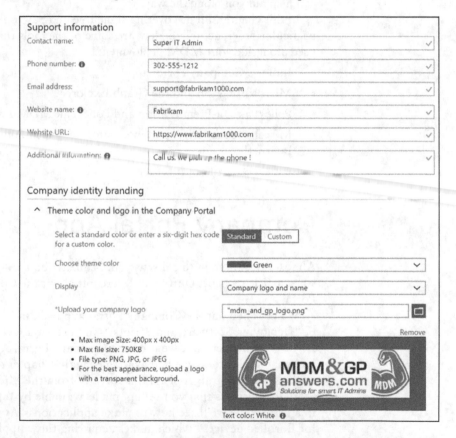

You can learn more about the configuration of the Company Portal app here: https://docs.microsoft.com/en-us/intune/company-portal-app.

Users Interacting with the Company Portal App

There are a lot of useful things users can do inside the Company Portal app. Beyond enabling users to download their own applications, we'll talk a walk around the park with the following functions:

- Getting help and support
- Checking Conditional Access problems
- Setting up/re–setting up a device for corporate use
- Enabling a user to change a password
- Enabling users to Managing their own applications
- Syncing, remote locking, or resetting a device

Users Getting Help and Support

After you set it up, when a user runs the Company Portal app, they can see your branding, as seen in Figure 11.2.

FIGURE 11.2 Seeing your company branding, some warnings, and how users can get around

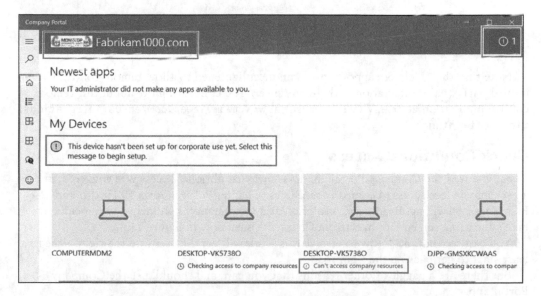

When users need help, they click on the little question mark icon (not shown.) When they click it, they can see your Help & Support information (shown in Figure 11.3).

FIGURE 11.3   Seeing your help and support branding

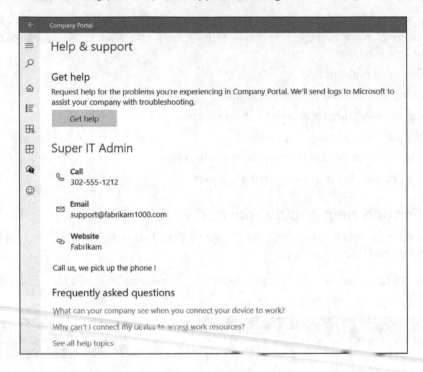

Note that the "Help & support" area can be enlightened to allow remote control via a third party (paid) integration with TeamViewer. You can learn more about this remote control integration at TeamViewer's website at www.teamviewer.com/en-us/integrations/ microsoft-intune/.

Check Conditional Access

Then, we used the Company Portal app to see why conditional access was triggered, and a user maybe lost access to company resources (Chapter 9, "Windows 10 Health and Happiness: Servicing, Readiness, Analytics, and Compliance"). To help you remember, here's the same screen shot back from Chapter 9, seen now in Figure 11.4.

You can see that the "How to resolve this" link will get the user into the right place to at least start to get back on the right road.

But there are a gaggle of other reasons that you can, and should, use the Company Portal app.

FIGURE 11.4   An end user can see what problem is triggering conditional access via the Company Portal app.

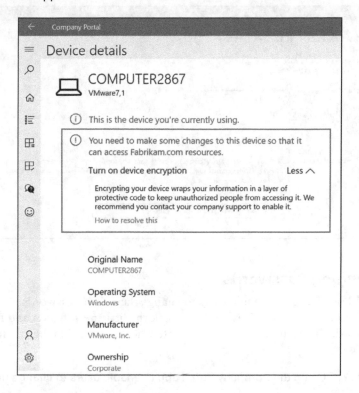

Setting Up a Device for Corporate Use

As you can see in Figure 11.2, a device might also have some issues and need to be enrolled or re-enrolled for corporate use. When they click on this notification, they are guided through the enrollment process.

You can see the "Set up your device" page in Figure 11.5, and the "Add work account to this device" page in Figure 11.6.

FIGURE 11.5   Getting started with device enrollment/re-enrollment

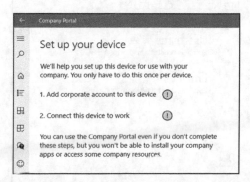

FIGURE 11.6   Adding a user's account to the device

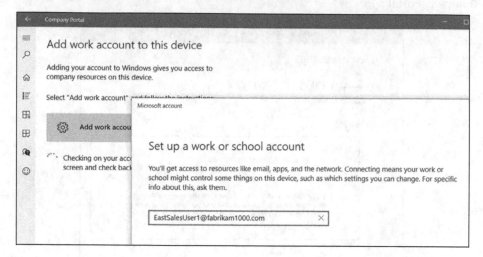

Users Changing Passwords

The Company Portal app can enable users to change their own passwords.

You can see this in Figure 11.7, where they click the little person icon and then click Change Password. The resultant page is a website where they can change their own password.

FIGURE 11.7   Using the Company Portal app to enable users to change their own passwords

Users Checking All Apps, Available Apps, and Installed Apps

The Company Portal can provide a one-stop shop of everything and anything you want to deploy using Intune. So items like these will be in one place:

- MSI applications
- APPX/MSIX applications
- Win32 applications
- Windows Store for Business applications
- Web links to interesting places

An example can be seen in Figure 11.8.

FIGURE 11.8   Users can see the available applications (which are not forcefully required).

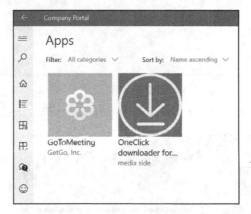

That said, if you don't see the full complement as expected in the Company Portal, there's likely a pretty good reason. First, remember that an application can be *assigned* or not. Assigned means there is going to be an attempt to install it. But you can also not assign an application and simply make it "Available for enrolled devices."

As a reminder of how to make an application available for enrolled devices, see Figure 11.9 which shows how to make an application "Available for enrolled devices" within Intune.

Syncing, Remote Lock, or Resetting a Device

We didn't go much into phones in this book, but if you're using Intune to manage them, users can jump into the Company Portal and lock or reset a mobile device. You can see this in Figure 11.10.

FIGURE 11.9   Making an application available for enrolled devices (without forcefully requiring it)

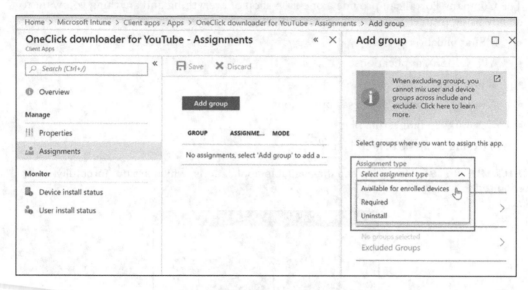

FIGURE 11.10   How to lock or reset a phone using the Company Portal

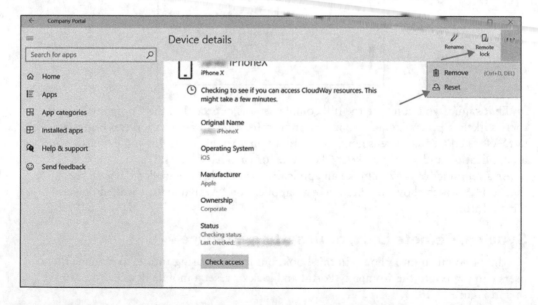

Additionally, instead of using the Windows settings app to trigger an MDM sync, you can use the Company Portal app to do it. This application can also tell Intune to perform a sync for other devices as well.

To do this, users can right-click over this device or another device they own and click "Check access." This is secret code for "sync with Intune now." You can see this in Figure 11.11.

FIGURE 11.11 Right-clicking over another device the user has access to enables them to check access, which is the same as an MDM sync.

If a user clicks into a device, however, they can then reset it, if they leave the machine in the back of a taxi, for instance. Next time the computer connects... goodnight Irene. You can see how to do that in Figure 11.12, and also note that the "Check access" button, which does the same thing as the button in Figure 11.11, is there too.

FIGURE 11.12 Sending the command to reset a device

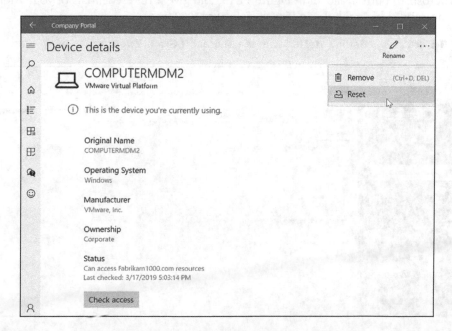

The blog entry I alluded to at the beginning of this section, along with extra details you might find interesting can be found at:

```
https://microscott.azurewebsites.net/2018/11/09/
microsoft-intune-windows-company-portal-app-yes-you-should-be-deploying-it/
```

Microsoft Graph and the Graph Explorer

You might have heard the word *graph* before if you've been poking around Azure- and MDM-land for a while. A graph is just a big ol' database that you can poke programmatically to learn about interesting things or make it do interesting things.

What kinds of interesting things? Well, that's up to you.

But largely, the items you see as click-y clicks in Azure and Intune are really just pokey-poking database items underneath the hood. And you can poke around too. And so can your programmers.

So anytime you think to yourself, "Man, this is taking like 802 clicks in Azure and Intune to do *this* job (add a user, report on status, deploy an application, etc.)," you can reframe it with, "Hey, Alice, can you please use the Graph API to program away these 802 clicks into three for me...or zero if I use a command line?"

The official Graph API documentation can be found here:

```
https://docs.microsoft.com/en-us/azure/active-directory/develop/
active-directory-graph-api
```

But there's a way for you to check out the graph yourself and give it a whirl, without having to do any coding at all. It's called the Graph explorer. Start out by going to https://developer.microsoft.com/en-us/graph/graph-explorer and click the "Sign in with Microsoft" button, shown in Figure 11.13, and give it the credentials of your Global Admin account, like Frank Rizzo (frank@fabrikam1000.com).

FIGURE 11.13 Getting started with the Microsoft Graph Explorer

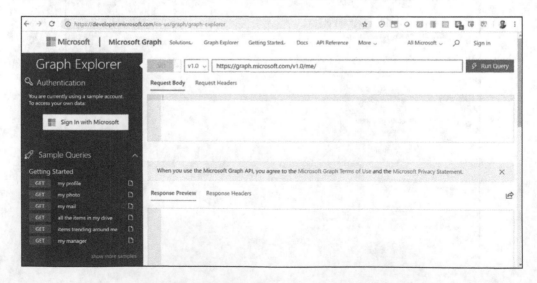

While this tool is generally geared toward developers, it can be used by mere mortals as well. In fact, Microsoft provides several sample queries, also seen in Figure 11.13, to click upon immediately.

After you're logged on, you can immediately click on, say, the "my profile" Getting Started sample query. When you do, the bar at the top will change to a pre-populated GET query: `https://graph.microsoft.com/v1.0/me/`. The sample code will be seen at the bottom, like what's seen in Figure 11.14.

FIGURE 11.14   Results of clicking on the "My profile" sample query

```
⊘ Success - Status Code 200,        132ms

Response Preview    Response Headers

▾ {
        "@odata.context": "https://graph.microsoft.com/v1.0/$metadata#users/$entity",
        "businessPhones": [
            "302-351-8408"
        ],
        "displayName": "Frank Rizzo",
        "givenName": "Frank",
        "jobTitle": null,
        "mail": null,
        "mobilePhone": null,
        "officeLocation": null,
        "preferredLanguage": "en",
        "surname": "Rizzo",
        "userPrincipalName": "frank@fabrikam1000.com",
        "id": "20db14aa-2687-424c-a09a-f2e716fb4040"
    }
```

You can see items contained and filled in in your profile, like userPrincipalName, Display name, ID and so on.

Another fun one is `https://graph.microsoft.com/v1.0/devicemanagement/manageddevices`, which gives you the list of all Intune devices and their properties. Just put that line of text next to the "Run Query" button, and then smack it! (The Run Query button, that is.)

You're welcome to click upon some of the other pre-populated sample queries, but some might work and others might not. And there could be two reasons why. The first problem you might encounter would be when you click upon "my photo" you will get a result like this.

```
⊗ Failure - Status Code 404,        2902ms

Response Preview    Response Headers

▾ {
    ▾   "error": {
            "code": "ResourceNotFound",
            "message": "Resource could not be discovered.",
        ▾   "innerError": {
                "request-id": "0b2c8874-014e-44c2-86d7-a9f0225070a6",
                "date": "2019-03-17T17:04:19"
            }
        }
    }
```

Since there is no photo, there's nothing to share.

Another problem could be not enough permissions. For this example, start by clicking "show more samples," which would be toward the bottom left of Figure 11.13, then pick the category of Groups (not shown).

After that, try out the "Groups I belong to" sample query. You will see it fail with a permissions problem. What permissions do you need? Of course, you have to look it up. The Graph API tells the tale. For a user (like you) to perform the operation of getMemberGroups they need to have extra permissions which can be learned about here:

```
https://docs.microsoft.com/en-us/graph/api/
user-getmembergroups?view=graph-rest-1.0
```

In checking this out, the answer is that for an application, you need Group.Read.All (least permissions needed), or if you add Directory.Read.All or Directory.ReadWrite .All permissions, those would work as well.

Here is the full Permissions reference:

```
https://docs.microsoft.com/en-us/graph/permissions-reference
```

In my case, I gave Frank (whom, as Global Admin I would have guessed would just have uber-rights but seems to require delegation anyway) the Group.Read.All and Directory.Read.All rights.

When I did…poof. Out popped the groups in the graph Response Preview like this.

Setting permissions isn't too hard. Simply click on "Modify Permissions" and a pop-up appears with all the permissions. Then pick the permission(s) you need, as seen in Figure 11.15.

FIGURE 11.15   Selecting the permission(s) you need to perform the work

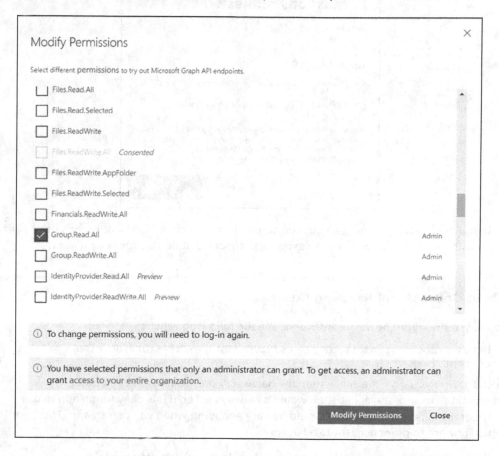

Some items require admin consent, even though you're an admin, as seen here:

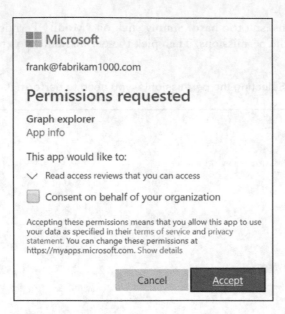

If you click Accept, you're saying you can do it. If you click "Consent on behalf of your organization," then Accept, you're saying that anyone can do this for your tenant.

About Consent and Revoking Consent

To learn more about how consent works, see the following article:

    https://docs.microsoft.com/en-us/azure/active-directory/develop/
    consent-framework

In short, first you give the application the necessary permissions. If you don't give consent, the user of the application would be always asked if it is okay for an app to use those granted permissions. This would be very annoying when you use an app. Thus, you typically want to grant consent to all users.

Additionally, it's possible to revoke consent. Here's an article to check out it:

    https://shawntabrizi.com/aad/
    revoking-consent-azure-active-directory-applications/

In tests, here's what I found:

1. Any particular user can go to myapps.microsoft.com. Then find Security & Compliance. Then select Remove as seen here:

2. An admin can un-consent someone else if desired. Inside Azure, if you want to try this, find the section named "Enterprise applications." If it's not on your left navigation, then search for it using the top navigation search as seen here:

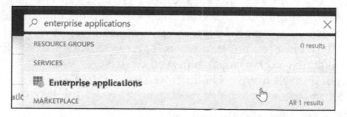

Then locate "Graph explorer" in the list of applications, as seen here:

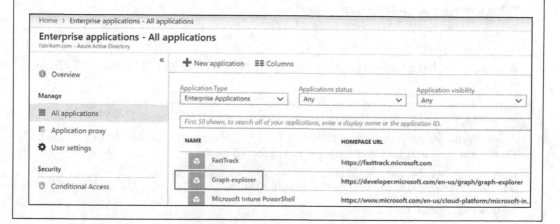

Click into Graph Explorer and nuke the person's access, as seen here:

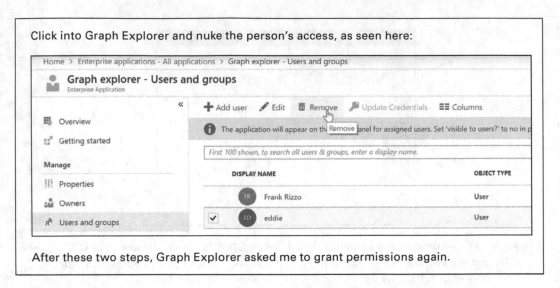

After these two steps, Graph Explorer asked me to grant permissions again.

The graph API isn't just for reading stuff (called a GET), it's also for making stuff happen (called a POST). Using a POST, you can do all sorts of programmatic goodies, like adding users to groups, changing roles, creating users, and more.

The Graph API isn't just for Intune; it works for Azure AD, Office 365, Enterprise Security and Mobility, and other cloud-connected services.

Some good "not insanely overly technical" overview on the Graph can be found at the YouTube videos:

- Intune APIs in Microsoft Graph, found at:
  `https://www.youtube.com/watch?v=1vAhRDq2lE0`

- What's new on Microsoft Graph, found at:
  `https://www.youtube.com/watch?v=3X10r2VVLCg`

  As for blog entries:

- A great intro that goes into the verbs like GET, POST, PUT, PATCH and DELETE can be found at:

  `https://techcommunity.microsoft.com/t5/Intune-Customer-Success/`
  `Support-Tip-Getting-Started-with-Microsoft-Graph-API/ba-p/364257?`

- A whopping 30-part blog series called "30 days of Microsoft Graph" can be found on Day 0, starting here and continuing onward for 30 posts:

  `https://developer.microsoft.com/en-us/graph/blogs/`
  `announcing-30-days-of-microsoft-graph-blog-series/.`

  In this blog, you'll find how to:

  - Update Exchange Online mailboxes.
  - Create a OneNote Notebook.
  - Create users in Azure AD.

  And 27 other interesting things. Wow.

PolicyPak On-Prem & MDM Edition

It's going to be hard not to read this section as a blatant commercial message. But I'll start off by saying I'm a proud papa of PolicyPak. Since my last book, PolicyPak has grown by hundreds of customers, managing nearly 2 million endpoints worldwide. We've expanded the team to include a significant number of developers, QA engineers, support specialists, and customer success managers. Maybe something in this section will help you out and you'll give it a try.

In these sections, we cannot cover all that PolicyPak can do, but I will cover some of our "greatest hits." And I'll be especially focused on MDM scenarios. That said, PolicyPak has three editions:

- **PolicyPak Group Policy Edition:** Computers must be domain joined to get these directives.

- **PolicyPak MDM Edition:** Computers must be MDM enrolled to get these directives.

- **PolicyPak Cloud Edition:** Computers may be domain joined, MDM enrolled, or non-domain joined to get these directives.

Why am I mentioning all three editions if we're going to focus on MDM?

Well, because if you like what PolicyPak can do, you might want to leverage more than one edition to cover your bases. The main use cases for PolicyPak alongside MDM managed devices are as follows:

Getting Nearly Any Group Policy, Group Policy Preferences, and Group Policy Security Setting Over to MDM   Not every Group Policy setting is in MDM. We covered this in huge detail in this book. The Administrative Template section in Intune is a nice step forward, but it contains a fraction of what's available in Group Policy right now.

Overcome UAC prompts (PolicyPak Least Privilege Manager).   When you use Autopilot to deploy new machines, you want your users to run as standard users. Yay! Now they cannot do lots of important things.

Boo. Use PolicyPak Least Privilege Manager to overcome UAC prompts and do admin-like things. Yay!

Dictate the right settings for applications (PolicyPak Application Manager).   Applications are deployed via Intune. Yay! Now those applications are not *actually* configured correctly.

Boo. Use PolicyPak Application Manager to give the "correct settings of the moment" alongside those applications. Yay!

Dictate the right Windows 10 features and optional features (PolicyPak Feature Manager for Windows).   You've rolled out with Autopilot. Yay!

Now the features and optional features aren't how you need them to be.

Boo. Use PolicyPak Feature Manager for Windows to implement the "correct features of the moment" you need to support the users' requirements. Yay!

"Start menu with brains."   You've dictated a new MSI or MSIX from Intune. Yay!

Now your application doesn't make any appearance on the right side of the Start Menu.

Boo. Use PolicyPak Start Screen & Taskbar Manager to place the application's icons into groups and/or onto the Taskbar. Yay!

MDM's scripting ability might not be enough.   I already covered this aspect of PolicyPak in Chapter 6. The problem with the built-in scripting engine for Intune is that it cannot do more than just PowerShell, and there are some size restrictions. Additionally, scripts are only applied once.

With the PolicyPak Scripts Manager component, your scripts can be .VBS (Visual Basic), JavaScript (.JS), Shell (.BAT or .CMD) or PowerShell. Scripts can be applied once, always (every hour), or once again (when re-triggered). There is no size restriction in the script. You can order the scripts. And, scripts can leverage Item Level Targeting (ILT) to detect when conditions are true and false (instead of you trying to bake it into your script).

Since it's already covered in Chapter 6, I won't cover it here. But the videos for PolicyPak Scripts can be found at www.policypak.com/products/scripts manager.html.

Windows 10's AppLocker ability might not be enough.   In Chapter 10, "Security with Baselines, BitLocker, AppLocker, and Conditional Access," I explained how AppLocker is great, but you might need to keep babysitting it to add rules again and again. As such, in Chapter 10 I showed PolicyPak Least Privilege Manager and it's SecureRun™ feature, which enables you to do one-click whitelisting. You can check out this feature at:

```
https://www.policypak.com/video/
stop-cryptolocker-and-other-unknown-zero-day-attacks-with-policypak-
secureruntm.html
```

MDM's file deployment features might need a little boost.   This is another topic I already covered in detail in Chapter 6, specifically with PolicyPak File Delivery Manager. PolicyPak File Delivery Manager enables you to download files (including really big ones) from a source like Amazon S3. And if the file is a ZIP, it can be auto-unpacked so a collection of files is always kept up-to-date. Again, see Chapter 6 for details and screen shots.

Getting Started with PolicyPak

To get started with PolicyPak (any edition), we do ask that you first attend a "Getting ready for a successful trial" webinar. This will set you up with the latest knowledge and explain the latest problems that PolicyPak can fix. After that we hand over the bits, and you can try it yourself. The PolicyPak download looks like what's in Figure 11.16.

FIGURE 11.16   Install the PolicyPak Client-Side Extension MSI to the endpoints, and install the Admin Console MSI on your machine, and that's it.

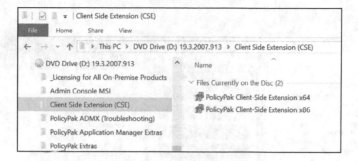

Installation is easy and looks like this:

- **Your machine:** Have the Group Policy Management console to make and edit Group Policy and PolicyPak items. Install the PolicyPak Admin Console MSI there. You can see the result seen in Figure 11.17.

- **Endpoint machines:** Use Intune or another MDM to deploy the PolicyPak Client-Side Extension (CSE).

- **PolicyPak license file:** It's an MSI. Upload to Intune and deploy it to your client machine.

For a cute overview cartoon, check out:

```
https://www.policypak.com/video/
policypak-and-mdm-deploying-real-group-policy-and-extra-policypak-settings-
overview.html
```

After you have the settings you want, you simply export them as XMLs. (We'll be doing more of that in a bit.) Once you have your "basket of XMLs," you need to wrap them up into a .MSI file. PolicyPak has a tool called the Group Policy Exporter utility that will do just that.

So, here's the plan:

- Use PolicyPak to make policy settings you cannot make any other way.

- Export those settings as XML files.

- Wrap the XML files into an MSI file.

- Upload the MSI to Intune or another MDM service.

- Assign the MSI to groups (users or computers).

- MSI is downloaded and magic is applied.

For a general flyover and overview of PolicyPak and Intune, check out this video:

```
https://www.policypak.com/video/policypak-and-microsoft-intune.html
```

FIGURE 11.17   PolicyPak hooks right into the Group Policy editor you already know.

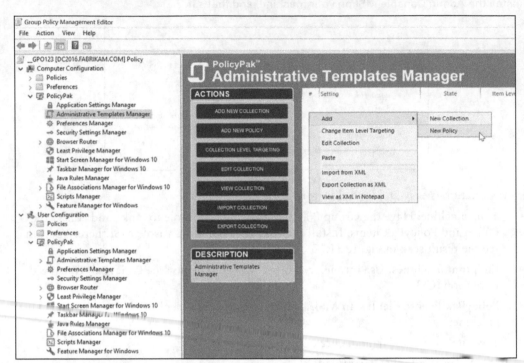

Using PolicyPak to Export Existing Group Policy to MDM

With over 4,000 Group Policy settings, 10,000 variations of Group Policy Preferences, and a myriad of security settings, MDM just cannot do it all. So PolicyPak enables you to take existing Group Policy, Group Policy Preferences, and Group Policy security settings and export them for use.

These would be the three components to export real Group Policy settings:

- PolicyPak Admin Templates Manager
- PolicyPak Preferences Manager
- PolicyPak Security Settings Manager

As you can see in Figure 11.18, you can create new policies born from ADMX/ Administrative Templates. This simply uses your existing ADMX store, local store or your domain's central store. So whatever templates you're using right now to create Group Policy ADMX settings, those are the ones you can use and export, right now. In Figure 11.18, I'm creating a policy that will **Prohibit access to Control Panel and PC settings**.

FIGURE 11.18 Using PolicyPak Admin Templates Manager to create and then export Group Policy ADMX settings

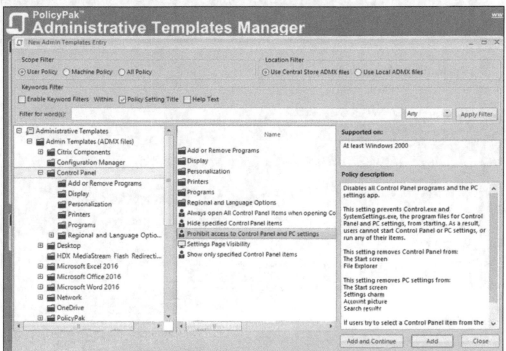

Settings can be either User or Computer side and are easily exported as XML. And, if you have any third-party ADMX templates, you can immediately use them (also seen in Figure 11.18) and export those settings. In this way, every Group Policy ADMX setting is covered, usable, and exportable to MDM. Remember: Microsoft's Policy CSP will only work with curated settings; with PolicyPak Admin Templates Manager, the superpower is that you can really leverage *any* ADMX setting you need.

If you have Group Policy Preferences settings, like Shortcuts, Services, Power Settings, Registry Settings, Environment Variables, Device Restrictions, Scheduled Tasks, and so on, you can use PolicyPak's built-in wizard to export those settings, as seen in Figure 11.19.

And, for Group Policy Security settings, the process is similar. In the GPOs which contain Security Settings, just use the PolicyPak Security Settings Manager to export existing Group Policy security settings, as seen in Figure 11.20. Most security settings will export. Some won't. You can see that in Figure 11.20.

FIGURE 11.19 Exporting Group Policy Preferences settings as XML files

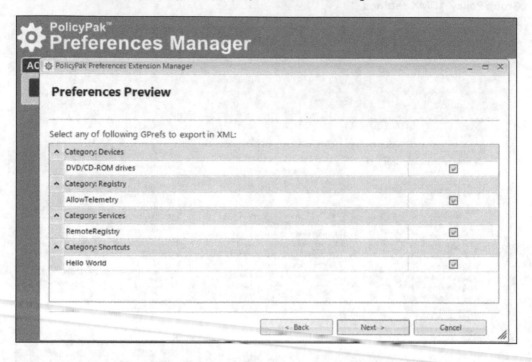

FIGURE 11.20 Exporting Group Policy Security settings as XMLs

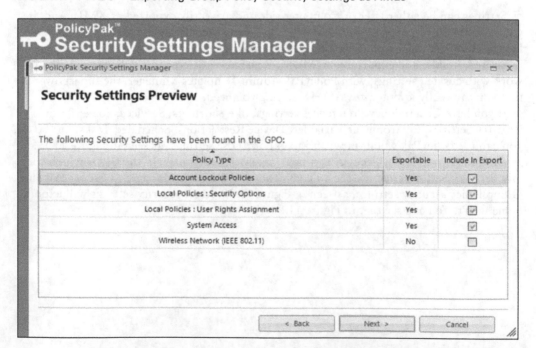

At this point, you use the PolicyPak Exporter tool to wrap up the XMLs to make them into an MSI. Then you deploy that MSI via Intune.

Seriously, it's that easy.

For an end-to-end video of PolicyPak and Intune where you can see the export of real Group Policy settings and using them in Intune, check out:

`https://kb.policypak.com/kb/article/482-policypak-and-microsoft-intune/`

Using PolicyPak to Overcome UAC Prompts

We saw PolicyPak in Chapter 10 when we talked about overcoming a UAC prompt when needing to manage BitLocker. Standard users cannot back up their own BitLocker recovery keys, and in that chapter I showed how to use PolicyPak Least Privilege Manager to overcome that.

There are however, almost certainly going to be instances when you deploy an application that is, well, old and cranky. Or maybe new and cranky. And when users run it, the app displays a UAC prompt that would prevent the user from running it as designed, or prevent the user from running it at all.

To overcome this, you can use PolicyPak Least Privilege Manager to elevate stubborn applications to bypass UAC prompts (Figure 11.21).

FIGURE 11.21   Running applications that require UAC prompts

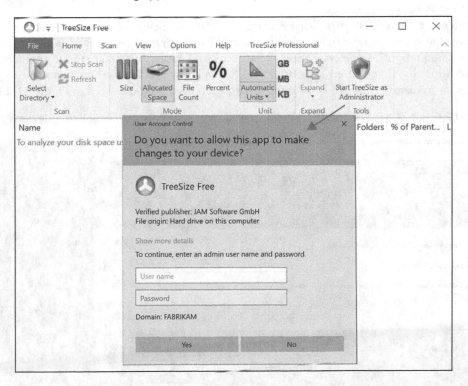

Using PolicyPak Least Privilege Manager, you just set up your rule. In Figure 11.22, I've made a rule to say, "Whenever I see TreeSizeFree higher than 4.0.3-ish, and also signed by JAM Software GmbH, then Run with elevated privileges."

FIGURE 11.22   Overcoming UAC prompts with PolicyPak Least Privilege Manager

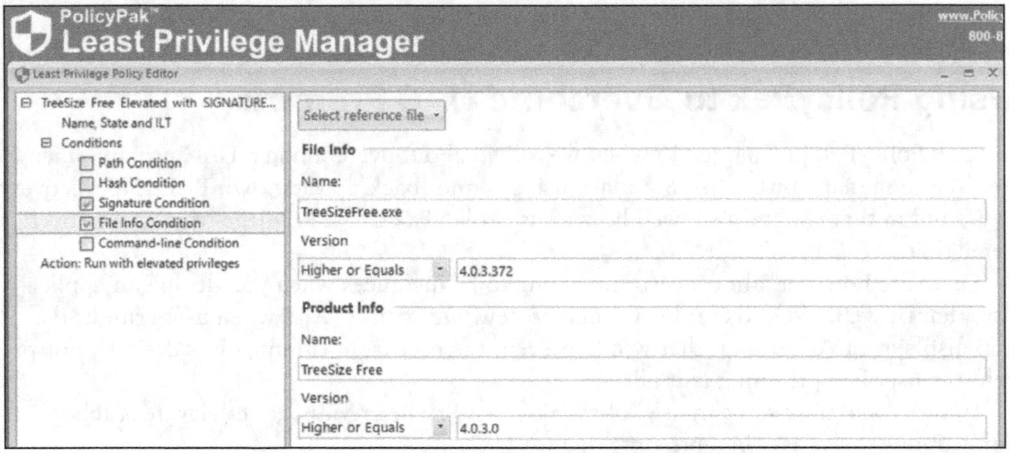

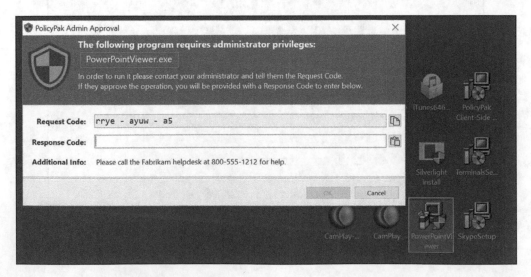

When I want to use this with Intune, just export as XML and wrap it up into the MSI using the PolicyPak Exporter.

You can also use PolicyPak Least Privilege Manager to elevate scripts that might perform actions that require admin rights, elevate Control Panel applets like Device Manager that require admin rights, and elevate the installation of MSI applications that require admin rights.

Additionally, if your users are out in the field and download something you *want* to permit them to install, they can be prompted with a challenge code, as seen in Figure 11.23.

FIGURE 11.23   The PolicyPak Least Privilege Manager Request/Response code dialog box

Then, they read out the challenge code to the help desk or other authorized person and their wish is granted. No local admin rights required, keeping your machine as secure as possible.

You can see a video of PolicyPak Least Privilege Manager basics and a video of PolicyPak Least Privilege Manager Admin approval (challenge codes) check out: `https://kb.policypak.com/kb/article/` `172-kill-local-admin-rights-run-applications-with-least-privilege` and `https://kb.policypak.com/kb/article/191-01-admin-approval-demo/`.

Using PolicyPak to Block and Allow UWP Applications

If you set up Windows Store for Business, you've got a nice curated library of applications to download and install on demand. But what about the consumer-facing Microsoft Store?

Maybe you want to allow the consumer Microsoft Store but allow users to install and run applications, say, from a specific vendor—like, greenlight all Adobe products but block everything else.

With PolicyPak Least Privilege Manager and the ability to block and allow UWP applications, but allow specific vendors or applications through, this is drop-dead easy.

The end-to-end video on this can be found here:

`https://www.policypak.com/video/` `policypak-manage-block-and-allow-windows-universal-uwp-applications.html`

Also, special note to those using Windows 10 Pro: PolicyPak Least Privilege Manager can block the consumer Microsoft Store (which typically cannot be done otherwise). Additionally, you could also block the running of Microsoft Edge, if that's what you wanted to do.

I get those two questions a lot.

Using PolicyPak to Manage Application, Browser, and Java Settings

After applications are deployed using Intune, those applications are born with whatever defaults are bestowed upon them. That's not likely what you want. Heck, even lowly Internet Explorer needs to be optimally configured for your security settings.

Here's a super-quick rundown of three components that can work together to manage applications, browsers, and Java.

- **PolicyPak Application Settings Manager:** Has 500 preconfigured Paks to manage darn near every setting in every application you could possibly deploy to a Windows 10 desktop. See Figure 11.24 to see PolicyPak Application Settings Manager manage nearly every setting of Firefox, Internet Explorer, Chrome, and Java as well as tons of other applications.

- **PolicyPak Browser Router:** Now you have two browsers, Internet Explorer and Edge. And likely Chrome and also Firefox. Some websites simply work better based upon the browser the website is open within. In Figure 11.25, you can see how to make a PolicyPak Browser Router "route" to specify that a specific website (or pattern) will open with the right browser.

- **PolicyPak Java Rules Manager:** Old apps stink. But many require Java. And specific versions of Java. With PolicyPak Java Rules Manager, you can force specific web applications to marry up to a specific version of Java. See this in Figure 11.26.

The gist is simple: Deploy your applications and browsers as simply as you can. Then layer on top the policy settings you need to ensure the right look-and-feel and settings, which then go to the right people at the right times.

FIGURE 11.24 Using PolicyPak Application Settings Manager to manage your browsers' and desktop applications' settings

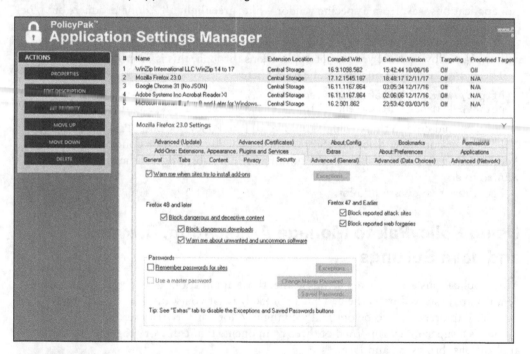

FIGURE 11.25   Use PolicyPak Browser Router to define which browser is best for what website or website pattern. Additionally, define which IE document mode to use for IE as necessary.

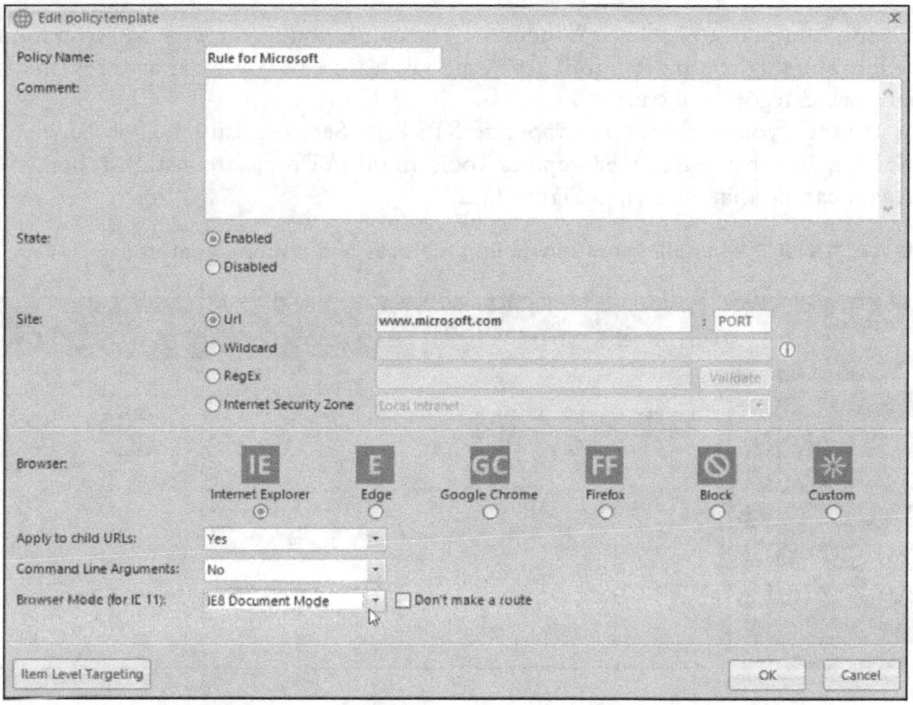

FIGURE 11.26   Map a specific website to a specific version of Java using PolicyPak Java Rules Manager.

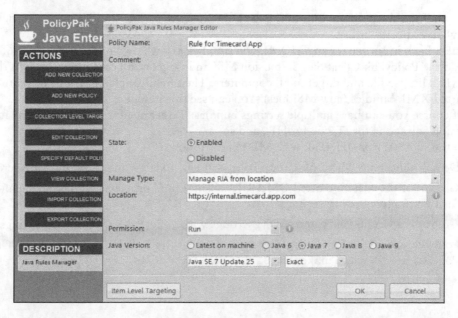

Using PolicyPak to Manage Windows Features (and Optional Features)

After using Autopilot to deploy a Windows 10 machine, you might want to "trim the sails" a little bit. You might want to install key Windows features or optional features (that's actually two categories of stuff!).

For instance, you might want to vaporize XPS Print Services features (does anyone really use those?!), and ensure that the Graphics Tools and RSAT tools are installed. In a few clicks, you can do that, as seen in Figure 11.27.

FIGURE 11.27   Installing or uninstalling features and optional features

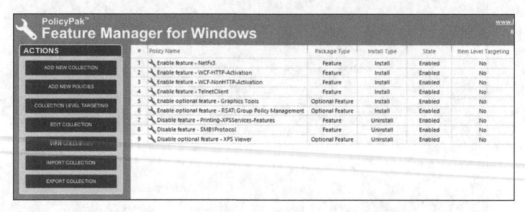

Again, when done, just export to XMLs, and you're almost there.

PolicyPak Deployment with Intune (or Any MDM)

After you have the policies you want, you can wrap them up into an MSI using the included PolicyPak Exporter utility.

Then, back in Intune (or any MDM), you simply learn what you used in Chapter 6. Upload the PolicyPak Client-Side Extension MSI and target to all computers. Upload the PolicyPak license file and target to all computers. Then finally, upload the one or more exported XML bundles (now MSI files). You can see this in Figure 11.28.

Of course you can have multiple settings bundles. Target one for Inside Sales, one for Roaming Sales, one for IT, one for HR, and so on.

So the summary of PolicyPak with MDM is as follows:

- Deploy almost any Microsoft Group Policy setting…today, without waiting for Microsoft.
- Get out of the custom-crafted OMA-URI business and problems with applying and then un-applying policy settings.
- Go beyond Group Policy and MDM settings with PolicyPak's own special settings.
- PolicyPak uses Item Level Targeting on all settings (PolicyPak's and Microsoft's Group Policy settings), which makes targeting super easy.

FIGURE 11.28   Upload and target the PolicyPak Client-Side Extension, PolicyPak license file, and the PolicyPak settings.

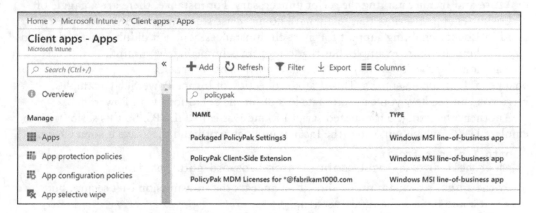

In short, we get lots of people using PolicyPak. Some people use the PolicyPak Group Policy edition to get their on-prem machines under control. Then they get the PolicyPak MDM Edition to deliver their exported policies for use with Intune or any MDM service.

Come check it all out at www.PolicyPak.com and really fill in the gaps you need to manage Windows 10.

Interesting Things I Found on the Internet

I admire anyone who gives away interesting free stuff on GitHib or the Internet for others to use. These guys just go the extra mile, for the glory of helping others. Seriously awesome stuff.

In the following sections are some items I think you might find useful in your journey.

Untested, but Seemingly Useful Scripts

I have used some, but certainly not all of these scripts. These are from MVP friends and colleagues who have put in some serious time and resources:

- **Aaron Parker:** https://github.com/aaronparker/Intune
- **Per Larsen:** https://github.com/PerLarsen1975
- **Eric Haavarstein:** https://github.com/haavarstein/Applications

All three house interesting scripts that can do interesting things in Intune. Typically these scripts use the PowerShell method, which takes advantage of the Intune Management Extension you learned about in Chapter 6.

These scripts are worth checking out and useful. I would say that because Azure and Intune is changing, sometimes the scripts might be superseded by something clicky-click in Azure and Intune, making the script unnecessary. For instance, there are a gaggle of BitLocker-enabling scripts that really have no more use since Intune now offers pretty good BitLocker-enabling support for most circumstances, where it didn't back in the "old days." There are more examples but that one springs immediately to mind.

Additionally, check out https://github.com/microsoftgraph/ powershell-intune-samples. This is a big collection of Intune PowerShell examples. Here you can see how you can automate lots of Intune operations with PowerShell.

Another interesting, but untested script I found was called iLAPS. So this script tries to emulate LAPS, which will rotate the local admin password and then save it somewhere.

http://blog.tofte-it.dk/
powershell-intune-local-administrator-password-solution-ilaps/

By the author's own admission though, it appears the transmission isn't secure, but maybe it could be in some future version.

Anyway, use the scripts when you have to, but if there's other ways to do it, I would typically recommend those because...you didn't write the script, and perhaps maintaining it could incur a degree of difficulty.

Yodamiitti Intune Management GUI

Petri Paavola, MVP, has created something called the Yodamiitti Intune Management GUI. I think it's pronounced *Yoda-meet-ee*, but since it's in Finnish, it's anyone's guess.

You can download it and take it for a spin at:

https://github.com/petripaavola/
yodamiitti_intunemanagementgui_communityedition

What this tool does is it uses the Graph API queries we explored earlier, but then it displays the data in a way that regular humans can read. And, get this: The columns are sortable!! Sortable? What is it, my birthday!??

To get started, you need to preinstall another script called the Microsoft.Graph .Intune.psd script. You can do this by first running install-script Microsoft.Graph. Intune as seen in Figure 11.29 and agreeing to the installation prompts.

Then after that run the tool with .\yodamiitti_intunemanagementgui_ communityedition.ps1, also seen in Figure 11.29.

FIGURE 11.29   Preinstalling Microsoft.Graph.Intune and then running Yodamiitti

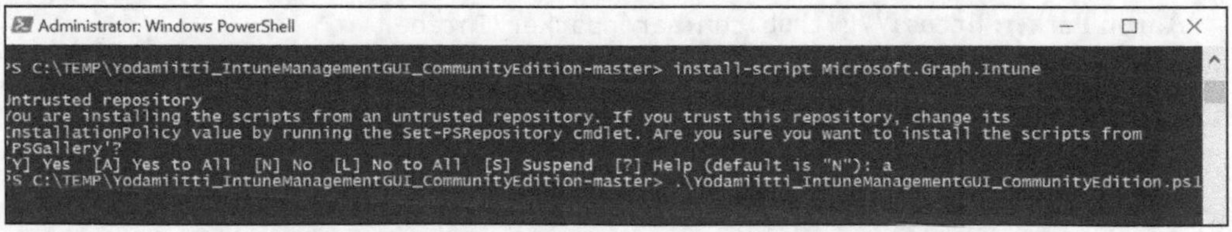

Then it opens into a nice GUI where you must first connect to your Intune. You do this via the Connect-MSGraph button and passing the credentials, like Frank Rizzo, as seen in Figure 11.30.

FIGURE 11.30   Connecting to your Intune

In the Overview pane, shown in Figure 11.31, you can see the device count of all your types of machines and the tenant ID. Across the top are useful tabs.

FIGURE 11.31   Yodamiitti navigation and content

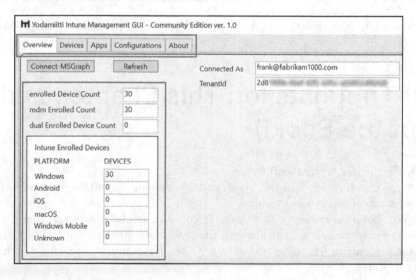

Just checking out the Devices tab, shown in Figure 11.32, you can see all the devices, last sync time, the owner (aka, userPrincipalName), and so on. You can also multi-select devices with the Ctrl key and then click Device Actions ➢ RebootNow (not shown).

FIGURE 11.32   You can multi-select devices in Yodamiitti and perform actions upon them.

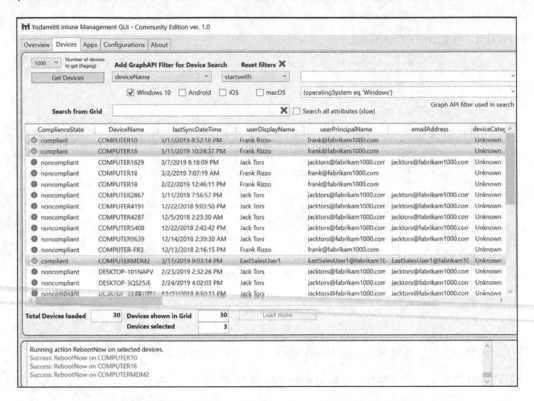

There's more to Yodamiitti, and it's really fun to use. So, check it out and start using it today.

Final Thoughts (on This Chapter, and about the Book!)

If you made it this far, my hat's off to you.

We covered oh oh so much in this book, and discovering the MDM free and pay tools is the cherry on top of a very large sundae.

I hope you got a lot of out of this book. If you did, send out a tweet! Just ping me at @jeremymoskowitz and use the hashtag #mdmbook and mention Chapter 11 for this chapter. Or ping me at @jeremymoskowitz with the hashtag #mdmbook for anything else you'd like to share.

As a final thought, and one I echoed earlier: This "cloud thing" is a journey. You start with a "pinch" of cloud, then become cloud-attached, and eventually, if needed or desired, you get to be fully in the cloud. Don't look at your neighbor and think, "I should be like him." Instead, find the path that works for you, go slowly and carefully, and light up the scenarios that make sense for your world to have the cloud functions you need.

Last, if you're not already signed up at MDMandGPanswers.com, please do so, as that's where I announce interesting things in both the MDM and Group Policy worlds, and it's the best way for us to stay in touch.

Thanks again for reading the book and having me along on the journey with you.

Jeremy
Moskowitz

Index